Labour Market Trends

incorporating **Employment** GAZETTE

Labour Market Trends,
Office for National Statistics, B3/5,
1 Drummond Gate,
London SW1V 2QQ.

Editorial office	0171 533 6126
Fax	0171 533 6185

Managing Editor	Frances Sly
Editor	David Bradbury
Assistant Editor	Annelise Jespersen
Design	Zeta Image to Print
	Geoff Francis
Labour Market Data	José Tomás
LFS Help-Line	Darren Stillwell
Statistics enquiries	See page S76

Advertising
Nigel Stephens
Tel: 01162 417300
Fax: 01162 416906

The Stationery Office

Labour Market Trends is available on subscription from:

Subscriptions Department
The Stationery Office Publications Centre,
PO Box 276, London SW8 5DT.
Tel: 0171 873 8499
Fax: 0171 873 8222

Single issues are available from the address above, and from The Stationery Office Bookshops.

Please remember to quote the publication title, and issue details (date, ISBN).

Payment may be made by Access/Visa/Connect credit cards, via your The Stationery Office account, or by cheque (made payable to 'The Stationery Office').

£63.50 Annual subscription
£6.00 Single issue
£89.50 Overseas

Printed by B.R. Hubbard Printers Ltd.,
Callywhite Lane, Dronfield, Sheffield S18 6XP.

ISSN 1361-4819

Contents

Volume 105   Number 9   Pages 305-364

CU00937814

News

News and research   306

Items include: *Social Focus on the Family*, indicators of regional competitiveness; a report on parents and the labour market; two government reports on maternity rights and 'family-friendly' practices; research into the National Record of Achievement; and the latest OECD outlook on employment.

Parliamentary questions   310

Bookshelf   311

Labour Market Update   313

This issue contains features on the labour market in the West Midlands; the definition of working-age households; workless households; temporary workers; and registered disabled people in the public sector.

Photos: Telegraph Colour Library and Birmingham City Council

Research brief

Review of information on the benefits of training to employers   317

Findings of DfEE research on the effects that training has on productivity, profitability and employee commitment.

Features

Spotlight on the West Midlands   323

The third in our series of features dealing with the labour market in the regions of the UK.

Economic activity of working-age households   333

An examination of different definitions of working-age households.

Workless households, unemployment and economic inactivity   339

What are the factors underlying the growth in the number of workless households since 1984?

Temporary workers in Great Britain   347

A look at temporary workers and the types of job they do.

Registered disabled people in the public sector and plans to improve the labour market position of disabled people   355

The latest statistics from public-sector employers under the former quota scheme, and the Government's approach to improving the labour market position for disabled people.

Statistics

LFS Help-Line   LFS45-48

This month's topics include: employees and self-employed people looking for a different or additional job; type of accommodation by economic activity; people born in the UK and outside, by ethnic origin; and employees in service industries by occupation.

Distribution of hourly earnings   320

A statistical report on the availability of regional and sub-regional data from the NES on the distribution of hourly earnings.

Labour Market Data   S1-76

The most recent figures for: employment, unemployment, vacancies, industrial disputes, earnings, government-supported training and other statistics.

ONS news

Social Focus on Families published

THE MOST WIDE-RANGING official study on families in the UK has been published by ONS. The report looks at families and how they live their lives today, as well as illustrating changes over the years. It also highlights the continuing importance of the family, despite changing social and economic characteristics.

Social Focus on Families shows that, in recent years, the family has experienced some major changes. For example, in one generation the number of first-time marriages has halved and the number of divorces has trebled. Cohabitation before marriage, once rare, is now the norm, and in 1995 lone parents headed 22 per cent of all families with children, nearly three times the proportion in 1971.

Other key findings of the report show that:

■ in 1994, 84 per cent of the population of Great Britain lived in one of its 15.8 million families;

■ traditional gender roles still persist, with mothers spending three hours a day on housework and cooking compared with fathers spending just three-quarters of an hour on these tasks; and

■ most absent fathers keep in contact with their families - 47 per cent of non-resident fathers saw their children at least once a week, and only 3 per cent never saw their children.

The chapter on family living standards focuses on four specific themes: economic activity; income; expenditure; and housing. With respect to economic activity, the report concludes that the traditional model of the husband as breadwinner and wife as homemaker has been eroded. The most significant change

has been the fall in the proportion of families living solely on a man's wages, and the related increase in the number of dual-earner households. In 1995 in 62 per cent of married couples of working age with children both adults were in work, compared with 50 per cent ten years earlier. The report also found that 37 per cent of mothers aged 25 to 34 said that they had returned to work within a year of the birth of their first child, compared with 14 per cent of mothers aged 60 to 64.

Other sections of the living standards chapter found that:

■ lone-parent families tend to have lower incomes, be more dependent upon benefits and have lower levels of savings than other types of families; and

■ where both partners work full-time, in 68 per cent of cases the man earns at least £50 a week more than his female partner.

The remaining two chapters of the

report look at: family structure and change; cohabitation, marriage and divorce; parenthood; lifestyles and relationships.

The report generally uses a standard definition of a family - either a married or cohabiting couple, with or without never-married children who have no children of their own, or a lone parent with such children. However, wider family relationships are also examined. 'Children' are here defined as people aged under 16, or single persons aged 16-18 and in full-time education.

Social Focus on Families draws on a wide range of data sources, including the General Household Survey, the Family Expenditure Survey, the Labour Force Survey, ONS registration data and the British Social Attitudes Survey.

• *Social Focus on Families*. ISBN 0 11 620919 4, £30. Published by The Stationery Office.

Work patterns for ethnic minorities

DETAILED ANALYSIS of employment, education and housing conditions for Great Britain's ethnic minorities is now available. Volume 4 of *Ethnicity in the 1991 Census* was published by ONS in late July.

The study, which follows earlier volumes on the ethnic minority populations of Great Britain, their demographic characteristics and social geography, is edited by Valerie Karn of the University of Manchester and has contributions from 21 other academics. Chapters relating

principally to the labour market include: labour force participation rates, self-employment and unemployment; patterns of ethnic minority employment in the context of industrial and occupational growth and decline; the impact of ethnic origins on educational and

occupational attainments; and monitoring equal employment opportunity.

• A fuller review of Volume 4 of *Ethnicity in the 1991 Census* is to be found on p311 of this issue of *Labour Market Trends*.

DfEE and DSS news

Families and work

TWO GOVERNMENT reports have highlighted the increasing prevalence of mothers returning to work after the birth of their children. The Policy Studies Institute carried out research on behalf of the Department for Education and Employment, the Department of Social Security and the Department of Trade and Industry, which has now been published as *Maternity*

Rights and Benefits in Britain 1996 and *Family-Friendly Working Arrangements in Britain 1996*. There was a high incidence of mothers returning to work after giving birth; by the time of the survey, 67 per cent of women had done so (compared with 45 per cent in 1988). The women most likely to return to work tended to be older, married, in higher-income families

and working for employers in the public sector or operating 'family-friendly' employment practices.

The first report, published by the DSS, concentrates on the effects of the 1994 changes to legislation affecting maternity rights and benefits. The research was designed to look at the effects both on women and on employers, as well as identifying any problems they had in understanding and complying with

legislation. Two large surveys were conducted in spring 1996 to examine this: a telephone survey consisting of 1,500 interviews with employers, and a postal survey of a sample of mothers who had given birth in June 1995 which produced 3,700 responses.

The survey of employers showed that they were generally aware of the legislation, and that it presented them with few problems - only 1 per cent of employers reporting difficulties.

(continued above right)

They also had a high awareness of new provisions introduced in October 1994 - 88 per cent being 'fully aware' of the employee's right not to be dismissed or selected for redundancy on grounds of maternity. Employers were, however, less aware of the long-standing right to extended maternity absence - only 61 per cent being fully aware of this - and provisions relating to statutory maternity pay. Smaller firms with few recent pregnancies were least likely to be aware of the maternity provisions.

Most mothers were aware of key aspects of maternity legislation, especially regarding employment protection and maternity leave. Thus, for example, 74 per cent were aware of their right to continuing non-wage benefits during maternity leave. Mothers most commonly mentioned their employer as the most useful source of information on maternity rights and benefits, but those in small workplaces more often mentioned government leaflets.

The findings pointed to a high degree of compliance with the legislation. The right to return to the same or a similar job appeared to have been honoured to a large degree, especially in the public sector. There were, however, some doubts about compliance in the small firms sector, where 21 per cent of employers with recent pregnancies among their employees reported that none of them had taken maternity leave.

Few employers had been caused problems by the right to return to work after maternity leave; however, 38 per cent of employers saw the right to 14 weeks of statutory maternity leave as causing a problem, mainly that of covering for the mother while she was away. Problems were most likely among small private-sector employers where 58 per cent reported difficulties. Of women entitled only to the 14 weeks' statutory maternity leave, 86 per cent took at least this amount. The remaining 14 per cent took less. The reasons for this are not known, but women who worked in non-union establishments were much more likely to take less than their 14 weeks entitlement. Extra-statutory maternity benefits were offered by 11 per cent of establishments, covering 30 per cent of women employees, and were commonest in establishments with a high proportion of young women or in large private- or public-sector organisations. Paternity leave was more common than extra-statutory maternity leave.

The second report, carried out for the DfEE, presents the findings of the research on what are often called 'family-friendly' employment practices - those features of employment that help employees combining family responsibilities with their job. It sought information on:
■ the range of such arrangements made available by employers;
■ the availability of the various arrangements to individual employees, especially parents of young children;
■ the take-up of the main types of arrangement by employees; and
■ employers' views of the utility of the arrangements.

Benefits available from employers included paternity leave; additional maternity leave; additional maternity pay; special leave at short notice for childcare reasons; career breaks and being allowed to work at home occasionally. Flexible or non-standard working time arrangements were provided by 71 per cent of establishments, and over half of mothers who had returned to work from a recent pregnancy had used such arrangements. Extra-statutory maternity leave was offered in 11 per cent of establishments employing women. In all, 31 per cent of establishments employing men granted paternity leave, usually limited to about four days.

Only 10 per cent of workplaces offered any form of practical assistance with childcare for parents with young children. Overall, 2 per cent offered a workplace nursery, 1 per cent supported a nursery elsewhere and 2 per cent operated a childcare allowance or voucher scheme. A third of establishments employing women had special leave arrangements to cover childcare emergencies

occurring at short notice. Career breaks were offered by 17 per cent of employers, but had relatively little take-up: only 1 per cent of mothers and 1 per cent of their partners reported having taken a career break.

There were a number of different types of non-standard working hours arrangements, of which the most common was flexible hours. This was available to full-time employees in 36 per cent of establishments. Temporary or permanent switches from full-time to part-time working were on offer in 22 per cent and 24 per cent respectively of establishments; women were much more likely than men to have switched permanently. Term-time only working was the least common type of non-standard working practice, available in 7 per cent of establishments.

- *Maternity Rights and Benefits in Britain 1996,* by C. Callender, N. Millward, S. Lissenburgh and J. Forth. DSS research report no. 67. ISBN 0 11 762536 1, £35. Available from The Stationery Office. *Family-Friendly Working Arrangements in Britain 1996,* by J. Forth, S. Lissenburgh, C. Callender and N. Millward. DfEE research report no. 16. ISBN 0 85522 615 3, £4.95. Available from DfEE Publications, PO Box 5000, Sudbury, Suffolk CO10 6YJ, tel 0845 6022260.

Parents and the labour market

A NEW report on parents and the labour market indicates that employment rates for mothers have increased faster than for other groups. Between 1984 and 1994 mothers' employment rose at twice the rate of that for other women, from 49 per cent to 59 per cent, with most of the growth being in full-time employment, from 17 per cent to 24 per cent.

The report, funded by the DfEE, is based on secondary analysis of the Labour Force Survey and examines changes in employment and working hours of mothers, fathers and parents

as a whole.

The greatest increase in mothers' employment was among women with a child under five, particularly among graduate women living with a partner. In contrast, the employment rate fell slightly among fathers (from 86 per cent to 85 per cent) and other men. Most employed mothers worked part-time, with a substantial proportion working shorter part-time hours (fewer than 16 hours a week), while the most common employment category for other women was shorter full-time hours (31 to 40 hours a week).

Over the decade there was an occupational move among mothers

towards higher status jobs, with this change again being most marked among women with a child under five. The proportion of mothers in non-manual occupations rose from 57 to 67 per cent, with a fall of similar proportions among those in semi- and unskilled work from 35 to 25 per cent. Mothers of children under five also featured in the rise in working hours, which grew by 4 hours per week for this group, compared with a rise of 2.3 hours among mothers in general and 0.4 hours for other women.

The increase in mothers' employment and working hours did not result in any compensating

changes for fathers, with no indications of a reduction in working hours nor of a substantial move towards more part-time employment. A feature by the report's authors, concentrating specifically on working fathers, appeared in July's *Labour Market Trends*, pp259-67.

- *Mothers, Fathers and Employment: Parents and the Labour Market in Britain 1984-1994,* DfEE research report RR10, ISBN 0 85522 595 5; £4.95. Available from DfEE Publications, PO Box 5000, Sudbury, Suffolk CO10 6YJ, tel 0845 6022260.

Research into the National Record of Achievement

AS PART OF THE review of the National Record of Achievement (NRA), the Department for Education and Employment commissioned several pieces of research. GHK Economics and Management studied the use of the NRA for reviewing progress, recording achievement and planning future action for school students. Social and Community Planning Research (SCPR) were asked to explore young people's perceptions, current use and likely future use of the NRA and the Institute for Employment Studies (IES) looked at employers' use of the NRA.

Most school leavers today are issued with an NRA - a document that allows individuals to set out their skills, record and achievements in a nationally-recognised format. The NRA system was reviewed following a recommendation in Sir Ron Dearing's report on qualifications for 16 to 19-year-olds. Extensive research was carried out by the DfEE as part of this process.

The GHK report looked at review, recording achievement and action planning (RRAP) in schools and was based on 700 telephone interviews and a series of 700 case studies. It found tremendous variations in the quality of RRAP, from minimalist approaches based on simply filling in the NRA to comprehensive approaches where the activity was integrated into the learning process. School teachers and students reported important benefits from effective RRAP, such as:

- greater self-esteem and confidence among students;
- improvements to performance;
- better relationships between staff and students;

- the opportunity to engage parents in the learning process; and
- pride in achievements at school.

Components which made RRAP effective in supporting the learning process were identified. These included: the need for clear learning objectives which encompassed academic and personal goals and the skills required to achieve them; setting achievable and measurable targets; identifying action for improvement; and regular assessment of progress. Similarly, a range of practices and tools which could help develop and implement effective RRAP were also noted. The report concludes with recommendations to help guide the development of coherent approaches to RRAP.

The SCPR study on individual use of the NRA was based on 20 focus groups. In all, 17 of these were with young people aged 16-24 selected to reflect a range of educational and employment sectors (at school, school leavers, in higher education, on government training schemes, employed and unemployed). The remaining three groups were with individuals taking part in development projects funded by DfEE.

The first contact with the NRA was generally through school, where young people's experience reflected that reported by the GHK study. There was little evidence of individuals being encouraged to update their NRAs after they left school; where this did occur, it was primarily at further education colleges or on a government-funded training scheme. The NRA appeared to be 'sold' to students almost exclusively as a document to present to prospective employers and college interviewers.

A number of key conclusions for encouraging the greater use of the NRA emerged, including that:

- individuals needed to be encouraged to consider the NRA as

a mechanism for identifying and considering their skills and future options;
- they needed to be encouraged to become used to reviewing their skills from a much earlier age;
- the NRA folders should continue to be produced, but with emphasis on the process by which individuals decided what to include in their NRA;
- NRA holders needed to be encouraged to maintain and update their NRAs, with easily accessible post-school guidance being made available; and
- the use of the NRA would be enhanced if education providers and employers recognised the NRA and encouraged individuals to use it as a tool to consider their future.

The IES study on employers' use of the NRA found that they saw benefits in seeing NRAs from job applicants, but that their current use was limited and tended to be restricted to school leavers. The research was centred on a telephone survey of 487 UK employers conducted in summer 1996, followed by 20 in-depth interviews. The sample of employers studied was not intended to be representative of all employers. It focused on those who were quite sophisticated in terms of their approach to recruitment and training.

The report found that NRAs were currently used by relatively few employers, mainly by those who regularly recruited young people. Firms did not generally seek NRAs when recruiting. Their use was instead driven by young people presenting them to prospective employers. However, the survey found that the more NRAs employers saw, the more they came to expect young people to present them as part of the recruitment process.

The NRA format includes information sheets on a number of areas, including personal details,

qualifications and credits, achievements and experiences, employment history, achievements in education, attendance record, and an individual action plan. Employers felt that all these were relevant, although the usefulness of specific pages varied by individual.

The study suggested that the benefits of using the NRA related more to the individual than the employer. However, employer benefits did include recording employee performance and motivating the workforce. Improvements that firms wanted to see to the NRA included more details on skills, work experience, career plans and personality. If the document were to be used for adults, employers wanted to see sections on competencies gained at work, and work-based achievements.

The conclusions drawn from these three pieces of research are reflected in the proposals from the NRA Review Steering Group, chaired by Sir Nicholas Goodison, for a new national record of achievement which is introduced earlier in schools and is an individually-owned tool for lifelong learning. These proposals are being taken forward and trials of the new materials will commence in autumn 1997.

- *Individual Use of the National Record of Achievement*, by Andrew Thomas and Rebecca Diba (SCPR). DfEE Research Study RS42. ISBN 0 11 270987 7. £25.95. *Employers' Use of the National Record of Achievement.* IES report 328. ISBN 1 85184 256 X. £35. *Review, Recording Achievement and Action Planning in Schools.* GHK1. ISBN 0 85522 604 8. All reports available from DfEE Publications, PO Box 5000, Sudbury, Suffolk CO10 6YJ, tel 0845 6022260.

DTI news

Regional competitiveness

CONSULTATION ON THE most appropriate range of indicators to illustrate the factors that determine regional competitiveness is being carried out by the Government. It has issued a consultation document outlining 13 proposed indicators and highlighting the potential difficulties involved in using them.

The indicators - developed by the Department of Trade and Industry in collaboration with ONS - include the Business Competitiveness Indicators and come under five main headings: overall competitiveness; labour market; education and training;

capital; and land and infrastructure.

For the labour market, the Government is particularly seeking views on whether earnings figures should be used as indicators of competitiveness and, if so, whether the relationship between average earnings and productivity would be useful. The document also looks at the two measures of unemployment - ILO and claimant count - and asks for comments on which would be preferred.

For 'overall competitiveness', the Government is looking for comments on the appropriate measure of gross domestic product per head; whether labour productivity should be measured for the economy as a whole

or only for the manufacturing sector; and whether the proportion of social security benefit claimants is an effective indicator of competitiveness and, if so, which benefit is the most appropriate measure.

Views are also specifically invited on the issues of research and development intensity, and road transport and congestion. The other indicators covered by the consultation document are manufacturing investment and output by foreign-owned companies; employment; educational and vocational attainment; Investors in People; VAT registrations and survival rates; and industrial property costs.

The regional competitiveness

indicators would be published regularly to help establish a framework for future work on regional competitiveness and identify underlying regional characteristics influencing regional competitiveness, says the document. They are designed to assist those responsible for regional development strategies and will also support the work of the proposed regional development agencies.

- *Regional Competitiveness Indicators: a Consultation Document* is available from Linda Oldfield, Statistics Directorate, DTI, Room G21, 10 Victoria Street, London SW1H 0NN, tel 0171 215 3279.

OECD news

International jobs outlook

THE ORGANISATION for Economic Co-operation and Development (OECD) has published its latest *Employment Outlook*. The annual publication concludes that unemployment in OECD countries is likely to fall only slightly next year.

The report's chapter on recent labour market developments and prospects suggests that GDP growth

in the OECD area is likely to average nearly 3 per cent in 1997 and 1998, but with substantial differences between member states. Growth should be robust in some countries, including the UK, but in others, such as Japan and the major continental European economies, it is likely to be more hesitant. The inflation outlook, the report believes, remains good nearly everywhere. Unemployment across the OECD will fall only slowly, down from its 1996 level of

36.3 million to a projected level of 35.7 million in 1997 and 35.2 million in 1998.

For the UK, the report projects GDP growth of 3.0 per cent in 1997 and 2.7 per cent in 1998. It projects a 1.3 per cent rise in employment in the UK in 1997, and 0.7 per cent in 1998. For UK unemployment, using the Eurostat definition, it projects a fall from 7.4 per cent in 1996 to 6.1 per cent in 1997 and 5.6 per cent in 1998.

Other chapters in the report cover:

a longer-run view of earnings mobility; economic performance and the structure of collective bargaining; the impact of trade with emerging economies on OECD labour markets; and whether job insecurity is on the increase in OECD countries. There is also a statistical annexe.

- *Employment Outlook: July 1997.* Organisation for Economic Co-operation and Development. ISBN 92 64 15579 1.

Expert help on the labour market is just a phone call away

Employment (see *Tables 1.1-1.5* and *1.9-1.13*)

Census of Employment	01928 792690
Employment and hours	01928 792563
Workforce in employment	01928 792563

Labour force, unemployment and vacancies (see *Tables 2.1-2.24, 3.1-3.3* and *7.1-7.24*)

Claimant count, vacancies notified to Jobcentres, and Labour Force Survey	0171 533 6176

Redundancy (see *Tables 2.32-2.36*)

Redundancy statistics	0171 533 6086

A selection of recent Parliamentary Questions concerning labour market statistics answered in letters from Dr Tim Holt, Director General of the Office for National Statistics. The date on which the answer was given is at the end of each PQ.

Earnings

MICHAEL FALLON (Sevenoaks) asked the Chancellor of the Exchequer what estimate he has made of the number of employees earning less than (a) £3.50 an hour, (b) £4.00 an hour and (c) £4.50 an hour; what estimate he has made of the number of self-employed people earning less than (a) £3.50 an hour, (b) £4.00 an hour and (c) £4.50 an hour; what estimate he has made of the number of people employed in the retail sector earning less than (a) £3.50 an hour, (b) £4.00 an hour and (c) £4.50 an hour; what estimate he has made of the number of people employed in (a) manufacturing and (b) services, earning less than (a) £3.50 an hour, (b) £4.00 an hour and (c) £4.50 an hour; what estimate he has made of the number of people employed in the agriculture, fishing and food industries earning less than (a) £3.50 an hour, (b) £4.00 an hour and (c) £4.50 an hour; what estimate he has made of the number of people employed by local authorities earning less than (a) £3.50 an hour, (b) £4.00 an hour and (c) £4.50 an hour; what estimate he has made of the number of people employed in the transport industries earning less than (a) £3.50 an hour, (b) £4.00 an hour and (c) £4.50 an hour; what estimate he has made of the number of people employed by charitable organisations earning less than (a) £3.50 an hour, (b) £4.00 an hour and (c) £4.50 an hour.

TIM HOLT: The latest information, from the Labour Force Survey, is given in the table below. Data for the self-employed are not available.

Employees on all rates including those whose pay for the survey pay-period was affected by absence; Labour Force Survey winter 1996/7 (December 1996- February 1997); Great Britain

Number of employees (thousands) with hourly earnings (including overtime) less than:

	£3.50	£4.00	£4.50
All			
Whole economy (SIC 1992 sectors A-Q)	3,174	4,786	6,557
Agriculture (SIC 1992 sectors A-B)	51	76	101
Manufacturing (SIC 1992 sector D)	400	680	972
Retail (SIC 1992 division 52)	703	1,094	1,427
Services (SIC 1992 sectors G-Q)	2,612	3,880	5,269
Transport (SIC 1992 divisions 60-63)	116	155	200
Charity, voluntary organisation or trust	60	91	130
Local government or council (including police, fire services and local authority controlled schools and colleges)	192	371	585
Full-time			
Whole economy (SIC 1992 sectors A-Q)	1,454	2,319	3,383
Agriculture (SIC 1992 sectors A-B)	45	60	84
Manufacturing (SIC 1992 sector D)	292	524	779
Retail (SIC 1992 division 52)	191	326	454
Services (SIC 1992 sectors G-Q)	1,026	1,618	2,350
Transport (SIC 1992 divisions 60-63)	86	119	155
Charity, voluntary organisation or trust	19	31	44
Local government or council (including police, fire services and local authority controlled schools and colleges)	47	80	163
Part-time			
Whole economy (SIC 1992 sectors A-Q)	1,720	2,467	3,174
Agriculture (SIC 1992 sectors A-B)	..	16	18
Manufacturing (SIC 1992 sector D)	108	155	192
Retail (SIC 1992 division 52)	512	768	973
Services (SIC 1992 sectors G-Q)	1,585	2,262	2,918
Transport (SIC 1992 divisions 60-63)	29	35	45
Charity, voluntary organisation or trust	41	61	86
Local government or council (including police, fire services and local authority controlled schools and colleges)	145	291	422

.. sample size too small to give a reliable estimate.
SIC 1992 - Standard Industrial Classification of economic activities 1992

(11 July)

Youth unemployment

GRAHAM BRADY (Altrincham and Sale West) asked the Chancellor of the Exchequer by how much youth unemployment levels have changed in each of the last four years; and by how much he expects them to change in each of the next four years.

TIM HOLT: The data you have requested for those under 25 years are shown in the attached table. ONS does not make forecasts of any of the labour market estimates data it produces.

Great Britain, not seasonally adjusted

Thousands

	Level	Change on year
1992/3	867	--
1993/4	785	-82
1994/5	695	-90
1995/6	656	-39
1996/7	633	-23

Source: Labour Force Survey
Figures are shown for winter of each year (December to February)

(15 July)

Temporary contracts

CHRISTOPHER FRASER (Mid Dorset and Poole North) asked the Chancellor of the Exchequer what estimate he has made of the proportion of people currently employed on temporary contracts in (a) the United Kingdom, (b) France, (c) Spain and (d) Italy; and to what extent this has changed since (i) 1987 and (ii) 1992.

TIM HOLT: Numbers of temporary employees and all employees are published in the Eurostat publication Labour Force Survey Results which is available in the House of Commons Library. The most recent edition is for 1995. The proportions for spring of each of the years 1987, 1992 and 1995 are shown in the table below. The latest figure for the United Kingdom, for winter 1996/7, is also shown.

Temporary employees as a proportion of all employees

Per cent

	United Kingdom	France	Spain	Italy
Spring 1987	6.2	7.1	15.6	5.4
Spring 1992	5.4	10.4	33.5	7.6
Spring 1995	6.8	12.2	35.0	7.2
Winter 1996/7	7.4	--	--	--

(29 July)

Unpaid work

JACKIE BALLARD (Taunton) asked the Chancellor of the Exchequer what statistics the Office for National Statistics compiles on the value of unpaid work to the economy.

TIM HOLT: ONS publishes no direct estimates of unpaid labour. It plans, however, to publish an experimental account of household production in the ONS publication Economic Trends in the next few months, based on time-use surveys. An article describing the approach was published in Economic Trends in July 1996.

(29 July)

Earnings (Blackpool)

GORDON MARSDEN (Blackpool South) asked the Chancellor of the Exchequer what estimate he has made of the number of employees in Blackpool currently earning less than (a) £3.50 per hour, (b) £3.75 per hour and (c) £4 per hour.

TIM HOLT: The latest information, from the New Earnings Survey (NES) April 1996, is given in the table below for the local authority district of Blackpool.

Employees on adult rates whose pay for the survey pay-period was not affected by absence, NES April 1996

Per cent

Employees with hourly earnings (excluding overtime) less than:

Blackpool	£3.50	£3.75	£4.00
Full-time	10.1	13.2	15.9
Part-time	18.4	25.0	30.3
All	12.2	16.2	19.5

(16 July)

Earnings (Stoke-on-Trent)

JOAN WALLEY (Stoke-on-Trent North) asked the Chancellor of the Exchequer how many people in the constituency of Stoke-on-Trent North earn (a) less than £4 per hour, (b) £3.50 per hour and (c) £3 per hour.

TIM HOLT: The latest available information, from the New Earnings Survey (NES) April 1996, is given in the table below for the parliamentary constituency of Stoke-on-Trent North.

Employees on adult rates whose pay for the survey pay-period was not affected by absence, NES April 1996

Per cent

Employees with hourly earnings (excluding overtime) less than:

Stoke-on-Trent North	£3.00	£3.50	£4.00
Full-time	0.5	1.5	11.1
Part-time	9.5	28.6	52.4
All	1.4	4.1	15.0

(16 July)

A selection of recent books which may be of interest to *Labour Market Trends* readers.

THE LATEST volume in a series exploring what the 1991 Census can tell us about ethnicity in Britain concentrates heavily on the labour market. Volume 4 of *Ethnicity in the 1991 Census* - 'Employment, education and housing among the ethnic minority populations of Britain' - devotes separate chapters, by various authors, to: labour force participation, self-employment and unemployment; patterns of ethnic minority employment in the context of industrial and occupational growth and decline; the impact of ethnic origins on education and occupational attainments; and monitoring of equal employment opportunity.

One of the questions the book aims to address is to what extent minority ethnic groups have worse or different experiences of education, housing and employment compared with the White population. It also asks to what extent ethnicity accounts for these differences and how much is related to other factors such as class, age, household characteristics, gender or geographical location. While acknowledging that the Census data are not designed to address causal questions - such as the effects, if any, of discrimination - the editors conclude that the evidence of the 1991 Census confirms that all minority ethnic groups "suffer a 'penalty', albeit of varying size, relative to the White population."

The 1991 Census was the first in which there was a question on ethnicity, as opposed to country of birth, and so provides the first nationally comprehensive information on the labour market participation and characteristics of men and women from ethnic minority groups. The third chapter of this volume, on labour market participation rates, says that the results largely confirm the Labour Force Survey in highlighting the disadvantages these groups face.

The patterns of involvement in the labour market are compared across all ten Census ethnic categories, contrasting the experience of men and women, and examining variations by age group, marital status, household status, educational attainment and family organisation. For example, a major influence on the lower economic activity rates of ethnic minority groups was their relative youth in comparison with the White population, as younger

people are less likely to be in the labour force, and people from some ethnic minority groups spent much longer in full-time education than White people. "However, highly qualified people from ethnic minority groups still suffered much higher unemployment rates than highly qualified White people," the authors add.

Although the degree of participation in the labour market by ethnic minority groups as a whole was markedly lower than that of Whites, for both men and women, there were noticeable differences between different minority groups. Generally, people from the Black ethnic groups were more likely than those from Asian or Other groups to be participating in the labour market.

A much higher percentage of economically active people were unemployed in the ethnic minority groups than in the White group. Among men, the unemployment rate (20 per cent) was nearly twice that for White men. The rates were highest for Bangladeshis (30.8 per cent), Black-Africans (28.9) and Pakistanis (28.5) and slightly lower, at around 25 per cent, for Black-Caribbean and Black-Other men. In contrast, unemployment among Indian men was 13.4 per cent and for Chinese men (10.5 per cent) it was slightly lower than for White men.

For women, unemployment among ethnic minority groups (15.6 per cent) was more than twice that for White women (6.5 per cent). The Pakistani and Bangladeshi groups again experienced the highest rates, even higher than men from the same ethnic groups, despite the fact that female unemployment rates were generally a lot lower than those of men. Unemployment rates for Black women (16.8 per cent) were well below those for Black men, with the exception of the Black-African group where a quarter of women were unemployed. Chinese women had the lowest unemployment rate (8.2 per cent) of all the ethnic minority groups, although this was still higher than the White female rate. Indian women also had relatively low unemployment rates at 12.6 per cent.

The chapter on industrial and occupational growth and decline looks at the implications of some ethnic groups being concentrated in particular sectors and outlines employment prospects over the medium term by using labour market projections. Although there

is no evidence that workers from ethnic minority groups are unequivocally concentrated in declining industries and occupations, some sub-groups are particularly vulnerable, according to forecast labour market trends. These include South Asian women in craft and plant and machine operative occupations in declining industries, and Black men and women in unskilled occupations and in clerical and secretarial occupations in public services. In contrast, Chinese men and women are particularly well-established in growth industries and occupations.

The impact of ethnic origins on education and occupational attainments is assessed in a chapter which asks whether members of ethnic minority groups have the same chances of securing desirable jobs and avoiding unemployment as do Whites of the same age and qualifications, and whether there is any difference between first and second generation minority groups.

Referring to 'ethnic penalties' (all sources of disadvantage, including discrimination), the authors find there are similar patterns between the generations, and little evidence that the second generation has an improved position in the labour market relative to British-born whites. Among the second generation, the relative chances of Black-Caribbean men reaching the salaried classes were 75 per cent of those of British-born Whites of the same age and qualifications. Their chances of avoiding unemployment were only 43 per cent of those of their White peers.

One of the reasons the Government gave for including an ethnic group question in the Census was to provide a benchmark against which the success of equal opportunity policies could be measured, and one chapter illustrates how the data can provide a basis for setting equal employment opportunity targets. Using Slough and its adjacent areas as a case study, the importance of geography is emphasised, with a key point being that each employer needs to be set targets reflecting conditions in their local area.

Other chapters examine various aspects of housing in relation to ethnic minority groups, and the final chapter addresses what the authors regard as appropriate responses to the findings of the Census, including the reform of race equality policy.

The authors also explain the technical aspects of using the Census to study ethnicity, including the use of Samples of Anonymised Records, Small Area Statistics and Local Base Statistics; look at the interpretation and possible problems of the ethnic group question; and examine the impact of under-enumeration on analyses of ethnic groups.

● *Ethnicity in the 1991 Census Volume 4: Employment, education and housing among the ethnic minority populations of Britain.* Valerie Karn (ed). The Stationery Office; 1997; £29.95; 296pp; ISBN 0 11 691658 3.

GIVEN THE large potential effects of European Union mandates related to the labour market, a 'thorough examination' of these effects should precede the introduction of any EU directive, according to a recent book assessing Europe's labour markets.

Ten authors address the issue of Community-level mandates, producing a range of interpretations which the editors hope will provide both a framework for evaluating EU social policy and insights into the consequences of social policy mandates. Confirming that the move towards labour market harmonisation in Europe is substantive and of consequence, the book examines two fundamental questions: whether government regulation in general and supranational regulation in particular can improve on individuals freely contracting with each other; and the extent to which government regulation improves the opportunities of some workers while harming the prospects of others. The different authors arrive at contrasting or opposing positions but all provide substantial evidence to support their conclusions.

The context is set by a chapter outlining both existing and prospective legislation, describing the course of policy from the 1970s onwards, followed by an analysis of the justifications for regulation of the labour market, together with an assessment of the likely impact of such regulation.

Against this background, the various factors affecting Community mandates are addressed from different perspectives. Chapters giving a

HOUSE OF COMMONS

Department of the Clerk of the House

Education and Employment Committee Specialist Assistant

A Specialist Assistant specialising in employment matters is required on the Education and Employment Committee. The duties will include giving assistance to the Clerk of the Committee, principally in preparing briefing material and draft reports for the Committee in support of their inquiries into a wide range of topics. Applications are invited from candidates with a good degree or an equivalent professional qualification in a relevant subject together with several years' relevant practical experience. An interest in public administration and a working knowledge of statistics would be an advantage.

Salary will be in the range of £18,256 - £28,906 pa (including Recruitment and Retention Allowance of £1,776 pa), according to qualifications and experience. The post is pensionable. Leave is generous. The appointment will commence as soon as possible after the satisfactory outcome of the normal post-interview enquiries, probably in January 1998, and will be for an initial period of two years with the possibility of extension for a further two years.

Strict political impartiality is required of all House of Commons staff and the persons appointed will be expected not to engage in political activities for the duration of the appointment.

Applications are sought from candidates with a good knowledge of policy matters which come within the employment responsibility of the Education and Employment Department and a good knowledge of labour market issues, possibly with a background in economics.

Strong computing and word processing skills are essential.

For further details and an application form (to be returned by 26th September 1997), write to **Recruitment & Assessment Services**, Innovation Court, New Street, Basingstoke, Hampshire RG21 7JB, or telephone Basingstoke (01256) 468551 (24 hours), or fax 01256 383786/383787. Please quote reference C3416 post C.

The House of Commons is an Equal Opportunities Employer.

Applications from registered disabled candidates will be welcomed

broad-based legal and economic analysis include an assessment of the role played by the European Court of Justice in the development of harmonisation of labour standards among member states. It is argued that the Court has both weakened and strengthened harmonisation, for example, by its 'direct effect' doctrine which confers rights on individuals against the state and, in contrast, by its ruling that different social standards are permissible among states - even if this interferes with trade - if the standards can be justified on public policy grounds.

Another chapter takes up the implications of EC labour regulation on industrial relations, arguing that the internationalisation of firms and industrial restructuring brought about by the Single European Market could destabilise co-operation between workers and employers, resulting in workplace conflicts and undermining economic performance. To counteract this threat, a social dimension to mandates is needed and it is claimed that certain measures - such as works councils - can help maintain employer-worker cooperation.

Two German contributors provide arguments that are most opposed to Community-level mandates. One contends that rules governing the social protection of workers in a country determine that country's competitive position as much as its raw materials and human capital - as with these other materials, so an individual country's social system has to stand a competitive 'market test'. Therefore, it is argued, a mandate that harmonises employment protection but leaves the other factors the same is illogical and damaging to competition.

The second German contribution looks at the tensions which have stemmed from the desire to preserve the corporatist nature of German institutions in an increasingly competitive international economy.

Spain is also taken as a case study in a chapter which addresses whether there is a link between the country's tightly regulated labour market and its high unemployment rates, while another section compares the EU with the North American Free Trade Agreement.

Finally, a brief overview of European labour markets, along with those of the USA and Japan, aims to provide empirical material relevant to the debate on the links between regulation and labour market outcomes. To this end, it includes comparative data on wage-fixing machinery, protection against dismissal, laws affecting labour contracts, employment statistics, earnings and income, and trends in unemployment inequality by education.

● *Labour Markets in Europe: Issues of Harmonization and Regulation*, edited J. T. Addison and W. Stanley Siebert. The Dryden Press; 1997; £17.95; 251pp; ISBN 0 03 099046 7.

PRIVATISATION

The rapid increase in privatisation in many countries since the 1980s has resulted in a number of consequences for individual labour markets. A recent study by the International Labour Organization assesses these consequences in developing countries (Republic of Korea, India and Mexico) and transition economies (Bulgaria, the Czech Republic, the former East Germany and Hungary) during the first half of the 1990s.

In the developing countries the key issues are usually how privatisation can promote efficiency and reduce the public debt, while in central and eastern Europe it has been a fundamental part of the transformation of a state-managed economy.

Based on more than 20 case studies, the study considers the effect of privatisation on productivity and on the level and structure of employment, and also examines the changes in wages, remuneration systems and industrial relations that evolved in newly-privatised firms.

Despite the differences in the countries and industries that make up the case studies, the book points to a number of conclusions.

In many cases, it was found that exposure to competition, rather than the nature of ownership itself, created the most pressure for improved efficiency. There was not sufficient evidence to say whether or not such improvements could be achieved without privatisation, but with other internal and external reforms which often accompanied privatisation, nor whether change in ownership per se increased efficiency.

● *Lessons from Privatization*, edited R. Van der Hoeven and G. Sziraczki. International Labour Organization; 1997; £14.85; 190pp; ISBN 92 2 109452 9.

Prepared by
the Government
Statistical Service

The Office for National Statistics
overview and update of trends in the
labour market, drawn from the Labour
Market Data section's detailed tables.

LABOUR MARKET UPDATE

LABOUR MARKET OVERVIEW

◆ **The latest statistics confirm continuing growth in the labour market, with falling unemployment and stable earnings growth. The Labour Force Survey figures indicate unemployment falling by around 20-35,000 a month. Recent claimant count figures are not inconsistent with this range.**

◆ **Unemployment levels continued to fall, as was indicated by both the spring 1997 LFS and the most recent claimant count figures.** Levels and rates on both measures were the lowest since 1990. Seasonally-adjusted unemployment in Great Britain on the ILO measure fell to a level of 2,037,000 in spring 1997, a decrease of 74,000 over the quarter and 285,000 over the year. The number of claimants in the UK (seasonally adjusted) fell by 49,800 in July to 1,550,000, an annual decrease of 576,000.

◆ **The ILO unemployment rate in Great Britain** (seasonally adjusted) was 7.2 per cent in spring 1997, down 0.3 percentage points over the quarter and 1.1 points over the year. The UK claimant count rate was 5.5 per cent in July, a decrease of 0.2 percentage points on the June rate.

◆ On the ILO measure, **long-term unemployed** (over one year) at 758,000 is now 717,000 lower than at its peak in spring 1984, but 127,000 higher than the start of the most recent upwards trend in spring 1991. The UK long-term claimant count fell by 85,500 over the quarter to 531,000 in July.

◆ The latest LFS results confirmed rising employment levels. In the quarter to spring 1997, the seasonally-adjusted **Great Britain total in employment rose by 91,000 to 26,076,000.** This represented an increase over the year of 431,000, and was the highest level since spring 1990. **UK Workforce in Employment** estimates (seasonally adjusted) showed an **increase of 86,000** in the quarter ending March to a level of **26,209,000** - the highest since September 1991 - resulting in an annual rise of 359,000.

◆ The seasonally-adjusted number of **employees in manufacturing industries** in Great Britain was **3,944,000** in June, a rise of 3,000 over the month. Employment in manufacturing rose by 25,000 over the year.

◆ The underlying annual **growth in average earnings** for the whole economy has **remained stable** in recent months. In the year to June, the underlying increase was 4.25 per cent (seasonally adjusted), the same as the year to May.

◆ The number of **new vacancies notified to UK Jobcentres fell by 1,000** in July to 224,900 (seasonally adjusted) but was 1,800 higher than the same month last year. The stock of unfilled vacancies in the UK in July was, at 284,400 (seasonally adjusted), at its highest level since the series began in 1980, reflecting an increase of 1,500 over the month and 54,300 over the year. The seasonally-adjusted number of placings by the employment service was 138,000 in July, down 4,000 over the month and down 10,000 since July 1996.

ECONOMIC ACTIVITY

Figure 1. *Tables 7.1-7.3*

◆ The economic activity rate for all people in Great Britain aged 16 and over from the spring (March to May) 1997 LFS (seasonally adjusted) stood at 62.9 per cent, the same rate as in winter (December to February) 1996/7 and 0.1 percentage points higher than spring 1996.

◆ The spring 1997 LFS recorded 84.9 per cent of men of working age as economically active (seasonally adjusted), compared with 71.9 per cent of women. The difference between the rates for men and women has decreased over the year to spring 1997. Over the

quarter, the rate did not change for men but fell by 0.2 points for women, while over the year the rates fell 0.2 percentage points for men and rose by 0.3 points for women.

◆ The LFS shows that the net increase in the number in employment of 431,000 in the year to spring 1997 was balanced by a decrease in the ILO unemployed of 285,000, an increase in the number of economically inactive of 8,000, and an increase in the total population aged 16 and over of 154,000 (all seasonally adjusted).

◆ In an analysis by age band, the spring 1997 LFS shows that the economic activity rate (not seasonally adjusted) remained highest for men among those aged 25-34 (93.4 per cent) and for women among those aged 35-49 (77.2 per cent).

◆ The seasonally adjusted economic inactivity rate for women of working age was 28.1 per cent in spring 1997, 0.3 percentage points lower than in spring 1996. The rate for men increased by 0.2 percentage points over the same period, standing at 15.1 per cent in spring 1997.

Figure 1   Economic activity rates by age group; spring 1997; Great Britain; not seasonally adjusted

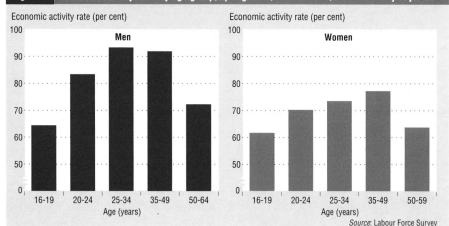

Source: Labour Force Survey

HOURS OF WORK

◆ The LFS estimate of the total number of actual hours worked per week (seasonally adjusted) was 866 million during spring 1997, up 1.7 per cent on spring 1996. This was a result of a rise of 1.7 per cent over the year in total employment and a decrease of 0.1 per cent in average actual weekly hours.

ECONOMIC BACKGROUND

Tables 0.5, 6.1-6.5

◆ Gross Domestic Product (GDP) in the second quarter of 1997 was 0.9 per cent higher than the previous quarter and 3.4 per cent higher than a year earlier.

◆ Excluding oil and gas, GDP in the second quarter of 1997 was 1.0 per cent higher than the previous quarter and 3.6 per cent higher than a year earlier.

◆ Retail sales volumes in the three months to June were 1.8 per cent higher than in the previous three months and 5.3 per cent higher than a year earlier.

◆ Manufacturing output in the three months to June was 0.1 per cent lower than in the previous three months but 1.6 per cent up on a year earlier.

◆ Construction output in the first quarter of 1997 was 1.1 per cent higher than the previous quarter and 3.6 per cent higher than a year earlier.

◆ Manufacturing investment in the first quarter of 1997 was 6.4 per cent higher than the previous quarter but 4.5 per cent lower than a year earlier.

◆ Government consumption in the first quarter of 1997 was 0.4 per cent lower than the previous quarter but 1.4 per cent higher than a year earlier.

◆ The balance of trade in goods in the three months to May was in deficit by £2.2 billion compared with a deficit of £2.3 billion in the previous three months and a deficit of £3.4 billion a year earlier.

◆ Excluding oil and erratics, export volumes in the three months to May were 2.7 per cent up on the previous three months and 6.6 per cent higher than a year earlier.

◆ Excluding oil and erratics, import volumes in the three months to May were 0.6 per cent up on the previous three months and 5.3 per cent higher than a year earlier.

◆ The increase over the 12 months to July in the 'all items' RPI was 3.3 per cent, up from 2.9 per cent for June. The main upward effect on the all items 12-month rate came from seasonal food prices and increased housing and motoring costs. Seasonal food prices fell less sharply than last year as adverse weather conditions restricted supplies. The rise in housing costs was principally due to increased mortgage interest payments following the increase in the base lending rates in June, although there was also an upward effect from house price increases. Within the motoring costs component, there was a strong upward effect from petrol price rises as a result of the increase in road fuel duty announced in the budget. This was partly offset by reductions in vehicle insurance premiums. There was also a small upward effect from charges for leisure services, which was offset by reduced fuel and light charges.

◆ The 'all items' RPI was unchanged over the month (between June and July), compared to a fall of 0.4 per cent between June and July last year.

◆ Excluding mortgage interest payments (RPIX), the 12-month rate of price increases was 3.0 per cent for July, up from 2.7 per cent for June.

◆ The index for all items excluding mortgage interest payments and indirect taxes (also known as RPIY) showed an increase over the latest 12 months of 2.2 per cent, unchanged from June.

◆ The 12-month rate of increase in the output price index for home sales of manufactured products is provisionally estimated at 1.4 per cent in July, compared with 1.1 per cent (provisional) in June. The input price index for materials and fuels purchased by manufacturing industry provisionally decreased by 9.0 per cent over the year to July, compared with a provisional decrease of 8.6 per cent for June.

EMPLOYMENT

Figure 2.
Tables 0.1-0.4, 1.1-1.5, 1.11, 7.1-7.4

◆ The latest results from the Labour Force Survey (LFS) for Great Britain, carried out in spring 1997, showed that total employment (seasonally adjusted) stood at 26,076,000, a rise of 91,000 since winter 1996/7 and a rise of 431,000 since spring 1996. Both male and female employment increased. The number of men in employment was up over the quarter by 42,000, and over the year by 259,000, reaching 14,395,000. The number of women in employment rose by 49,000 over the quarter, and 172,000 over the year, to 11,681,000. *(Table 7.1)*

◆ According to the LFS, the number of employees in Great Britain rose by 422,000 to 22,507,000 (seasonally adjusted) between spring 1996 and spring 1997, while the number of self-employed was 47,000 higher at 3,260,000. Over the quarter to spring 1997, the number of employees rose by 106,000 but the number of self-employed fell by 17,000.

◆ The LFS also showed that the numbers of both full-time and part-time employees rose over the quarter (by 99,000 and 8,000 respectively) and over the year (283,000 and 139,000) to spring 1997. *(Table 7.4)*

◆ In an analysis by industry sector, the LFS shows that over the year to spring 1997, the numbers in employment (not seasonally adjusted) increased by 2.8 per cent in the service industries but fell by 1.4 per cent in the manufacturing industries. These industries together accounted for nearly nine-tenths of those in employment. The increase in service employment was greater for men than women (up 3.1 per cent and 2.6 per cent respectively), while the decrease in manufacturing employment was smaller for men than women (down 1.0 per cent and 2.4 per cent respectively).

◆ The UK Workforce in Employment (unchanged from figures published in June) rose by 86,000 (0.3 per cent) over the quarter to March, and by 359,000 over the year, to 26,209,000. This is the fourth consecutive quarterly rise, and was entirely in male employment. The increase was all in employees (104,000), while there were falls in participants in work-related government-supported training schemes (10,000), the self-employed (6,000) and armed forces (3,000). *(Table 1.1)*

◆ Manufacturing jobs in Great Britain rose by 3,000 in June to 3,944,000. Over the year the series has risen by 25,000 (0.6 per cent), compared with a fall of 3,000 (-0.1 per cent) the year before. Over the month to June the largest increase was in textiles and leather, and other machinery and equipment, both up by 3,000 employees. The industry group showing the largest monthly fall was electrical and optical equipment, down by 8,000 employees. *(Table 1.2)*

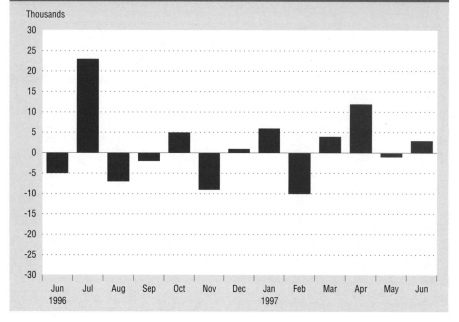

| Figure 2 | Monthly changes in manufacturing employees; June 1996 to June 1997; Great Britain; seasonally adjusted |

Thousands

UNEMPLOYMENT

Figures 3 and 4.
Tables 0.1-0.4, 2.1-2.24 (except 2.18), 7.1-7.6 (except 7.4)

◈ **On the ILO basis,** the LFS recorded that the seasonally-adjusted number unemployed in Great Britain in spring 1997 stood at 2,037,000, with quarterly and yearly falls of 74,000 and 285,000 people respectively. *(Table 7.1)*

◈ The seasonally-adjusted ILO unemployment rate fell over both the quarter and the year to spring 1997, by 0.3 and 1.1 percentage points respectively, to 7.2 per cent. *(Table 7.3)*

◈ The LFS also shows that 1,294,000 men and 743,000 women (seasonally adjusted) were ILO unemployed in spring 1997 - down 32,000 for men and down 42,000 for women since winter 1996/7, and down 231,000 and 53,000 respectively since spring 1996. *(Table 7.1)*

◈ The LFS recorded 595,000 ILO unemployed young people (those aged 16 to 24) in spring 1997, 63,000 fewer than in spring 1996. The youth ILO unemployment rate was 13.6 per cent.

◈ The LFS reports a fall in the number of long-term (over one year) ILO unemployed people over the year to spring 1997, both in total (by 135,000 to 758,000) and as a proportion of all ILO unemployed people (by 1.1 percentage points to 38.3 per cent).

◈ On the ILO basis, seasonally-adjusted unemployment in Great Britain (spring 1997) stood at 2 million (or 7.2 per cent), which is 435,000 higher than the Great Britain claimant count for the same period.

◈ **Claimant count unemployment statistics** are no longer affected by changes in the benefit regime. However, it is possible that labour market behaviour will continue to be influenced to some extent for some time to come. The recorded claimant unemployment falls sustained over the last six months

suggest that the rate of fall in unemployment is now higher than it was in mid-1996.

◈ The UK seasonally-adjusted claimant count level fell by 49,800 in July 1997 to stand at 1,550,000. *(Table 2.1)*

◈ The claimant count level was 43,900 lower than in April 1990 when it reached its last trough, and also 1,431,100 (48 per cent) lower than in December 1992 when it last reached a peak.

◈ The seasonally-adjusted claimant count rate, at 5.5 per cent of the workforce, is down 0.2 percentage points over the previous month. This is the lowest rate since April 1990. *(Table 2.1)*

◈ The UK claimant count rate is 2.1 percentage points lower than 12 months ago and, over the year, has fallen in every region for both men and women. *(Tables 2.1 and 2.3)*

◈ Between June and July 1997 the total level of seasonally-adjusted claimant count fell in every region. The largest regional percentage falls were in the South West, London, Scotland and the South East (GOR). *(Table 2.3)*

◈ The UK unadjusted claimant count level fell by 572,801 over the year to stand at 1,585,272, or 5.6 per cent of the workforce, down 2.1 percentage points over the year. *(Table 2.1)*

◈ The unadjusted UK long-term (more than one year) claimant count fell by 85,500 over the quarter ended July 1997 to 531,000. *(Tables 2.6 and 2.8)*

◈ The unadjusted UK youth (18-24 years old) claimant count rose by 1,200 over the quarter ended July 1997 to 422,900. *(Tables 2.5 and 2.6)*

JOBCENTRE VACANCIES

Figure 4.
Tables 3.1-3.3

◈ The number of vacancies remaining unfilled at Jobcentres (UK, seasonally adjusted) rose by 1,500 between June and July to 284,400. *(Table 3.1)*

◈ The seasonally-adjusted number of new vacancies notified to Jobcentres fell by 1,000 in July to 224,900. *(Table 3.1)*

◈ On a seasonally-adjusted basis, the number of people placed into jobs by the Employment Service fell by 3,600 in July to 137,500. *(Table 3.1)*

AVERAGE EARNINGS

Figure 5.
Tables 5.1, 5.3

◈ The underlying rate of increase in average earnings for the whole economy in the year to June 1997 was provisionally estimated to be 4¼ per cent. This was unchanged from the May figure. *(Table 5.1)*

◈ The September to November 1993 rate of 3 per cent was the lowest since 1967.

◈ The actual increase in whole economy average earnings was 4.1 per cent in the year to June 1997. *(Table 5.1)*

◈ In the manufacturing industries the underlying increase was 4¼ per cent. This was unchanged from the May figure. *(Table 5.1)*

◈ The November 1993 and September to December 1995 rates are the lowest since 1967 for the manufacturing industries.

◈ The production industries increase was 4¼ per cent. This is unchanged from the May figure and is the fifth successive month at 4¼. *(Table 5.1)*

◈ In the service industries the increase was 4½ per cent in June, unchanged from the May rate. *(Table 5.1)*

◈ The September and October 1993 figure of 2¼ per cent for the service sector was the lowest rate since the series began in 1985.

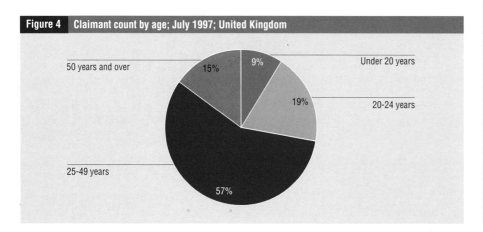

| Figure 3 | Claimant count by duration; July 1997; United Kingdom |

| Figure 4 | Claimant count by age; July 1997; United Kingdom |

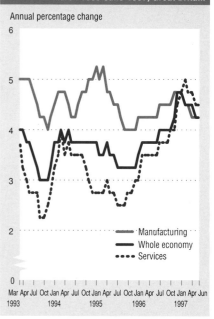

| Figure 5 | Underlying average earnings index; March 1993-June 1997; Great Britain |

PRODUCTIVITY AND UNIT WAGE COSTS

Figure 6.
Tables 1.8, 5.8

◈ Manufacturing output was 1.6 per cent higher in the three months ending June 1997 compared with a year earlier. *(Table 1.8)*

◈ Manufacturing productivity in terms of output per head was 1.4 per cent higher in the three months ending June 1997 compared with a year earlier. *(Table 1.8)*

◈ Manufacturing unit wage costs rose by 2.8 per cent in the three months ending June 1997 compared with a year earlier. *(Table 5.8)*

◈ Whole economy output per head was 1.9 per cent higher in the first quarter of 1997 compared with a year earlier. *(Table 1.8)*

◈ Whole economy unit wage costs were 2.8 per cent higher in the first quarter of 1997 compared with a year earlier. *(Table 5.8)*

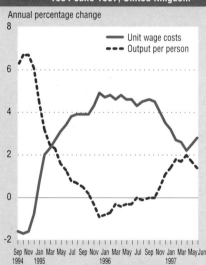

| Figure 6 | Manufacturing unit wage costs and output per person; September 1994-June 1997; United Kingdom |

Annual percentage change

TRAINING

Tables 7.7, 8.1-8.11

◈ Seasonally adjusted, three million (14.3 per cent) employees of working age received job-related training in the four weeks prior to LFS interview during winter 1996. This suggests a very slight increase on autumn 1996. *(Table 7.7)*

◈ The number participating in Training for Work (TfW) in England and Wales at the beginning of June 1997 was 19 per cent lower than it was 12 months earlier. *(Table 8.1)*

◈ The proportion of leavers from TfW between November 1995 and October 1996 who were in a job six months after leaving, was 3 percentage points higher than the figures for leavers between November 1994 and October 1995. This proportion continues to show an upward trend. *(Table 8.3)*

◈ The proportion who gained a qualification in the same period was 4 percentage points lower than the equivalent for leavers a year earlier. *(Table 8.4)*

◈ The number of Youth Training (YT) participants in England and Wales in June 1997 was 9 per cent lower than in the previous year. *(Table 8.1)*

◈ The proportion of YT leavers in the 12 months to October 1996 who were in a job six months after leaving was 4 percentage points higher than for leavers in the 12 months to October 1995. *(Table 8.5)*

◈ The proportion of YT leavers in the 12 months to October 1996 who gained a qualification while on the programme was the same as for 12 months earlier. The proportion who gained a full qualification rose by 1 percentage point. *(Table 8.1)*

◈ The number of people on Modern Apprenticeships in England and Wales was 82,200 in June 1997. Although this represents a small fall over the previous month, the overall trend is for the programme to continue to increase steadily in size. *(Table 8.1)*

INTERNATIONAL COMPARISONS

Tables 2.18, 5.9, 6.8-6.9

◈ Compared with our EU partners, the internationally comparable ILO unemployment rate for the UK is lower than in Spain, Finland, France, Ireland, Italy, Sweden, Belgium, Germany and Portugal. *(Table 2.18)*

◈ The UK ILO rate is higher than in the Netherlands, Denmark, Austria and Luxembourg. *(Table 2.18)*

◈ The UK rate is below the EU average using the latest available data (6.9 per cent for the UK in May 1997 compared to 10.8 per cent for the EU as a whole).

◈ Manufacturing average earnings increase was higher for Great Britain than in five OECD countries. *(Table 5.9)*

◈ Harmonised indices of consumer prices (HICPs) are being calculated in each member state of the European Union for the purpose of international comparisons. This is in the context of one of the convergence criteria for monetary union as required by the Maastricht treaty. Eurostat published HICPs for the 15 European Union member states on 7 March 1997. To coincide with the transmission of UK HICP indices to Eurostat, UK HICP figures were released by ONS on 26 February in First Release ONS (97) 50. A more detailed breakdown of the UK HICP is given in the RPI Business Monitor MM23. For non-EU countries, consumer price indices excluding housing costs remain the best available basis of comparison. The RPI remains the best indicator of UK consumer price inflation.

◈ In EU countries there was an average rise in consumer prices of 1.6 per cent (provisional) over the 12 months to June, compared with an increase of 1.7 per cent in the UK. Over the same period consumer prices rose in France by 1.0 per cent and in Germany by 1.5 per cent. Outside the EU, consumer prices rose by 1.9 per cent in the USA, by 2.4 per cent in Canada and by 1.1 per cent (provisional) in Japan.

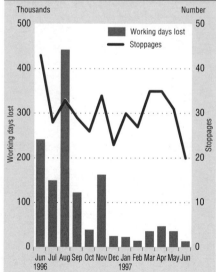

| Figure 7 | Working days lost due to labour disputes; June 1996-June 1997; United Kingdom |

LABOUR DISPUTES

Figure 7.
Tables 4.1-4.2

◈ It is provisionally estimated that 13,000 working days were lost because of stoppages of work in June 1997, which is lower than the revised estimate for May 1997 (36,000). It compares with 241,000 in June 1996 and a June average of 83,000 over the period 1990 to 1996.

◈ The number of working days lost in the 12 months to June 1997 is provisionally estimated to be 1,109,000 - equivalent to 49 days lost per 1,000 employees. Although the latest estimate is higher than the corresponding period a year ago (607,000), it is lower than the average over the ten year period 1987 to 1996 (1,721,000).

◈ Some 60 per cent of the 1,109,000 days lost were in the transport, storage and communication group industries (667,000), 13 per cent were lost in education (147,000), and a further 12 per cent were lost in manufacturing (137,000).

◈ A provisional total of 240 stoppages were recorded as being in progress in the 12 months to June 1997, which is lower than the corresponding period last year (246). The provisional single month figure for June is 20, which compares with 43 in June 1996.

If you have any comments or suggestions on the Labour Market Update please ring Cathy Baker at the Office for National Statistics, tel: 0171 533 6086

FOR DETAILED FIGURES SEE THE LABOUR MARKET DATA SECTION

LABOUR FORCE SURVEY

0171 533 6176

HELP-LINE

Prepared by
the Government
Statistical Service

---

*T*he Labour Force Survey (LFS) is a sample survey, conducted by the Social Survey Division of ONS, of around 60,000 households each quarter which provides a wide range of information about the labour force using internationally standard definitions. This feature presents some analyses carried out in response to enquiries on the Office for National Statistics' Labour Market Enquiry Helpline (incorporating the LFS Helpline).

CONTENTS FOR SEPTEMBER 1997 - PRESENTING RESULTS FROM WINTER (DECEMBER TO FEBRUARY) 1996/7 LFS

1 Employees and self-employed looking for a different or additional job

- *In winter 1996/7, 1.5 million employees and self-employed (around 6 per cent of all employees and self-employed) were looking for a different job.*

2 Type of accommodation by economic activity

- *The proportion of heads of household who owned their accommodation outright was greatest for the group who were economically inactive.*

3 People born in the UK and outside, by ethnic origin

- *For most groups, those born in the UK had higher activity rates than those born elsewhere.*

4 Employees in service industries, by occupation

- *For both men and women, the occupations with the lowest proportion of employees in a service industry were the craft and related occupations and plant and machine operatives.*

---

1 EMPLOYEES AND SELF-EMPLOYED WHO ARE LOOKING FOR A DIFFERENT OR ADDITIONAL JOB

The LFS asks people who are in employment whether they have been looking for a different or additional job, and their reasons for doing so. *Table 1* shows that in winter 1996/7, 1.5 million employees and self-employed (around 6 per cent of all employees and self-employed) were looking for a different job, and 0.2 million (less than 1 per cent of all employees and self-employed) were looking for an additional job.

Respondents can give up to three reasons why they are looking for a different job. *Table 2* gives the *main* reason that people gave in winter 1996/7. For both men and women the most common reason was that pay was unsatisfactory in their present job; 27 per cent of employees and self-employed looking for a different job gave this response. Around 5 per cent of employees and self-employed wanted longer hours than at present and around 3 per cent wanted shorter hours.

Table 1 Employees and self-employed looking for a different or additional job (Great Britain, winter 1996/7, not seasonally adjusted)

Thousands	All	Men	Women
Total number of employees and self-employed	**25,576**	**14,113**	**11,463**
of whom			
are looking for a different/additional job[a]	1,729	1,010	719
-different job	1,508	906	602
as a percentage of all employees and self-employed	*5.9*	*6.4*	*5.3*
-additional job	215	103	113
as a percentage of all employees and self-employed	*0.8*	*0.7*	*1.0*

a Includes a small number of people who did not state if the job they were seeking was different or additional.

Table 2 Main reason employees and self-employed gave for looking for a different job (Great Britain, winter 1996/7, not seasonally adjusted)

Per cent	All	Men	Women
Reasons for looking for a different job			
Pay unsatisfactory in present job	27	29	23
Other aspects of present job unsatisfactory	22	21	25
Present job may come to an end	14	15	13
Present job to fill time before finding another	10	10	10
Wants longer hours than in present job	5	3	8
Journey unsatisfactory in present job	3	3	4
Wants shorter hours than in present job	3	3	2
Other reason	15	16	15
Base: All employees and self-employed looking for a different job (thousands) (=100%)	**1,508**	**906**	**602**

2 TYPE OF ACCOMMODATION BY ECONOMIC ACTIVITY

The LFS is able to examine household characteristics according to the labour market status of the head of household. *Table 3* looks at housing accommodation types according to the economic activity of the heads of households for winter 1996/7.

The proportion of heads of households who owned their accommodation outright was greatest for the group who were economically inactive (over four in ten). A similar proportion of inactive heads of households rented their accommodation. Nearly all of the economically inactive heads who owned outright were aged 50 or over;

they were likely to have had longer to pay off any mortgage or loan than younger homeowners. This can be compared with ILO unemployed heads of households, where the majority rented and with those in employment where the majority were in the process of buying accommodation with a mortgage or loan.

Among the heads of households in employment, around a quarter who were part-time employees owned their accommodation. This group included a large proportion of heads of households who were aged 50 or over and were thus more likely to own their accommodation outright.

A further large proportion of part-time employees (over four in ten) rented their accommodation.

From spring 1996 onwards, new categories were introduced to the housing tenure question in the LFS (see red box). In winter 1996/7, around 308,000 heads of households (1 per cent of all heads of households) were in accommodation that was rent-free. This proportion was highest among heads of household who were temporary employees and is partly explained by the type of jobs that are temporary (for example, a quarter of heads of households who worked in agriculture and fishing lived rent-free).

There were also 60,000 heads of household (less than 1 per cent of all heads) who had part-rent part-mortgage accommodation; around three-quarters of these heads were in employment.

Figure 1 shows the type of rented accommodation, by economic activity for winter 1996/7. Heads of households who were renting or living rent-free were most likely to live in council or housing association accommodation (see red box) if the head was economically inactive. Over eight in ten inactive heads were in this group, compared with around half of heads of households who were in employment.

Table 3 Accommodation type of households, by economic activity of head

(Great Britain, winter 1996/7, not seasonally adjusted)

Per cent	All heads of households[a] (thousands) (= 100%)	Owned outright	Being bought with mortgage or loan	Rented	Rent-free
All in employment	13,715	13	64	20	1
All employees	11,288	12	65	21	1
Full-time employees	10,157	10	69	19	1
Part-time employees	1,130	26	30	43	1
Permanent employees	10,580	11	67	20	1
Temporary employees	603	14	45	38	2
Self-employed	2,344	21	62	16	1
ILO unemployed	1,095	9	24	66	*
Economically inactive	9,185	45	10	44	1
All heads of households	23,995	25	42	31	1

a Includes around 60,000 heads of household (less than 1 per cent of all heads of households) whose accommodation was part-rent, part-mortgage. Bases for calculation of percentages exclude heads of households who did not state their accommodation and a very small number of heads who gave squatting as a response.
* Sample size too small for a reliable estimate.

Housing tenure in the LFS

Prior to spring 1996, respondents were asked whether they owned their accommodation outright, were buying their accommodation with a mortgage or loan, or whether their accommodation was rented/rent-free. From spring 1996 onwards, rented/rent-free was split into two distinct categories and two more categories were added: part-rent part-mortgage, and squatting.

Those who said that their accommodation was rented/rent-free were asked who it was rented from or provided by:

● 'council or housing association' includes those who replied that their accommodation was rented from a local authority or council, Scottish Homes, New Town corporation, housing association, co-operative or housing charitable trust; and

● 'other' includes those who said that they rented their accommodation from an employing organisation, another organisation, relative of household member, individual employer or other individual private landlord.

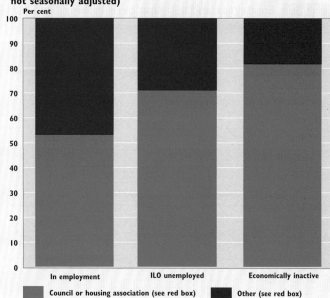

Figure 1 Type of rented accommodation, by economic activity of heads of household (Great Britain, winter 1996/7, not seasonally adjusted)

Per cent

In employment ILO unemployed Economically inactive

■ Council or housing association (see red box)   ■ Other (see red box)

3 | PEOPLE BORN IN THE UK AND OUTSIDE, BY ETHNIC ORIGIN

Figure 2 gives the economic activity rates for people of working age born in the UK and elsewhere, by ethnic origin, for an annual average of spring 1996 through to winter 1996/7. Averaging over four quarters increases the reliability of estimates of groups like ethnic minorities, where sample sizes are often too small for detailed analysis (see February 1997 LFS Help-Line).

Economic activity rates were higher for men than women and slightly higher for Whites than most other ethnic groups. For most ethnic groups, those born in the UK had higher activity rates than those born elsewhere. The exceptions were men of 'other origins', where the rates were the same, and Indian and Pakistani/Bangladeshi men, where activity rates were higher for those born elsewhere. The age structure has an important influence on economic activity rates because young people are more likely to be in full-time education. For all groups, those born in the UK had a higher proportion of 16 to 24-year-olds than those born elsewhere. The difference between those born in the UK and those born elsewhere (in the proportion of 16 to 24-year-olds) was greatest for the Indian and Pakistani/Bangladeshi groups. Among 16 to 24-year-olds, Pakistani/Bangladeshi men and Indian men (and women) were more likely than other groups to be inactive and in full-time education. This partly explains why men from these ethnic groups born in the UK had lower activity rates.

The lowest activity rates of those born in the UK and elsewhere were for Pakistani/Bangladeshi women, where around two in five of those born in the UK were economically active compared with around one in five of those born elsewhere. As for all groups, this may reflect differences in age and culture between those born in the UK and those born elsewhere.

Figure 3 gives the ILO unemployment rates for spring 1996 to winter 1996/7 of Whites and the other ethnic minority groups combined, for people of working age. ILO unemployment rates were lower for Whites than the ethnic minority groups combined (although there were differences in rates between the different minority groups). For the latter, rates were higher for those born in the UK. This is associated with youth unemployment. However, the age distribution explains only part of the difference in the ILO unemployment rates between Whites and ethnic minorities combined. Other possible reasons for the difference were suggested in 'Trends in the labour market participation of ethnic groups, 1984 to 1996', *Labour Market Trends,* August 1997, pp 295-303.

Figure 2 | **Economic activity rates for people of working age[a] by ethnic group and whether born in the UK[b]**

(Great Britain, annual average of spring 1996 through to winter 1996/7, not seasonally adjusted)

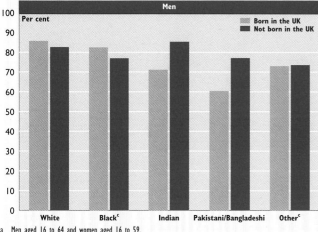
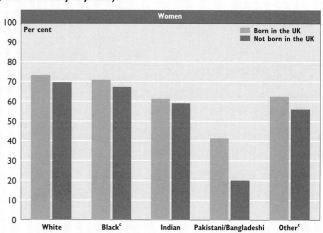

a   Men aged 16 to 64 and women aged 16 to 59.
b   UK (Great Britain and Northern Ireland) plus the Channel Islands and the Isle of Man.
c   People of 'Black-mixed' are included in the 'other' category for consistency with previous LFS articles, although the GSS harmonised output categories includes these people in the 'Black' category.

Figure 3 | **Unemployment rates for people of working age[a] by ethnic group and whether born in the UK[b]**

(Great Britain, annual average of spring 1996 through to winter 1996/7, not seasonally adjusted)

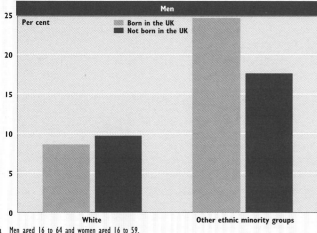

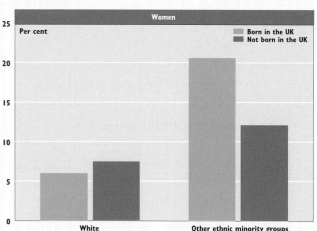

a   Men aged 16 to 64 and women aged 16 to 59.
b   UK (Great Britain and Northern Ireland) plus the Channel Islands and the Isle of Man.

4 EMPLOYEES IN SERVICE INDUSTRIES, BY OCCUPATION

The LFS classifies employment both by the type of activity engaged in by the employer (industry) and by the type of work done by the employee (occupation). It is of interest to look at the range of occupations undertaken by people employed in service industries.

Figure 4 gives the proportions of employees in each occupation group that work in service industries and other industries, for winter 1996/7. For both men and women, the occupations with the lowest proportion of employees in a service industry were the craft and related occupations and plant and machine operatives. Nevertheless, around a third of men and around a fifth of women in these occupations worked in a service industry. In each of the remaining occupations, the proportion of male employees in service industries was lower than that for women, although over nine in ten male employees in the personal and protective occupation group worked in a service industry.

Figure 4 | **Employees in service industries, by occupation** (Great Britain, winter 1996/7, not seasonally adjusted)

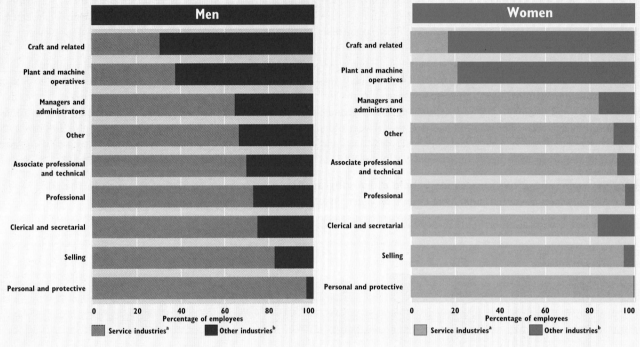

a Includes distribution, hotels and restaurants, transport and communication, banking, finance and insurance, public administration, education and health and other services.
b Includes agriculture and fishing, energy and water, manufacturing and construction industries.

Standard Occupational Classification

An accurate occupational classification is essential for identifying occupational trends and developments in the labour market. At the most detailed level of classification, the LFS uses around 500 codes to distinguish between different occupations (the Standard Occupational Classification - SOC). These codes are then grouped together, with reference to the skills, qualifications, training and experience needed competently to perform tasks in each occupation, to produce the broad groups seen in the LFS Help-Line and most other *Labour Market Trends* features. Some examples of the sorts of occupations included in each group are given below.

● Managers and administrators (SOC code 1) - for example, general managers of large companies or administrations, local government officers, officers in the armed forces, the police force and the fire service and managers and proprietors in service industries such as restaurants, garages and hairdressers;

● Professional occupations (SOC code 2) - for example, mechanical, electronic and chemical engineers, scientists, medical practitioners, teachers, judges, barristers and accountants;

● Associate professional and technical occupations (SOC code 3) - for example, scientific technicians, computer analysts, nurses and literary, artistic and sports professionals;

● Clerical and secretarial occupations (SOC code 4) - for example, receptionists, telephonists, clerks, personal assistants and secretaries;

● Craft and related occupations (SOC code 5) - for example, bricklayers, plasterers, glaziers and other construction trades, electronic/electric trades and wood and metalwork trades;

● Personal and protective service occupations (SOC code 6) - for example, NCOs and other ranks in the armed forces, police officers below the rank of sergeant, security guards, chefs, waiters/waitresses, hairdressers, and medical assistants such as ambulance staff and dental nurses;

● Sales occupations (SOC code 7) - for example, sales representatives, sales assistants, market and street traders, buyers and brokers.

● Plant and machine operatives (SOC code 8) - for example, drivers of buses, trains, taxis and lorries and operatives in chemical, metal making, textiles and food and drink processes; and

● Other occupations (SOC code 9) - for example, farm workers, coal miners, labourers, porters, postal workers and kitchen hands.

What effect does training have on productivity, profitability and employees' commitment to the organisation?

A recent report by **Francis Green,** Professor of Economics at Leeds University Business School, reviews the formal evidence available on the benefits of training to employers.

Review of information on the benefits of training for employers

Key findings

- There are large gaps in our knowledge about the way the training market is functioning.
- No research has been carried out, either in Britain or abroad, which attempts to measure the impact of training on company profitability.
- Research into the link between training and labour productivity is also lacking in Britain.
- Studies carried out abroad in most cases indicate that training has a direct and positive impact on productivity; there is little agreement, however, about the magnitude of the effect.
- Several British studies have found that the skills of an establishment's workforce do have a positive impact on productivity. To the extent that training raises skill levels, these studies therefore provide indirect evidence of the link between training and productivity.
- There is some evidence, both from Britain and abroad, to show that training reduces labour turnover and, therefore, helps to increase job tenure. However, the impact of training on labour mobility has been found to be relatively small.
- Few studies have examined the impact of training on raising employee commitment to corporate objectives. What evidence there is, however, does indicate a positive correlation between training and employee commitment.

THE REPORT reviews the formal evidence on the benefits of training for employers, in order to contribute to the overall evaluation of the functioning of the skill formation system in Britain. Formal evidence is defined as evidence derived from quantitative data drawn from large samples, using formal statistical methods of analysis.

The report concludes that there are large gaps in our knowledge about the way the training market is functioning. The potential importance of enterprise-based training for upgrading the skills of the British workforce is not in doubt, but no formal studies of companies have been completed in Britain which investigate the links between training and profits or productivity.

In Britain, enterprise training plays a pivotal role in the skill formation system. Job-related training has been organised around the principle of a training market in which the forces of supply and demand are allowed, as much as possible, to determine the level and quality of training that is provided. While the Government provides considerable support for the training of young people, for the most part the training of adult workers is left to employers or employees to fund and arrange. The Government provides encouragement to

firms to train, and substantial infra-structural support through the Training and Enterprise Councils and the Local Enterprise Councils. Especially important in this approach is the Investors in People standard. But it is primarily up to employers and their workforces to determine their training needs. Given this emphasis on enterprise training, it will be useful to understand the incentives that companies face when determining the level, the quality, and the purpose of any training they provide.

Attributed benefits of training

There are several reasons commonly offered by companies for training, and a number of benefits are correspondingly claimed. In addition to the aim of raising the skills of employees in their regular jobs, training is used for multi-skilling, to engender commitment or enthusiasm for corporate objectives, to implement change, to meet health and safety and other external standards, to prepare employees for promotion, or to attract good recruits. New skills that training is aimed at producing are typically quoted as computing, customer care and problem solving skills, ability to work in teams, and reliability and working to deadlines.

Whatever the benefits to the employees trained, the bottom line question for companies operating in the private sector is whether training is profitable. There are, however, no existing formal studies of the impact of training on profitability. Instead, there are studies which focus instead on 'intermediate' variables, that is, organisation-wide variables that are important in the determination of profits. The primary intermediate variable for this purpose is the productivity of the labour force, defined as output (measured in some suitable way) divided by employment. The value of these studies is that they can assess whether the claimed benefits for the workforce, as listed above, translate into real benefits for the company. Their dis-advantage is that, since they do not measure the costs of training, they cannot definitively assess the rate of return.

There is also some evidence on two other intermediate variables. The first concerns labour turnover, and the second is the degree of 'organisational commitment' of a company's workforce. In addition, the report considers two kinds of indirect evidence. First, it considers existing evidence about the relationship between the stock of skills of the workforce and productivity. Second, it briefly considers the evidence concerning the distribution of training opportunities among firms, and among employees within firms.

The findings

The report describes in non-specialist terms the findings of 21 formal research studies from Britain and abroad, providing an overview of these studies and of some other related evidence. It looks at the statistical and measurement problems that commonly occur in studies of the impact of training on companies before reviewing the overall findings.

Evidence about the link between training and labour productivity is lacking in Britain. Studies from abroad show in most, but not all, cases that training does have a positive impact on productivity. There is little agreement, however, about the magnitude of this effect. Estimates range from very large (about an 80 per cent increase attributed to training) to a negligible effect. One of the best studies, especially in terms of its representativeness and its standards of data collection, found no significant overall impact from training on company turnover or on productivity in a survey that sampled American establishments with at least 20 employees.[1] Nevertheless, it did find that certain kinds of training were effective in raising productivity, notably computer training in the non-manufacturing sector.

Because training may have an impact on labour turnover, and because the latter has a theoretical connection with organisational objectives, the report includes some evidence on this matter. The general finding is that the impact of training on labour mobility is comparatively small, in relation to other factors determining mobility, and for the most part is in the downward direction. This finding applies equally to British and American studies. Whether the training is for youths or for adults, the effect is mostly to reduce the probability of employees quitting their jobs in any one period, and thereby to increase the tenure of jobs, but not by much. The significance of this general conclusion is two-fold. First, it provides some reassurance that the danger of skilled workers being poached is not increased by offering them training, and is probably reduced somewhat. Second, it shows that there may be a minor contribution of training via this route (in addition to its impact via other routes) to meeting organisational goals.

Organisational commitment is typically measured by combining the responses to a set of questions to employees about their attitudes to their employer. Evidence on the impact of training on organisational commitment is surprisingly scarce. Among the now quite large number of studies that have looked at the antecedents and effects of organisational commitment, few have treated the presence of training opportunities as a possible variable. This omission is surprising because a number of commentators have suggested that such a link exists. Only two studies, one British the other American, provide relevant evidence. Both confirm a positive correlation between training and commitment. However, neither develops a suitable multivariate analysis to examine the influence of training separately from the influence of other variables. So it is not possible to conclude robustly that training increases commitment.

Since the amount of direct formal evidence on the question of training's impact on organisations is not all that large, it is useful to turn to some indirect formal evidence.

The main route through which training might be beneficial for companies is by raising the skills of the workforce, and hence productive efficiency. Hence, it seems relevant to check empirically whether a higher skilled workforce is substantially more productive. But this is only indirect evidence for any effect of training, for two reasons. First, it would need to be assumed that the company's training does indeed contribute to a significant rise in workforce skills. Second, the skills that companies acquire can be - and frequently are - obtained through recruitment, and by the same token any skilled workers obtained by the company's training might quit. It is therefore probably best to see any evidence about the link between skills and performance as a necessary though not sufficient condition for training to be thought of as benefiting companies through this route.

The evidence to date on this issue is that higher level skills normally lead to greater productivity. Most energetic in providing evidence on this issue has been the National Institute of Economic and Social Research. Many of its studies have compared the productivity and skills at workplaces in Britain with those at similar workplaces in continental Europe and they point to traditional deficiencies in Britain's supply of intermediate-skilled workers at the craft and technician levels. However, the impact of skills should not be overstated: there are many other sources of productivity differences, and one study reviewed is a reminder of this. The productive superiority of American establishments may, according to this evidence, be due not so much to better skills but mainly to economies of scale.

There are many groups of workers who tend to receive little or no training, and it is likely that firms have calculated that it does not benefit the company to fund such training. By the same token, much of the training actually undertaken is presumably done because it is perceived to pay off.

However, great care is needed when using evidence about who receives training to infer something about the returns of training. It may not be the case that training is always a response to economic incentives and, vice versa, there may be situations when there is an incentive to train but firms do not respond to it.

With heavy qualifications, this report includes in its review two studies on the distribution of training at a British company and one from the United States. The general evidence suggests the following: training is greater for those who have good qualifications or more education, for younger people, for new recruits to jobs, in larger establishments, in establishments that are introducing technological changes, and in establishments that have union representation. Training also varies considerably across occupational groups, with those in the less skilled groups receiving less training.

Missing knowledge

The report indicates that there are large gaps in our knowledge about the way the training market is functioning. The potential importance of enterprise-based training for upgrading the skills of the British workforce is not in doubt. But it is disarming that there are no formal studies of companies in Britain which can be called on to provide evidence of any direct link between training and productivity. The evidence from abroad is also patchy, though for the most part it does suggest that there is some positive link.

It is recommended, therefore, that future research should be devoted to examining the benefits of training on profitability, as well as to improving our knowledge of its effects on productivity and on other intermediate variables.

Footnotes

1 Lynch, L M and Black, S E: *Beyond the Incidence of Training: Evidence from a national employers survey,* Working Paper No. 5231 (1995), National Bureau of Economic Research.

Review of Information on the Benefits of Training for Employers, DfEE research report RR7, is available from Cambertown Ltd, tel 01709 888688. Price £4.95. ISBN 0 85522 592 0.

PREPARED BY
THE GOVERNMENT
STATISTICAL SERVICE

Distribution of hourly earnings

Growing interest in regional earnings has resulted in the Office for National Statistics producing new regional tables on the proportions of employees earning below specific pay thresholds.

By **Derek Bird,** Earnings and Employment Division, Office for National Statistics.

IN RESPONSE to a lot of interest in regional earnings data, the ONS has produced summary analyses showing the proportions of employees earning below specific pay thresholds.

The data have been derived from the 1996 New Earnings Survey (NES) for Great Britain, and relate to the hourly earnings of employees on adult rates whose pay was not affected by absence; they also exclude overtime earnings. The data refer to location of employment, not the residence of employees. The information is useful in assessing the number of employees who might be affected by a minimum wage were it to be set at any one of five levels. The levels chosen for analysis replicate those pay bands most frequently asked about by MPs in Parliamentary Questions, although the NES can be used to obtain estimates for any rate of pay. The value of £4.42 per hour, representing a half of male median earnings, is the figure often quoted in the context of a minimum wage by the trade union movement.

This statistical report provides data for Government Office Regions (GOR), but similar information is also available for local and unitary authorities and parliamentary constituencies. Information is available for individuals by sex, industry or occupation, but this report concentrates on looking at full- and part-time workers as a whole.

Findings

The data in *Table 1* show that around 1 per cent of full-time employees earned less than **£2.50** per hour in 1996. Wales had the highest proportion of full-time employees earning below £2.50 (1.1 per cent), with London having the lowest (0.5 per cent).

For part-time employees earning less than £2.50 an hour, London again had the lowest proportion compared with other GORs, but at 3.6 per cent it was more than seven times higher than the figure for full-time workers. There was a higher proportion of part-time employees earning less than £2.50 in Scotland (5.5 per cent) than the rest of Great Britain.

At the other end of the earnings scale there are some quite pronounced regional disparities. Just 3.3 per cent of full-time employees in London earned less than **£4.00** in 1996, a proportion which is lower than all other regions and less than one third the proportion in Wales, which had the highest (11.3 per cent).

Generally, about two-fifths of part-time employees earned less than £4.00, although the proportion in London was less than half this (18.7 per cent). The North East had the highest proportion of part-time employees earning below £4.00, with nearly half of all workers (48 per cent) earning below the threshold. Most other regions had broadly similar proportions of both full- and part-time employees earning less than £4 per hour, with the exception of the South East and, to a lesser extent, the Eastern region, where the proportions were smaller. This distribution reflects the figures from the NES for average hourly earnings, which also showed that London and the South East had the highest average hourly earnings and Wales the lowest.

By location of employment, the parliamentary constituency with the highest proportion of full-time employees earning less than £4 per hour was St Ives, with 31.3 per cent. This contrasts with Bexleyheath, Fulham and Islington North constituencies where there were no full-time employees reported as earning below this threshold.

The constituency with the highest proportion of part-time employees earning below £4.00 per hour was East Lothian where more than three-quarters (76.2 per cent) earned less than this.

There is a small number of cases where the sample size is too small to provide reliable estimates and there are some limitations to the coverage of the NES which should be considered when looking at the data for employees with low earnings. Because of this ONS advises users to read the description of the survey which is given in Volume A of the *New Earnings Survey 1996.* Copies are available on request.

Information on the earnings of employees is also available from the Labour Force Survey but, because of its smaller sample size, reliable estimates for small areas cannot be produced. An article which compared the two sources appeared in *Labour Market Trends,* April 1996, pp161-74.

The NES is available via The Stationery Office (ISBN 011620818) and is priced at £19.95 per volume or £100 for the complete set of six volumes. Results from the 1997 NES will be published in September 1997, and a summary article is scheduled to appear in the November edition of *Labour Market Trends.*

Table 1   Hourly earnings[a] of employees on adult rates, by Government Office Region, April 1996

Government Office Region	Percentage earning less than				
	£2.50	£3.00	£3.50	£4.00	£4.42
North East					
Full-time	0.8	2.2	6.0	11.2	17.1
Part-time	4.5	8.9	28.0	48.2	58.3
All	1.6	3.7	10.9	19.5	26.3
North West					
Full-time	0.7	1.7	4.6	9.3	14.9
Part-time	3.7	6.8	21.7	38.7	49.3
All	1.4	2.8	8.3	15.6	22.3
Merseyside					
Full-time	0.6	2.0	5.1	8.7	14.0
Part-time	3.2	6.8	20.8	41.1	51.8
All	1.2	3.1	8.7	16.1	22.7
Yorkshire and the Humber					
Full-time	0.6	1.7	5.2	10.8	17.2
Part-time	3.9	7.8	21.7	41.2	55.5
All	1.4	3.2	9.3	18.2	26.6
East Midlands					
Full-time	0.8	2.0	5.3	11.0	17.2
Part-time	4.6	8.4	21.6	40.4	51.3
All	1.6	3.4	8.8	17.3	24.5
West Midlands					
Full-time	0.8	1.7	4.2	9.1	15.0
Part-time	4.0	7.4	23.0	41.4	54.9
All	1.4	2.9	8.1	15.8	23.3
Eastern					
Full-time	0.9	1.6	3.7	7.9	12.9
Part-time	5.1	8.6	20.5	35.7	47.4
All	1.8	3.2	7.6	14.3	20.8
London					
Full-time	0.5	0.8	1.7	3.3	5.7
Part-time	3.6	5.4	11.3	18.7	30.2
All	1.0	1.5	3.2	5.8	9.5
South East					
Full-time	0.7	1.2	3.1	6.6	11.3
Part-time	4.9	6.9	17.4	31.4	43.2
All	1.6	2.5	6.3	12.2	18.5
South West					
Full-time	0.9	1.8	4.8	10.3	16.3
Part-time	4.4	8.2	24.0	41.5	51.8
All	1.7	3.2	9.2	17.6	24.5
Wales					
Full-time	1.1	2.0	5.4	11.3	18.3
Part-time	5.1	8.1	25.3	43.5	55.1
All	1.9	3.3	9.5	18.0	25.9
Scotland					
Full-time	1.0	1.9	5.0	10.1	15.6
Part-time	5.5	8.6	22.7	40.4	53.3
All	1.9	3.2	8.6	16.2	23.2

Source: New Earnings Survey

Note: Survey is of those whose pay is not affected by absence.
a   Hourly earnings exclude overtime.

Further information:
For more data,
available for virtually all areas, contact:

ONS
Earnings Information and Analysis
Room 249
PO Box 12
East Lane
Runcorn WA7 2GJ
tel 01928 792077
fax 01928 792408
e-mail dbird.ons.run@gtnet.gov.uk

YOUR INSIGHT INTO THE LABOUR MARKET

THE LABOUR FORCE SURVEY

LFS FIRST RELEASE AND LFS QUARTERLY BULLETIN

LFS results are first published in printed form in an Office for National Statistics (ONS) First Release just six weeks after each quarterly reference period. A wide range of analyses and tables are included. **(£20 per annum)**

Further LFS analyses are included in the 60-page full colour publication LFS Quarterly Bulletin together with explanatory charts and text. **(£30 per annum)**

LFS USER GUIDE

The LFS User Guide consists of six volumes - 1) Background & Methodology, 2) LFS Questionnaire, 3) Details of LFS Variables, 4) LFS Standard & Eurostat Derived Variables, 5) LFS Classifications and 6) LFS Local Area Data. **Volumes 1, 2, 5 & 6 cost £5 each. Volumes 3 & 4 cost £10 each. Complete LFS User Guide is £30. Subscription or User Guide contact: Barbara Louca (Tel 0171 533 6179)**

LFS DATA via QUANTIME

Quantime now offers you:
- Bureau services
- LFS data to use on your PC
- Full training & technical support
- Direct dial-up facilities
- Export data in a range of formats (SPSS, SIR, SAS)

For more information and a free information pack, contact: QUANTIME Ltd. (Tel 0171 625 7222)

LFS DATA via NOMIS®

Nomis® now offers you:
- LFS data for TECs/LECs
- LFS data for counties and local authority districts
- Efficient computer mapping
- User support services

For more information and a free information pack, contact: NOMIS® (Tel 0191 374 2468/2490)

HELPLINE

For further information about the LFS, **contact the LABOUR MARKET ENQUIRY HELPLINE Tel 0171 533 6176**

RESEARCH USE OF LFS

For research users, copies of all LFS databases are available from the Data Archive. **For information Tel 01206 872001**

PREPARED BY
THE GOVERNMENT
STATISTICAL SERVICE

Spotlight on the West Midlands

This article on the West Midlands region is the third in the 'Spotlight' series examining the labour market from a regional perspective, following features on the South West and Yorkshire and the Humber.

By **Kelly Field**, Labour Market Division, Office for National Statistics.

THE WEST MIDLANDS Government Office Region (GOR) and Standard Statistical Region (SSR) are identical, including the counties of Hereford and Worcester, Shropshire, Warwickshire, and West Midlands (a metropolitan county), and the former county of Staffordshire (see *technical note*). It comprises 5 per cent of the total land mass of the UK.

After London, the West Midlands metropolitan county is the second most densely populated county in the UK, with around 3,000 people per square kilometre. The region as a whole has a higher population density than the UK average. In total, there are 5.3 million residents of the region, with a workforce of approximately half this number.

The recovery in the labour market since 1993 has been gradual but steady, with small but consistent falls in unemployment – the outcome of generally low levels of labour turnover – and slightly above-average growth in employment. However, some sectors – particularly in

CONTENTS

INTRODUCTION: A broad overview of the West Midlands and its labour market.

DEMOGRAPHY: The resident population in the region over the past few years, and labour force projections.

EMPLOYMENT: Comparing the region's employment trends with the national picture, with an analysis by industry.

VACANCIES: A look at the level of Jobcentre vacancies in the region from 1987 to 1997.

UNEMPLOYMENT: Unemployment rates together with age and duration analyses.

REDUNDANCIES: The region's redundancy rate in comparison with the national average.

EARNINGS: Average gross weekly earnings in the region, analysed by gender and industry.

QUALIFICATIONS AND TRAINING: Economically active in the region by their highest qualification, and the numbers receiving job-related training.

manufacturing industries – have been faring less well than others.

For several years, the region's claimant count unemployment rate was some way above that for the UK. However, in the last

couple of years the region has experienced one of the highest percentage decreases in the number of claimants in the country, and for the past year the claimant rate has been lower than the UK average.

The region is among the most manufacturing-dependent of all the UK regions, with a higher proportion of people employed in – and more GDP directly attributable to – the sector than for the rest of the UK. Many of the service industries in the region are directly dependent upon manufacturing, and so the sector's prospects are fundamental to the regional economy as a whole. However, the performance of the services sector is also important, as most of the region's residents are employed in the service industries.

The levels of in- and out-commuting to and from the region are low. Around 3 per cent of employed residents work outside the region, and likewise 3 per cent of jobs in the region are taken by people living outside the area. This means that the region as a whole functions as a highly self-contained labour market, i.e. the majority of people both live and work within the West Midlands.

Spotlight on the West Midlands

DEMOGRAPHY

THE POPULATION in the West Midlands grew at a slower rate than the average for Great Britain over the decade to 1995 – 2 per cent compared with 3 per cent.

In general, the region's population grew steadily over the decade – however, growth was slow between 1985 and 1986, and also 1993 and 1994. In Great Britain as a whole, the number of residents has increased steadily each year.

Resident population
Between 1985 and 1995, the rate of increase in population differed across the region. The number of residents in Shropshire grew by 7 per cent, while the metropolitan county of West Midlands recorded a slight decrease over the decade. (*Table 1*)

The region has a slightly higher proportion of residents aged under 15 than the Great Britain average, but the rest of the population structure – by both age and sex – follows the national pattern. (*Table 2*)

Although there are more females than males in the region (*Table 2*), the percentage increase in male residents between 1985 and 1995 was higher than that for females. This was also the case in the country as a whole, with the percentage rises for both sexes being higher nationally than regionally.

In all, 8 per cent of the region's population belong to an ethnic minority group – the highest proportion after London. However, the majority are resident in the West Midlands metropolitan county, with the proportion of ethnic minority communities in the region's other counties being lower than the national average of 6 per cent.

The labour force
The region had the same economic activity rate for those aged 16 and over in winter 1996/7 as the UK as a whole, but a slightly lower rate for those of working age. Economic activity rates in the region varied widely between counties. (*Table 3*)

There was a 2 per cent increase in the region's labour force between 1986 and 1996, compared with the UK average of 4 per cent. Following the national trend, the number of women in the labour force increased by 7 per cent in the region over the decade, while the number of men fell slightly. Despite this, there continue to be more men than women in the labour force, with the region's proportion of women in the labour force, at 44 per cent, being one of the lowest in the country. (*Table 4*)

A shift can be seen over the decade in the age structure of the labour force, with a rise in the number of workers aged 35 to 59, but a decrease of around a quarter in those aged between 16 and 24. This was the pattern for both sexes, both regionally and nationally, and reflects the small number of births in the 1970s following the 'baby boom' of the 1960s. (*Table 4*)

Future trends
The labour force in the region is projected to increase by 4 per cent between 1996 and 2006, compared with 5 per cent in the UK as a whole. The ongoing trend of an increasing number of women in the labour force is expected to continue, with a projected rise of 8 per cent in the region over the decade – similar to the UK average. However, over the same period there is a projected regional increase of only 0.5 per cent in the number of men in the labour force – lower than the national rise of 2 per cent. These projections result in a further slight increase, to 45 per cent, in the proportion of women in the labour force in 2006. A continued shift in the age structure of the labour force also seems likely. Projected falls in the numbers aged under 35, and to a lesser extent in those aged 65 and over, are more than offset by projected increases in numbers in the labour force at intervening ages – particularly at ages 35 to 44 and 60 to 64. (*Table 4*)

Table 1 Resident population

Thousands and percentages

| | Population (thousands) | | | | | | | Population percentage change | | |
	1985	1990	1991	1992	1993	1994	1995	1985-1995	1990-1995	1994-1995
Great Britain	55,127	55,972	56,207	56,388	56,559	56,753	56,957	3.3	1.8	0.4
West Midlands	**5,195**	**5,250**	**5,265**	**5,278**	**5,290**	**5,295**	**5,306**	**2.2**	**1.1**	**0.2**
Hereford and Worcester	653	682	685	690	695	700	694	6.3	1.9	-0.8
Shropshire	392	410	412	413	414	416	420	7.0	2.4	0.8
Stoke-on-Trent UA[a]	251	252	253	253	253	254	254	1.3	0.8	0.1
Staffordshire[a]	771	792	797	799	801	800	802	4.1	1.2	0.2
Warwickshire	481	487	489	492	494	496	499	3.6	2.4	0.5
West Midlands[b]	2,646	2,626	2,629	2,631	2,634	2,628	2,637	-0.3	0.4	0.4

Source: Mid-year population estimates, Nomis®, ONS

a   Comprise the former county of Staffordshire.
b   The metropolitan county of West Midlands.

Table 2 Resident population: by age and sex, 1995

Thousands and percentages

| | West Midlands | | | Great Britain | | |
	Males	Females	All	Males	Females	All
Percentage aged:						
0-14	**20.6**	**19.1**	**19.8**	20.2	18.4	19.3
15-19	**6.2**	**5.7**	**6.0**	6.1	5.6	5.9
20-29	**15.1**	**13.9**	**14.5**	15.3	14.1	14.7
30-39	**15.1**	**14.2**	**14.7**	15.8	14.8	15.3
40-49	**13.7**	**13.1**	**13.4**	13.8	13.2	13.5
50-59	**11.5**	**11.1**	**11.3**	11.0	10.7	10.8
60 and over	**17.8**	**22.9**	**20.4**	17.8	23.2	20.6
All ages (=100 per cent) (thousands)	**2,621**	**2,686**	**5,306**	27,922	29,035	56,957

Source: Mid-year population estimates, Nomis®, ONS

Table 3 Economic activity, winter 1996/7

Thousands and percentages

| | In employment (percentages) | | | ILO unemployment rate | Total economically active (=100 per cent) (thousands) | Economic activity rate for all 16 and over[b] (percentages) | Economic activity rate for all of working age[b] (percentages) |
	Employees (as a percentage of all in employment[a])	Self-employed (as a percentage of all in employment[a])	All in employment (as a percentage of the economically active)				
United Kingdom	86.2	12.5	92.6	7.4	28,690	62.6	78.3
West Midlands	**87.6**	**10.9**	**92.9**	**7.1**	**2,585**	**62.6**	**78.2**
Hereford and Worcester	86.6	12.0	93.3	6.7	380	67.6	84.5
Shropshire	80.5	16.4	94.6	5.4	195	59.1	78.3
Staffordshire[c]	87.8	11.0	94.4	5.6	548	65.6	79.2
Warwickshire	85.5	13.5	96.6	*	261	66.7	83.2
West Midlands[d]	89.5	9.0	91.1	8.9	1,201	59.6	75.0

Source: Labour Force Survey, ONS

*   Sample size too small for reliable estimate.
a   As a percentage of all in employment – including unpaid family workers, those on government training programmes and those who did not state whether they were employees or self-employed.
b   Working age: 16-59 for women; 16-64 for men.
c   The former county of Staffordshire.
d   The metropolitan county of West Midlands.

Table 4 The projected labour force: by age and sex[a]

Thousands and percentages

| | West Midlands | | | | | | | | |
| | All | | | Men | | | Women | | |
	1986	1996	2006	1986	1996	2006	1986	1996	2006
Percentage aged:									
16-24	22.6	16.3	15.2	21.2	16.1	15.2	24.5	16.5	15.2
25-34	22.6	26.1	20.8	23.3	26.6	21.3	21.6	25.4	20.0
35-44	23.8	23.2	27.4	23.2	22.7	26.5	24.6	23.9	28.5
45-59	25.7	29.5	31.0	25.8	28.7	30.3	25.5	30.5	31.8
60-64	3.9	3.4	4.3	4.8	4.1	4.9	2.6	2.6	3.5
65 and over	1.5	1.5	1.4	1.6	1.8	1.7	1.3	1.1	1.0
All of working age[b] (thousands)	2,479	2,537	2,625	1,463	1,449	1,456	1,015	1,087	1,169
All aged 16 and over (= 100 per cent) (thousands)	2,543	2,605	2,705	1,487	1,475	1,481	1,056	1,129	1,224

| | United Kingdom | | | | | | | | |
| | All | | | Men | | | Women | | |
	1986	1996	2006	1986	1996	2006	1986	1996	2006
Percentage aged:									
16-24	22.9	16.0	15.0	21.6	15.7	14.8	24.8	16.6	15.3
25-34	23.1	26.9	21.2	24.0	27.4	21.9	21.9	26.2	20.4
35-44	23.3	23.6	27.3	22.9	23.3	26.8	23.9	24.1	27.9
45-59	25.3	28.3	30.7	25.0	27.7	30.2	25.6	29.1	31.4
60-64	3.9	3.5	4.3	4.9	4.1	4.7	2.6	2.8	3.8
65 and over	1.5	1.5	1.4	1.6	1.7	1.6	1.2	1.3	1.1
All of working age[b] (thousands)	26,861	27,747	29,154	15,791	15,713	16,109	11,070	12,034	13,045
All aged 16 and over (= 100 per cent) (thousands)	27,566	28,554	30,092	16,055	15,986	16,376	11,511	12,546	13,715

Source: Labour Force Survey and labour force projections, ONS

a   The projections for 2006 are 1994-based. These will be updated to take account of actual events since 1994 when the next set of sub-national population projections have been prepared.
b   16-59 for women and 16-64 for men.

Table 5 Employment, spring quarters

Thousands and percentages

	Population (thousands)					Percentage change				
	1986	1990[a]	1993[b]	1995	1996	1986-1996	1990-1996	1990-1993	1993-1996	1995-1996
All in employment aged 16 and over										
West Midlands	2,234	2,481	2,274	2,347	2,348	5.1	-5.4	-8.3	3.3	0.0
Great Britain	23,984	26,324	24,907	25,350	25,578	6.6	-2.8	-5.4	2.7	0.9
Employees										
West Midlands	1,976	2,112	1,964	2,036	2,057	4.1	-2.6	-7.0	4.7	1.0
Great Britain	20,852	22,388	21,313	21,675	22,020	5.6	-1.6	-4.8	3.3	1.6
Self-employed										
West Midlands	204	321	269	280	258	26.5	-19.6	-16.2	-4.1	-7.9
Great Britain	2,729	3,482	3,108	3,269	3,205	17.4	-8.0	-10.7	3.1	-2.0

Source: Labour Force Survey, ONS

a   Chosen to represent an employment peak.
b   Chosen to represent an employment trough.

Figure 1   Full- and part-time employment,[a] winter 1996/7

All persons aged 16+

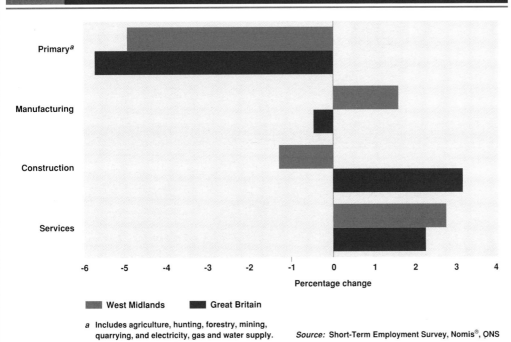

Great Britain
North East
North West (GOR) and Merseyside
North West (GOR)
Merseyside
Yorkshire and the Humber
East Midlands
West Midlands
Eastern
London
South East (GOR)
South West
England
Wales
Scotland

Percentages (0, 20, 40, 60, 80, 100)

Legend: ■ Full-time ■ Part-time ■ Full-time ■ Part-time

a Defined by self-assessment.   Source: Labour Force Survey, ONS

Figure 2   Annual change in employees in employment by major industry group, March 1996 to March 1997

Primary[a]
Manufacturing
Construction
Services

Percentage change (-6, -5, -4, -3, -2, -1, 0, 1, 2, 3, 4)

Legend: ■ West Midlands ■ Great Britain

a Includes agriculture, hunting, forestry, mining,
   quarrying, and electricity, gas and water supply.   Source: Short-Term Employment Survey, Nomis®, ONS

EMPLOYMENT

A TOTAL OF 2.3 million people aged 16 and over were in employment in the region in spring 1996, according to the LFS. This was up from 2.2 million a decade earlier – a rise of 5 per cent compared with the Great Britain average of 7 per cent.

Over the past decade, the Workforce in Employment estimates have indicated that there has been a structural shift from manufacturing to the service industries, both regionally and nationally.

Employment trends

For those aged 16 and over, changes in employment levels in the region between 1986 and 1996 broadly followed the national trends. Between the employment peak in 1990 and the trough in 1993, the level fell more sharply regionally than nationally, but since then has recovered slightly. (*Table 5*)

Between spring 1986 and 1996, the number of women aged 16 and over in employment rose by 11 per cent in the region, while the number of men increased by just 1 per cent. The equivalent average increases for Great Britain as a whole were higher over the decade, at 13 and 2 per cent respectively.

There was a 4 per cent rise in the number of employees in the region over the decade to spring 1996 – up 0.1 million to 2.1 million. Again, the national increase over the same period was higher – 6 per cent. In line with the trend for Great Britain as a whole, the number of female employees in the region rose by 10 per cent between 1986 and 1996; there was a small decrease in the number of male employees. (*Table 5*)

In all, 258,000 people were self-employed in the region in spring 1996 – 26 per cent higher than a decade earlier, compared with a national increase of 17 per cent. However, the level in Great Britain followed a broadly upwards trend between spring 1993 and 1996, whereas in the West Midlands the opposite was true. The number of self-employed women in the region has increased more over the decade than self-employed men, as it also has nationally. The proportion of all aged 16 and over in employment who were self-employed in winter 1996/7 was 11 per cent regionally, less than the national average of 13 per cent. (*Table 5*)

Full- and part-time employment

Three-quarters of all aged 16 and over in employment work full-time, both regionally and nationally. This proportion has decreased slightly in recent years, indicating a rising trend in the employment of part-time workers. (*Figure 1*)

Of women in employment, 48 per cent worked part-time in winter 1996/7 – a higher proportion than the national average of 45 per cent. However, the converse was true among men, with the percentages being 8 and 10 per cent respectively. Some 83 per cent of part-time workers in the region are female, compared with 80 per cent nationally.

Part-time employment in the region increased by 14 per cent between winter 1992/3 and 1996/7, compared with a national rise of 12 per cent. Over this period, the increases in full-time employment were 5 and 3 per cent respectively. This is further indication of the growth in part-time working – a trend which is expected to continue.

EMPLOYMENT Continued

Analysis by industry

Between March 1987 and 1997, there was a fall in the number of employees in manufacturing in the region, but the percentage decrease was less than the national average – 10 compared with 16 per cent. This was because, although the region experienced a greater proportionate fall in the early 1990s, the increase in employees over the past few years has been larger than in Great Britain as a whole. Over the year to March 1997, there was a rise in the level regionally, compared with a slight decrease nationally. (*Figure 2*)

In the region's service industries, there was a 19 per cent increase in the number of employees over the decade to March 1997 – higher than the national rise of 16 per cent. Over the year to March 1997, the increases in the level of employees were similar regionally and nationally. (*Figure 2*)

The number of employees in construction has fluctuated around an average of 78,000 over the past few years in the region, with a slight fall being recorded between March 1996 and 1997. Nationally, however, there was a downwards trend in the level from late 1994 till March 1996, but then a 3 per cent increase in numbers over the next year. (*Figure 2*)

In September 1995, the region had the highest proportion of employees in manufacturing in the country – 27 per cent compared with a national average of 18 per cent. For local authority districts within the region, however, concentrations varied from 10 per cent in both Solihull and Shrewsbury and Atcham, to 41 per cent in The Wrekin. (*Figure 3*)

For Great Britain as a whole, the largest proportion of employees are in the public administration, education, and health sector, with just over a quarter of employees in March 1997 compared with 23 per cent regionally. (*Figure 4*)

Analysis by occupation

In the region in winter 1996/7, three occupational groups shared the highest proportion of workers – managers and administrators, clerical and secretarial, and craft and related, each with 15 per cent of those aged 16 and over in employment. Nationally, the greatest proportion – 16 per cent – were managers and administrators. The region has a larger proportion of both plant and machine operatives, and those in craft and related occupations, than Great Britain, with this higher concentration of manual workers being linked to the region's large manufacturing sector. (*Figure 5*)

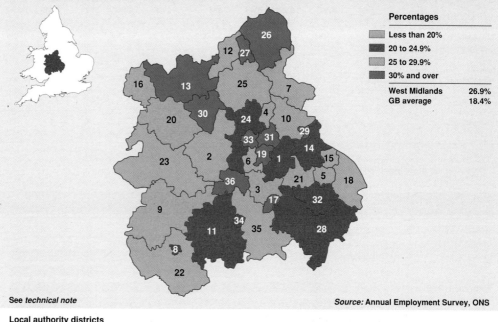

Figure 3 Percentage of employees in manufacturing industries by local authority district, September 1995

Percentages
- Less than 20%
- 20 to 24.9%
- 25 to 29.9%
- 30% and over

West Midlands 26.9%
GB average 18.4%

See *technical note*

Source: Annual Employment Survey, ONS

Local authority districts

1	Birmingham	9	Leominster	16	Oswestry	23	South Shropshire
2	Bridgnorth	10	Lichfield	17	Redditch	24	South Staffordshire
3	Bromsgrove	11	Malvern Hills	18	Rugby	25	Stafford
4	Cannock Chase	12	Newcastle-under-Lyme	19	Sandwell	26	Staffordshire Moorlands
5	Coventry	13	North Shropshire	20	Shrewsbury and Atcham	27	Stoke-on-Trent*
6	Dudley	14	North Warwickshire	21	Solihull	28	Stratford-on-Avon
7	East Staffordshire	15	Nuneaton and Bedworth	22	South Herefordshire	29	Tamworth*
8	Hereford*					30	The Wrekin

31	Walsall
32	Warwick
33	Wolverhampton*
34	Worcester*
35	Wychavon
36	Wyre Forest

Estimates have been calculated as a percentage of total employment, except those marked*.

* Estimates have been calculated using totals which exclude agriculture and horticulture (MAFF confidentiality restrictions apply here).

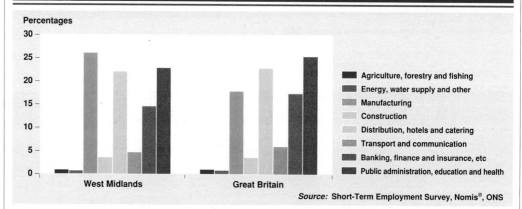

Figure 4 Employees in employment by industry, March 1997

Percentages

West Midlands   Great Britain

- Agriculture, forestry and fishing
- Energy, water supply and other
- Manufacturing
- Construction
- Distribution, hotels and catering
- Transport and communication
- Banking, finance and insurance, etc
- Public administration, education and health

Source: Short-Term Employment Survey, Nomis®, ONS

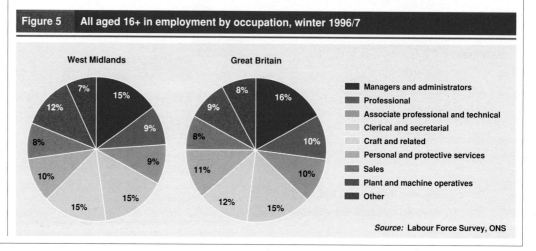

Figure 5 All aged 16+ in employment by occupation, winter 1996/7

West Midlands   Great Britain

- Managers and administrators
- Professional
- Associate professional and technical
- Clerical and secretarial
- Craft and related
- Personal and protective services
- Sales
- Plant and machine operatives
- Other

Source: Labour Force Survey, ONS

Figure 6 — Vacancies notified to Jobcentres,[a] seasonally adjusted

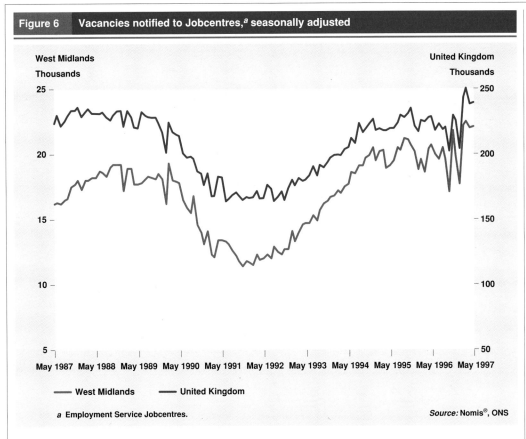

West Midlands
Thousands

United Kingdom
Thousands

May 1987 May 1988 May 1989 May 1990 May 1991 May 1992 May 1993 May 1994 May 1995 May 1996 May 1997

— West Midlands   — United Kingdom

a Employment Service Jobcentres.

Source: Nomis®, ONS

Figure 7 — Notified vacancies and placings[a] by occupation, West Midlands, quarter ending April 1997

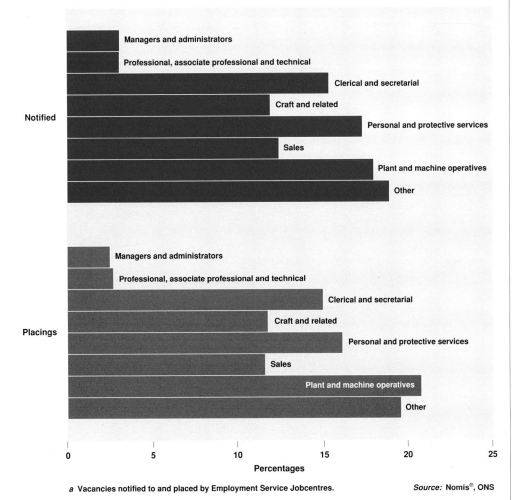

Notified

Managers and administrators
Professional, associate professional and technical
Clerical and secretarial
Craft and related
Personal and protective services
Sales
Plant and machine operatives
Other

Placings

Managers and administrators
Professional, associate professional and technical
Clerical and secretarial
Craft and related
Personal and protective services
Sales
Plant and machine operatives
Other

0   5   10   15   20   25
Percentages

a Vacancies notified to and placed by Employment Service Jobcentres.

Source: Nomis®, ONS

VACANCIES

IN EMPLOYMENT SERVICE Jobcentres in the region, the fluctuating levels of notified vacancies, placings, and unfilled vacancies over the past few years have provided an indication of the state of the economy and its recovery since the recession of the early 1990s.

Seasonally-adjusted trends since 1987
Although the overall pattern in the number of vacancies notified was similar in the West Midlands to the UK average, as a consequence of a stronger period of growth between 1992 and 1994, the West Midlands has seen an increase in level over the previous peak in the late 1980s. The number of vacancies in the region has fluctuated around 20,000 a month since the end of 1994. (*Figure 6*)

Analysis by occupation
In the quarter ending April 1997, the highest proportion of notified vacancies in the region, apart from the 'other occupations' group, was in the plant and machine operatives occupational group, at 18 per cent. In Great Britain, the highest percentage – also 18 per cent, and again excluding 'other occupations' – was for the personal and protective occupations. (*Figure 7*)
In the same quarter, the highest percentage of placings in the region was again for plant and machine operatives with 21 per cent – going against the national trend by being higher than that for 'other occupations' (20 per cent). For the country as a whole, the 'other occupation' group contributed 23 per cent of placings, with the personal and protective group having the next highest proportion of 17 per cent. (*Figure 7*)

UNEMPLOYMENT

THE SEASONALLY-ADJUSTED claimant count rate in the region in May 1997 was 5.7 per cent, similar to the UK percentage of 5.8.

In winter 1996/7, the unemployment rate on the ILO measure was also lower regionally than nationally, 7.1 per cent compared with a UK average of 7.4 (not seasonally adjusted).

The number of claimants in the region fell by 52 per cent over the decade to May 1997, compared with 43 per cent for the UK. The level of claimant unemployment, both regionally and nationally, is close to the level of the previous trough in 1990. Over the year to May 1997, levels decreased by around a quarter both regionally and nationally (seasonally adjusted).

The number of unemployed on the ILO measure in the region in winter 1996/7 was 182,000, with a percentage decrease in the level over the year of 18 per cent (not seasonally adjusted). This was one of the largest percentage falls in the country, and compares with a figure of 10 per cent for the UK as a whole.

Trends since 1987

Levels of both claimants and ILO unemployed have in the region, as in the UK as a whole, followed similar trends over the past decade.

Over the decade May 1987 to 1997, the peak number of claimants (seasonally adjusted) in the region was in May 1987, while the lowest level was recorded in May 1997. From the peak in 1987, the claimant count followed a downwards trend for three years, then rose again till the end of 1992, and since then has generally been decreasing. This was similar to the national pattern (all seasonally adjusted). (*Figure 8*)

The percentage increases and decreases in the seasonally-adjusted claimant count rate over the past decade have been higher in the region than nationally. The region's rate in May 1997 was less than half that in May 1987. (*Figure 8*)

Since 1987, the region has recorded one of the highest percentage falls in the number of claimants in the UK.

Unemployment rates

The region had the fifth lowest unadjusted claimant count rate in the country in May 1997, which at 5.7 per cent was slightly lower than the UK average of 5.8. At 7.1 per cent, the ILO unemployment rate in the region for winter 1996/7 was also the fifth lowest in the UK. (*Figure 9*)

On the ILO measure, the unemployment rate in the region was 3.4 points lower in spring 1996 than 1986, compared with a national decrease of 3.0 points over the decade. Between spring 1986 and 1996, the levels of unemployment fell by a quarter both regionally and nationally.

Among men, the rates on both measures were lower in the region than nationally. Among women, the regional ILO rate was lower than the UK average, but the converse was true for the claimant count measure (all unadjusted).

The ILO unemployment rate among the ethnic minority groups in the region in winter 1996/7 was 16.4 per cent, slightly lower than the Great Britain figure of 16.6. ILO rates for White people were 6.4 per cent regionally and 6.9 nationally.

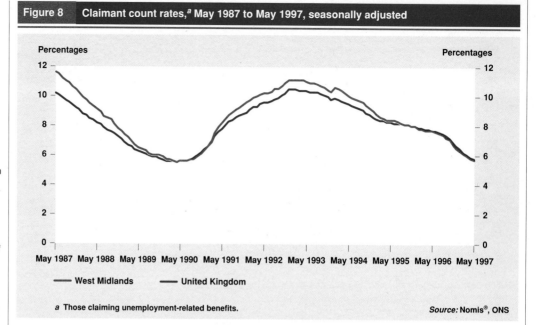

Figure 8   Claimant count rates,[a] May 1987 to May 1997, seasonally adjusted

— West Midlands   — United Kingdom

a Those claiming unemployment-related benefits.

Source: Nomis®, ONS

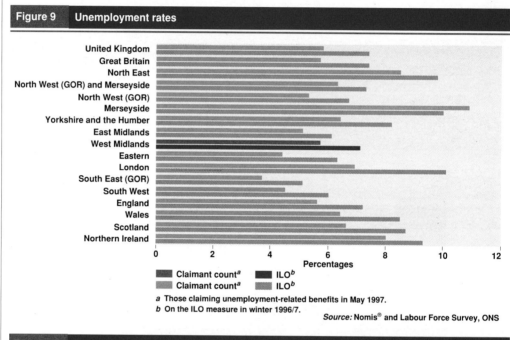

Figure 9   Unemployment rates

- Claimant count[a]   ILO[b]
- Claimant count[a]   ILO[b]

a Those claiming unemployment-related benefits in May 1997.
b On the ILO measure in winter 1996/7.

Source: Nomis® and Labour Force Survey, ONS

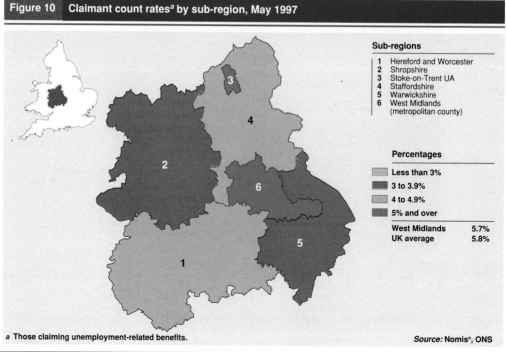

Figure 10   Claimant count rates[a] by sub-region, May 1997

Sub-regions

1 Hereford and Worcester
2 Shropshire
3 Stoke-on-Trent UA
4 Staffordshire
5 Warwickshire
6 West Midlands (metropolitan county)

Percentages

- Less than 3%
- 3 to 3.9%
- 4 to 4.9%
- 5% and over

| West Midlands | 5.7% |
| UK average | 5.8% |

a Those claiming unemployment-related benefits.

Source: Nomis®, ONS

Figure 11 — Claimant count rates[a] by travel-to-work area, May 1997

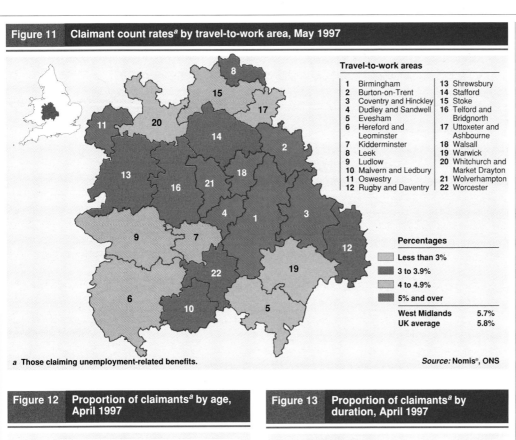

Travel-to-work areas

1	Birmingham	13	Shrewsbury
2	Burton-on-Trent	14	Stafford
3	Coventry and Hinckley	15	Stoke
4	Dudley and Sandwell	16	Telford and
5	Evesham		Bridgnorth
6	Hereford and	17	Uttoxeter and
	Leominster		Ashbourne
7	Kidderminster	18	Walsall
8	Leek	19	Warwick
9	Ludlow	20	Whitchurch and
10	Malvern and Ledbury		Market Drayton
11	Oswestry	21	Wolverhampton
12	Rugby and Daventry	22	Worcester

Percentages

- Less than 3%
- 3 to 3.9%
- 4 to 4.9%
- 5% and over

West Midlands	5.7%
UK average	5.8%

a Those claiming unemployment-related benefits.

Source: Nomis®, ONS

UNEMPLOYMENT Continued

Sub-regional analysis

In May 1997, the claimant count rate for the West Midlands metropolitan county was 7.2 per cent – twice that recorded in Shropshire (3.5 per cent) and Warwickshire (3.6 per cent). (*Figure 10*)

By travel-to-work area, the lowest claimant rate in May was 2.6 per cent, recorded in Evesham, Uttoxeter and Ashbourne, and Warwick. The highest rate was in Wolverhampton, with 7.3 per cent. (*Figure 11*)

Analysis by age group

At April 1997, the number of claimants in the region was lower than a decade previously for all age groups, with the highest percentage falls in the youngest and oldest age groups. This was also the situation for the UK as a whole – however the proportionate decreases were larger regionally, particularly for the middle age groups.

The highest proportion of claimants was in the 20 to 29-year-old age group in April, both regionally (35 per cent) and in the UK as a whole (34 per cent). (*Figure 12*) This was also the case with the ILO measure in winter 1996/7, with the proportions being 32 and 31 per cent respectively.

However, there is a difference between the two measures when analysed by age group, in that more people in the youngest and oldest age groups are included in the ILO measure than in the claimant count, whereas for the intermediate age groups the reverse is true.

Analysis by duration

For all durations, the number of claimants in the region in April 1997 was lower than that in 1987. For all groups apart from those claiming for less than four weeks, the percentage falls in the level over the decade were higher regionally than for the UK as a whole.

In April 1997, when analysed by duration, the highest proportion of claimants – a quarter – had been claiming benefits for between 8 and 26 weeks, both regionally and nationally. The region had a higher proportion of claimants who had been claiming benefits for over five years than the national average – 10 and 8 per cent respectively. (*Figure 13*)

Overall, 38 per cent of claimants in the region were classified as long-term – claiming for over one year – compared with 37 per cent in the UK. For local authority districts within the region, concentrations of long-term claimants ranged from 22 per cent in Hereford to 45 per cent in Sandwell. (*Figure 14*)

Figure 12 — Proportion of claimants[a] by age, April 1997

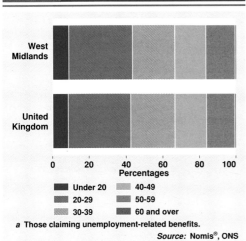

Percentages

- Under 20
- 20-29
- 30-39
- 40-49
- 50-59
- 60 and over

a Those claiming unemployment-related benefits.

Source: Nomis®, ONS

Figure 13 — Proportion of claimants[a] by duration, April 1997

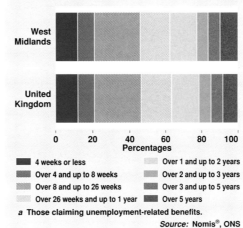

Percentages

- 4 weeks or less
- Over 4 and up to 8 weeks
- Over 8 and up to 26 weeks
- Over 26 weeks and up to 1 year
- Over 1 and up to 2 years
- Over 2 and up to 3 years
- Over 3 and up to 5 years
- Over 5 years

a Those claiming unemployment-related benefits.

Source: Nomis®, ONS

Figure 14 — Concentrations of long-term claimants[a] by local authority district, April 1997

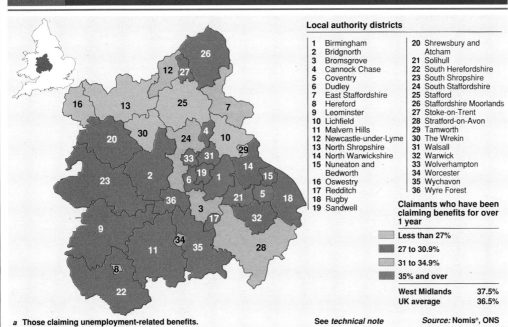

Local authority districts

1	Birmingham	20	Shrewsbury and
2	Bridgnorth		Atcham
3	Bromsgrove	21	Solihull
4	Cannock Chase	22	South Herefordshire
5	Coventry	23	South Shropshire
6	Dudley	24	South Staffordshire
7	East Staffordshire	25	Stafford
8	Hereford	26	Staffordshire Moorlands
9	Leominster	27	Stoke-on-Trent
10	Lichfield	28	Stratford-on-Avon
11	Malvern Hills	29	Tamworth
12	Newcastle-under-Lyme	30	The Wrekin
13	North Shropshire	31	Walsall
14	North Warwickshire	32	Warwick
15	Nuneaton and	33	Wolverhampton
	Bedworth	34	Worcester
16	Oswestry	35	Wychavon
17	Redditch	36	Wyre Forest
18	Rugby		
19	Sandwell		

Claimants who have been claiming benefits for over 1 year

- Less than 27%
- 27 to 30.9%
- 31 to 34.9%
- 35% and over

West Midlands	37.5%
UK average	36.5%

a Those claiming unemployment-related benefits.

See *technical note*

Source: Nomis®, ONS

Spotlight on the West Midlands

REDUNDANCIES

THE TREND IN the level of redundancies in the region has followed that in Great Britain over the past few years. Both regionally and nationally, the number of redundancies reached a peak in 1991, and then followed a downwards trend until the end of 1994. For the last couple of years, the level of redundancies in each quarter has fluctuated around 19,000 in the region, less than half the number recorded at the peak.

Over the last few years, the redundancy rate in the region has been similar to the national average at around 10 redundancies per 1,000 employees, but has recorded a larger percentage decrease since the peak in 1991. It should be noted, however, that regional estimates of redundancies and regional rankings vary from quarter to quarter. (*Figure 15*)

EARNINGS

FROM THE 1996 New Earnings Survey, average gross weekly earnings of full-time employees in the region were £324, £28 less than the Great Britain average of £352.

Over the year to April 1996, the average gross weekly earnings for both men and women in the region increased by 4 per cent, whereas in Great Britain the rise was 4 per cent for men and 5 per cent for women.

Analysis by sex
In April 1996, average gross weekly full-time earnings for men in the region were £360, compared with a national average of £391. The regional figure for women was £257, £26 less than for Great Britain (see *technical note*). (*Figure 16*)

Within the region in April 1996, there were variations in earnings, with the counties of Warwickshire and West Midlands having higher averages. Shropshire recorded a particularly low average for women of £233 a week. (*Figure 16*)

Analysis by occupation
For men in full-time manual employment, average gross weekly earnings in the region in April 1996 were close to the Great Britain figure – £297 and £301 respectively. For non-manual employment, the differential was greater – £425 regionally compared with £464 nationally. The average gross weekly pay for women in manual jobs in the region in April 1996 was £192 – among the highest of all the regions in Great Britain. For those with non-manual jobs, the average pay of £276 was £26 less than the national figure. (*Table 6*)

In the region in April 1996, average earnings for men were particularly low in clerical and secretarial occupations, but high for sales occupations. For women, average pay was low compared with other regions for managers and administrators, but high in the professional occupations. (*Table 6*)

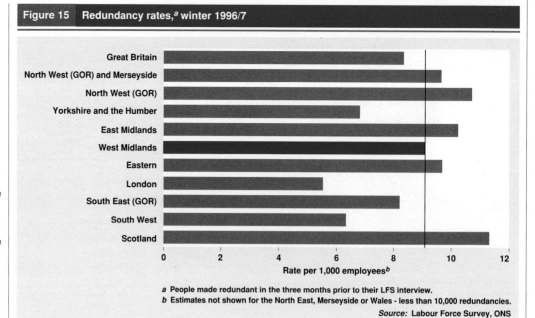

Figure 15 Redundancy rates,[a] winter 1996/7

a People made redundant in the three months prior to their LFS interview.
b Estimates not shown for the North East, Merseyside or Wales - less than 10,000 redundancies.

Source: Labour Force Survey, ONS

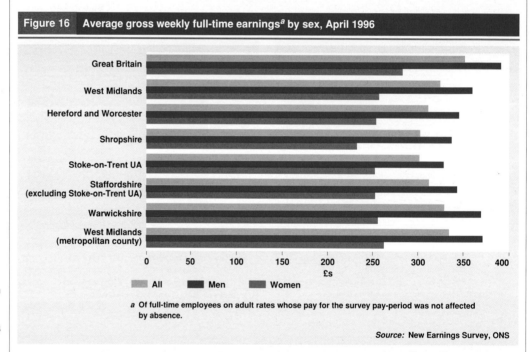

Figure 16 Average gross weekly full-time earnings[a] by sex, April 1996

a Of full-time employees on adult rates whose pay for the survey pay-period was not affected by absence.

Source: New Earnings Survey, ONS

Table 6 Average gross weekly full-time earnings[a] by sex and occupation, April 1996

	West Midlands		Great Britain	
	Men	Women	Men	Women
Managers and administrators	522.8	324.4	569.2	389.4
Professional	491.8	416.1	520.6	421.1
Associate professional and technical	377.8	325.4	463.5	349.9
Clerical and secretarial	256.9	218.7	274.9	239.1
Craft and related	319.2	207.9	331.6	200.1
Personal and protective	299.5	187.7	317.2	207.0
Sales	319.4	202.8	321.9	208.5
Plant and machine operatives	301.4	207.0	303.8	208.8
Other	246.7	165.7	253.6	174.5
All manual occupations	297.1	191.5	301.3	195.2
All non-manual occupations	425.0	276.4	464.0	302.4
All occupations	360.1	256.9	391.3	283.0

Source: New Earnings Survey, ONS

a   Of full-time employees on adult rates whose pay for the survey pay-period was not affected by absence.

Table 7 Economically active of working age: by highest qualification, winter 1996/7

Thousands and percentages

	West Midlands	Great Britain
Degree or equivalent	11.7	14.5
Higher education below degree	9.4	9.9
GCE A-level or equivalent	15.4	15.9
Apprenticeship	9.7	10.9
GCSE or equivalent	19.0	19.9
CSE below grade 1	7.6	6.2
Other	9.6	8.9
None	17.7	13.9
Total (= 100 per cent) (thousands)	2,515	27,810

Source: Labour Force Survey, ONS

Table 8 Persons of working age receiving job-related training,[a] winter 1996/7

Percentages

	West Midlands	Great Britain
Total persons of working age:	12.7	12.8
men	11.7	12.1
women	13.8	13.5
Employees and self-employed:	13.3	13.3
in managerial and professional occupations	19.3	18.1
in service industries	15.6	15.1

Source: Labour Force Survey, ONS

a   In the four weeks before their interview.

QUALIFICATIONS AND TRAINING

RESULTS FROM the winter 1996/7 LFS revealed that the West Midlands had an above-average proportion of economically active with no qualifications. The West Midlands also had a slightly lower than national average proportion educated to A-level or above.

The winter 1996/7 LFS results showed that 408,000 people of working age had received job-related training in the four weeks prior to their interview, representing 13 per cent of everyone of working age. This proportion was the same as the average for Great Britain as a whole.

Qualifications
Regionally in winter 1996/7, 18 per cent of the economically active of working age held no qualifications. This was the highest proportion of all the regions in Great Britain, and compares with the national average of 14 per cent. (*Table 7*).

Training
The level of those receiving job-related training follows a seasonal pattern depending on the academic year. In winter 1996/7, 306,000 employees and self-employed of working age had participated in job-related training in the region in the last four weeks. This represented 13 per cent of the total number of employees and self-employed, the same as the national average. The level has shown an upwards trend recently both regionally and nationally. (*Table 8*)

In the region over the past few years, there has generally been a greater proportion of women of working age receiving training than men. However, only recently has the number of women undergoing job-related training been higher than the number of men. This situation was the same across the country.

Further information

- For more information on the Nomis® database, see p319.
- For information on the annual New Earnings Survey, phone 01928 792077/8.
- LFS data is also available from Quantime, see p322.
- *Regional Trends* is an annual publication examining the regions of the UK, covering a wide range of statistics. For enquiries, phone 0171 533 5796.
- Further information and statistics for the West Midlands are available from both the Government Office for the West Midlands and the West Midlands Employment Information Unit. The Government Office publishes a yearly document called *West Midlands Labour Market and Skill Trends*, and for more details contact Paul Bayliss on 0121 212 5157. The EIU produces a twice-yearly publication, *Labour Market Review*, for details contact Ray Brookes on 0121 452 5404.
- If you have any comments on this regional profile, please contact Steve Hickman at the Office for National Statistics, on 0171 533 6113.

Spotlight on the West Midlands

TECHNICAL NOTE

Regions

Government statistical policy is that since 1st April 1997 GORs have replaced SSRs as the primary classification for the presentation of official statistics at regional level. The West Midlands region is defined identically as a GOR and an SSR.

There are ten GORs in England, but the North West region and Merseyside are usually combined into one region for statistical purposes. There were eight SSRs in England before the change. London is also a GOR, but was not a separate SSR, instead forming part of the South East.

Nomis® builds GOR data from local authority wards on either a 1981 or 1991 basis, according to the dataset. This is done either on a county basis or on a TEC basis.

Currently, LFS data for GORs are based on estimates weighted to mid-year population estimates and projections relating to SSRs (see p 253, *Labour Market Trends*, July 1997). The issue of weighting to GOR population figures will be considered as part of a wider review of LFS grossing to take place later this year.

The third phase of the local government reorganisation in England came into effect in April 1997, with parts of some two-tier areas (comprising counties and local authority districts) being replaced by a single-tier unitary authority. Within the West Midlands, one new unitary authority was formed. The district of Stoke-on-Trent, along with part of a ward in the Stafford local authority district, separated from the former county of Staffordshire and became a unitary authority. The rest of Staffordshire remained as a county, as did Hereford and Worcester, Shropshire, Warwickshire, and the metropolitan county of West Midlands.

Figures 3 and *14* refer to local authority districts. From April 1997, as detailed above, the district of Stoke-on-Trent was replaced by a unitary authority.

LFS data for local authorities

A further source of LFS data is the annual local area database. This makes it possible to carry out cross-sectional analyses of local area data from the survey using 14 key variables for each of the 184,000 people on the database. It was first released in May 1996, covering the period March 1994-February 1995. An updated version was released at the beginning of 1997, covering March 1995-February 1996.

LFS quarterly data is not available for unitary authorities, and so in *Table 3* the former counties of the West Midlands have been used. However, the local area database does contain some unitary authority information for the period spring 1995 to winter 1995/6 (March 1995-February 1996), covering the unitary authorities created in April 1995 and 1996. This was the first time that any LFS estimates have been produced for unitary authorities. For further

details, phone Steve Hickman on 0171 533 6113.

Employment

The LFS is considered to be the better source for estimates of overall employment, while the Workforce in Employment (i.e. the Annual Employment Survey and the Short-term Employment Survey) is the better source for employment by industry. Details of the two data sources are given in the 'Notes on summary tables' in the Labour Market Data section, pS3.

Vacancies

Vacancy statistics during 1996 were affected by the introduction of a new vacancy circulation computer system, LMS. In effect, the introduction of this system meant that staff in Jobcentres were distracted by having to learn to use new software and therefore had less time to place people into jobs. This consequently led to a temporary rise in the level of unfilled vacancies (i.e. the stock). The effect of LMS has now completely bottomed out.

Unemployment

ONS produces two measures of unemployment. The first is derived from the quarterly LFS, and is defined on a consistent and internationally recognised basis set out by the International Labour Organization (ILO). ONS also publishes the monthly claimant count, which is based on the administrative system and includes all people claiming unemployment-related benefits at Employment Service offices on the day of the monthly count.

The claimant count rate uses workforce estimates as its denominator, which are based mainly on the employer-based (and hence workplace-based) estimates of employees in employment, whereas the LFS provides residence-based unemployment rates. Further details of the two sources are given in the 'Notes on summary tables' in the Labour Market Data section, pS3.

Jobseeker's Allowance was introduced in October 1996, and between then and April 1997 this had an effect on the claimant count. It is believed that LFS figures give a better indication of movements in that period.

Earnings

When comparing figures from the New Earnings Survey, a region could have a lower level of average earnings than another if it has a higher proportion of employees in industries or occupations with relatively lower earnings. This is because average earnings from the Survey do not take into account different mixes of occupations, and therefore cannot be used to claim that pay for like work is lower. Earnings comparisons take no account of differing price levels between regions and therefore do not indicate differences in the standard of living.

PREPARED BY
THE GOVERNMENT
STATISTICAL SERVICE

Economic activity of working-age households

There has been growing interest recently in analysis of economic activity at the household level. This article examines different definitions of working-age households, looks at their effects on the proportions of workless households and other sub-groups of interest and recommends a standard definition for general use.

By **David Hastings**,
Labour Market Division,
Office for National Statistics.

Photo: Telegraph Colour Library

Introduction

EMPLOYMENT and unemployment have tended to be regarded only in relation to individual people, but over the last few years there has been growing interest in how they affect whole households and families. This is much more complex than simply looking at individuals. Recent *Labour Market Trends* articles have presented some household and family data from the Labour Force Survey (LFS) and discussed some of the methodological problems involved in using LFS household and family data, including the issue of grossing.[1] The LFS is grossed at an individual level and there can be problems when analysing at household or family level (see LFS Help-Line report, 'Family analysis,' *Labour Market Trends*, June 1996, for further details).

Analyses can be complex even when using just the main economic activity categories of in employment, ILO unemployed and economically inactive. There are many possible ways in which these can be combined in households and families. Attention so far, however, has concentrated mostly on one particular phenomenon, the increasing number of households with all adults in employment ('work-rich') or no adults in employment ('work-poor'), at the expense of the traditional household of married couple with the husband as the breadwinner and an economically inactive housewife.

Analysis of this is further complicated by social and demographic factors. *Table 1* shows the composition of households from 1961 to 1996. As marriages and cohabiting partnerships break up more often, so more lone parent families and more single

Key findings

- It is recommended that the standard definition of working-age households includes all households that contain at least one person of working age.
- 19.6 per cent of households had no one in employment in spring 1996 - this proportion fell throughout the rest of the year.
- Changes in household structure have increased the number and proportion of workless households quite separately from the effect of the overall levels of employment and unemployment.
- The proportion of non-pensioner single person households has trebled since 1961; the proportion of single pensioner households has doubled in that time.
- Around 40 per cent of working-age households containing one working-age adult are workless; about 10 per cent of working-age households containing two working-age adults and around 6 per cent of working-age households with three or more working-age adults have no one in employment.
- More than half of all working-age households have all adults in employment; one in ten of all working-age households contain at least one person who is ILO unemployed.
- About half of all working-age households containing someone who is ILO unemployed contain at least one other person in employment.
- Some 69 per cent of all workless households consist of adults who are all inactive; 16 per cent contain only ILO unemployed adults.

Table 1   **Composition of households by type of household and family, 1961-1996, Great Britain**

Per cent

Type of household	1961	1971	1981	1991	Sum 1996[a]
One-person households					
Under pensionable age	4	6	8	11	13
Over pensionable age	7	12	14	16	14
Two or more unrelated adults	5	4	5	3	3
One-family households[b]					
Married couples with:					
No children	26	27	26	28	28
1-2 dependent children[c]	30	26	25	20	20
3 or more dependent children[c]	8	9	6	5	4
Non-dependent children only	10	8	8	8	7
Lone parent with:					
Dependent children[c]	2	3	5	6	7
Non-dependent children only	4	4	4	4	3
Two or more families	3	1	1	1	1
Number of households (Millions) (=100%)	16.2	18.2	19.5	22.4	na

Source: Population Censuses and Labour Force Survey

a   Labour Force Survey data is unweighted.
b   These households may contain some individuals who are not members of the nuclear family.
c   May also include non-dependent children.

person households are formed. The proportion of lone parents with dependent children has risen substantially over this period. Young single people living alone rather than with their parents also form more single person households. The proportion of non-pensioner single person households has trebled since 1961 and the proportion of single pensioner households has doubled (note that the term 'pensioners' is used as being synonymous with people of pensionable age). The growth in the population of pensionable age means an increasing proportion of households consisting of retired and hence economically inactive people. (Haskey describes the changes that have affected household and family composition in recent decades in more detail.[2]) All these factors will tend to increase the number and proportion of work-poor households quite separately from the effect of the overall levels of employment and unemployment. This will distort comparisons with other countries and between regions, as well as comparisons over time.

Workless households

Recent commentary in this area has concentrated even more narrowly on a single summary measure, the proportion of 'workless households', or households with no one in employment. There seems now to be a consensus that this measure should be based on the population of working age only (i.e. men aged 16 to 64 and women aged 16 to 59), excluding people of pensionable age, most of whom are retired (LFS data shows that around 750,000 pensioners are in employment, about 8 per cent of all pensioners.) However, some households include adults both of working

age and of pensionable age. A variety of approaches has been tried to achieve a practicable and reasonable definition of 'working-age households' or 'non-pensioner households', based on the variables available for LFS data.

Definitions of working-age households

Box 1 shows four definitions of working-age households. The first definition, based on household composition (HC), was first used by the House of Commons Library in its research on behalf of MPs. It was subsequently used by ONS (in order to maintain consistency) to answer parliamentary questions on workless households. This definition was also used for an LFS Help-Line report – 'The economic status of people in non-pensioner households' – in *Labour Market Trends*, February 1997.

Box 1   Definitions of working-age households

Household composition (HC) – based on the household composition variable, excludes all households consisting of one or two adults, with no children, where at least one person is of pensionable age.

Someone of working age (1WA) – includes all households containing at least one person of working age.

Head of household/non-students (HoH) – excludes households where the head of the household is of pensionable age and households containing only (full-time) students.

No pensioners (NP) – excludes households that contain at least one person of pensionable age.

A second approach – someone of working age (1WA) – was used by ONS in 'Data on households and families from the Labour Force Survey' in *Labour Market Trends*, March 1997. The third definition, based on the head of household (HoH), has been used by the Employment Policy Institute.[3] A fourth definition – no pensioners (NP) – includes households which contain working-age adults only.

Assessment of the different definitions

The ideal definition would be one that covers the entire working age population and minimises the number of pensioners included in the definition, that is appropriate for addressing likely issues of policy relevance, and that can be practically applied. Possible distortions to analyses of sub-groups of particular interest, which might be caused by excluding any working-age adults and by including non-working age adults, also have to be considered.

Table 2, for illustration, shows the number of working-age and non-working age persons included and excluded by various definitions for two separate quarters, spring 1993 and summer 1996. Spring 1993 data have been adjusted by excluding households where there are missing members (see *technical note*).

Numbers of working-age adults and pensioners included and excluded

The working age population is fully covered by the 1WA definition. Just over 2 million pensioners are included in both spring 1993 and summer 1996 as they live in 'mixed' households with working-age adults.

The HC definition includes only about

Table 2   Working-age and non-working-age adults by working-age household definitions, United Kingdom

000s and per cent

Definitions[b]	Spr 1993[a]				Sum 1996			
	Working-age adults		Non-working age adults		Working-age adults		Non-working age adults	
	Included	Excluded	Included	Excluded	Included	Excluded	Included	Excluded
All households								
Number (000s)	34,420	0	9,995	0	35,576	0	10,198	0
Percentage	100.0	0.0	100.0	0.0	100.0	0.0	100.0	0.0
1WA								
Number (000s)	34,420	0	2,006	7,990	35,576	0	2,074	8,124
Percentage	100.0	0.0	20.1	79.9	100.0	0.0	20.3	79.7
HC								
Number (000s)	33,369	1,051	1,066	8,929	34,510	1,066	1,101	9,098
Percentage	96.9	3.1	11.1	89.3	97.0	3.0	10.8	89.2
HoH								
Number (000s)	32,884	1,536	908	9,087	34,224	1,353	899	9,299
Percentage	95.5	4.5	9.0	90.9	96.2	3.8	8.8	91.2
NP								
Number (000s)	32,027	2,393	0	9,995	33,172	2,404	0	10,198
Percentage	93.0	7.0	0.0	100.0	93.2	6.8	0.0	100.0

Source: Labour Force Survey

a   Adjusted by excluding all households with missing members.
b   See *Box 1* opposite for details of definitions.

97 per cent of all working-age adults in spring 1993 and summer 1996, but also includes more than 1 million pensioners. Similar numbers of working-age adults are excluded in both quarters.

The HoH definition achieves only about 96 per cent coverage of the working age population in both quarters. More than 1.5 million working-age people are excluded in spring 1993 and nearly 1.4 million in summer 1996. Around 900,000 pensioners are included by this definition.

The NP definition, which excludes any household with a pensioner, includes about 93 per cent of all working-age adults in both spring 1993 and summer 1996 but excludes about 2.4 million working-age adults.

Coverage

The second criterion is that the definition should cover all groups which are of interest from a policy point of view. We would wish to include all the households that contain someone of working age in order to cover everyone who would normally be expected to be potentially active in the labour market.

The HC definition excludes those working-age adults who are members of two adult households where only one adult is over pensionable age. But any households of more than two adults are included as the household composition variable does not distinguish between pensioners and non-pensioners for these categories.

The 1WA definition, which includes all households with at least one working-age adult, would include all working-age adults.

The HoH definition excludes working-age adults who live in households where

the head of the household is over pensionable age. Thus, households with someone in employment may be excluded solely on the basis of the age of the head of the household. Households containing only students were excluded from this definition in order to produce time-series starting before 1984. For 1996, between 200,000 and 400,000 working-age adults – depending on the time of year – who are in all-student households are excluded.

The NP definition excludes those households that have both working- and non-working age adults. Again, this excludes some people of working age who may be active in the labour market.

Practicality

The recommended definition should be able to be easily applied on a consistent basis over time. The HC and HoH definitions are both complicated to apply and difficult to maintain a consistency over time. The 1WA and NP definitions are very clearly defined, easily applicable, interpretable and would be straightforward to keep on a consistent basis.

Effects of definitions on sub-groups

Table 3 presents a time-series of proportions of working-age households in various sub-groups for each of the definitions of working-age households. *Table 3(a)* shows that for the overall percentage of workless households the 1WA definition consistently results in the highest proportion (at least 1.2 percentage points higher), the NP definition gives the lowest proportions, and the other two fall in between. The level of worklessness has been falling throughout 1996.

One factor that affects worklessness in a

household is the number of working-age adults in the household. *Table 3(b-d)* shows that around 40 per cent of households with one working-age adult are workless compared with just over 10 per cent of two working-age adult households and about 5-6 per cent of households with more than two working-age adults. The proportions of workless households produced by the different definitions are much closer to each other within each of these size categories than for all households together.

For households containing dependent children (see *Table 3(e)*), the level of worklessness is slightly lower than overall except for the HC definition which shows a higher level for households with children. The HoH definition produces the lowest figures as some households with children will be excluded because the head of the household is over working age and some all-student households will have children.

Another important figure is the proportion of households with everyone in employment. *Table 3(f)* shows that this has increased steadily from spring 1992 onwards as the numbers in employment, particularly among women, have increased. The NP definition shows the highest percentage whereas the 1WA definition has the lowest proportion. This is because the 1WA definition includes all those mixed households with working-age adults and pensioners but the 'no pensioners' definition excludes all such households.

Table 3(g) shows the proportion of households with at least one member who is ILO unemployed. The percentage has risen and fallen since 1992, broadly in line with trends for individuals, but there is little difference between the four definitions,

Table 3 Proportions of working-age households, in various sub-categories, by working-age definition,[a] United Kingdom

Per cent

	Spr 1992[b]	Spr 1993[b]	Spr 1994[b]	Spr 1995[b]	Spr 1996	Sum 1996	Aut 1996	Win 1996
(a) Workless households as a proportion of all households								
1WA	17.7	19.0	19.3	19.4	19.6	19.2	19.0	18.7
HC	16.4	17.6	18.1	18.1	18.3	17.9	17.7	17.5
HoH	16.6	17.8	18.0	18.2	18.4	18.1	17.9	17.5
NP	16.3	17.4	18.0	18.1	18.1	17.6	17.5	17.2
(b) Workless households with one working-age adult as a proportion of all households with one working-age adult								
1WA	39.8	40.6	40.6	40.4	40.6	40.5	39.9	40.0
HC	40.0	40.1	40.2	40.1	40.1	40.0	39.4	39.7
HoH	40.3	40.6	40.0	40.3	40.6	40.6	39.9	39.7
NP	41.0	40.8	40.9	40.7	40.7	40.5	39.9	40.1
(c) Workless households with two working-age adults as a proportion of all households with two working-age adults								
1WA	10.6	11.5	11.4	11.0	11.3	10.5	10.5	10.0
HC	10.6	11.5	11.4	11.0	11.3	10.5	10.5	10.0
HoH	10.3	11.2	11.1	10.7	11.0	10.3	10.3	9.7
NP	10.5	11.4	11.4	11.0	11.2	10.4	10.3	9.8
(d) Workless households with three or more working-age adults as a proportion of all households with three or more working-age adults								
1WA	5.2	5.7	6.0	5.9	6.0	5.3	6.0	6.3
HC	5.2	5.7	6.0	5.9	6.0	5.3	6.0	6.3
HoH	4.4	5.0	4.9	4.7	5.1	4.9	5.4	5.4
NP	5.2	5.7	6.0	5.8	5.9	5.2	5.9	6.2
(e) Workless households with dependent children as a proportion of households with dependent children								
1WA	16.8	17.7	18.3	18.3	18.3	18.0	17.3	16.9
HC	16.8	17.8	18.4	18.4	18.4	18.1	17.4	17.0
HoH	16.4	17.4	18.0	17.9	17.9	17.7	17.2	16.5
NP	16.7	17.6	18.4	18.3	18.2	17.9	17.2	16.8
(f) Households with all in employment as a proportion of all households								
1WA	50.8	51.1	51.9	53.0	53.7	54.1	54.7	54.7
HC	53.3	53.4	54.2	55.3	56.1	56.5	57.4	57.1
HoH	53.5	53.7	54.7	55.7	56.5	56.7	57.4	57.5
NP	55.5	55.7	56.3	57.4	58.3	58.7	59.3	59.3
(g) Households with at least one person ILO unemployed as a proportion of all households								
1WA	13.7	14.3	13.2	11.9	11.1	11.5	10.9	10.2
HC	14.1	14.6	13.6	12.2	11.4	11.8	11.2	10.4
HoH	13.8	14.4	13.4	11.9	11.2	11.6	11.0	10.2
NP	14.0	14.6	13.6	12.1	11.4	11.8	11.2	10.4
(h) Workless households with at least one person ILO unemployed as a proportion of (g)								
1WA	48.2	51.5	53.9	55.1	54.5	50.3	52.2	53.1
HC	46.9	50.2	52.8	54.1	53.5	49.2	51.2	52.1
HoH	47.2	50.6	53.1	54.1	53.6	49.4	51.2	52.0
NP	47.4	50.5	53.1	54.5	53.9	49.6	51.5	52.0

Source: Labour Force Survey

a   See *Box 1* on p334 for details of definitions.
b   Adjusted for missing household members.

Table 4 All-student households, United Kingdom

				Per cent
	Spr 1996	Sum 1996	Aut 1996	Win 1996
Total all-student households (000s) (= 100%)	205	123	136	206
Proportion of working-age adults				
One working-age adult	54.0	63.1	60.2	56.8
Two working-age adults	21.4	19.0	18.2	16.0
Three or more working-age adults	24.6	17.9	21.6	27.3
Proportion of workless households	58.7	57.5	63.2	59.8

Source: Labour Force Survey

although the 1WA definition seems to be consistently lower than the other three.

Table 3(h) shows that around half of all the households with at least one ILO unemployed member are households with at least one other household member in employment.

Table 4 shows some analysis of all-student households which are excluded by the HoH definition. Over a half to two-thirds of these households in 1996 contained only one working-age adult. Around 60 per cent of all-student households were workless. If these households are included within the HoH definition then the overall workless household proportion would increase by between one quarter and one half of a percentage point for the 1996 quarters.

Recommended definition

It is recommended that the 1WA definition – households containing at least one working-age adult – be used as the standard way to define working-age households (although other definitions may be more suitable for certain specific specialised analyses). This definition covers the entire working-age population, thus including all working-age adults who are active in the labour market, and can be used simply and consistently. It does produce the highest proportion of workless households and the lowest proportion of work-rich ones, which may suggest that it is producing a distorted impression of these categories, but in practice it is in any case necessary to look at them in much more detail in order to interpret them correctly.

Interpretation

More detailed analysis is especially important for the interpretation of workless household estimates as workless households have different household compositions.

People can be without employment for a variety of different reasons. In addition to the ILO definition of unemployment, the LFS identifies 24 separate categories of economic inactivity in three broad groupings: seeking work but unavailable to start work; not seeking work but would like work; and not seeking nor wanting to work. Reasons for inactivity coded by the LFS include student, looking after family or home, temporarily sick or injured, long-term sick or disabled, waiting for results of job application, believes no job available, not started looking, not looked, not need or want a job, retired or other reason.

The number of working-age adults contained in a household should be looked at separately in order to interpret the results clearly. *Table 5* shows a breakdown of the overall estimate of workless households by economic activity, for spring 1996, using the recommended definition of working-age households. It shows that 69 per cent of all workless households consist of adults who are all inactive compared with 16 per cent who only contain ILO unemployed adults. The remaining 15 per cent contain both ILO unemployed and inactive adults. About two-thirds of all workless households contain only one working-age adult. Nearly 30 per cent contain two working-age adults and the remaining 5 per cent contain three or more working-age adults. Half of all workless households contain only one working-age adult, and have all adults (whether of working-age or pensionable-age) inactive.

For more information see 'Workless households, unemployment and economic inactivity' on pp339-45 of this issue. ■

Footnotes

1 'Household and family data from the Labour Force Survey: recent improvements in approach', *Labour Market Trends*, June 1997, pp209-216. 'Data on households and families from the Labour Force Survey', *Labour Market Trends*, March 1997, pp89-98.

2 Haskey, J: Population review: (6) Families and households in Great Britain, *Population Trends* 85, HMSO (London, 1996).

3 Employment Policy Institute: *Employment Audit*, summer 1996.

Table 5 Workless households by economic activity and household composition, spring 1996, United Kingdom

				Per cent
	All ILO unemployed	ILO unemployed and inactive	All inactive	Total
One working-age adult, no children	10.5	na	18.9	29.4
One working-age adult, with children	3.3	na	18.2	21.5
One working-age adult, no children, with pensioners	*	1.9	12.2	14.1
One working-age adult, with children, with pensioners	*	*	0.4	0.5
One working-age adult	**13.8**	**1.9**	**49.8**	**65.5**
Two working-age adults, no children	1.1	3.0	9.6	13.7
Two working-age adults, with children	1.2	6.7	6.1	14.0
Two working-age adults, with or without children, with pensioner	*	0.5	0.8	1.3
Two working-age adults	**2.3**	**10.2**	**16.4**	**29.0**
Three or more working-age adults	*	**2.5**	**2.9**	**5.5**
All workless households	**16.3**	**14.6**	**69.1**	**100.0**

Source: Labour Force Survey

na   not applicable.
*   Sample size too small for a reliable estimate.

Adjustment for households with missing members

Figures for the spring 1992 to spring 1995 quarters have been adjusted for households with missing members. The *technical note* to 'Data on households and families from the LFS' (*Labour Market Trends*, March 1997, pp89-98) describes the inconsistencies and discontinuities of household data in the Labour Force Survey in detail. From spring 1992 to winter 1995, if a member of a household was not present and if the respondent was unable or unwilling to give any information about that person then there was no record of that person in the survey. Thus, there could be households with missing members. In the case of a married or cohabiting couple, the algorithm used to calculate family type would have assumed that no data for a partner meant no partner, classifying the responding member to be either a single person or a lone parent, depending on whether they had any children. The introduction of the household matrix approach from spring 1996 has eliminated this problem.[1] Thus, for analysis based on spring 1992 to spring 1995, households with missing members have been excluded.

Errors in household composition data

In 1995, some errors were discovered in the programs deriving some of the household and family variables for 1992 to 1994. The variable most affected was household composition, which is the basis for the HC definition of working-age households. This definition was affected by the inclusion of households with two adults and no children with at least one person of pensionable age in the number of working-age households, instead of excluding them from the definition of working-age households. Other variables affected to a lesser extent were household type, age of oldest dependent child in family aged under 16 and under 19, and age of youngest dependent child in family under 19. It was decided not to correct these variables as the effects were thought to be small and household data were of little interest at that time. Analysis in this article for spring 1992, spring 1993 and spring 1994 uses the corrected data which ONS released in July 1997.

Relationship to head of household

Introduction of the household matrix approach has also enabled new and revised household and family unit variables to be derived. One variable that was revised was relationship to head of the household. For the spring 1996 quarter only, the old version is also available in order to include imputed cases where data has been carried forward (for one quarter only) because of the respondent being unavailable. This has been used in the HoH definition of working-age households. From summer 1996, the revised relationship to head of household variable has been used.

Seasonality

Estimates of economic activity at the individual level are subject to the effects of seasonality. Thus, it is likely that estimates of economic activity at the household level may be affected seasonally in a similar way.

Footnotes

1 'Household and family data from the Labour Force Survey: recent improvements in approach', *Labour Market Trends*, June 1997, pp209-216.

Further information:
Any enquiries arising from this feature
should be referred to
David Hastings
tel 0171 533 6146.

Workless households, unemployment and economic inactivity

The population can be divided into those in employment, unemployed and economically inactive. Most attention has been paid to employment and unemployment. This article examines what has been happening to economic inactivity since 1984 at both the individual level and the household level.

By **Iain Bell**, **Nicola Houston** and **Robert Heyes**,
Analytical Services:
Labour Market Analysis Division,
Department for Education
and Employment

Photo: Telegraph Colour Library

Key findings

- In spring 1996, just under 20 per cent of working-age households were workless.
- Between 1984 and 1991, the proportion of working-age households with nobody in employment remained roughly constant at around 16 per cent. Between 1991 and 1996, the proportion of households that were workless rose to just under 20 per cent.
- In 1984, 13 per cent of workless households consisted of one adult with children under 16. By 1996, this had risen to 22 per cent. The proportion of workless households which had more than one adult fell from 63 per cent in 1984 to 48 per cent in 1996.
- 75 per cent of single-adult households with the youngest child under 5 were workless in 1996, compared with 50 per cent of single-adult households with the youngest child aged 5 to 15.

- In 1993/4 three-quarters of adults living in workless households lived in family units in receipt of state benefit.
- There were 7.5 million economically inactive working-age people in spring 1996 – 22 per cent of the working-age population. Almost two-thirds were women.
- Between 1984 and 1996, economic inactivity remained at just over a fifth. However, over this period the proportion of men who are inactive has increased, while the proportion of women who are inactive has declined.
- Between 1984 and 1996, there has been a large increase in the number and proportion of people giving their reason for inactivity as being long-term sick or disabled. This increase may, however, just reflect changed reporting patterns over time.

Introduction

THE FIRST PART of this article looks at unemployment and inactivity within households. Unemployment here is defined as people who are out of work, have actively sought work in the last four weeks and are available to start a job within a fortnight (the ILO definition). People who are economically inactive are those not in work who are either not seeking work or unavailable to start a job or both. Labour Force Survey (LFS) data from the spring quarter (March-May) is used to analyse trends in inactivity at the household level. This part of the article identifies how many households in Great Britain have nobody in employment; what type of households these are; the reasons why there is no one in employment and how the number of households with nobody in employment has changed over the past decade.

The article mainly focuses on changes in workless households over the period 1986 to 1996. However, evidence presented in research papers by Gregg and Wadsworth of the Centre for Economic Performance shows that there was a large rise in the number of workless households between the mid-70s and the mid-80s. This was mainly driven by increasing levels of worklessness across all types of household.

The article also looks at inactivity at the individual level. Characteristics of the unemployed and trends over time are already widely available from the LFS. Inactivity impacts on a large number of people and not just those who live in households where nobody works. In spring 1996 there were 7.5 million people of working age who were inactive; only 50 per cent of them lived in households where nobody worked. This section looks at LFS data showing what has been happening to inactivity at the individual level over the past decade; the reasons why people are inactive and the type of people who are likely to be inactive.

It should be noted at this point that the household data presented here are not very robust. The figures should be treated as guidance to levels and trends, not definitive estimates. For more details of the reasons, see the *technical note*.

Definition of a working-age household

Some of the results on household issues can be affected by the definition of a working-age household selected. There are several choices. For details of these and their relative merits, see 'Economic activity of working-age households' by David Hastings on pp333-8 of this issue of *Labour Market Trends*. For this article, the definition that has been used is any household which contains at least one person of working age. This definition was chosen because we wished to examine all households that had working-age members. Note that this will include households where at least one person of pensionable age lives with at least one person of working age. It will also include households made up entirely of students.

Periods considered

The LFS has been in existence since 1973. However, only since 1984 has a reasonably consistent set of data been available. In what follows, most of the comparisons will be between 1986 and 1996, which represent roughly equivalent points in the economic cycle. 1991 is also included as roughly the trough of the last economic cycle. Although 1986 and 1996 represent similar points in the economic cycle, they are not similar points in the employment cycle. The employment rate in 1996 was higher than in 1986.

Trends in the number of households with nobody in employment

In spring 1996, 20 per cent of working-age households contained no working members, 52 per cent contained only people who were in employment and 28 per cent contained a mixture of working and non-working members.

While workless households have increased as a proportion of all working-age households over the past decade and households with all members employed have also increased slightly, there has been a large fall in the proportion of households with some people in employment and some not (*Figure 1*).

Although the proportion of households with nobody in employment rose over this period, the rise was not continuous. The proportion of working-age households that had nobody in employment remained roughly constant at around 16 per cent between 1984 and 1991, but increased to just under 20 per cent in spring 1996. There is some evidence that the proportion of workless households has fallen by around 1 percentage point between spring and winter 1996. This level of change is liable to be stronger than any seasonal effects.

The impact of changing household size

Over this period, there has been a large increase in the number of households, reflecting, in part, the increase in the divorce rate, a growing trend for people to live in single-adult households and other social and demographic factors. Over the last decade the number of single-adult households (with and without children) has increased by over 70 per cent. Single-adult households are also much more likely to have nobody in employment than households with more than one adult. *Table 1* shows the changes that have taken place in household size for working-age households.

Table 2 shows the number of workless households by size of household. Lone par-

Figure 1   Economic activity of working-age households; Great Britain; spring quarters

Per cent

Legend: All in employment | Mixed | Nobody in employment

Source: Labour Force Survey

Table 1   **Working-age households by number of adults[a] and presence of children; Great Britain; spring quarters**

	Households (thousands)				
	1984	1986	1991	1996	Percentage change 1984 to 1996
One adult, children under 16	556	654	885	1,267	128
One adult, no children under 16	1,725	1,984	2,407	3,253	89
Two adults, children under 16	4,681	4,605	4,583	4,729	1
Two adults, no children under 16	4,509	4,636	5,199	5,283	17
Three or more adults, children under 16	1,576	1,477	1,279	1,214	-23
Three or more adults, no children under 16	2,717	2,817	2,703	2,608	-4
All households	**15,764**	**16,172**	**17,055**	**18,355**	**16**

[a] The number of adults in a working-age household includes anyone aged 16 or older.

Source: Labour Force Survey

Table 2 Workless working-age households[a] by household composition; Great Britain; spring quarters

Per cent

	1984	1986	1991	1996
One adult, children under 16	13	15	20	22
One adult, no children under 16	23	24	27	30
Two adults, children under 16	21	20	15	14
Two adults, no children under 16	31	30	29	26
Three or more adults, children under 16	4	4	3	2
Three or more adults, no children under 16	7	8	7	6
All workless households	100	100	100	100
All workless households (000s = 100%)	**2,526**	**2,800**	**2,692**	**3,578**

a The number of adults in a working-age household includes anyone aged 16 or older.   Source: Labour Force Survey

ents and single-person households accounted for 39 per cent of workless households in 1986. By 1996, they accounted for over half of all workless households. Over the same period, workless households with two adults decreased as a share of all workless households from 50 per cent in 1986 to 40 per cent in 1996, and workless households with three or more adults fell from 12 per cent to 8 per cent over this period. This can be compared with the employment rate of individuals. In 1984, the employment rate of working-age adults was 68.6 per cent, and in 1986 it was 69.6 per cent. In 1991, it was 73.2 per cent and in 1996 it was 71.8 per cent.

Marital status and presence of children

In 1996, 55 per cent of children living in workless households lived in lone-parent households. In 1986, only 36 per cent of children living in workless households lived in these households. Lone parents are more likely to be out of work if they have children under 5. In 1996 over three-quarters of lone-parent households (one adult only, with at least one child under 16) where the youngest child was under 5 were workless; whereas just under half of lone-parent households where the youngest child was between 5 and 15 were workless. Regardless of the age of children, lone-parent households have a higher proportion with nobody in employment than any other group.

Table 3 sets out the workless household rate by presence of married couples and children in the household. The stereotypical household of a married couple with or without children actually comprises a low proportion of all workless households. In 1986, 12 per cent of households containing a married or cohabiting couple had nobody in employment. By 1996, 11 per cent of such households were workless – higher than in 1991 but lower than in 1986. The proportion of households containing lone parents (with or without other non-married members) with nobody in employment was higher in 1996 than in 1991 and higher in 1991 than in 1986. Note this excludes households with married or cohabiting members which contain a lone-parent family. A higher proportion of households with nobody married or cohabiting and no children under 16 were workless in 1996 than in 1986 – 30 per cent in 1996 compared with 27 per cent in 1986.

Divorced and separated people without partners have higher non-employment rates than those who are married or cohabiting. Increased divorce rates over the last decade (plus other factors) mean that more older people are living alone. Analysis by age shows that almost half of the increase in workless one-person households is due to people aged between 45 and retirement age. For women over 45, the increase in single-person households has been associated with increased proportions in employment, despite an absolute rise in the number of workless households. However, for men over 45, the increased number of single person households has also seen an increase in their non-employment rate.

Reasons for non-employment in workless households

The proportion of workless households that had at least one member unemployed on the ILO definition has fallen from 41 per cent in 1986 to 31 per cent in 1996. There has been a large increase in the proportion of households where all members are inactive (*Figure 2*). This has happened for all household types. For example, there has been a large increase in the number of workless households with a married or cohabiting couple and children under 16 where all working-age members are inactive. In 1986, only 25 per cent of these households had all working-age members inactive. In 1996, 44 per cent of these households were completely inactive.

A major reason behind the increase in workless households is the increase in long-term sickness and disability. *Table 4* gives the reasons for inactivity for households where all members are inactive, by marital status of household. Across all household types, the

Table 3 Working age households with nobody in employment; Great Britain; spring quarters

Thousands

	Thousands/percentage of all such households		
	1986	1991	1996
All households	16,172	17,055	18,355
with nobody in employment	2,800	2,692	3,578
percentage	*17*	*16*	*20*
of which:			
Households, nobody married/cohabiting, no under-16s	3,556	3,653	4,606
with nobody in employment	965	959	1,401
percentage	*27*	*26*	*30*
Households, nobody married/cohabiting, with under-16s	958	1,081	1,531
with nobody in employment	488	586	847
percentage	*51*	*54*	*55*
Households with married/cohabiting members, no under-16s	5,879	6,656	6,538
with nobody in employment	769	719	804
percentage	*13*	*11*	*12*
Households with married/cohabiting members and under-16s	5,778	5,665	5,680
with nobody in employment	578	427	525
percentage	*10*	*8*	*9*

Source: Labour Force Survey

Thousands

	Nobody married/ cohabiting, under-16s			Nobody married/ cohabiting, with under-16s			Includes married/ cohabiting couple, no under-16s			Includes married/ cohabiting household, with under-16s			All households		
	1986	1991	1996	1986	1991	1996	1986	1991	1996	1986	1991	1996	1986	1991	1996
All working age household members inactive	579	626	902	360	484	690	562	539	647	145	141	233	1,645	1,789	2,472
- all members retired	51	65	80	0	0	*	67	104	127	*	0	*	120	169	209
- all members long-term sick/disabled	147	220	411	13	18	43	29	46	104	*	*	13	195	289	571
- all members looking after family/home	11	20	17	278	388	525	*	*	*	14	14	37	306	423	583
- all members students	82	94	108	*	13	30	*	*	13	*	*	*	95	114	155
- all members inactive for other reasons	174	131	150	34	42	55	69	42	24	11	11	*	287	226	235
- mixture of above reasons	113	95	135	28	23	37	389	340	376	113	110	171	643	567	719
-of which have at least one long-term sick	62	54	88	*	*	*	190	199	271	34	50	115	291	310	481
All working-age members ILO unemployed	284	254	405	87	78	124	40	33	31	62	39	47	473	403	606
Mixture of ILO unemployed and inactives	102	80	95	42	25	33	167	147	126	371	248	245	682	499	500
All households with nobody in employment	965	959	1,402	488	586	847	769	719	804	578	427	525	2,800	2,692	3,578

Source: Labour Force Survey

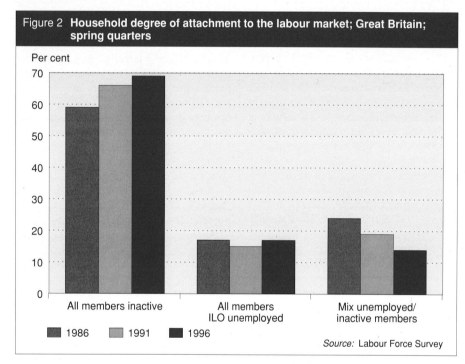

Figure 2   Household degree of attachment to the labour market; Great Britain; spring quarters

Per cent

Legend: 1986, 1991, 1996

Categories: All members inactive; All members ILO unemployed; Mix unemployed/ inactive members

Source: Labour Force Survey

proportion of households with all members inactive has increased. Overall, the number of households with at least one member long-term sick or disabled has doubled between 1986 and 1996 and the number where all members are long-term sick or disabled has more than doubled. While 45 per cent of the increase in households with all members long-term sick or disabled is accounted for by over-45s living by themselves, every group has shown an increase in long-term sickness irrespective of age, marital status of household or the presence of children.

Interpreting changes in inactivity due to long-term sickness and disability over time is difficult. This is because, over time, there are improvements in diagnosis of certain types of illnesses, more awareness of certain types of illness and more willingness on the part of the respondent to say they have an illness which may have had more of a stigma attached to it in the past.

The General Household Survey (GHS) measures limiting long-standing illnesses and this survey also showed an increase in number of people with long-term sickness. It also asked about reduced activity due to acute sickness in the last fortnight and converted this into average number of days of acute illness per person per year. The GHS showed that for the economically inactive the average number of restricted activity days per person per year for men aged 16-44 increased from 25 to 45 between 1985 and 1995, from 62 to 87 for men 45-64, from 25 to 30 for women 16-44, and 40 to 61 for women 45-64. This suggests an increase in acute long-term sickness among working-age inactive people.

There are other pieces of evidence which suggest that the working-age population are not getting healthier: first, the LFS shows a general increase in long-term sickness and disability in the working-age population as a whole – not just those who are inactive; and, secondly, findings released in *Social Trends 27* show that 'healthy life years' have not improved over the last 20 years.

Overall, there is evidence to suggest that the working-age population is not getting healthier. Reported long-term illness and disability in the LFS (and other surveys) is increasing, but the extent to which this actually represents a genuine increase in long-term sickness is not clear.

Sickness benefits

Long-term sickness is strongly related to age. Around 60 per cent of men aged 35-64 who are inactive give the reason for their inactivity as being long-term sick. There are a number of benefits that may be claimed by people who are inactive because of sickness or disability. One example of such benefits is Incapacity Benefit, formerly Invalidity Benefit (IVB). Although this only represents one particular benefit paid to the long-term sick, the trends shown are similar to those for the other sickness benefits – although not identical.

The numbers of men aged 35-64 on IVB increased from around 550,000 in 1984 to 950,000 in 1995. This rise of over 70 per cent in 11 years is similar both to the trend in male IVB claimants of all ages (see *Figure 3*) and to the trend in the numbers receiving all types of sickness benefits. Looking at the reasons for this increase in the numbers on IVB, *Figure 4* shows the yearly male inflows to IVB in the 35-64 age group.

The steady increase in IVB claimants is not mirrored by a consistent rise in people starting to claim (inflows). In fact, inflows remained stable over the period 1983-84 to 1990-91, after which they rose substantially at the same time as the UK economy entered recession. However, the flows onto Invalidity Benefit are small compared with the stock. While the numbers flowing onto IVB began falling in 1993-94, the number of people claiming continued to rise. It follows, therefore, that the increase in the stock is more a product of people staying on IVB longer rather then more people joining.

The increase in average duration occurs because once on IVB for more than one

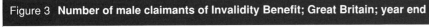

Figure 3 Number of male claimants of Invalidity Benefit; Great Britain; year end

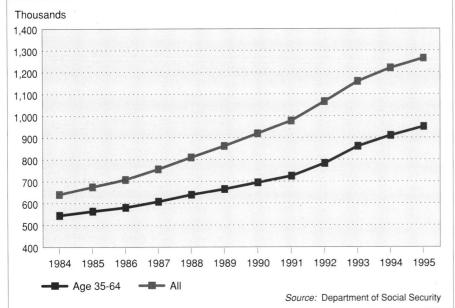

Thousands

Age 35-64   All

Source: Department of Social Security

Figure 4 Number of new male claimants of Invalidity Benefit; Great Britain; financial years

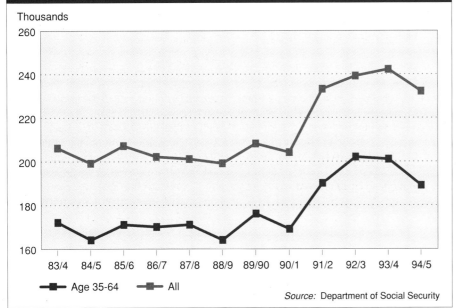

Thousands

Age 35-64   All

Source: Department of Social Security

year the proportion leaving is very low, generally less than 10 per cent a year. The steady increase in men aged 35-64 claiming IVB is not fully explained by rising inflows. Claimants are on the benefit for long periods of time and few leave.

The Family Expenditure Survey gives detailed information on benefit receipt among adults in workless households. It shows that in 1993/4, 29 per cent of adults in workless households were in a family unit which was in receipt of some form of sickness benefit.

Benefits and workless households

The Family Expenditure Survey shows that in 1993/4, around three-quarters of adults in workless households lived in a family unit that received social security. The extent to which lone parents affect these figures is clear from the fact that 94 per cent of children living in workless households are living in a family unit which receives state benefits.

Inactivity in the working-age population

Inactivity is not just confined to workless households – only 50 per cent of all inactive people live in workless households. In spring 1996 21.7 per cent of the working-age population were economically inactive. This represents around 7.5 million people, 2.8 million men and just over 4.7 million women.

In spring 1996, the largest proportion of inactive men previously worked in craft and related occupations and plant and machine operative jobs. These jobs are manual and many require only low-level skills. Among inactive women, the majority came from clerical or secretarial occupations, personal or protective occupations and sales occupations. Again, these sectors are predominantly low skilled.

Table 5 shows that the economic inactivity rate (proportion of working-age population who are economically inactive) of working-age men without qualifications in spring 1996 is more than double that of working-age men with qualifications (28.4 per cent compared with 12.4 per cent). *Table 5* also shows that the same is true for women of working age with and without qualifications. Those with no qualifications have an inactivity rate of 44.7 per cent compared with 23.5 per cent for those with qualifications.

Trends in individual economic inactivity

The proportion of people of working age who are inactive has remained fairly constant between 1984 and 1996, at just over a fifth of the working-age population (*Figure 5*). However, this aggregate figure masks significant changes in the participation of men and women in the labour market. Between spring 1984 and spring 1996 the male working-age inactivity rate has gradually risen from 11.9 per cent to 15.3 per cent. The majority of this increase occurred between spring 1991 and spring 1996. In contrast, the female working-age inactivity rate has fallen from 33.7 per cent in spring 1984 to 28.7 per cent in spring 1996. The majority of this fall occurred between spring 1984 and spring 1991 – since then the female working-age inactivity rate has remained fairly constant. Around 30 per cent of the total were men and about 70 per cent were women. In 1986, almost 40 per cent of the total were men and around 60 per cent of them were women.

Qualifications and inactivity

Male and female inactivity rates for those of working age with and without

Table 5   **Economic inactivity rates of people of working age with and without qualifications; Great Britain; spring quarters**

	Percentage of working-age population			
	1984	**1986**	**1991**	**1996**
Men				
With qualifications	9.4	9.4	9.4	12.3
Without qualifications	16.3	18.0	19.8	28.6
Women				
With qualifications	28.0	25.9	22.9	23.1
Without qualifications	40.8	40.2	40.1	45.3

Source: Labour Force Survey

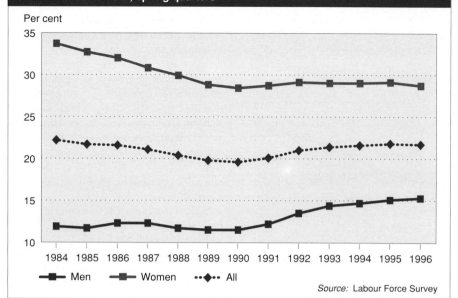

Figure 5 Proportion of working age population who are economically inactive; Great Britain; spring quarters

Per cent

Legend: Men, Women, All

Source: Labour Force Survey

qualifications have also changed significantly over the last decade. *Table 5* shows that inactivity rates for men both with and without qualifications have increased since 1984. However, the percentage point increase for men with qualifications has been significantly less than for men without qualifications. Men with qualifications have experienced an increase in their inactivity rate from 9.4 per cent in spring 1984 to 12.3 per cent in spring 1996 (around 3 percentage points). Men without qualifications have experienced a 12 percentage point increase in their inactivity rate. Their inactivity rate increased from 16.3 per cent in 1984 to 28.4 per cent in 1996.

Figure 5 shows that the working-age female inactivity rate has been declining since 1984, but this fall has been confined to women with qualifications. In spring 1984 the inactivity rate for working-age women with qualifications was 28 per cent; by spring 1996 this had fallen to 23.1 per cent. In contrast, the inactivity rate for working-age women with no qualifications remained fairly static between 1984 and 1991, but increased by just over 5 percentage points between 1991 and 1996.

Although inactivity rates have increased among those without qualifications, the proportion of the population who have no qualifications has fallen. Overall, though, inactivity has increased among those without qualifications.

Reasons for inactivity among men

Among working-age men the main reason for the growth in inactivity is long-term sickness and disability. The number of working-age men who are inactive has increased between 1984 and 1996, and so has the proportion of these who are long-term sick. *Table 6* shows that the proportion of inactive men who are long-term sick has increased from 31 per

cent in 1984 to 41 per cent in 1996. The largest percentage point increase occurred between 1991 and 1996.

There has also been a threefold increase (from a low base) in the proportion of men giving 'looking after family or home' as their reason for inactivity. This may reflect the increase in female participation in the labour force. If we look only at inactive married or cohabiting men, there has been a fourfold increase in the proportion giving looking after family or home as their reason for inactivity (from 2 per cent to 8 per cent). Economic activity of wives or partners of heads of married or cohabiting family units has also increased by 9 percentage points between 1986 and 1996,

suggesting that for some the traditional roles of 'breadwinner' and those undertaking domestic duties may be reversed.

In 1996 around half of working-age inactive men were heads of married or cohabiting households. Of these 55 per cent of them were inactive because they were long-term sick. The inactivity rate of heads of married or cohabiting households has remained fairly constant at around 10 per cent over the last ten years. However, the reasons for inactivity among this group have changed over time. The proportion giving long-term sick or disabled as their reason for inactivity has increased by 14 percentage points in the last ten years – from 41 per cent in 1986 to 55 per cent in 1996. The proportion giving looking after family or home has also increased from 2 per cent in 1986 to 8 per cent in 1996. There was a decline in the proportion of discouraged workers.

The second largest group of inactive men are those who live on their own. Around a quarter of inactive men live alone. In 1996 the main reasons for inactivity in this group were long-term sickness (43 per cent) and being a student (29 per cent).

Reasons for inactivity among women

Table 7 shows that between 1984 and 1996 there has been a fall in the absolute number of inactive women and a 12 percentage point fall in the proportion of inactive women looking after family or home. The largest fall has been in the 20-24 age group. Between 1984 and 1996 there has been a 23 percentage point reduction in the proportion of inactive women aged 20-24 giving looking after family home as their reason for inactivity. This

Table 6   Reasons for inactivity, working-age men; Great Britain; spring quarters

				Per cent
	1984	1986	1991	1996
Student	33	30	29	28
Looking after family or home	2	3	3	6
Long-term sick/disabled	31	29	35	41
Does not want/need a job	5	4	2	1
Discouraged workers	7	9	3	2
Other	22	26	28	22
All inactive men (thousands = 100%)	**2,065**	**2,157**	**2,172**	**2,765**

Source: Labour Force Survey

Table 7   Reasons for inactivity, working-age women; Great Britain; spring quarters

				Per cent
	1984	1986	1991	1996
Student	11	10	12	16
Looking after family or home	63	60	57	51
Long-term sick/disabled	8	8	11	18
Does not want/need a job	10	10	9	3
Discouraged workers	2	2	1	1
Other	5	9	10	12
All inactive women (thousands = 100%)	**5,316**	**5,086**	**4,687**	**4,727**

Source: Labour Force Survey

partly reflects an increase in the participation of young women in full-time education. Between 1984 and 1996 there has been a 22 percentage point increase in the proportion of women in this group who are inactive because they are students.

Between 1984 and 1996 there has been a 10 percentage point increase in the proportion of inactive working-age women who are long-term sick or disabled. There has been an increase in the proportion of inactive women who are long-term sick across all age groups. The largest increases have been in the older age groups, 14 percentage points in the 35-49 age group and 17 percentage points in the 50-59 age group.

Around 60 per cent of inactive women are married or cohabiting. The main reason for inactivity in this group is looking after family or home. In 1996, 63 per cent of inactive married or cohabiting women gave looking after family or home as their reason for inactivity – down 8 percentage points between 1986 and 1996. This has been accompanied by a sharp increase in labour market participation among married or cohabiting women. Their economic activity rate has increased by 9 percentage points between 1986 and 1996. However, there has also been an increase in inactivity due to long-term sickness among married or cohabiting women.

In 1996, just under a fifth of inactive women were lone parents. In 1996, women represented 92 per cent of inactive lone parents. Three-quarters of inactive female lone parents gave looking after family or home as the main reason for their inactivity in 1996. Over the past decade, lone parents (men and women) have been the least economically active group. Just over 40 per cent of all lone parents are inactive. This figure has increased slightly over the past ten years, from 41 per cent in 1986 to 43 per cent in 1996. This is mainly due to a growth in inactivity due to long-term sickness.

Just over 10 per cent of inactive women live in single-person households, compared with almost a quarter of inactive men. In 1996 the main reasons for inactivity among women living alone were long-term sickness (41 per cent) and being a student (33 per cent). Across all single-person households (men and women) the proportion who are inactive has grown over the past decade. The main reason for the growth in inactivity in this group is the increase in long-term sickness. In 1986 the proportion who were long-term sick was 26 per cent; by 1986 this had increased to 42 per cent.

Conclusion

Between 1984 and 1991, the proportion of working-age households which had no members in employment remained roughly constant, at around 16 per cent. Between 1991 and 1996, the proportion rose to just under 20 per cent. Changing household size is very important in describing the increase in the workless household rate. Between 1984 and 1991, there were large increases in the numbers of single-adult households and in particular, single-adult households with at least one person under 16.

Single-adult households have high non-employment rates, and increases in their numbers over time, coupled with a worsening in their employment rate, has contributed to the rise in workless households. For lone parents, the age of the youngest child is an important factor in the level of economic activity. Lone-parent households where the youngest child is under 5 are more likely to be workless than those where the youngest child is between 5 and 15.

Workless households are largely dependent upon state benefits. In 1993/4 three quarters of adults living in workless households lived in family units that were in receipt of benefit.

Only 50 per cent of inactive people live in workless households. Between 1984 and 1996, economic inactivity increased for men but decreased for women. The LFS asks the reasons why people are inactive. This showed that over time increasing numbers of inactive people are reporting that they are inactive because of long-term illness or disability. Results from other surveys also back this up. However, while there is no evidence that the population is getting healthier, it is thought that much of the reported increase in sickness and disability is due to changing response patterns rather than genuine changes to the health of the population. ∎

Technical note

Household data quality
There have been several feature articles on the quality of household data from the Labour Force Survey, namely: 'Data on households and families from the Labour Force Survey', Pam Tate, *Labour Market Trends*, March 1997, pp89-98; 'Household and family data from the Labour Force Survey: recent improvements in approach', David Hastings, *Labour Market Trends*, June 1997, pp209-16; and 'Economic activity of working-age households', David Hastings, *Labour Market Trends*, September 1997, pp333-8. The main problem with household data in terms of this article is that the current LFS grossing system only takes account of individual characteristics. It therefore may not reproduce with full accuracy the distribution of household types in the population. This means that the results presented in this document should be treated as a guide to the levels and trends and not as definitive estimates.

Data on reasons for inactivity
Prior to 1992, the Labour Force Survey was carried out annually, focused on the spring quarter. Since 1992, the LFS has been carried out quarterly. For the purposes of comparison over time data for spring quarters have been used.

However, there were many changes to the questionnaire when the survey moved from being annual to quarterly. One of the major changes was in the way reasons for inactivity were identified. As part of this article a consistent time-series on reasons for inactivity was created. The categories that were linked were: students; looking after family/home; long-term sick/disabled; not needing a job; discouraged workers; and other.

In general, a consistent series could be produced for most of these categories between 1991 and spring 1993. Linkage with data for 1992 is not possible due to teething problems with the new survey (for further details, see *LFS User Guide, Volume 3*). The one area where the linkage does not look consistent is for people who do not want or need a job. The numbers in this category fell dramatically over this period. It is likely that the differences were absorbed into a lot of the remaining categories and so no other series appear to show a discernible discontinuity. For this reason, users are advised that the category 'not want/need a job' does not provide a consistent time-series. More detailed information on the changes in methodology which occurred when the survey went from being annual to quarterly are contained in *Employment Gazette*, October 1992, pp483-90.

Definitions

household	a single person or group of people who have the same address as their only or main residence and who either share one meal a day or share the living accommodation.
family unit	a single person, or a married or cohabiting couple on their own, or with their never-married children who have no children of their own, or lone parents with such children.
state benefit	those in receipt of Invalidity Benefit, War Disability Pension, Attendance Allowance, Industrial Injuries Disablement Pension, Invalid Care Allowance, Mobility Allowance, Severe Disability Allowance, Sickness Benefit and Industrial Injuries Benefit, Disability Living Allowance, Income Support or Unemployment Benefit. The period covered by this article predates Jobseeker's Allowance, so this is not included.
ILO unemployed	those who were out of work, had actively sought work in the four weeks before the interview and were able to start a new job within a fortnight of the interview.
economically inactive	those who are not in employment or ILO unemployed.
workless	those who are either ILO unemployed or economically inactive i.e. not in employment.

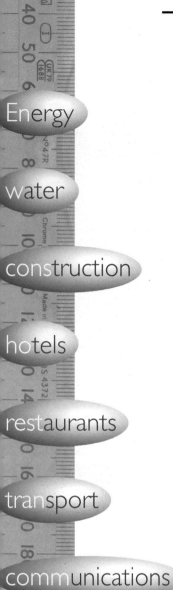

Energy

water

construction

hotels

restaurants

transport

communications

Take the measure of the British workforce

Getting a clear picture of how the employed workforce changed between 1993 and 1995 is a 'must' for any labour market planner or analyst. But where do you go for the latest data?

Look no further than the Annual Employment Survey 1995, new from ONS. Based on a sample of 130,000 businesses across Great Britain, AES breaks down employee jobs by local area, industrial activity, sex and full or part-time status.

AES is the **only** source of employment data giving such detail for all sectors of the economy, providing a unique profile of employment patterns across Great Britain today.

The new AES series replaces the old Census of Employment, last conducted in 1993. The 1995 results are is now available in a series of three booklets. These are:

Part 1: GB & Regions summary
Results for GB & Regions to 92 class (4 digit) male female/part-time split. Plus a GB & Regions summary table.
ISBN 1 857 74 227 3

Part 2: Local Authority Districts and Counties
Broad Industry Groups for each Local Authority District and County and GB, male, female full/part-time split.
ISBN 1 85774 229 X

Part 3: Government Office Regions and TEC/LEC areas; Size Analysis of Local Units
Broad Industry Groups for each Government Office Region, TEC/LEC areas and GB, male, female full/part-time split. Results for GB & Regions for local units by size- Broad Industry Groups
ISBN 1 85774 230 3

All booklets cost **£35.99** each. Order the whole set and get a **10 per cent** reduction: pay **£97.20**.

For copies of any of the booklets please ring the **Office for National Statistics** Sales Office on **0171 533 5678** or fax **0171 533 5689**. For information about the contents of the booklets, please contact Earnings and Employment Division, ONS on **01928 792563**.

Temporary workers in Great Britain

Temporary work has increased from 5.5 per cent of employees in the mid to late 1980s to more than 7 per cent today. This article presents information from the spring 1996 Labour Force Survey, on the types of temporary work and the people engaged in these jobs, and makes comparisons with 1984 and 1992.

By **Frances Sly** and **Darren Stillwell**, Labour Market Division, Office for National Statistics.

Photo: Telegraph Colour Library

Key findings

- Since 1990, there has been an increase in both the number of temporary employees and the proportion of all employees who were temporary, reaching 7.1 per cent of all employees (1.6 million) in spring 1996, compared with around 5.5 per cent during the mid to late 1980s.
- In 1996, 8 per cent of women employees and 6 per cent of men employees were temporary; since 1991, the increase in the proportion of employees who were temporary has been greater for men than for women.
- Temporary jobs have accounted for at least one-third of new engagements since 1984.
- Since 1992, around half of temporary employees have been on a fixed-term contract or task.
- Some 49 per cent of men and 36 per cent of women in a temporary job said this was because they could not find a permanent job. Among women in temporary employment, 34 per cent said that they did not want a permanent job, compared with 20 per cent for men.
- Around 10 per cent of employees in the public sector are temporary, compared with around 6 per cent in the private sector.
- The greatest concentrations of temporary employees are in the professional occupations, where one in seven employees is temporary, and in the public administration, education and health industry sector and the 'other services' industry sector where around one in ten employees is temporary.
- The UK has the third lowest proportion of temporary employees in the EU.

Introduction

TEMPORARY JOBS have periodically been the focus of attention from both academic researchers and the media. In the 1980s the interest in temporary work was largely associated with the prevailing labour market segmentation theories. These viewed the use of temporary workers as a means by which employers were able to vary the size of their workforce more easily and rapidly in response to supply and demand patterns, the various stages of their production cycle, and changes in economic circumstances.[1] Statistical information on the early 1980s is not clear, but it is believed that temporary work increased at this time, suggesting that in the early stages of recovery from recession the number of temporary employees grew faster than permanent employees as employers were hesitant about taking on new permanent employees.[2] This certainly appears to have happened in Great Britain in the 1990s when the number of temporary employees increased as a proportion of all employees by 1 percentage point between spring 1993 and 1995 (see *Figure 1*), increasing less rapidly in other years.

In the 1990s there is continuing interest in temporary jobs as one form of 'flexible' working (alongside others such as part-time work and work of varying weekly or monthly hours). It can offer benefits not only to employers but also to employees, who might prefer a non-standard working arrangement in order to fit paid work more easily around other responsibilities, such as looking after a family or undertaking full-time education. Indeed, it is now recognised that people do not spend all their lives in permanent, full-time jobs, but move through a variety of working arrangements, which may at times, particularly in their early years, include temporary jobs.

In addition to overall trends for 1984 to 1996, this article presents more detailed analyses from the Labour Force Survey (LFS), giving the proportions of employees who are temporary, the proportions in each type of temporary work and the reasons they gave for working on a temporary basis. There is also a breakdown of temporary workers into broad industry and occupation groups, and finally there is a comparison with other EU countries.

What is temporary work?

Temporary jobs can take a variety of forms. These have in common the fact that the jobs are held by someone who has been recruited to do them for a finite period of time (although this may be up to several years). They include seasonal work, casual work, non-permanent jobs obtained through a temporary employment agency ('agency temps') and jobs carried out under a fixed-term contract. Temporary jobs in Great Britain have traditionally been common in certain industries and occupations: the 1986 LFS showed, for example, that there were high concentrations of temporary workers in distribution, hotels and repairs and other services and in clerical work, catering and some professional occupations, such as teaching.[3]

Within a general increase in both the number and proportion of employees who are temporary, the nature of temporary work that people are undertaking in Britain has changed since 1992. There have been increases in the proportions of temporary workers who are agency temps, those on fixed-term contracts or tasks, and temporary employees who could not find a full-time job. Analysis of occupation and industry groups shows that different forms of temporary work were concentrated within different occupations and industries. The main industrial sectors employing temporary workers were public administration, education and health industries and the professional occupations. These industry and occupation groups include jobs in both nursing and education – high users of

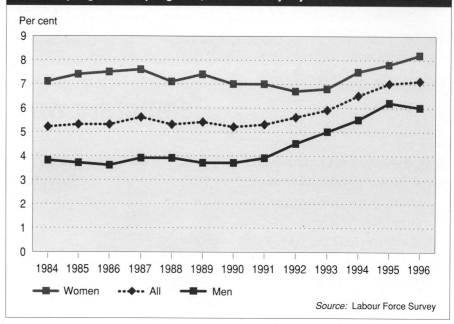

Figure 1 **Percentage of employees who were temporary; Great Britain; spring 1984 to spring 1996; not seasonally adjusted**

Source: Labour Force Survey

temporary work. The growth since 1992 has also been greatest in these areas, with clerical/secretarial and personal/protective service occupations and the banking, finance and insurance industry sector also showing above average growth in temporary employment.

Overall trends 1984-1996

Figure 1 gives the proportion of employees who were temporary, from spring 1984 to spring 1996. Between spring 1984 and spring 1991, the proportion of all employees who were temporary remained around 5 per cent. As unemployment fell and employment rose between 1986 and 1990 the proportion of employees in temporary jobs fell slightly. It started to rise during the recession and then continued to rise in the first years of the recovery, although between 1995 and 1996 the rate of growth slowed. Between 1993 and 1995 there was an increase of 1 percentage point, and by 1996 both the proportion and the number of employees who were temporary were at the highest level since at least 1984: 1,557,000 temporary employees, accounting for 7.1 per cent of all employees in the labour force.

There were more women than men in temporary jobs in spring 1996 (861,000 compared with 696,000) and they represented a greater proportion of employees (8.2 per cent of women employees) than did men (6.0 per cent). However, since 1991 the increase in the proportion of employees who were temporary has been greater among men than women. From 1991 to 1995 the proportion of male employees who were temporary increased by over 2 percentage points compared with around 1 percentage point during the same period for women. There was, however, a drop in the proportions for men between 1995 and 1996.

Despite this growth, temporary jobs are still a small fraction of employment. As such, it is not a sign that job tenure is falling. In 1996, 10 per cent of all employees had been in their job for less than six months, 19 per cent for less than a year: these figures are exactly the same as in 1986. In general, temporary jobs are lasting longer. In 1996, around 40 per cent of temporary jobs had a total duration of more than one year.[4]

The significance of temporary jobs in the labour market may be greater than their numbers suggest. The LFS shows that temporary jobs account for at least a third of new engagements (a proportion which has not varied much since at least 1984) which suggests that a large proportion of jobs taken by the unemployed and new entrants to the labour market may be temporary. Information from the claimant count supports this hypothesis, as nearly half of the people who leave the count return within a year, though this includes people leaving so-called permanent jobs too.[5] These figures reflect instability at the fringes of the labour market, particularly in entry jobs, and there is concern among some analysts about both the high rate of return to non-employment from temporary jobs and the quality of temporary entry jobs.

Types of temporary jobs

Table 1 gives the proportions in the different types of temporary jobs, within the rising total, between 1992 and 1996. Over this period, most temporary workers (about half) were on a fixed-term contract or performing a fixed task. Around a quarter were casual or seasonal workers, although this proportion had declined from 29 per cent in 1992 to 25 per cent in 1996. There was an increase in the proportion of temporary workers who were agency temps, almost doubling to 13 per cent in 1996.

Table 1 Temporary employees by type of temporary job; Great Britain; spring 1992 to spring 1996; not seasonally adjusted

					Per cent
	1992	1993	1994	1995	1996
Fixed-term contract/task	48	50	54	54	51
Agency temping	7	7	8	11	13
Casual or seasonal	29	28	27	25	25
Other	16	15	11	11	10
All (thousands = 100%)	1,195	1,251	1,386	1,512	1,557

Source: Labour Force Survey

While there were more women than men temporary employees, they were similarly distributed across the age groups and the various forms of temporary work (see *Table 2*). Overall, the proportion of employees who were temporary was greatest among those aged 16 to 24 and those over retirement age (see *Table 3*). Temporary employees in these two age groups were also more likely to be in casual or seasonal work than those in other age groups, and less likely to be on fixed-term contracts. The 16 to 24-year-old age group will contain students in weekend or vacation work, while the group aged over retirement age may contain people who have retired from full-time work but wish to remain economically active or supplement their existing income.

Part-time temporary workers

Almost half of temporary workers were part-time, although the proportion has fallen slightly since spring 1992 (see *Table 4*). Part-time work has been most common among temporary employees who are casual or seasonal workers, comprising about three-quarters of this group. Over the same period, there has been a decrease in the proportion of agency temps working part-time, from 35 per cent to 29 per cent, coupled with an increase in the proportion of part-time temporary employees in 'other' forms of temporary work (to more than half of all temporary employees in this group by spring 1996).

Women were much more likely than men to work part-time in a temporary job; around 60 per cent of female temporary employees in spring 1996 were part-time (considerably more than among female permanent employees), compared with less than 30 per cent of men. Around three-quarters of part-time temporary employees were women and a fifth of part-time temporary workers were full-time students.

Reasons for employers' use of temporary workers

The reasons that are most commonly given by employers for recruiting temporary workers include: providing cover for the absence of permanent staff (e.g. on maternity leave); to cope with seasonal fluctuations in the workload; to staff short-term projects; and to acquire people with specialist skills which are only needed on a short-term basis or which are only available on a non-permanent basis.[6]

A comparison of LFS data from 1984 and 1994 shows that there has been a greater increase in the proportions of employees in 'flexible' employment (e.g. temporary workers, part-time workers or people working variable hours) in establishments of 25 or more employees than in smaller establishments.[7] Whereas small establishments were the relatively greater users of temporary workers in 1984, larger establishments had caught up with them ten years later, having doubled their proportions of temporary employees. There was growth in these flexible labour market forms in smaller establishments (those with less than 25 employees), but the increase in proportions was less.

Why employees work on a temporary basis

There are a wide range of reasons why employees might take jobs on a temporary basis. In the case of highly-skilled workers, temporary contracts can provide a higher income and greater autonomy than a permanent job. Some people might prefer the flexibility of temporary work because they wish to combine working with other responsibilities, for example looking after children during school holidays or undertaking a course of higher education. Others may be in temporary work because they have been unable to obtain a permanent job.[8] For employees in this category, temporary jobs can offer, in addition to

Table 2 Distribution of male and female temporary workers, by type of temporary job; Great Britain; spring 1996; not seasonally adjusted

		Per cent
	Men	Women
Fixed-term contract/task	55	49
Agency temping	13	13
Casual or seasonal	23	27
Other	10	11
All (thousands = 100%)	696	861
As a percentage of all employees	6.0	8.2

Source: Labour Force Survey

Table 3 Distribution of temporary workers, by age and type of temporary job; Great Britain; spring 1996; not seasonally adjusted

			Age (years)			Per cent
	All	16-24	25-34	35-49	50-59 (women) 64 (men)	60+ (women) 65+ (men)
Fixed-term contract/task	51	37	61	60	53	29
Agency temping	13	15	14	12	11	*
Casual or seasonal	25	37	17	18	25	49
Other	10	11	9	10	11	*
All (thousands = 100%)	1,557	448	399	438	209	63
As a percentage of all employees	7.1	12.9	6.5	5.5	5.4	11.7

Source: Labour Force Survey

* Sample size too small for a reliable estimate.

Table 4 Part-time temporary workers, by type; Great Britain; spring 1992 to spring 1996; not seasonally adjusted

					Per cent
	1992	1993	1994	1995	1996
Fixed-term contract/task	34	33	35	36	35
Agency temping	35	29	28	25	29
Casual or seasonal	77	77	75	76	76
Other	46	50	51	50	51
All temporary employees	48	48	47	46	46

Source: Labour Force Survey

Table 5 Reason for being in a temporary job; Great Britain; spring 1992 to spring 1996; not seasonally adjusted

					Per cent
	1992	1993	1994	1995	1996
Could not find permanent job	37	43	43	44	42
Did not want permanent job	28	26	26	27	28
Contract included training	6	6	7	6	5
Other reason	31	25	24	23	26
All (thousands = 100%)	1,195	1,251	1,386	1,512	1,557

Source: Labour Force Survey

Table 6 Reason for being in a temporary job, by type of job; Great Britain; spring 1996; not seasonally adjusted

				Per cent
	Fixed-term contract/task	Agency temping	Casual or seasonal	Other
Could not find permanent job	45	57	33	29
Did not want permanent job	17	27	50	26
Contract included training	8	*	*	7
Other reason	30	16	17	37
All (thousands = 100%)	801	201	395	159

Source: Labour Force Survey

*   Sample size too small for a reliable estimate.

income, an opportunity to acquire skills and experience – and in some cases training – which are likely to help them to find a permanent job in the future. Further, there is recent evidence that some employers recruit staff on a non-permanent basis to cope with a temporary increase in the workload, but subsequently offer them permanent jobs when such vacancies become available.[9]

The reasons respondents to the LFS gave for being in a temporary job are shown in *Table 5*. The proportion of people saying they were in temporary work because they could not find a permanent job increased from 37 per cent in spring 1992 to 42 per cent in spring 1996. Men were more likely than women to be in temporary work because they could not find a permanent job. Around a half of men in temporary work gave this response, compared with a little over a third of women (see *Figure 2*). For both men and women, this proportion was higher in the groups aged 25 to 34 and 35 to 49 than in other age groups. Around six in ten men aged

25 to 49 and four in ten women aged 25 to 49 could not find a permanent job. Women in temporary employment were more likely than men to say that they did not want a permanent job (around a third compared with a fifth).

Table 6 shows the cross-analysis of the reasons people gave for being in a temporary job, by type of temporary job in 1996. Agency temporary workers were the group most likely to say that they had not been able to find a permanent job – more than half gave this response. Almost half of those on fixed-term contracts and a third of those in casual or seasonal jobs also said that they could not find a permanent job. Those in casual or seasonal work were most likely to have said that they did not want a permanent job (50 per cent).

Occupations of temporary workers

Table 7 gives the percentage of employees who were temporary in each occupational group, for spring 1992 to spring 1996. The small increase in the overall percentage of temporary workers was outstripped in the professional occupations. In 1992 around one in ten professional employees was temporary – this proportion had reached one in seven by 1996. There were also relatively strong increases in temporary workers among clerical and secretarial occupations and in the personal and protective services. These occupations are largely to be found in the services sector, where all of the recent growth in employment has occurred.

There were also clear differences in the types of temporary contract associated with different occupations (see *Table 8*), which might be expected as a result of

Figure 2 Reason for temporary work, by age; Great Britain; spring 1996; not seasonally adjusted

Men / Women stacked bar charts, Per cent (0–100) by Age (years): Men — All, 16-24, 25-34, 35-49[a], 50-64; Women — All, 16-24, 25-34, 35-49, 50-59.

Legend: Other reason / Did not want permanent job / Could not find permanent job

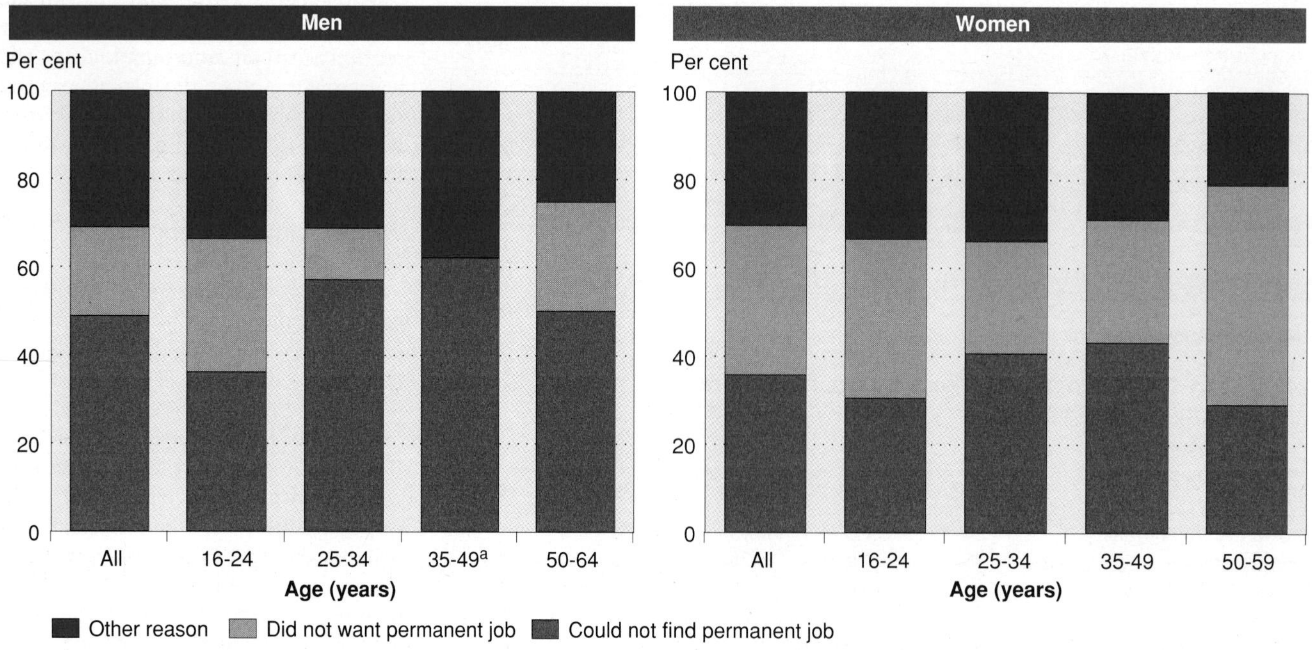

a 'Other reason' includes a small number of temporary employees who did not want a permanent job.

Source: Labour Force Survey

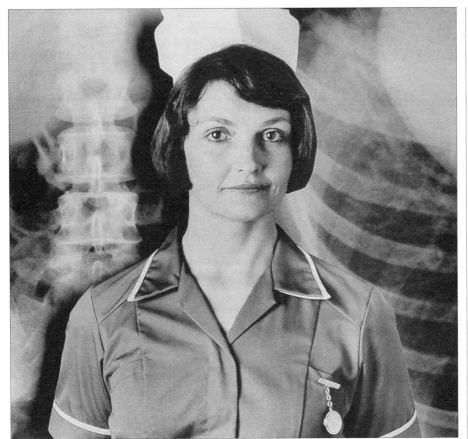

Photo: Telegraph Colour Library

differences in the level of qualifications and skills required to carry out different occupations. Of all temporary employees, around a fifth were in each of professional occupations and clerical and secretarial occupations. Of the temporary workers in the professional occupations, around six in ten worked in education, where short courses and research projects which employ a lot of staff on a temporary basis are quite common. Of the temporary workers in personal and protective services, over a third were in childcare occupations and over a quarter were in catering occupations. A third of all fixed-term contract workers were in professional occupations and nearly a half of all agency temporary workers were in clerical and secretarial occupations. Seasonal and casual workers were found in their largest numbers in personal and protective services with around a quarter of temporary employees.

A common perception is that most temporary jobs are of poor quality, particularly for new entrants into the labour market. However, *Table 8* suggests that temporary jobs, far from all being low-paid and unstable, fall into a number of categories, ranging from the casual and seasonal personal and protective service jobs (which may be relatively low-paid and unstable) to the often highly-paid professional employees, typically working on fixed-term contracts in specialist fields. Clerical and secretarial temps are typically employed through an agency, which may confer many of the benefits of permanent working with relatively few disadvantages.

Temporary work in the public and private sectors

Since spring 1994 (the first spring quarter for which information is available) the public sector has employed a higher proportion of temporary employees than the private sector, at around one in ten compared with one in 20 (see *Table 9*). Almost three-quarters of all temporary jobs in the public sector were fixed-term contracts, compared

Table 7 **Percentage of temporary employees in each occupational group; Great Britain; spring 1992 to spring 1996; not seasonally adjusted**

					Per cent
Standard Occupational Classification	1992	1993	1994	1995	1996
Major occupation group					
Managers and administrators	2	2	2	2	3
Professional	10	11	14	14	14
Associate professional and technical	6	7	7	7	7
Clerical and secretarial	5	6	6	7	8
Craft and related	4	4	4	5	4
Personal and protective service	7	7	8	8	9
Sales	5	5	5	5	5
Plant and machine operatives	5	5	6	7	6
Other	8	8	9	10	9
All temporary employees	**6**	**6**	**6**	**7**	**7**

Source: Labour Force Survey

Table 8 **Distribution of temporary workers, by occupation group and type of temporary work; Great Britain; spring 1996; not seasonally adjusted**

						Per cent
Standard Occupational Classification	All temporary employees	Fixed-term contract/task	Agency temping	Casual or seasonal	Other	All employees
Major occupation group						
Managers and administrators	6	8	*	*	7	15
Professional	21	32	*	7	17	11
Associate professional and technical	9	13	8	4	7	9
Clerical and secretarial	19	14	49	13	15	16
Craft and related	6	6	*	6	9	10
Personal and protective service	15	12	10	24	17	12
Sales	6	2	*	13	7	9
Plant and machine operatives	9	7	16	10	9	10
Other	10	6	6	20	11	8
All temporary employees (thousands = 100%)	**1,557**	**801**	**201**	**395**	**159**	**22,020**

Source: Labour Force Survey

* Sample size too small for a reliable estimate.

Figure 3 **Temporary work in the public and private sectors, by type; Great Britain; spring 1996; not seasonally adjusted**

Public sector	Private sector
Fixed-term contract/task 71%	Fixed-term contract/task 39%
Casual or seasonal 6%	Casual or seasonal 33%
Agency temping 15%	Agency temping 17%
Other 8%	Other 11%

Source: Labour Force Survey

with only two-fifths of temporary jobs in the private sector (see *Figure 3*). Private sector organisations were heavier users of the other forms of temporary work, with a third of all their temporary employees in casual or seasonal work compared with an eighth in the public sector. The growth in the proportion of temporary workers over the last two years has been similar in both the public and private sectors, as *Table 9* shows.

Industries employing temporary workers

Table 10 shows that from spring 1992 to 1996 the largest increases in the percentage of employees who were temporary workers were in the energy and water industries, 'other services', the banking, finance and insurance group and the public administration, education and health industry group. Similar to the professional occupation category, this latter category includes both the nursing and teaching professions. In 1996 more than half of the temporary workers in this industry group were employed in the education sector.

The distribution of the different types of temporary work by broad industry grouping in spring 1996 is shown in *Table 11*. Just under two-fifths of all temporary workers were found in the public administration, education and health industry; a half of those on fixed-term contracts worked in this industry. A third of agency temps worked in banking, finance and insurance, and a third of casual and seasonal workers were in the distribution, hotels and restaurant industries.

Hotels and catering – included in the distribution, hotels and restaurants industry grouping – is characterised by both seasonal demand and one-off events (over two-fifths of temporary workers in this sector were in the hotel and catering group). Seasonal demand in agriculture is well documented, and 'other services' includes cultural, sporting and similar activities, which also sometimes employ large numbers of temporary workers for one-off events.

The research cited earlier has found that fixed-term contracts for highly-skilled workers can provide greater autonomy and

Table 9 **Use of temporary workers by the public and private sectors; Great Britain; spring 1994ᵃ to 1996; not seasonally adjusted**

			Per cent
	1994	1995	1996
Public sector	9.8	10.2	10.4
Private sector	5.2	5.8	5.7
All	**6.5**	**7.0**	**7.1**

Source: Labour Force Survey

a   The public/private sector variable was introduced in autumn 1993.

Table 10 **Percentage of temporary employees in each industry sector; Great Britain; spring 1992 to spring 1996; not seasonally adjusted**

					Per cent
Standard Industrial Classification 1992	1992	1993	1994	1995	1996
Industry sector					
Agriculture and fishing	7	6	7	8	8
Energy and water	5	6	7	8	8
Manufacturing	4	3	4	4	4
Construction	6	5	6	7	6
Distribution, hotels and restaurants	5	5	5	5	5
Transport and communication	3	4	4	5	5
Banking, finance and insurance etc.	5	6	6	7	7
Public administration, education and health	8	8	10	10	10
Other services	8	9	11	10	11
All temporary employees	**6**	**6**	**6**	**7**	**7**

Source: Labour Force Survey

Table 11 **Distribution of temporary workers, by industry; Great Britain; spring 1996; not seasonally adjusted**

						Per cent
Standard Industrial Classification 1992	All temporary employees	Fixed-term contract/task	Agency temping	Casual or seasonal	Other	All employees
Industry sector						
Agriculture and fishing	1	*	*	3	*	1
Energy and water	2	2	*	*	*	1
Manufacturing	13	12	19	11	15	21
Construction	4	4	3	*	7	4
Distribution, hotels and restaurants	15	6	10	35	17	20
Transport and communication	5	4	8	5	*	6
Banking, finance and insurance etc.	14	12	35	8	10	14
Public administration, education and health	38	53	16	20	35	27
Other services	8	6	*	15	9	5
All temporary employees (thousands) (=100%)	**1,557**	**801**	**201**	**395**	**159**	**22,020**

Source: Labour Force Survey

*   Sample size too small for a reliable estimate.

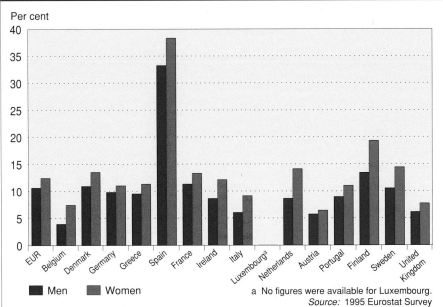

Figure 4 Levels of temporary employment in 15 EU countries; spring 1995; not seasonally adjusted

Men   Women

a No figures were available for Luxembourg.
Source: 1995 Eurostat Survey

earnings than a permanent post.[10] Such contracts are also likely to involve specialised work. Since 45 per cent of temporary employees on fixed term contracts say that they are in a temporary job because they could not find a permanent job, this may indicate that some who are unable to find permanent work in their area of specialisation would rather take a fixed-term temporary post in the same area than choose to look more widely for permanent work. In some cases the temporary job may lead to a permanent post, though in many cases the employer will want to employ the specialist skills for a fixed period only.

Temporary work in the European Union

It is possible to compare broad LFS figures for the UK with a corresponding series of European Labour Force Surveys. *Figure 4* presents the incidence of temporary work among employees for the 15 EU member states in 1995 (the latest year for which Eurostat have published the data).[11] It shows that Spain experiences the greatest occurrence of temporary employment of any of the 15 EU member states and the UK has the third lowest percentage of employees in temporary work, after Belgium and Austria (no recent figure was available for Luxembourg, where temporary work had previously been less common than in the UK). While differences in the pattern of employment between countries is likely to depend on a variety of factors, the regulatory governance of the labour market (including collective agreements) is likely to have an important impact on the degree of labour market flexibility. The highest levels of temporary employment tend to exist in countries where there are relatively high levels of employment legislation (such as Spain). A

significant factor here is the level of employment protection afforded to permanent staff in preference to temporary workers. Whereas it is relatively costly to dismiss a permanent employee, it is likely to be less costly to hire a worker on a temporary contract, therefore permitting the firm greater flexibility. The relative scarcity of temporary employment in the UK in comparison to its EU partners can thus in part be ascribed to the less regulated nature of its labour market.[12]

The European LFS also gives data showing the reasons given by employees for being in temporary work (see *Table 12*). These figures should be treated with caution, however, as in certain countries respondents were presented with a more restricted range of options – France and Germany, for example, both had very high proportions of respondents giving no reason for being in temporary employment.

In countries where temporary work is most common and the labour market is highly regulated, high levels of dissatisfaction with temporary employment were recorded – notably in Spain, where 86 per cent of respondents were in temporary work because they could not find any permanent employment. A number of countries exhibit peculiarities in the reasons given for being in temporary employment which are probably due to the unique characteristics of the workings and regulations of their labour markets. The Netherlands, for example, has a high proportion of respondents in temporary employment because they do not want permanent work. Denmark and Austria have high incidences of people being in temporary employment because it involved training.

In summary, the UK has a relatively low level of temporary employment compared to other European countries, but with a similar gender breakdown – women being slightly more likely to be in temporary work than men. The most probable reason for this is the more flexible and unregulated state of

Table 12 Reason for being in a temporary job; EU countries; spring 1995

Per cent

	Contract covering a period of training	Could not find a permanent job	Did not want a permanent job	Contract for probationary period	No reason given
EU 15	**17.0**	**39.0**	**7.2**	**2.5**	**34.4**
Belgium	18.7	41.9	*	8.2	30.3
Denmark	31.2	43.8	24.9	*	*
Germany	38.0	*	*	*	62.0
Greece	5.2	78.3	4.6	9.0	2.9
Spain	3.9	86.0	0.3	0.6	9.2
France	16.6	*	*	7.2	76.2
Ireland	14.6	63.2	17.8	*	*
Italy	23.9	51.3	4.3	3.4	17.1
Luxembourg	*	*	*	*	*
Netherlands	1.4	48.1	43.4	*	7.1
Austria	50.4	13.8	11.1	24.7	*
Portugal	5.0	83.3	*	9.6	*
Finland	4.8	57.0	11.0	3.9	23.3
Sweden	*	79.2	20.8	*	*
United Kingdom	5.3	44.5	27.3	*	22.9

Source: 1995 Eurostat Survey

* Figures unavailable or sample size too small for a reliable estimate.

the UK labour market, where there is not such a distinction between the rights of permanent and temporary employees. This explanation is reflected in the fact that a relatively low proportion of temporary workers in the UK are so employed because they are unable to find any permanent work. The data on temporary work across Europe remain patchy, and hence are a prime area in which research could be expanded. ■

Footnotes

1 McGregor, A and Sproull, AC: *Employer Labour Use Strategies: Analysis of a national survey*, Department of Employment Research Paper No 83, 1991.

2 Casey, B, Metcalf, H and Millward, N: *Employers' use of flexible labour*, Policy Studies Institute.

3 King, S: 'Temporary workers in Britain: Findings from the 1986 Labour Force Survey', *Employment Gazette*, April 1988.

4 LFS Help-Line, *Labour Market Trends*, May 1997.

5 The claimant count is the monthly administrative measure of those claiming unemployment benefits. Information is published each month in *Labour Market Trends*. See 'Destination of leavers from claimant unemployment', *Labour Market Trends*, October 1996, pp443-52 for proportions returning to count (*Table 7*).

6 ELUS; Casey, B: 'The extent and nature of temporary employment in Great Britain', *Policy Studies* Vol. 8, Part I, July 1987; Meager, N: 'Temporary work in Britain', *Employment Gazette*, January 1986. 'Employers' use of temporary workers', *Labour Market Trends*, September 1996, pp403-12.

7 Casey, B, Metcalf, H and Millward, N: op. cit.

8 Casey, B: op. cit.; Meager, N: op. cit.

9 *Temporary Workers*, IDS Study 579, June 1995. 'Employers' use of temporary workers', *Labour Market Trends*, September 1996, pp403-12.

10 Casey, B: op. cit.; Meager, N: op. cit.

11 *Labour Force Survey Results 1995*, Eurostat.

12 Grubb and Wells (1993), as cited in Beatson, M: *Labour Market Flexibility*, Employment Department Group, Research Series No. 48, April 1995, p23. Grubb and Wells found correlations between the severity of employment regulation and the composition of type of employment to be statistically significant.

Acknowledgements

The authors wish to acknowledge the considerable assistance of Phillip Lee at the Office for National Statistics, Paul Teasdale at the Department of Trade and Industry, and Tristan Slinger and others at the Department for Education and Employment.

Technical note

Questions in the LFS

From spring 1992 onwards, the LFS section on the temporary/permanent status of employment takes the form of four questions that are asked of employees only. The first question asks whether a job is 'permanent' or 'not permanent in some way' (i.e. temporary). Whether a job is temporary or permanent is based on the respondent's own assessment of their employment. The LFS does not stipulate a duration that defines a temporary job.

Respondents who say that their job is temporary are then asked a further three questions. Firstly, the type of temporary job, where the responses available are: seasonal work; work done under contract for a fixed period or task; agency temping (where the employee is leased out by a temporary workers bureau and remains the employee of the bureau rather than of the company with which they are placed); casual work; or some other reason for the job being temporary. Secondly, they are asked about their reasons for taking a temporary job. Four responses are available: contract that includes a period of training; could not find a permanent job; did not want a permanent job; or some other reason. Finally – in the spring (March to May) quarters only – respondents are asked about the total duration of their temporary job. They can respond with a duration of between 'less than one month' to 'over five years', or state that the duration of their temporary employment has 'not yet been fixed'.

Data quality issues

Recoding from self-employed to employee status

In the LFS, some self-employed people are recoded as employees if they give occupation details which ONS judges are inconsistent with being self-employed (for example, if a respondent states they are a member of the police service). This process increases the number of employees and decreases the number of self-employed. However, from 1992 onwards, since the questions on the temporary/permanent status of jobs are asked only of employees, anybody replying that they are self-employed at the interview will *not be asked* the temporary employees section of the questionnaire. If they are recoded later as an employee, they will be classed as 'does not apply'. This category is a relatively large group of people (usually around 200,000 employees) for whom we have no information about their temporary/permanent status. The LFS excludes these people, i.e. they are assumed to be in permanent employment. Prior to 1992, the temporary work questions were also asked of self-employed people so the reclassification of employment status has no effect on the availability of this information.

Change in questions

Between spring 1991 and spring 1992 a discontinuity occurred in the responses to reasons why a job is not permanent. From 1992 onwards, respondents have a choice of one of the five responses as to why a job was temporary (see 'Questions in the LFS', above). Prior to 1992, the three categories of seasonal, casual and agency temps were grouped as one response. Hence, data on the totals of temporary workers remain consistent from spring 1991 to spring 1992, despite the change of question, but the totals of the responses given for the type of temporary job prior to spring 1992 are not comparable with estimates after this date.

Variability

When studying temporary workers, data from the spring quarters remain the most stable. Summer and winter data on temporary workers are highly seasonal due to, for example, summer jobs in the tourist industry or additional jobs in the retail industry during the Christmas period. No grossed-up estimates from the LFS of less than 10,000 are published because the relative sampling error of the estimates is greater than 20 per cent. This particularly affects combinations of temporary workers with other LFS variables that have several sub-categories, for example, occupation and industry groups.

Further information:
Labour Market Enquiry Helpline
Office for National Statistics
Room B4/10
1 Drummond Gate
London SW1V 2QQ
tel 0171 533 6176

*ual feature Special feature Special feature Special feature Special feature Special featu
ure Special feature Special feature Special feature Special feature Special feature Speci
cial feature Special featu*
Special feature *eature Special feature Special featu*
ure Special feature Speci *ature Special feature Speci
cial feature Special feature Special feature Special feature Special featu*

Registered disabled people in the public sector and plans to improve the labour market position of disabled people

This article shows the latest statistics from a cross-section of public sector employers who agreed to disclose the number of registered disabled people they employed. They relate solely to registered disabled people and are not, therefore, a complete guide to the employment of people with disabilities. The article also outlines the Government's approach to improving the labour market position of disabled people.

By **Christine Jukes**, Employment Service.

Photo: Employment Service

Key findings

- The 1,022 public sector employers surveyed in this article employed 26,850 registered disabled people (staff units) in 1996.
- Only 14 of these employers reached or exceeded the 3 per cent quota of registered disabled people laid down in the Disabled Persons (Employment) Act 1944.
- Registration was voluntary; many employers will have employed more non-registered disabled people.

- The Disabled Persons (Employment) Act 1944 quota and registration provisions were repealed in December 1996.
- The employment provisions of the Disability Discrimination Act 1995 came into force on 2 December 1996.
- The labour market position of disabled people will be monitored using a baseline survey and the Labour Force Survey.

Quota and registration

THE DISABLED Persons (Employment) Act 1944 (DP(E)A) placed a duty on employers with 20 or more workers to employ a quota of registered disabled people. The quota stood at 3 per cent of the employer's total workforce.

Although the quota duties were not binding on the Crown, government departments agreed to accept the same responsibilities as other employers. The National Health Service and Community Care Act 1990 removed crown immunity from the National Health Service (NHS), which

means it was also legally bound by the quota provisions of the DP(E)A 1944 until 2 December 1996.

A full set of figures for government departments has been supplied by the Cabinet Office's Office of Public Services and Science. They relate to the position on 1 December 1996. The figures for other public sector employers have been obtained during the annual enquiry into the position of all employers subject to quota regulations; this was carried out by the Employment Service during the summer of 1996.

This article reports the number of registered disabled people employed in public sector organisations in 1996, and expresses these as percentages of the total workforce in each case. The figures have been collected from a cross-section of public sector employers and are disclosed with their agreement.

The quota and registration provisions of the DP(E)A 1944 were repealed when the employment provisions of the Disability Discrimination Act 1995 (DDA) came into effect on 2 December 1996. These are therefore the final tables of figures to be compiled in this series. The tables have been produced annually since 1976. They relate only to people who were *registered* as disabled and are not a complete guide to all the people with disabilities who were employed by these employers when the figures were collected.

This year there have been some changes to the lists covering England, Scotland and Wales. All Scottish regional and district councils and Welsh county and district councils have been replaced by unitary authorities. Some local authorities in England changed to unitary status on 1 April 1996. Where possible these changes have been included in the tables. Although the changes appear substantial, the overall registered disabled employment figures shown in the tables are relatively unaffected.

The Disability Discrimination Act 1995

The quota and registration provisions of the DP(E)A 1944 were limited in scope and did not meet the needs of disabled people in a modern labour market.

The employment provisions of the DDA 1995, which came into force on 2 December 1996, apply to employers with 20 or more employees, including government departments and agencies. The Act provides a statutory right for disabled people not to be discriminated against or treated less favourably than other people in any aspect of employment including recruitment, transfer, promotion, training, retention and dismissal. Among other things, this means that an employer may have to make a reasonable adjustment if the premises or employment arrangements substantially disadvantage a disabled person compared with a non-disabled person.

The future for disabled people's employment legislation

The Government is committed to ensuring that disabled people get a fair deal in the labour market. Although the DDA is providing disabled people with very significant rights in the area of employment, there are fundamental flaws in the Act. The Government therefore has a manifesto commitment to support enforceable, comprehensive civil rights for disabled people. This broadly means that ministers will be considering two things: how a commission might offer disabled people help and support and how to ensure the proper scope for legislation to protect disabled people from discrimination, including in the area of employment.

There will be consultations on the implementation of the manifesto commitment but, in the mean time, the DDA will continue. Ministers will be considering whether there are any improvements that can practically be made to its protection for disabled people through its regulation-making powers. By monitoring the operation of the DDA it will be possible to gain a valuable insight into the way in which anti-discrimination legislation for disabled people operates in Great Britain and this will help with decisions on change.

Ministers are also looking at ways in which services for disabled people and their employers can be improved. Some small, but important, changes to Access to Work have already been made to help disabled people get and retain employment and the scope for further improvements will be considered.

Ministers' decisions will be informed by evidence about disabled people's situation in the labour market. The picture provided by registration statistics was very inadequate. In future, the Labour Force Survey will be a main source of statistics with a revised module based on the DDA definition. This is currently being evaluated and will, it is hoped, be available later this year. A range of research is also being commissioned, such as a survey of 2,000 disabled people which is now nearing completion. This should help provide a baseline against which changes in the labour market position of disabled people can be measured.

Information about the DDA

If you require leaflets or information on the DDA 1995, the Government has set up an information line. The DDA Information Line can be accessed in a number of ways: for live operator service call 0345 622633; text telephone 0345 622644; faxback 0345 622611; or automated line 0345 622688. If you wish to write, there is a freepost address: DDA Information, Freepost MID02164, Stratford-upon-Avon CV37 9BR. *A Brief Guide to the Act* and a DDA information catalogue are also available on the internet at: www.disability.gov.uk.

FACTORS TO BE KEPT IN MIND WHEN CONSIDERING THE STATISTICS

- They reflect only the people with disabilities who were registered as disabled under the terms of the DP(E)A 1944. It was not compulsory for disabled people to register and many of the people who were eligible did not do so.
- The winter 1996/7 Labour Force Survey showed there were approximately 2.4 million economically active people with a long-term health problem or disability in Great Britain. However, in 1996 the total number of people who were registered as disabled under the DP(E)A was only 374,000.

- Less than a quarter of the public sector organisations listed employed the statutory 3 per cent quota of registered disabled people, but many would probably have had a far higher percentage of disabled employees due to the number of disabled people who were employed but not registered.
- The column headed 'registered disabled people' in the tables includes some figures which end in '.5'. This is because registered disabled people employed for between 10 and 30 hours per week counted as half a 'staff unit' for the purpose of the quota scheme.

Photo: B. Busco/Image Bank

Number and percentage of registered disabled people employed in public sector organisations, 1996

Great Britain

English and Welsh county councils/ unitary authorities

	Registered disabled people (staff units)	Per cent
Bath and North East Somerset	–	–
Bedfordshire	121	1.5
Berkshire	90	0.5
Blaenau Gwent	18	1.6
Bristol[a]	87	0.6
Buckinghamshire	60	0.5
Cambridgeshire	18	0.1
Cardiff	48	0.4
Ceredigion	5	0.2
Cheshire	77	0.4
Cleveland	44	0.7
Conwy	3	0.1
Cornwall	184	1.7
Cumbria	47.5	0.5
Denbighshire	50	1.0
Derbyshire	154.5	0.5
Devon	315	1.6
Dorset	204.5	1.8
Durham	80	0.6
East Sussex	270.5	2.1
Essex	54	0.2
Flintshire	18	0.3
Gloucestershire	168	1.5
Hampshire	83	0.3
Hereford and Worcester	92	0.8
Hertfordshire	90	0.3
Isle of Anglesey	15	0.5
Isle of Wight	17	0.8
Isles of Scilly	1	0.7
Kent	28	0.1
Lancashire	347	1.0
Leicestershire	103.5	0.5
Lincolnshire	31.5	0.4
Merthyr Tydfil	16	1.9
Norfolk	41	0.3
Northamptonshire	176	1.4
Northumberland	35	0.6
North Yorkshire	70	0.4
Nottinghamshire	484	1.5
Oxfordshire	63.5	0.6
Pembrokeshire	15	0.3
Rhondda, Cynon, Taff	39	0.3
Shropshire	13	0.2
Somerset	103	1.2
South Gloucestershire	9	0.1
Staffordshire	150	0.7
Suffolk	86.5	0.6
Surrey	28	0.2
Swansea	91	1.0
Warwickshire	89	0.8
West Sussex	30	0.2
Wiltshire	114	0.9
Wrexham	19	1.6
All	**4,597**	**0.7**

English and Welsh borough and district councils

	Registered disabled people (staff units)	Per cent
Adur	1	0.3
Allerdale	5	1.5
Alnwick	7.5	3.7
Amber Valley	7	1.1
Arun	3	0.6
Ashfield	12	1.4
Ashford	7	1.5
Aylesbury Vale	6	1.0
Babergh	1	0.3
Barnsley	94.5	1.2
Barrow-in-Furness	13	4.4
Basildon	9	0.6
Basingstoke and Deane	1	0.2
Bassetlaw	3	0.4
Berwick-upon-Tweed	5	3.2
Birmingham	615	1.8
Blaby	1	0.4
Blackburn	19	1.3
Blackpool	39	3.5
Blyth Valley	8	1.3
Bolsover	5	1.1
Bolton	131.5	1.5
Boston	4	1.1
Bournemouth	14	0.8
Bracknell	6.5	0.9
Bradford	209	1.2
Braintree	12	1.5
Breckland	4	1.4
Brentwood	14	3.2
Bridgnorth	2	0.8
Brighton	14	1.8
Broadland	2	1.3
Bromsgrove	1	0.2
Broxtowe	8	1.2
Burnley	10	1.0
Bury	30	0.5
Calderdale	50	0.6
Cambridge	16	1.4
Cannock Chase	4	0.5
Canterbury	9.5	1.3
Caradon	11	2.7
Carlisle	5.5	0.6
Carrick	11	2.4
Castle Morpeth	5	1.6
Castle Point	4	1.0
Charnwood	4	0.6
Chelmsford	5	0.6
Cheltenham	11	1.1
Cherwell	1	0.2
Chester	16	2.0
Chester-le-Street	2	0.3
Chesterfield	20	1.5
Chichester	9	1.6
Chiltern	1	0.3
Chorley	3	0.6
Christchurch	0	0
Colchester	18	1.8
Congleton	2	0.4
Copeland	9	1.6
Corby	9.5	1.6

English and Welsh borough and district councils (cont.)

	Registered disabled people (staff units)	Per cent
Cotswold	1	0.2
Coventry	98	0.6
Craven	8	2.6
Crawley	7	0.8
Crewe and Nantwich	6	0.8
Dacorum	9	0.9
Darlington	10	0.9
Daventry	2	0.5
Derby	37	2.3
Derbyshire Dales	1.5	0.4
Derwentside	14	1.5
Doncaster	50	0.4
Dover	11	2.5
Dudley	64	0.7
Durham	9	1.0
Easington	26	2.2
East Cambridgeshire	0	0
East Devon	1	0.2
East Dorset	0	0
East Hampshire	0	0
East Hertfordshire	2	0.5
East Lindsey	12	1.4
East Northamptonshire	8	4.7
East Staffs/Lichfield	4	0.7
East Yorkshire	94	0.8
Eastbourne	8	1.3
Eastleigh	7	1.6
Eden	1.5	0.6
Ellesmere Port and Neston	19	2.6
Elmbridge	65	1.0
Epping Forest	7	1.0
Epsom and Ewell	1	0.3
Erewash	7	0.9
Exeter	12	1.4
Fareham	2	0.4
Forest Heath	5.5	2.1
Forest of Dean	1	0.3
Fylde	5	1.4
Gateshead	79	0.7
Gedling	2	0.3
Gillingham	1	0.2
Gloucester	12	1.4
Gosport	3	0.6
Gravesham	5	1.0
Great Yarmouth	16	2.5
Guildford	8	0.9
Halton	25	2.4
Hambleton	0	0
Harborough	4	1.0
Harlow	32	2.4
Harrogate	14.5	1.4
Hart	2	0.6
Hartlepool	13	0.4
Hastings	12	3.2
Havant	6	0.9
Hertsmere	1	0.2
High Peak	4	0.8
Hinckley and Bosworth	7	2.5
Horsham	4	0.8
Hove	5	1.0

Number and percentage of registered disabled people employed in public sector organisations, 1996   (cont.)

English and Welsh borough and district councils (cont.)

	Registered disabled people (staff units)	Per cent
Hull	160	1.3
Huntingdon	9	1.3
Hyndburn	5	0.9
Ipswich	21	1.6
Kennet	1	0.3
Kerrier	7	1.5
Kettering	7	1.4
King's Lynn & West Norfolk	4	0.6
Kirklees	140.5	1.2
Knowsley	40	0.6
Lancaster	15	1.5
Leeds	379	1.5
Leicester	86	2.1
Leominster	0	0
Lewes	2	0.5
Lincoln	12	0.9
Liverpool	319	1.3
Luton	20	1.4
Macclesfield	16	1.7
Maidstone	1	0.2
Maldon	1	0.6
Malvern Hills	1	0.3
Manchester	250.5	1.1
Mansfield	14	1.3
Melton	4	1.6
Mid Bedfordshire	1	0.3
Mid Devon	1	0.2
Middlesbrough	97.5	1.5
Mid Suffolk	0	0
Mid Sussex	2	0.6
Milton Keynes	17	1.4
Mole Valley	0	0
New Forest	4	0.3
Newark and Sherwood	2	0.3
Newbury	1	0.2
Newcastle-under-Lyme	4	0.6
Newcastle-upon-Tyne	123	0.9
North Bedfordshire	8	1.2
North Cornwall	5	1.0
North Devon	4	0.7
North Dorset	1	0.5
North East Derbyshire	16	1.7
North East Lincolnshire	45	0.6
North Hertfordshire	5	0.6
North Kesteven	2.5	0.6
North Lincolnshire	62	1.0
North Norfolk	4	0.9
North Shropshire	3	1.4
North Somerset	20	0.4
North Tyneside	47	0.7
North Warwickshire	1	0.2
North West Leicestershire	4	0.8
North Wiltshire	2	0.4
Northampton	18.5	1.2
Norwich	45	2.2
Nottingham	102	2.7
Nuneaton and Bedworth	9	1.0
Oadby and Wigston	1	0.5
Oldham	35	0.4

English and Welsh borough and district councils (cont.)

	Registered disabled people (staff units)	Per cent
Oswestry	0	0
Oxford	22	1.7
Pendle	9	1.2
Penwith	5	1.9
Peterborough	11	0.8
Plymouth	23	1.0
Poole	9	1.1
Portsmouth	10	0.7
Preston	26	1.9
Purbeck	0	0
Reading	22.5	2.0
Redditch	18	2.4
Reigate and Banstead	7	1.6
Restormel	11	1.9
Ribble Valley	4	1.3
Richmondshire	4	1.4
Rochdale	46	0.5
Rochester-upon-Medway	5	0.8
Rochford	1	0.4
Rossendale	12	1.9
Rother	1	0.3
Rotherham	32	0.4
Rugby	0	0
Runnymede	5	1.2
Rushcliffe	3	0.6
Rushmoor	1	0.3
Rutland	2	2.9
Ryedale	1	0.4
Salford	69	0.9
Salisbury	11	2.2
Sandwell	182	2.1
Scarborough	17	1.5
Sedgefield	8	0.9
Sedgemoor	6	0.8
Sefton	70	0.8
Selby	2	0.5
Sevenoaks	7	1.4
Sheffield	315	1.5
Shepway	3.5	0.7
Shrewsbury and Atcham	3	0.5
Slough	17	1.6
Solihull	20	0.6
South Bedfordshire	1	0.2
South Buckinghamshire	1.5	0.8
South Cambridgeshire	6	1.4
South Derbyshire	5	1.3
South Hams	3	0.6
South Herefordshire	0	0
South Holland	4	1.1
South Kesteven	10	2.0
South Lakeland	6	0.9
South Norfolk	3	0.8
South Northamptonshire	1	0.2
South Oxfordshire	3	1.0
South Ribble	4	1

English and Welsh borough and district councils (cont.)

	Registered disabled people (staff units)	Per cent
South Shropshire	1	0.7
South Somerset	4	0.4
South Staffordshire	3	0.5
South Tyneside	69	0.9
Southampton	41	1.8
Southend-on-Sea	14	1.2
Spelthorne	6	1.7
St Albans	4	0.9
St Edmundsbury	3	0.3
St Helens	26	0.5
Stafford	3	0.4
Staffordshire Moorlands	3	0.6
Stevenage	5	0.6
Stockport	50	0.7
Stockton-on-Tees	16	0.9
Stoke-on-Trent	49	1.9
Stratford-on-Avon	4	0.8
Stroud	1	0.2
Suffolk Coastal	0	0
Sunderland	72	0.5
Surrey Heath	2	0.8
Swale	4	0.9
Tameside	91	1.3
Tamworth	1	0.2
Tandridge	4	1.4
Taunton Deane	9	1.2
Teesdale	3	2.1
Teignbridge	4	0.6
Tendring	12	2.0
Test Valley	5	0.8
Tewkesbury	3	0.8
Thamesdown	18.5	1.0
Thanet	1	0.2
Three Rivers	4	1.2
Thurrock	11	1.0
Tonbridge and Malling	2	0.5
Torbay	15	1.9
Torridge	8	2.3
Trafford	36.5	0.8
Tunbridge Wells	4	1.0
Tynedale	6	1.4
Uttlesford	4	1.2
Vale of White Horse	3	0.9
Vale Royal	9	1.0
Wakefield	74	0.6
Walsall	157	1.5
Wansbeck	3	0.6
Warrington	25	1.6
Warwick	0	0
Watford	11	1.2
Waveney	11	1.5
Waverley	2	0.5
Wealden	5	0.9
Wear Valley	5	0.8
Wellingborough	5	1.2
Welwyn Hatfield	4	0.5
West Devon	3	2.3
West Dorset	2	0.5
West Lancashire	14	1.6
West Lindsey	1	0.3

Number and percentage of registered disabled people employed in public sector organisations, 1996 (cont.)

Great Britain

English and Welsh borough and district councils (cont.)

	Registered disabled people (staff units)	Per cent
West Oxfordshire	0	0
West Somerset	0	0
West Wiltshire	5	0.8
Weymouth and Portland	5	1.1
Wigan	108	1.9
Winchester	6	1.3
Windsor and Maidenhead	3	0.6
Wirral	155	1.4
Woking	5	1.2
Wokingham	2	0.5
Wolverhampton	187	1.3
Worcester	3	0.4
Worthing	7	1.2
Wrekin, The	19	1.2
Wychavon	2	0.7
Wycombe	7	1.0
Wyre	8	1.6
Wyre Forest	20	2.2
York	60	1.1
All	**7,257**	**1.1**

London borough councils

	Registered disabled people (staff units)	Per cent
Barking and Dagenham	49	0.7
Barnet	43	0.5
Bexley	9	0.4
Brent	79	1.5
Bromley	21	0.5
Camden	88	1.4
City of London	20	0.5
Croydon	105	1.3
Ealing	57	0.6
Enfield	38	0.5
Greenwich	66	0.6
Hackney	46	0.5
Hammersmith and Fulham	112	1.7
Haringey	74	1.0
Harrow	113	1.9
Havering	30	0.4
Hillingdon	38	0.5
Hounslow	42.5	0.6
Islington	74	0.8
Kensington and Chelsea	19	0.5
Kingston-upon-Thames	17	0.5
Lambeth	178	2.7
Lewisham	124.5	1.4
Merton	49	1.0
Newham	96	0.9
Redbridge	39	0.5
Richmond-upon-Thames	18	0.3
Southwark	86	1.1
Sutton	9	0.2
Tower Hamlets	46	0.4

London borough councils (cont.)

	Registered disabled people (staff units)	Per cent
Waltham Forest	135	1.9
Wandsworth	32	0.6
Westminster	29	0.5
All	**1,985**	**0.9**

Scottish city authorities

	Registered disabled people (staff units)	Per cent
Aberdeen City	–	–
Dundee City	33	0.4
City of Edinburgh	182.5	1.1
Glasgow City	464	0.6
All	**679.5**	**0.7**

Scottish island councils

	Registered disabled people (staff units)	Per cent
Orkney Islands	11	0.8
Shetland Islands	14	0.6
Western Isles	16.5	0.9
All	**41.5**	**0.8**

Scottish unitary authorities

	Registered disabled people (staff units)	Per cent
Aberdeenshire	66	0.6
Angus	11	0.3
Argyll and Bute	–	–
Borders	9	0.2
Clackmannan	2	0.1
Dumbarton/Clydebank	58	2.7
Dumfries and Galloway	59	0.9
East Ayrshire	40	0.7
East Dunbartonshire	3	1.0
East Lothian	23.5	0.6
East Renfrewshire	3	1.1
Falkirk	11	0.7
Fife	33.5	1.6
Highland	81.5	0.9
Inverclyde	30	0.6

Scottish unitary authorities (cont.)

	Registered disabled people (staff units)	Per cent
Midlothian	10	0.3
Moray	9	1.0
North Ayrshire	200	3.1
North Lanarkshire	83	0.5
Perth and Kinross	20	0.5
Renfrewshire	26	1.2
South Ayrshire	22.5	0.5
South Lanarkshire	100.5	8.1
Stirling	13	1.0
West Lothian	12.5	1.0
All	**1,228.5**	**1.0**

Regional health authorities

	Registered disabled people (staff units)	Per cent
East Sussex Health Authority	1	0.5
Northern and Yorkshire[b]	2	0.2
Northern and Yorkshire	1	0.8
Oxford	0	0
West Midlands	3	1.2
All	**7**	**0.3**

District health authorities

	Registered disabled people (staff units)	Per cent
Barking, Havering and Brentwood	2.5	0.1
Barnsley	0	0
Basingstoke and North Hampshire	3	0.2
Bedford	0	0
Calderdale and Kirklees	2	1.4
Cornwall and Isles of Scilly	0	0
Coventry	3	1.4
Dartford and Gravesham	4	0.2
Doncaster	3.5	3.1
Dorset Health Commission	1	0.6
Dudley	1	1.0
Dyfed and Powys Health Authority	0	0
Ealing, Hammersmith and Hounslow	2	0.6
East Kent Health Authority	0	0
East Lancashire Consortium	0.5	0.6
East Riding	1	0.6
East Sussex	1	0.5
Grimsby and Scunthorpe	0	0
Harrow	1	0.05

Number and percentage of registered disabled people employed in public sector organisations, 1996   (cont.)

Great Britain

District health authorities (cont.)

	Registered disabled people (staff units)	Per cent
Leeds	1	0.5
Leicestershire District Health Authority	0	0
Lincolnshire Health Authority	0	0
Manchester Health Commission	1	0.6
Medway	16.5	0.7
Mid Essex	11	0.3
New River Health Authority	3	1.3
NHS Executive Anglia & Oxford	0	0
Norfolk Health	1	0.5
Northampton Health Authority	0	0
North Bedfordshire	0	0
North Derbyshire Health Authority	1	0.9
North Hertfordshire	7	0.4
North Worcestershire	1	0.1
North Yorkshire	0	0
Nottingham Health	0	0
Plymouth Health Authority	5.5	0.2
Prince Charles Hospital	9	0.3
Redbridge & Waltham Forest	0	0
Rotherham	1	0.7
Royal Bethlem and Maudsley	10	0.5
Sandwell	0	0
Sandwell Family Health Services Authority	1	1.6
Sheffield	1	0.2
Shropshire	0	0
Solihull	6	0.2
Southampton and South West Hants	2	1.4
South Bedfordshire	0	0
South Derbyshire Health Authority	2	0.5
Southend	3	0.1
Suffolk Health Authority	0	0
Wakefield	1	0.7
Walsall	0	0
Warwickshire Health Authority	1	1
West Surrey Health Commission	3	1.2
Wilts and Bath	1	0.5
Wirral	0	0
Worcester (Headquarters)	1	0.5
All	**121.5**	**0.3**

Scottish health boards

	Registered disabled people (staff units)	Per cent
Argyll and Clyde	6	0.1
Ayrshire and Arran	1	0.6
Borders	12	1.2
Dumfries and Galloway	1	1.2
Fife	0	0

Scottish health boards (cont.)

	Registered disabled people (staff units)	Per cent
Forth Valley	1	1.0
Grampian	1	0.3
Greater Glasgow	6	0.02
Highland	1	0.4
Lanarkshire	3.5	0.1
Lothian	3	0.6
Orkney	0	0
Shetland	2	0.6
Tayside	1.5	0.4
Western Isles	5	0.9
All	**44**	**0.1**

English and Welsh NHS Trusts

	Registered disabled people (staff units)	Per cent
Aberdare Hospital	3	1.1
Addenbrooks NHS Trust	25	0.6
Aintree Hospitals	8	0.3
Airedale	6.5	0.3
Alexandra Healthcare	2.5	0.2
Allington Trust	3	0.3
Andover Community NHS Trust	1	0.2
Anglian Harbours	4	0.3
Ashford Hospital	1	0.1
Avalon Somerset NHS Trust	3	0.3
Avon Ambulance Service	1	0.3
Aylesbury Community Healthcare	1	0.1
Barking, Havering and Brentwood Community Unit	3	0.2
Barnet Community Healthcare Trust	8	0.3
Barnet Family Health Service Authority	0	0
Barnsley Community Priority Services	1	0.1
Barnsley District General Hospital	4	0.2
Basildon and Thurrock General Hospitals	5	0.3
Basingstoke Priority Services Unit	0	0
Bassetlaw Hospital and Community Health Service	6	0.4
Bath and West Community	5	0.4
Bath Mental Health Care	1	0.1
Bath Royal National Hospital for Rheumatic Diseases	0	0
Bedfordshire and Herts Ambulance Service	0	0
Bedford Hospitals	2	0.1
Beds and Shires Healthcare NHS Trust	0	0
Birmingham Heartlands Hospital	5.5	0.2
Birmingham Women's Healthcare	0	0
Bishop Auckland Hospital	3	0.2
Blackburn Hyndburn and Ribble Valley	8	0.3

English and Welsh NHS trusts (cont.)

	Registered disabled people (staff units)	Per cent
Blackburn Communicare NHS Trust	3	0.3
Blackpool Victoria Hospital Trust	4	0.2
Blackpool, Wyre and Fylde Community Health Service	7	0.4
Bolton Community Healthcare Trust	1	0.1
Bolton Hospitals Trust	10	0.3
Bournewood Community and Mental Health	9	0.5
Bradford Community Health	4.5	0.3
Bradford Hospitals	9	0.2
Bridgend and District	4	0.1
Brighton Healthcare	26	1.3
Bromley Hospitals NHS Trust	3	0.2
Burnley Healthcare	33	0.8
Burton Hospitals	1	0.1
Bury and Rochdale District Health Authority NHS Trust	1	0.9
Calderdale Healthcare	16	0.7
Calderstones NHS Trust	12	0.9
Cambs and Huntingdon Health Commission	1	0.1
Camden and Islington Health Services Trust	45	1.4
Canterbury and Thanet Community Healthcare	5.5	0.4
Cardiff Community NHS Trust	6	0.3
Cardiothoracic Centre (Liverpool)	0	0
Carlisle Hospitals	4	0.3
Carmarthen and District	2	0.1
Central Nottinghamshire Healthcare Trust	7	0.3
Central Manchester Health Care Trust	7	0.2
Central Middlesex Hospital	2	0.2
Central Sheffield University Hospital	15	0.4
Ceredigion and Mid Wales	7	0.8
Chase Farm Hospital	5	0.4
Chester and Halton	1	0.1
Chester Acute Hospitals	4	0.2
Chesterfield and North Derbyshire Royal Hospital	7	0.3
Cheviot and Wansbeck NHS	3	0.1
Chichester Priority Care Service	4.5	0.3
Chorley and South Ribble	5	0.3
Christie Hospital	6	0.5
Churchill John Radcliffe (Oxford)	18	0.5
City and Hackney Community Service Trust	3	1.6
City Hospitals Sunderland	8	0.2
Clatterbridge Centre for Oncology	0	0
Cleveland Ambulance	1	0.4
Community Health Care North Durham	5	0.4
Community Health Services NHS Trust	4.5	0.3
Cornwall and Isles of Scilly Healthcare Trust	7	0.3

Number and percentage of registered disabled people employed in public sector organisations, 1996 (cont.)

English and Welsh NHS trusts (cont.)

	Registered disabled people (staff units)	Per cent
Cornwall & Isles of Scilly Learning Disabilities NHS Trust	2	0.4
Coventry Healthcare	2	0.2
Crawley & Horsham NHS Trust	5	0.4
Croydon Health Authority	2	1.6
Cumbria Ambulance Service	0	0
Dacorum and St Albans Community	3.5	0.2
Darlington Memorial Hospital	6	0.5
Derby City Hospital	1	0.1
Derbyshire Ambulance Service	0	0
Derbyshire Royal Infirmary	2.5	0.1
Derwen NHS Trust, St Davids Hospital	6	0.7
Dewsbury Health Care	0.5	0.03
Doncaster Healthcare	5	0.3
Doncaster Royal Infirmary and Montagu Hospital	7	0.2
Dorset Ambulance Service	2	0.6
Dorset Community NHS Trust	4	0.4
Dorset Health Care	3	0.1
Dorset Trust	0	0
Dudley Group of Hospitals	2	0.1
Dudley Priority Health	3	0.2
Durham Ambulance Service	0	0
Durham Health Commission	2	1.6
Ealing Hospital	6	0.5
East Anglian Ambulance NHS Trust	0	0
East Berkshire Community Health Unit	1.5	0.1
East Berkshire Trust for People with Learning Difficulties	3.5	0.9
Eastbourne Hospitals	17.5	0.6
East Cheshire	3	0.2
East Glamorgan NHS Trust	3	0.2
East Gloucestershire	5	0.1
East Somerset	6	0.3
East Surrey Learning Disability and Mental Health Service NHS Trust	5	0.7
East Wiltshire Health Care	0	0
East Yorkshire Hospital	0	0
East Yorkshire Hospitals NHS Trust (Castle Hill Hospital)	4	0.4
Enfield Community Care NHS Trust	3	0.2
Epsom Health Care	1	0.1
Essex Ambulance Service	3	0.4
Essex and Herts Community NHS Trust	1	0.1
Essex Rivers Health Care	5	0.2
Exeter Community Services	9	0.3
Fareham College	1	0.3
First Community Health (Stafford)	3	0.8
Forest Healthcare	16	0.5
Fosse Health Trust	15	0.4
Frenchay Health Care	22	0.7
Frimley Park Hospital	5	0.3
Furness Hospitals	1.5	0.1
Gateshead Health Care	0	0
Gateshead Hospitals	5	0.2

English and Welsh NHS trusts (cont.)

	Registered disabled people (staff units)	Per cent
George Elliot Hospital	5	0.3
Glan Clwyd District General Hospital	7	0.3
Glan Hafren NHS Trust	10	0.3
Glanymor NHS Trust	12	0.5
Glenfield Unit NHS Trust	3	0.2
Gloucester Royal NHS Trust	10	0.5
Gloucester Ambulance	1	0.3
Gofal Cymuned Clwydian Community Care	15	0.5
Good Hope Hospital NHS Trust, Sutton Coldfield	3	0.2
Grantham and District Hospital Trust	3	0.5
Great Ormond Street Hospital for Children	2	0.1
Greenwich Healthcare	22	0.8
Grimsby Health	1	0.04
Guild Community Health Care	8	0.5
Guys and St Thomas Hospital	42	0.6
Gwent Community Health	1.5	0.1
Gwynedd Community Health NHS Trust Llanfaifechan	0	0
Gwynedd Hospital NHS Trust Bangor	6	0.3
Halton General Hospital	1	0.1
Hampshire Ambulance NHS Trust	0	0
Harefield Hospital (London)	0	0
Haringey Health Care	74	1.0
Harrogate Health Care	3.5	0.2
Harrow and Hillingdon Health Care	2	0.2
Hartlepool and Peterlee Hospitals	1	0.04
Hastings and Rother	5	0.2
Heatherwood and Wexham Park Hospitals	70	2.9
Heathland Mental Health	4	0.5
Hereford and Worcester Ambulance	0	0
Hereford Hospitals	3	0.2
Herefordshire Community Health	5	0.5
Highbury College	5	1.0
Hillingdon Hospital	3	0.2
Hinchingbrooke Health Care NHS Trust	1	0.1
Horizon, Hertfordshire	3	0.3
Horton General Hospital	1	0.1
Hounslow and Spellthorne Community	1	0.1
Huddersfield NHS Trust	6.5	0.3
Hull and Holderness Community Health	1	0.04
Humberside Ambulance Service	1	0.2
Iechyd Morgannwg Health Trust	1.5	1.2
Ipswich Hospital	7	0.2
Isle of Wight Acute	60	4.8
Isle of Wight Community Health Care	1	0.04
James Paget Hospital, Great Yarmouth	2	0.1

English and Welsh NHS trusts (cont.)

	Registered disabled people (staff units)	Per cent
Kent and Canterbury Hospitals	4	0.2
Kettering General Hospital	14	0.9
Kidderminster General Health Services Unit	0	0
King Edward VII Hospital	4.5	1.1
Kings Healthcare	7	0.2
King's Lynn and Wisbech Hospitals	4	0.2
Kings Mill Centre for Health Care Services	10	0.4
Kingston and Esher Community Health	2	0.3
Kingston Hospital	3.5	0.3
Lancashire Ambulance Service Trust	4	0.7
Lancashire College of Nursing and Health Studies	1	0.6
Lancaster Acute Hospitals	6	0.4
Lancaster Priority Services	9	0.9
Landough Hospital	11	0.5
Leeds Community and Mental Health Services	7.5	0.2
Leicestershire Ambulance NHS Trust	3	0.7
Leicester General Hospital	2	0.1
Leicester Mental Health	7	0.3
Leicester Royal Infirmary	13	0.3
Lewisham Hospital	11	0.5
Lifecare (Caterham)	0	0
Lifespan Healthcare	16	1.6
Lincoln and Louth NHS Trust	5	0.2
Lincoln District Health Care	4.5	0.5
Lincolnshire Ambulance	1	0.2
Liverpool Women's Hospital	4	0.8
Llanelli Dinefwr	8	0.7
Luton and Dunstable Hospital	1	0.03
Mancunian Community and Mental Health Unit	3	0.3
Mayday NHS Trust	2	0.1
Mental Health and Learning Disabilities (South Surrey and Area)	5	0.7
Mental Health Foundation of Mid Staffs	0	0
Mersey Regional Ambulance Service	8	0.8
Merton and Sutton Community Health Services	4	0.3
Mid Anglia Community Health	1	0.1
Mid Cheshire Hospitals	3	0.1
Mid Essex Community Health Service	3	0.3
Mid Essex Hospital Services	11	0.3
Mid Glamorgan Ambulance Trust	1	0.3
Mid Staffordshire Acute Services Unit	4	0.3
Mid Staffordshire General Hospitals	4	0.2
Milton Keynes General Hospital	4	0.3
Milton Keynes Community Health	0	0
Moorfield Eye Hospital	3	0.3
Morecambe Bay NHS Trust	0	0

Number and percentage of registered disabled people employed in public sector organisations, 1996   (cont.)

Great Britain

English and Welsh NHS trusts (cont.)

	Registered disabled people (staff units)	Per cent
Morriston Hospital	4.5	0.2
Mount Vernon Hospital	2	0.1
Mulberry, Lincolnshire	1	0.3
Nevill Hall District Trust	4	0.3
New Possibilities	2	0.2
Newcastle City Health NHS Trust	10	0.4
Newham Healthcare	3	0.2
Norfolk and Norwich Health Care	6	0.2
Northallerton Health Services	3.5	0.3
North Birmingham Community Health	1	0.1
North Birmingham Mental Health	0	0
North Cumbria Health Authority	1	1.3
North Downs Community Health	2	0.2
North Durham Acute Hospital	4	0.2
North East Essex Mental Health	0	0
North East Worcester Healthcare Trust	2	0.3
Northern Devon Healthcare	7	0.4
Northern General Hospital	11.5	0.3
Northgate and Prudhoe	5	0.3
North Hertfordshire	9	0.4
North Kent Health Care Trust	1	0.1
North Lakeland Healthcare	7	0.7
North Middlesex Hospital	6	0.4
North Manchester Health Care NHS Trust	9	0.4
North Mersey Community	34	1.1
North Staffordshire Combined Healthcare	7.5	0.3
North Staffordshire Hospital	13	0.3
North Tees NHS Trust	2.5	0.1
North Tyneside Health Care	0.5	0.5
Northumberland Mental Health Trust	1	0.2
Northumberland Community Health NHS Trust	1	0.2
Northumbria Ambulance Service	3	0.4
North Wales Ambulance Trust Mold	6	1.1
North Warwickshire NHS Trust	4	0.2
North West Anglia Health Commission	0.5	0.02
North Yorkshire Ambulance Service	0	0
Norwich Community Health Partnership	7	0.2
Nottingham City Hospital NHS Trust	8	0.2
Nottingham Community Health Trust	2	0.1
Nottingham Healthcare NHS Trust	2	0.1
Nottinghamshire Ambulance Service	2	0.4
Nuffield Orthopaedic (Oxford)	3	0.5
Optimum Health Services	7	0.6
Oxford Ambulance	3	1.2

English and Welsh NHS trusts (cont.)

	Registered disabled people (staff units)	Per cent
Oxford Community Health	3	0.3
Oxfordshire Family Health Service	1	1.0
Oxfordshire Mental Healthcare	0	0
Oxleas NHS Trust	2	0.2
Papworth Hospital	0	0
Parkside Mental Health Services	2	0.2
Parkside Health	12	0.7
Pathfinder NHS Trust	10	1.1
Pembrokeshire	3	0.2
Peterborough Hospitals Unit	13	0.7
Phoenix NHS Trust	11	0.5
Pilgrim Health Trust	5	0.3
Pinderfields Hospital Trust Wakefield	3	0.1
Plymouth Community Services	7	0.5
Pontefract Hospitals	3	0.3
Poole General Hospital	7	0.3
Portsmouth Health Care NHS Trust	2.5	0.1
Portsmouth Hospital Trust	2	0
Powys Health Care	8	0.8
Premier Health	6	0.3
Preston Acute Hospital	5	0.2
Princes Alexandra Hospital	6	0.3
Princess Royal Hospital, Telford	2	0.2
Queen Elizabeth II Hospital, East Herts	6	0.4
Queen Mary's, Sidcup – Bexley Health	2	0.1
Queen Mother Hospital	0	0
Queens Medical Centre	11	0.2
Queen Victoria Hospital	3	0.6
Ravensbourne Priority Health	4	0.2
Redbridge and Waltham Forest Family Practitioners	0	0
Redbridge Health Care Trust	4	0.2
Redcliffe Infirmary	6	0.6
Rhondda NHS Trust	2	0.1
Richmond Twickenham Health Care Trust	12	0.6
Robert Jones and Agnes Hunt	0	0
Rochdale Health Care	12	0.5
Rockingham Forest NHS Trust	3	0.2
Rotherham General Hospitals	7	0.2
Rotherham Priority Health Services	7	0.5
Royal Berks & Battle Hospital	30	0.9
Royal Berkshire Ambulance	2	0.6
Royal Bournemouth and Christchurch	7.5	0.3
Royal Cornwall Hospital & West Cornwall Hospital	9	0.3
Royal Devon and Exeter NHS Trust Exeter Specialist Services	18	0.7
Royal Free Hampstead	6	0.2

English and Welsh NHS trusts (cont.)

	Registered disabled people (staff units)	Per cent
Royal Hospitals NHS Trust	9	0.2
Royal Hull Hospital	2	0.04
Royal Liverpool Children's Hospital	8	0.4
Royal Liverpool University Hospital	4	0.1
Royal London Hospital and Association Community Service	8	0.1
Royal National Orthopaedic Hospital	11	1.6
Royal Oldham Hospital	14	0.4
Royal Shrewsbury Hospital	15	0.6
Royal Surrey and St Lukes Hospital	0	0
Royal United Hospital Bath Health	8	0.3
Royal Victoria Infirmary and Association Hospitals	5	0.1
Royal West Sussex Trust, now St Richards Hospital Trust	7	0.5
Royal Wolverhampton NHS Trust	6	0.2
Rugby	2	0.3
Salford Community Health Care NHS Trust	2	0.3
Salford Mental Health Services NHS Trust	17	1.3
Salford Royal Hospital	5	0.2
Salisbury Health Care	1	0
Scarborough & North East Yorkshire Health Care	5	0.2
Scunthorpe and Goole Hospitals	1	0.1
Scunthorpe Community Health Unit	0	0
Severn NHS Trust	14	0.5
Sheffield Childrens Hospital	7.5	0.7
Sheffield Community Health Trust	13.5	0.5
Shropshire Community Health	4	0.3
Shropshire Mental Health Service	4	0.6
Somerset NHS Trust	1	0.8
South & East Wales Ambulance	3	0.5
Southampton University Hospital Trust	14.5	0.3
South Bedfordshire Community Health Care	3	0.2
South Birmingham Community Health	12	0.6
South Birmingham Mental Health	15	0.8
South Bucks	1	0.04
South Cumbria Community and Mental Health Unit	0	0
South Devon Healthcare	8	0.2
South Downs Health NHS Trust	0	0
South Durham Health Care	1	0.1
Southend Community Care	3	0.3
Southend Health Club	2	0.2
Southern Derbyshire Mental Health Unit	1	0.1

Number and percentage of registered disabled people employed in public sector organisations, 1996 (cont.)

English and Welsh NHS trusts (cont.)

	Registered disabled people (staff units)	Per cent
South Kent Community Health Care Trust	2	0.2
South Kent NHS Trust Hospitals	5.5	0.2
South Lincolnshire Community and Mental Health	1.5	0.2
South Manchester University Hospitals	25	0.4
Southmead Health Services	18	0.5
Southport and Formby	7	0.5
Southport Priority and Family Services Unit	3	0.5
South Tees Acute Hospital	4.5	0.1
South Tees Community and Mental Health	1	0.1
South Tyneside Health Care	4	0.2
South Warwickshire General NHS Trust	3	0.1
South Warwickshire Health Care	3.5	0.3
South Warwickshire Mental Health	1	0.2
South Yorkshire Metropolitan Ambulance and Paramedic Service	1	0.2
St George's Health Care Trust	7	0.2
St Helens and Knowsley Community Trust	3	0.1
St Helens and Knowsley NHS Trust	2	0.3
St Helier's Health Care Trust	5	0.2
St James' University Hospital	10.5	0.2
St Mary's	2	0.1
St Peter's Hospital NHS Trust	1	0.1
Staffordshire Ambulance Service	3	0.8
Stockport Acute Services	6	0.4
Stockport Healthcare	4	0.2
Stoke Mandeville Hospital	11	0.7
Surrey Heartlands Health Care Trust	4	0.2
Swansea NHS Trust	4.5	0.2
Swindon & Molborough NHT	0	0
Tameside and Glossop Acute Services	7	0.5
Tameside and Glossop Community and Priority	3	0.2
Taunton and Somerset Hospital	23	0.9
Teddington Memorial Hospital	0	0
Thameslink Healthcare Services	0.5	0.1
The Bury Healthcare NHS Trust	12	0.6
The Freeman Group	11	0.3
The Royal London Homeopathic Hospital	0	0
The Tavistock and Portman NHS Trust	3	1.3
Tower Hamlets Healthcare NHS Trust	4	0.2
Trafford Healthcare NHS Trust	13	0.6
UCL Hospitals	8	0.2

English and Welsh NHS trusts (cont.)

	Registered disabled people (staff units)	Per cent
United Bristol Healthcare	13	0.3
Unit of Learning Disability, Oxford	3	0.5
Unit of Leeds Teaching Hospitals	18	0.4
Velindre Hospital NHS Trust	0	0
Wakefield and Pontefract Community Health	4	0.3
Walsall Community Health Trust	0.5	0
Walsall Hospital	5	0.2
Walsgrave Hospital	9	0.2
Walton Centre for Neurology and Neurosurgery	0	0
Wandsworth Community Health NHS Trust	0	0
Warks Ambulance Service	0	0
Warrington Acute Unit	1	0.1
Warrington Priority Care Unit	7	0.5
Weald of Kent NHS Trust	1	0.1
Wearside Priority Health Care	1	0.1
Wellhouse	6	0.3
West Berkshire Priority Care	8	0.4
West Cheshire NHS Trust (Priority Care Unit)	3	0.4
West Country Ambulance Service	1	0.1
West Cumbria Health Authority	5	0.2
West Dorset General Hospitals	1	0.1
West Herts Community Health Trust	4	0.2
West Lambeth Community Health Care	4	0.3
West Lancashire	6	0.3
West Lindsay NHS Trust	0	0
West London Health Care NHS Trust	3	0.2
West Middlesex University Hospital	7	0.6
West Midlands Ambulance Service	2	0.2
Westmoreland Hospitals	2	0.4
Weston Area Health	2	0.2
Weston Park Hospital	1	0.2
West Suffolk Hospital NHS Trust	5	0.2
West Wales Ambulance NHS Trust	0	0
West Yorkshire Metropolitan Ambulance Service	3	0.3
Weybourne Community NHS Trust	2	0.4
Whittington & Royal Northern Hospital	6	0.3
Wigan and Leigh Health Service Trust	10	0.2
Wiltshire Ambulance	0	0
Wiltshire Health Service	2	0.2
Winchester and Eastleigh Healthcare Trust	7	0.3

English and Welsh NHS trusts (cont.)

	Registered disabled people (staff units)	Per cent
Wirral Hospitals	8	0.2
Wolverhampton Primary Healthcare	3	0.2
Worcester Royal Infirmary	2	0.1
Worcester Community Unit	1	0.1
Worthing and Southlands Hospital	13	0.6
Worthing Priority Care Unit	4	0.4
Wrexham Maelor Hospital	3	0.2
Wrightington Hospital	4	0.8
Yardley Green Unit	0	0
York Health Services	8.5	0.2
All	**2,404**	**0.3**

Scottish NHS trusts

	Registered disabled people (staff units)	Per cent
Angus NHS Trust	8	0.4
Borders Community Health Services NHS Trust	0	0
Caithness and Sutherland	2	0.4
Central Scotland Healthcare	0	0
Dumfries Galloway Acute and Maternity Hospital NHS Trust	8	0.6
Dumfries and Galloway Community Care	5	0.3
Dundee Healthcare NHS Trust	0	0
Dundee Teaching Hospital	4.5	0.1
Dykebar Hospital Trust Paisley	5	0.2
East and Midlothian NHS Trust	4	0.2
Edinburgh Healthcare Trust	7	0.2
Edinburgh Sick Children's NHS Trust	1	0.1
Falkirk and District Royal Infirmary NHS Trust	2	0.1
Fife Healthcare NHS Trust	8	0.3
Glasgow Royal Infirmary NHS Trust	0	0
Grampian Healthcare NHS Trust	10	0.2
Gt Glasgow Community and Mental Health Service NHS Trust	–	–
Hairmyres and Stonehouse Hospitals NHS Trust	2.5	0.2
Highland Communities NHS Trust	6	0.3
Inverclyde Royal NHS Trust	3	0.2
Kirkcaldy Acute Hospital NHS Trust	3	0.2
Law Hospital NHS Trust	2	0.1
Monklands and Bellshills Hospitals	24.5	0.7
Moray Health Services NHS Trust	0	0
North Ayrshire and Arran	12	0.4

Number and percentage of registered disabled people employed in public sector organisations, 1996 (cont.)

Scottish NHS trusts (cont.)

	Registered disabled people (staff units)	Per cent
Perth and Kinross Healthcare NHS Trust	1.5	0.1
Queen Margaret Hospital NHS Trust	0	0
Raigmore Hospital	4.5	0.3
Renfrewshire Healthcare NHS Trust	–	–
Royal Aberdeen Hospital Trust	4.5	0.1
Royal Alexandra Hospital	3	0.2
Royal Infirmary of Edinburgh NHS Trust	11	0.3
South Ayrshire Hospitals NHS Trust	6.5	0.5
Southern General Hospital	4.5	0.2
Stirling Royal Infirmary	3	0.2
Stobhill NHS Trust	1	0.1
Victoria Infirmary NHS Trust	2	0.1
Western General Hospitals NHS Trust	10	0.4
West Glasgow Hospitals University NHS Trust	1	0
West Lothian	5	0.1
Yorkhill NHS Trust	2.5	0.1
All	**177.5**	**0.2**

Other bodies within the NHS

	Registered disabled people (staff units)	Per cent
Dental Practice Board	20	3.6
London Ambulance Service	7	0.2
Prescription Pricing Authority	13.5	0.8
Scottish Health Common Services Agency	12	0.5
Welsh Health Common Services Organisation	4	0.3
All	**56.5**	**0.6**

Nationalised industries and public authorities

	Registered disabled people (staff units)	Per cent
British Broadcasting Corporation	150	0.7
Civil Aviation Authority	25	0.4
All	**175**	**0.6**

Government departments

	Registered disabled people (staff units)	Per cent
Agriculture, Fisheries & Food	145	1.4
Crown Office, Scotland	9	0.8
Crown Prosecution Service	43	0.7
Customs and Excise	346	1.5
Defence	1,172	1.0
Education and Employment	1,513	3.5
Environment	51	1.1
Forestry Commission	53	1.3
Foreign and Commonwealth Office	17	0.3
Health	57	1.2
Health and Safety Executive	101	2.4
Home Office	105	0.9
Inland Revenue	1,205	2.0
Intervention Board	38	4.2
Land Registry	236	2.7
Lord Chancellor's Dept.	200	1.7
National Savings	142	2.8
Office for National Statistics	59	1.8
Ordnance Survey	14	0.7
Overseas Development Administration	22	1.6
Prison Service	58	0.2
Registers of Scotland	27	2.4
Scottish Office	59	1.1
Scottish Prison Service	7	0.2
Social Security	1,959	2
Trade and Industry	110	1.1
Transport	117	1.0
Welsh Office	19	0.9
Other government departments	157	0.8
All	**8,076**	**1.6**

Source: Cabinet Office

Note: A staff unit is a registered disabled person who is employed for more than 30 hours a week, and half a staff unit is a person employed for between 10 and 30 hours per week.
- No figures available.
a Estimated figure.
b Now amalgamated health authority.

LABOUR MARKET *data*

PREPARED BY
THE GOVERNMENT
STATISTICAL SERVICE

SUMMARY TABLES
	Notes	S3
0.1	Labour Force Survey: UK	S4
0.2	Workforce: UK	S4
0.3	Labour Force Survey: GB	S5
0.4	Workforce: GB	S5
0.5	Background economic indicators	S6

EMPLOYMENT
1.1	Workforce	S7
1.2	Employees in employment: industry time series	S8
1.3	Employees in employment: administrative technical and clerical in manufacturing	S10
1.8	Output, employment and productivity	S12

UNEMPLOYMENT
2.1	UK summary	S14
2.2	GB summary	S14
2.3	Regions	S16
2.4	Assisted and local areas	S21
2.5	Age and duration: UK	S22
2.6	Regions: summary	S24
2.7	Age: time series UK	S26
2.8	Duration: time series UK	S26
2.9	Counties and local authority areas	S27
2.10	Parliamentary constituencies	S30
2.15	Age: estimated rates	S35
2.18	International comparisons	S36
2.19	UK flows	S38
2.20	GB flows by age	S39
2.23	Claim history: interval between claims	S40
2.24	By sought and usual occupation	S40
2.32	Redundancies in Great Britain	S41
2.33	Redundancies by region	S41
2.34	Redundancies by age	S41
2.35	Redundancies by industry	S41
2.36	Redundancies by occupation	S41

VACANCIES
3.1	UK summary: seasonally adjusted: flows	S42
3.2	Summary: seasonally adjusted: regions	S42
3.3	Summary: regions	S43

LABOUR DISPUTES
4.1	Totals; industries; causes	S44
4.2	Stoppages of work: summary	S45

EARNINGS
5.1	Average Earnings Index: industrial sectors	S47
5.3	Average Earnings Index: industries	S48
5.8	Unit wage costs	S51
5.9	International comparisons	S52

RETAIL PRICES
6.1	Recent index movements	S54
6.2	Detailed indices	S54
6.3	Average for selected items	S55
6.4	General index: time series	S56
6.5	Changes on a year earlier: time series	S57
6.8	International comparisons	S58
6.9	International comparisons: all items exc housing costs	S60

LABOUR FORCE SURVEY
7.1	Economic activity: seasonally adjusted	S62
7.2	Economic activity: not seasonally adjusted	S63
7.3	Economic activity by age: not seasonally adjusted	S64
7.4	Full-time and part-time workers	S65
7.5	Alternative measures of unemployment (seasonally adjusted)	S66
7.6	Alternative measures of unemployment (not seasonally adjusted)	S67
7.7	Job-related training received by employees	S68
7.8	Average actual weekly hours by industry sector	S69

GOVERNMENT-SUPPORTED TRAINING
8.1	Number of people participating in the programmes	S70
8.2	Number of starts on the programmes	S70
8.3	Destinations and qualifications of TFW/ET leavers	S71
8.4	Destinations and qualifications of YT leavers	S71
8.5	Destinations and qualifications of TFW/ET leavers who completed their agreed training	S73
8.6	Destinations and qualifications of YT leavers who completed their agreed training	S73

OTHER FACTS AND FIGURES
A1	Disabled jobseekers: GB	S74

DEFINITIONS	S74
REGULARLY PUBLISHED STATISTICS	S75
STATISTICAL ENQUIRY POINTS	S76

Publication dates of main economic indicators September – November

Labour market statistics

Unemployment, employment, vacancies, earnings, hours, unit wage costs, productivity and industrial disputes.

September . . . . 17 Wednesday
October . . . . 15 Wednesday
November . . . . 12 Wednesday

Retail prices index

September . . . . 9 Tuesday
October . . . . 7 Tuesday
November . . . . 11 Tuesday

In the information age . . .
. . . you need fast access
to facts and figures.

Information about the Office for National Statistics, its services and data is available on the Internet. ONS's site on the World Wide Web is at: http://www.emap.com/ons/

You will find information on:
- THE WORK OF THE ONS ■ OFFICIAL STATISTICS CODE OF PRACTICE
- STATSFAX SERVICE ■ PRESS RELEASES ■ ONS DATABANK/NAVIDATA
- PRODUCT CATALOGUE

ONS's Socio-Economic Statistics and Analysis Group (SESAG) has a separate site at: http://www.open.gov.uk/lmsd/lmsdhome.htm.

Look here for information on:
- SAMPLE SOCIO-ECONOMIC DATA, INCLUDING LABOUR MARKET AND LABOUR FORCE SURVEY (LFS) DATA ■ SUBSCRIPTIONS TO LABOUR MARKET TRENDS ■ NOMIS
- HELPLINES ON LABOUR MARKET AND LFS DATA

You can also email SESAG on sesag.cso.cax@gtnet.gov.uk

NOTES ON SUMMARY TABLES

The Office for National Statistics publishes two regular and complementary measures of both employment and unemployment. One series is based on results from the Labour Force Survey (LFS) which is a sample survey of households in the United Kingdom; the other uses employ-ment information collected from employers and information on unemployment from the count of people claiming unemployment related benefits. The quarterly series of LFS data has been available for Great Britain since spring 1992; prior to this an annual LFS was conducted in the spring of each year. Quarterly information for the United Kingdom is only available from winter 1994/5 when the first quarterly LFS was conducted in Northern Ireland; prior to this the LFS in Northern Ireland (and therefore the United Kingdom) was conducted annually.

In the following summary tables the LFS and Workforce series have been used to give, as far as possible, separate overall pictures of the labour force; the construction of the 'economically active' in the LFS table and the total 'workforce' in the Workforce table represent different approaches to estimating the total number either in employment or seeking employment.

EMPLOYMENT

The two measures of employment are compiled on very different bases. The LFS classifies people according to their main job; those in employment are people who did at least one hour's work in the reference week (or had a job they were temporarily away from). In contrast, the Workforce in Employment (WiE) counts jobs which contribute to Gross Domestic Product (GDP). Further, all LFS estimates come from a single source and are necessarily consistent. This is not the case with the WiE estimates, which depend on several sources - estimates for employees and for the Armed Forces are based on data from employers; figures for the self-employed are taken from the LFS; and estimates of those on work-related government training schemes are obtained from administrative sources. Additionally, the LFS is based on an average over 13 weeks, while the WiE is a point-in-time estimate.

GOVERNMENT-SUPPORTED TRAINING

Both the LFS and WiE series have separate components for people on government-supported training. Neither of these components represent everyone on programmes. Some people on programmes do not have an element of work experience in their training so are excluded from the workforce. Others are either self-employed or have a contract of employment so are counted as self-employed or employees. For more information on government-supported training and how they are treated see the statistical note published in the October 1994 *Employment Gazette*.

UNEMPLOYMENT

ILO (International Labour Organization) unemployment, estimated from the LFS, is based on internationally standard definitions. It includes as unemployed all those people without a job, who were available to start work within the two weeks following their interview and had either looked for work in the four weeks prior to interview or were waiting to start a job they had already obtained.

Because interviews are conducted throughout each quarter, ILO unemployment from the LFS is based on an average over a 13-week period. The claimant unemployment figures are based on those claiming unemployment-related benefits at Employment Service offices on a particular day each month who are out of work, available for, capable of and actively seeking employment. A detailed comparison of the two measures of unemployment is shown in *Table 7.5* and an article giving further information was published in the October 1993 *Employment Gazette*.

STRENGTHS

The different sources each have their have own advantages and are useful in different circumstances. The following gives a brief indication of the advantages and disadvantages of each source.

Labour Force Survey: The LFS is very useful for providing an articulated view of the labour market on the basis of internationally agreed ILO concepts and definitions - the totals of the LFS estimates of people in employment, ILO unemployed and economically inactive add to the estimated total population* aged 16 and over. The LFS also includes a wealth of demographic information so that people's economic status can be cross-referenced with such information as age, occupation, ethnic origin and qualifications. Labour Force Surveys are conducted in all countries of the EU and OECD and also now in many of the new democracies of eastern and central Europe and so are very useful for making international comparisons. The disadvantages of the LFS are: first that, being a sample survey, it is subject to sampling error and is therefore very limited in what is available at local area level; and second, as mentioned below, it is not ideal for industrial classifications.

Workforce in Employment: The WiE series for employees is particularly useful for analysis by industry since it is based on information supplied by employers and is consistent with other government surveys of businesses. Additionally, the sample provides information which is consistent in industry coverage and quality from one quarter to the next. Industry classification within the LFS is based on statements by individuals who may have a different perception of the sector in which they work to that of their employer. The WiE series also feeds into National Accounts and the workforce in employment total is used in the denominator for calculating claimant unemployment rates. The disadvantages of the WiE are that, to give an overall picture of employment, a number of figures from different sources have to be added together. Although the WiE has a much higher coverage rate than the LFS, with over 50 per cent of employees explicitly covered, there is some evidence that the employment figures from the WiE are not as comprehensive in their scope as those from the LFS.

Claimant unemployment: The claimant count is a timely and regular indicator of the number claiming unemployment-related benefits. It is particularly useful as an up-to-date indicator of latest unemployment trends and is therefore a valuable economic indicator. Since it covers all those claiming benefits (as opposed to the LFS which is only a representative sample) it is also able to provide unemployment figures for very small areas. The disadvantages of the claimant count are that: first, being an administrative by-product the coverage of the count can change whenever there is a change to the benefit system upon which it is based and compensating adjustments are necessary whenever the change is significant and relevant; and second, it is not internationally comparable.

---

* Population in private households, student halls of residence and NHS accommodation.

0.1 SUMMARY TABLE
The Labour Force Survey in the United Kingdom: seasonally adjusted

THOUSANDS

		In employment					ILO unemployed	Total econ. active	Econ. inactive	All aged 16 & over
		Employees	Self-employed	Government-supported training programmes	Unpaid family workers	Total				
All										
1992	Spr	22,077	3,227	377	181	25,862	2,832	28,694	16,615	45,310
1993	Spr	21,871	3,186	356	151	25,564	2,998	28,561	16,838	45,400
1994	Spr	21,968	3,304	336	146	25,754	2,797	28,551	16,913	45,465
1995/6	Win	22,603	3,301	259	122	26,285	2,405	28,690	16,995	45,685
1996	Spr	22,619	3,294	248	127	26,288	2,392	28,679	17,045	45,724
1996	Sum	22,641	3,369	247	118	26,374	2,327	28,702	17,074	45,775
1996	Aut	22,787	3,372	223	122	26,505	2,293	28,798	17,019	45,816
1996/7	**Win**	**22,949**	**3,366**	**223**	**114**	**26,653**	**2,180**	**28,833**	**17,024**	**45,857**
Changes										
Aut 96-Win96/7		163	-7	-1	-8	148	-113	35	6	41
Win95/6-Win96/7		346	65	-36	-8	367	-225	143	29	172
Males										
1992	Spr	11,622	2,443	246	55	14,366	1,897	16,263	5,661	21,924
1993	Spr	11,414	2,390	232	43	14,079	2,019	16,098	5,888	21,985
1994	Spr	11,459	2,487	220	49	14,216	1,858	16,074	5,976	22,050
1995/6	Win	11,797	2,488	162	36	14,484	1,590	16,074	6,131	22,206
1996	Spr	11,822	2,473	156	41	14,493	1,577	16,070	6,162	22,232
1996	Sum	11,821	2,534	156	38	14,549	1,521	16,070	6,193	22,262
1996	Aut	11,915	2,532	136	41	14,624	1,481	16,105	6,183	22,288
1996/7	**Win**	**12,024**	**2,525**	**134**	**39**	**14,722**	**1,375**	**16,097**	**6,218**	**22,315**
Changes										
Aut 96-Win96/7		110	-7	-2	-2	98	-107	-9	35	26
Win95/6-Win96/7		227	36	-28	3	238	-215	23	86	109
Females										
1992	Spr	10,455	784	131	126	11,497	935	12,431	10,955	23,386
1993	Spr	10,457	796	123	108	11,485	979	12,464	10,951	23,415
1994	Spr	10,509	817	116	97	11,539	939	12,478	10,938	23,416
1995/6	Win	10,806	813	97	86	11,801	814	12,616	10,864	23,480
1996	Spr	10,797	821	92	85	11,795	814	12,609	10,883	23,492
1996	Sum	10,820	835	91	81	11,825	806	12,632	10,881	23,512
1996	Aut	10,872	840	87	81	11,881	812	12,692	10,835	23,527
1996/7	**Win**	**10,925**	**841**	**89**	**76**	**11,931**	**805**	**12,736**	**10,806**	**23,542**
Changes										
Aut 96-Win96/7		53	1	1	-5	50	-7	44	-29	15
Win95/6-Win96/7		119	28	-8	-10	129	-9	120	-57	63

Note: LFS seasonal quarters are defined as follows: spring (March-May); summer (June-August); autumn (September-November); winter (December-February).

0.2 SUMMARY TABLE
The Workforce in the United Kingdom: seasonally adjusted

THOUSANDS

		Workforce in employment					Claimant unemployed	Workforce
		Employees in employment	Self-employed	Work-related Government-supported training	HM forces	Total		
All								
1994	Mar	21,656	3,274	323	254	25,508	2,729	28,236
1995	Mar	21,923	3,371	270	233	25,797	2,352	28,149
1996	Mar	22,111	3,302	214	222	25,849	2,187	28,036
1996	Sep	22,304	3,367	191	218	26,080	2,071	28,151
1996	Dec	22,355	3,361	190	216	26,122	1,880	28,002
1997	**Mar**	**22,459**	**3,355**	**180**	**214**	**26,209**	**1,711**	**27,919**
Changes								
Dec 96 - Mar 97		104	-6	-10	-3	86	-169	-83
Mar 96 - Mar 97		348	53	-34	-8	359	-476	-117
Males								
1994	Mar	10,943	2,453	203	237	13,835	2,093	15,929
1995	Mar	11,079	2,550	166	217	14,011	1,797	15,809
1996	Mar	11,179	2,490	135	207	14,010	1,666	15,676
1996	Sep	11,263	2,532	120	203	14,118	1,572	15,690
1996	Dec	11,326	2,525	120	201	14,172	1,430	15,603
1997	**Mar**	**11,430**	**2,520**	**114**	**199**	**14,262**	**1,308**	**15,570**
Changes								
Dec 96 - Mar 97		103	-5	-6	-2	90	-123	-33
Mar 96 - Mar 97		251	30	-21	-8	252	-359	-107
Females								
1994	Mar	10,714	821	120	18	11,672	635	12,308
1995	Mar	10,844	821	104	17	11,785	555	12,340
1996	Mar	10,933	812	79	16	11,839	520	12,360
1996	Sep	11,041	835	71	15	11,962	499	12,461
1996	Dec	11,029	835	70	15	11,950	449	12,399
1997	**Mar**	**11,030**	**835**	**66**	**15**	**11,946**	**403**	**12,350**
Changes								
Dec 96 - Mar 97		1	-0	-4	-0	-4	-46	-49
Mar 96 - Mar 97		97	23	-13	-1	107	-117	-10

| | | In employment | | | | | | | | |
		Employees	Self-employed	Government-supported training programmes	Unpaid family workers	Total	ILO unemployed	Total econ. active	Econ. inactive	All aged 16 & over
All										
1996	Spr	22,085	3,213	225	122	25,645	2,321	27,966	16,556	44,522
	Sum	22,096	3,289	225	114	25,724	2,255	27,978	16,582	44,560
	Aut	22,252	3,283	200	115	25,851	2,221	28,072	16,527	44,599
1996/97	Win	22,401	3,277	199	108	25,985	2,111	28,096	16,542	44,638
1997	**Spr**	**22,507**	**3,260**	**197**	**111**	**26,076**	**2,037**	**28,113**	**16,564**	**44,677**
Changes										
Win 96/97-Spr97		106	-17	-1	3	91	-74	17	22	39
Spr96-Spr97		422	47	-27	-11	431	-285	146	8	154
Males										
1996	Spr	11,551	2,403	142	40	14,137	1,525	15,662	5,992	21,654
	Sum	11,542	2,466	143	37	14,187	1,472	15,659	6,019	21,678
	Aut	11,637	2,459	122	40	14,258	1,432	15,690	6,014	21,703
1996/97	Win	11,743	2,454	119	37	14,353	1,326	15,679	6,050	21,728
1997	**Spr**	**11,817**	**2,421**	**121**	**37**	**14,395**	**1,294**	**15,689**	**6,064**	**21,753**
Changes										
Win 96/97-Spr97		74	-33	2	0	42	-32	11	14	25
Spr96-Spr97		266	18	-21	-4	259	-231	28	72	99
Females										
1996	Spr	10,534	810	83	82	11,509	796	12,305	10,564	22,869
	Sum	10,554	823	82	77	11,537	782	12,319	10,562	22,881
	Aut	10,615	824	79	75	11,593	789	12,382	10,513	22,895
1996/97	Win	10,658	824	79	71	11,632	785	12,417	10,492	22,909
1997	**Spr**	**10,690**	**840**	**76**	**75**	**11,681**	**743**	**12,424**	**10,500**	**22,923**
Changes										
Win 96/97-Spr97		32	16	-3	3	49	-42	7	7	14
Spr96-Spr97		**156**	**30**	**-6**	**-7**	**172**	**-53**	**119**	**-64**	**55**

Note: LFS seasonal quarters are defined as follows: spring (March-May); summer (June-August); autumn (September-November); winter (December-February).

| | | Workforce in employment | | | | | | |
		Employees in employment	Self-employed	Work-related Government-supported training	HM forces	Total	Claimant unemployed	Workforce
All								
1995	Dec	21,566	3,238	210	226	25,240	2,149	27,389
1996	Mar	21,536	3,219	197	222	25,175	2,101	27,276
	Jun	21,597	3,213	165	221	25,197	2,064	27,261
	Sep	21,728	3,289	170	218	25,405	1,985	27,390
	Dec	21,774	3,283	169	216	25,442	1,809	27,251
1997	**Mar**	**21,878**	**3,277**	**161**	**214**	**25,530**	**1,644**	**27,174**
Changes								
Dec 96 - Mar 97		104	-6	-8	-3	88	-165	-77
Mar 96 - Mar 97		341	59	-36	-8	355	-458	-102
Males								
1995	Dec	10,919	2,448	135	210	13,712	1,637	15,349
1996	Mar	10,893	2,419	124	207	13,643	1,600	15,243
	Jun	10,912	2,403	103	206	13,625	1,565	15,189
	Sep	10,978	2,466	106	203	13,753	1,506	15,259
	Dec	11,039	2,459	106	201	13,805	1,375	15,180
1997	**Mar**	**11,142**	**2,454**	**101**	**199**	**13,896**	**1,255**	**15,151**
Changes								
Dec 96 - Mar 97		104	-5	-5	-2	91	-120	-29
Mar 96 - Mar 97		249	35	-23	-8	253	-345	-92
Females								
1995	Dec	10,647	789	75	16	11,528	512	12,040
1996	Mar	10,643	800	73	16	11,531	502	12,033
	Jun	10,685	810	62	16	11,573	499	12,072
	Sep	10,749	823	64	15	11,652	479	12,131
	Dec	10,735	824	63	15	11,637	434	12,070
1997	**Mar**	**10,735**	**824**	**60**	**15**	**11,634**	**389**	**12,022**
Changes								
Dec 96 - Mar 97		0	-0	-3	-0	-3	-45	-48
Mar 96 - Mar 97		92	24	-13	-1	102	-113	-10

Output / Income

	GDP			GDP 1990 prices			Index of output UK — Production industries [1,2]		Manufacturing industries [1,3]		Index of production OECD countries [1]		Real personal disposable income		Gross trading profits of companies [4]	
	1990=100			£ billion	%		1990=100	%	1990=100	%	1990=100	%	1990=100	%	£ billion	%
1991	98.0			468.9	-2.1		96.6	-3.4	95.0	-5.0	99.6	-0.4	99.9	-0.1	68.7	0.1
1992	97.5			466.5	-0.5		97.0	0.4	94.9	-0.1	99.3R	-0.3	101.9	2.0	69.0	0.5
1993	99.5			476.8	2.2		99.1	2.2	96.3	1.5	98.7R	-0.6	103.9	2.0	76.3	10.5
1994	103.8			498.2	4.5		104.4	5.3	100.8	4.7	103.0R	4.4	105.5	1.5	87.3	14.4
1995	106.7			511.9	2.8		106.7	2.2	102.5	1.7	106.1	3.0	108.9	3.2	92.8	6.3
1996	**109.2**			**524.5**	**2.5**		**107.9**	**1.1**	**102.8**	**0.3**	**108.2**	**2.0**	**113.0**	**3.8**	**103.4**	**11.4**
1996 Q2	108.7			130.6	2.5		107.5	1.1	102.1	-0.2	107.6	1.7	112.4	4.3	25.2	10.6
Q3	109.3			131.3	2.5		108.2	1.0	103.2	0.4	108.8	2.6	112.7	3.6	26.2	12.2
Q4	110.5			132.7	2.9		108.6	1.5	103.3	0.7	109.7r	3.1	114.0	2.8	27.3	12.4
1997 Q1	111.6			133.9	3.1		108.4	1.1	103.8	1.4	110.9	3.8	113.7	0.8	27.5	11.3
Q2	..			..	..		**108.8**	**1.2**	**103.7**	**1.6**	..	..	**114.7**	**2.0**	**28.5**	**13.3**
1996 Dec	..			..	..		109.1	1.5	103.4	0.7	109.9r	3.0				
1997 Jan	..			..	..		108.8	1.7	103.6	1.0	110.8	3.3	..	..	..	..
Feb	..			..	..		108.3	1.6	104.0	1.4	110.8	3.3	..	..	..	..
Mar	..			..	..		108.1	1.1	103.9	1.4	111.0	3.8	..	..	..	..
Apr	..			..	..		109.1	1.2	104.2R	1.8	112.1	4.0	..	..	..	..
May	..			..	..		108.0R	0.7	103.2R	1.6	112.2	4.2	..	..	..	..
Jun	..			..	..		**109.5**	**1.3**	**103.7**	**1.5**	..	..	..	..	..	..

Expenditure

	Consumer expenditure 1990 prices		Retail sales volumes [1]		Fixed investments [5] — All industries 1990 prices [6]		Manufacturing industries 1990 prices [3,6]		General government consumption at 1990 prices		Stock changes 1990 prices [7]		Base lending rates + [8]		Effective exchange rate + [1,9]	
	£ billion	%	1990=100	%	£ billion	%	£ billion	%	£ billion	%	£ billion	%			1990=100	%
1991	340.0	-2.2	98.7	-1.3	75.4	-7.9	12.8	-10.0	115.8	2.6	-4.21		10.50		100.7	0.7
1992	339.7	-0.1	99.4	0.7	74.1	-1.8	11.8	-7.6	115.7	-0.1	-0.97		7.00		96.9	-3.8
1993	348.2	2.5	102.4	3.0	73.1	-1.2	11.2	-5.1	115.5	-0.2	-0.88		5.50		88.9	-8.3
1994	357.8	2.8	106.2	3.7	76.4	4.4	12.0	6.8	118.1	2.2	3.12		6.30		89.2	0.3
1995	364.0	1.7	107.5	1.2	78.2	2.4	13.2	9.9	119.6	1.3	3.73		6.80		84.8	-4.9
1996	**376.6**	**3.5**	**110.6**	**2.9**	**80.0**	**2.3**	**12.4**	**-5.6**	**122.4**	**2.4**	**1.01**		**5.97**		**86.3**	**1.8**
1996 Q2	93.7	3.0	110.0R	2.6	20.3	2.4	2.9	-13.2	30.6	2.1	-0.49		5.92		84.8	0.6
Q3	94.4	3.6	111.1	3.4	19.8	0.6	3.0	-11.5	30.6	2.1	-0.63		5.75		85.5	1.5
Q4	95.6	4.3	112.3	3.8	20.0	2.3	3.1	-6.1	30.8	2.4	1.76		5.92		91.4	9.5
1997 Q1	96.4	3.7	113.8	4.8	20.5	2.6	3.3	..	30.7	0.9	1.29		6.00		96.9	16.0
Q2	..	..	**115.8**	**5.3**	**21.5**	**6.0**	**4.3**	..	**31.7**	**3.8**	**1.29**		**6.25**		**96.9**	**14.3**
1996 Dec	..	..	112.1	3.9	..	..	..	..	..	..	..		6.00		93.8	9.5
1997 Jan	..	..	113.0	4.1	..	..	..	..	..	..	..		6.00		95.9	13.0
Feb	..	..	113.6	4.2	..	..	..	..	..	..	..		6.00		97.4	14.9
Mar	..	..	114.5	4.7	..	..	..	..	..	..	..		6.00		97.4	16.0
Apr	..	..	114.6R	4.7	..	..	..	..	..	..	..		6.00		99.5	17.2
May	..	..	115.9R	5.0	..	..	..	..	..	..	..		6.25		99.0	17.5
Jun	..	..	**116.6**	**5.3**	..	..	..	..	..	..	..		**6.50**		**100.4**	**17.5**

Trade in goods / Balance of payments / Prices

	Export volume [1]		Import volume [1]		Trade in goods balance	Current balance		Tax and price index + [1,10]		Producer price index + [1,3,10] — Materials and fuels		Home sales	
	1990=100	%	1990=100	%	£ billion	£ billion		Jan 1987=100	%	1990=100	%	1990=100	%
1991	101.2	1.2	94.7	-5.3	-10.3	-8.0		126.2	5.4	97.9	-2.1	105.4	5.4
1992	103.7	2.5	100.9	6.5	-13.1	-10.1		129.8	2.9	97.4	-0.5	108.7	3.1
1993	107.4	3.6	104.8	3.9	-13.5	-10.8		131.4	1.2	101.8	4.5	112.9	3.9
1994	118.5	10.3	109.4	4.4	-11.1	-1.7r		135.2	2.9	104.4	2.6	115.8	2.6
1995	127.7	7.8	114.3	4.5	-11.6	-3.7		140.4	3.8	114.4	9.6	120.6	4.1
1996	**136.3**	**6.7**	**124.1**	**8.6**	**-12.6**	**-0.4**		**142.4**	**1.4**	**113.1**	**-1.1**	**123.8**	**2.7**
1996 Q2	136.0	9.4	123.1	8.8	-3.1	0.7		141.9	0.8	114.8	-	123.9	2.9
Q3	136.9	5.8	124.7	7.0	-3.2	-0.4		142.2	0.7	111.2	-2.7	123.7	2.1
Q4	139.1	6.2	126.1	7.5	-2.6	0.5		143.2	1.2	110.3	-4.6	124.4	2.0
1997 Q1	142.0	6.5	126.5	3.3	-2.1	1.5		143.4	0.8	107.9	-7.1	124.9	1.2
Q2	..	..	..	..	..	..		..	..	**103.8P**	**-9.6**	**125.1P**	**1.0**
1996 Dec	138.3	6.3	126.1	7.5	-0.9	..		143.6	1.2	110.3	-4.6	124.7	2.0
1997 Jan	144.0	5.6	128.4	8.0	-0.6	..		143.6	1.3	109.4	-5.9	125.0	1.7
Feb	141.7	7.3	127.2	6.2	-0.8	..		144.2	1.3	107.9	-6.4	124.9	1.4
Mar	140.4	6.6	124.0	3.4	-0.7	..		144.6	1.3	106.4	-7.1	124.8	1.2
Apr	149.3R	7.2	136.9R	4.6	-1.0	..		143.8	1.3	103.9R	-8.6	125.0	1.0
May	145.4	7.1	129.2	5.4	-0.5	..		144.4	1.4	104.5	-9.4	125.2R	0.9
Jun	..	..	..	..	..	..		**145.0**	**1.7**	**103.0P**	**-9.6**	**125.0P**	**1.0**

P	=	Provisional
R	=	Revised
r	=	Series revised from indicated entry onwards.
		Data values from which percentage changes are calculated may have been rounded.
*		For most indicators two series are given, representing the series itself in the units stated and the percentage change in the series on the same period a year earlier.
+		Not seasonally adjusted.

1 The percentage change series for the monthly data is the percentage change between the three months ending in the month shown and the same period a year earlier.
2 Production industries: SIC divisions 1 to 4.
3 Manufacturing industries: SIC divisions 2 to 4.
4 Industrial and commercial companies (excluding North Sea oil companies) net of stock appreciation.
5 Gross domestic fixed capital formation, excluding fixed investment in dwellings, the transfer costs of land and existing buildings and the national accounts statistical adjustment.
6 Including leased assets.
7 Value of physical increase in stocks and work in progress.
8 Base lending rate of the London clearing banks on the last Friday of the period shown.
9 Average of daily rates.
10 Annual and quarterly figures are average of monthly indices.

	Employees in employment					Self-employed persons (with or without employees) **	HM Forces #	Work-related government-supported training programmes ++	Workforce in employment ##	Workforce *
	Male		Female		All					
	All	Part-time +	All	Part-time +						
UNITED KINGDOM										
Unadjusted for seasonal variation										
1993 Jun	10,952	1,093	10,660	4,827	21,613	3,189	271	311	25,384	28,249
Sep	10,993	1,104	10,663	4,808	21,656	3,196	267	306	25,424	28,336
Dec	10,972	1,128	10,762	4,926	21,734	3,245	258	329	25,566	28,348
1994 Mar	10,884	1,109	10,669	4,852	21,553	3,246	254	323	25,376	28,154
Jun	10,947	1,127	10,754	4,896	21,700	3,298	250	302	25,551	28,136
Sep	11,079	1,148	10,759	4,858	21,838	3,306	246	289	25,679	28,259
Dec	11,061	1,163	10,895	4,990	21,956	3,371	237	296	25,860	28,277
1995 Mar	11,013	1,153	10,794	4,908	21,807	3,341	233	270	25,652	28,050
Jun	11,123	1,193	10,905	4,989	22,028	3,351	230	227	25,836	28,090
Sep	11,158	1,179	10,855	4,895	22,013	3,330	228	220	25,791	28,083
Dec	11,232	1,252	10,997	5,031	22,229	3,348	226	227	26,030	28,258
1996 Mar	11,106	1,242	10,884	4,980	21,990	3,270	222	214	25,697	27,928
Jun	11,199	1,282	10,996	5,052	22,195	3,283	221	181	25,881	27,977
Sep	11,311	1,305	11,016	5,019	22,326	3,373	218	191	26,108	28,212
Dec	11,360	1,336	11,089	5,073	22,449	3,389	216	190	26,244	28,113
1997 Mar	**11,368**	**1,294**	**10,974**	**4,986**	**22,341**	**3,322**	**214**	**180**	**26,057**	**27,802**
UNITED KINGDOM										
Adjusted for seasonal variation										
1993 Jun	10,951	1,086	10,636	4,809	21,588	3,190	271	311	25,360	28,279
Sep	10,960	1,122	10,700	4,864	21,660	3,192	267	306	25,425	28,313
Dec	10,953	1,116	10,706	4,871	21,659	3,220	258	329	25,467	28,250
1994 Mar	10,943	1,119	10,714	4,871	21,656	3,274	254	323	25,508	28,236
Jun	10,941	1,125	10,723	4,868	21,663	3,302	250	302	25,517	28,160
Sep	11,034	1,160	10,793	4,912	21,828	3,302	246	289	25,664	28,219
Dec	11,040	1,153	10,834	4,938	21,874	3,345	237	296	25,752	28,176
1995 Mar	11,079	1,166	10,844	4,929	21,923	3,371	233	270	25,797	28,149
Jun	11,115	1,189	10,872	4,959	21,987	3,357	230	227	25,801	28,114
Sep	11,110	1,188	10,889	4,943	21,999	3,325	228	220	25,772	28,036
Dec	11,205	1,239	10,936	4,978	22,141	3,321	226	227	25,914	28,150
1996 Mar	11,179	1,253	10,933	5,004	22,111	3,302	222	214	25,849	28,036
Jun	11,197	1,279	10,975	5,034	22,172	3,291	221	181	25,865	28,015
Sep	11,263	1,313	11,041	5,065	22,304	3,367	218	191	26,080	28,151
Dec	11,326	1,320	11,029	5,027	22,355	3,361	216	190	26,122	28,002
1997 Mar	**11,430**	**1,309**	**11,030**	**5,017**	**22,459**	**3,355**	**214**	**180**	**26,209**	**27,919**
GREAT BRITAIN										
Unadjusted for seasonal variation										
1993 Jun	10,676	1,054	10,390	4,713	21,066	3,108	271	295	24,740	27,502
Sep	10,715	1,065	10,390	4,693	21,105	3,115	267	288	24,774	27,579
Dec	10,693	1,087	10,484	4,805	21,177	3,164	258	311	24,910	27,593
1994 Mar	10,605	1,068	10,392	4,732	20,997	3,165	254	305	24,722	27,401
Jun	10,666	1,086	10,475	4,774	21,141	3,216	250	286	24,893	27,383
Sep	10,797	1,107	10,479	4,736	21,276	3,224	246	270	25,016	27,497
Dec	10,775	1,119	10,607	4,861	21,382	3,289	237	278	25,186	27,513
1995 Mar	10,730	1,110	10,508	4,780	21,238	3,259	233	252	24,982	27,292
Jun	10,836	1,148	10,616	4,859	21,452	3,269	230	210	25,161	27,330
Sep	10,870	1,135	10,567	4,766	21,437	3,247	228	205	25,118	27,320
Dec	10,945	1,206	10,706	4,898	21,651	3,266	226	210	25,352	27,496
1996 Mar	10,822	1,197	10,594	4,848	21,416	3,188	222	197	25,023	27,170
Jun	10,915	1,238	10,707	4,920	21,622	3,205	221	165	25,214	27,226
Sep	11,025	1,260	10,726	4,887	21,751	3,295	218	170	25,434	27,448
Dec	11,071	1,289	10,792	4,935	21,864	3,311	216	169	25,560	27,357
1997 Mar	**11,081**	**1,247**	**10,680**	**4,851**	**21,761**	**3,244**	**214**	**161**	**25,380**	**27,059**
GREAT BRITAIN										
Adjusted for seasonal variation										
1993 Jun	10,675	1,048	10,365	4,695	21,039	3,109	271	295	24,715	27,530
Sep	10,683	1,083	10,427	4,749	21,110	3,111	267	288	24,775	27,560
Dec	10,675	1,075	10,431	4,751	21,106	3,140	258	311	24,814	27,498
1994 Mar	10,663	1,079	10,436	4,751	21,099	3,193	254	305	24,852	27,481
Jun	10,660	1,083	10,443	4,745	21,103	3,219	250	286	24,858	27,404
Sep	10,752	1,118	10,512	4,790	21,265	3,220	246	270	25,000	27,460
Dec	10,755	1,110	10,549	4,808	21,303	3,263	237	278	25,081	27,413
1995 Mar	10,794	1,123	10,558	4,801	21,353	3,289	233	252	25,126	27,388
Jun	10,827	1,145	10,583	4,829	21,410	3,274	230	210	25,125	27,350
Sep	10,822	1,144	10,600	4,814	21,422	3,242	228	205	25,098	27,275
Dec	10,919	1,194	10,647	4,845	21,566	3,238	226	210	25,240	27,389
1996 Mar	10,893	1,208	10,643	4,872	21,536	3,219	222	197	25,175	27,276
Jun	10,912	1,234	10,685	4,902	21,597	3,213	221	165	25,197	27,261
Sep	10,978	1,268	10,749	4,933	21,728	3,289	218	170	25,405	27,390
Dec	11,039	1,273	10,735	4,890	21,774	3,283	216	169	25,442	27,251
1997 Mar	**11,142**	**1,262**	**10,735**	**4,881**	**21,878**	**3,277**	**214**	**161**	**25,530**	**27,174**

Note: Definitions of terms used will be found at the end of the section.
* Workforce in employment plus claimant unemployed. For the claimant unemployment series see *Tables 2.1* and *2.2* and their footnotes.
# HM Forces figures, provided by the Ministry of Defence, represent the total number of UK service personnel, male and female, in HM Forces, wherever serving and including those on release leave. The numbers are not subject to seasonal adjustment.
** Estimates of the self-employed are based on the results of the Labour Force Survey. The Northern Ireland estimates are not seasonally adjusted.
++ Includes all participants on government training and employment programmes who are receiving some work experience on their placement but who do not have a contract of employment (those with a contract are included in the employees in employment series). The numbers are not subject to seasonal adjustment.
Employees in employment, the self-employed, HM Forces and participants in work-related government training programmes. See *Employment Gazette*, pS6, August 1988.
+ Estimates of part-time employees in the United Kingdom are only available on a quarterly basis since December 1992. The Northern Ireland component is not seasonally adjusted.

EMPLOYMENT
Employees in employment in Great Britain

THOUSANDS

GREAT BRITAIN SIC 1992 Section, subsection, group	All industries and services A-Q		Manufacturing industries D		Production industries C-E		Production and construction industries C-F	
	All employees unadjusted	Seasonally adjusted	All employees unadjusted	Seasonally adjusted	All employees unadjusted	Seasonally adjusted	All employees unadjusted	Seasonally adjusted
1983 Jun	20,572	20,562	5,034	5,052	5,644	5,664	6,685	6,706
1984 Jun	20,741	20,735	4,928	4,946	5,504	5,524	6,542	6,564
1985 Jun	20,920	20,909	4,882	4,895	5,431	5,446	6,457	6,474
1986 Jun	20,886	20,874	4,763	4,777	5,262	5,277	6,263	6,280
1987 Jun	21,080	21,071	4,697	4,713	5,157	5,174	6,179	6,197
1988 Jun	21,740	21,736	4,735	4,754	5,170	5,192	6,233	6,254
1989 Jun	22,134	22,133	4,723	4,747	5,140	5,166	6,242	6,267
1990 Jun	22,382	22,370	4,605	4,628	5,000	5,026	6,114	6,142
1991 Jun	21,728	21,707	4,196	4,215	4,566	4,588	5,592	5,616
1992 Jun	21,387	21,359	3,983	3,995	4,316	4,331	5,242	5,260
1993 Jun	21,066	21,039	3,808	3,814	4,097	4,106	4,937	4,950
1994 Jun	21,141	21,103	3,823	3,827	4,078	4,084	4,917	4,928
1995 Feb			3,889	3,908	4,126	4,142		
Mar	21,238	21,353	3,893	3,912	4,129	4,148	4,932	4,961
Apr			3,881	3,909	4,113	4,142		
May			3,898	3,922	4,129	4,157		
Jun	21,452	21,410	3,918	3,922	4,149	4,155	4,963	4,973
Jul			3,930	3,922	4,159	4,153		
Aug			3,943	3,924	4,171	4,152		
Sep	21,437	21,422	3,945	3,919	4,173	4,146	4,982	4,948
Oct			3,955	3,938	4,180	4,161		
Nov			3,965	3,942	4,188	4,163		
Dec	21,651	21,566	3,981	3,962	4,204	4,184	5,014	4,991
1996 Jan			3,915	3,934	4,133	4,150		
Feb			3,918	3,936	4,135	4,149		
Mar	21,416	21,536	3,932	3,950	4,148	4,166	4,940	4,967
Apr			3,903	3,930	4,089	4,118		
May			3,902	3,924	4,085	4,112		
Jun	21,622	21,597	3,913	3,919	4,102	4,111	4,904	4,909
Jul			3,950	3,942	4,128	4,125		
Aug			3,955	3,935	4,133	4,115		
Sep	21,751	21,728	3,950	3,933	4,136	4,119	4,944	4,924
Oct			3,959	3,938	4,146	4,124		
Nov			3,952	3,929	4,138	4,113		
Dec	21,864	21,774	3,955	3,930	4,141	4,114	4,971	4,936
1997 Jan			3,920	3,936	4,111	4,123		
Feb			3,905	3,926	4,096	4,110		
Mar	21,761	21,878	3,913	3,930	4,104	4,118	4,920	4,942
Apr P			3,915	3,942	4,106	4,135		
May P			3,916	3,941	4,107	4,136		
Jun P			**3,934**	**3,944**	**4,125**	**4,139**		

GREAT BRITAIN

SEASONALLY ADJUSTED

SIC 1992 Section subsection, group	Service Industries G-Q		Agriculture, hunting, forestry and fishing A,B 01-05	Mining and quarrying, supply of electricity, gas and water C,E 10-14,40-41	Food products beverages and tobacco DA 15-16	Manufacture of clothing, textiles, leather and leather products DB/DC 17-19	Wood and wood products DD 20	Paper, pulp, printing, publishing & recording media DE 21-22	Chemicals, chemical products & man-made fibres DG 24
	All employees unadjusted	Seasonally adjusted							
1983 Jun	13,541	13,502	355	610	546	550	78	459	327
1984 Jun	13,863	13,825	346	577	531	549	78	455	326
1985 Jun	14,126	14,089	346	550	525	552	80	458	322
1986 Jun	14,297	14,261	334	500	508	557	83	448	313
1987 Jun	14,584	14,549	325	461	504	546	85	454	306
1988 Jun	15,198	15,166	317	437	495	549	89	457	311
1989 Jun	15,596	15,563	303	419	485	519	92	466	317
1990 Jun	15,974	15,931	297	398	479	476	91	467	305
1991 Jun	15,849	15,802	289	373	481	404	80	456	276
1992 Jun	15,855	15,808	291	336	455	388	78	447	268
1993 Jun	15,822	15,783	307	292	442	382	84	439	255
1994 Jun	15,944	15,894	281	258	432	373	86	453	244
1995 Feb				234	435	368	79	454	256
Mar	16,063	16,136	256	236	428	367	77	456	251
Apr				234	434	362	76	455	252
May				234	433	363	77	454	253
Jun	16,236	16,184	253	233	431	358	77	459	252
Jul				231	437	358	77	453	253
Aug				229	436	357	77	453	254
Sep	16,175	16,219	255	227	432	354	77	450	253
Oct				223	438	351	78	454	253
Nov				221	440	351	78	455	252
Dec	16,389	16,317	259	222	442	353	86	454	252
1996 Jan				216	434	352	75	449	250
Feb				214	436	350	74	450	250
Mar	16,228	16,310	259	215	438	349	87	450	251
Apr				187	439	352	82	446	250
May				188	439	352	82	446	252
Jun	16,471	16,438	250	192	439	349	77	447	253
Jul				183	439	355	84	451	251
Aug				180	440	354	85	447	248
Sep	16,536	16,555	248	186	441	352	79	440	250
Oct				186	439	354	83	443	246
Nov				184	438	352	84	442	246
Dec	16,651	16,585	253	184	440	350	83	443	245
1997 Jan				186	436	362	82	445	248
Feb				184	437	361	80	443	247
Mar	16,593	16,678	257	188	440	359	80	443	246
Apr P				193	434	364	80	442	247
May P				195	438	362	81	443	246
Jun P				**195**	**440**	**365**	**80**	**444**	**248**

GREAT BRITAIN	Rubber and plastic products	Non-metallic mineral products, metal & metal products	Machinery and equipment nec	Electrical and optical equipment	Transport equipment	Coke, nuclear fuel and other manufacturing nec	Construction	Wholesale and retail trade, and repairs	Hotels and restaurants
SIC 1992 Section, subsection, group	DH 25	DI/DJ 26-28	DK 29	DL 30-33	DM 34-35	DF,DN 23,36-37	F 45	G 50-52	H 55
1983 Jun	196	954	504	617	583	220	1,042	3,189	917
1984 Jun	201	925	491	615	540	217	1,040	3,268	959
1985 Jun	202	911	492	613	523	219	1,029	3,287	989
1986 Jun	203	866	480	596	506	223	1,002	3,287	988
1987 Jun	208	844	475	588	485	226	1,022	3,291	993
1988 Jun	218	854	485	586	482	232	1,063	3,395	1,068
1989 Jun	222	870	489	582	474	238	1,101	3,530	1,158
1990 Jun	216	856	488	550	470	238	1,116	3,597	1,216
1991 Jun	190	765	457	488	425	209	1,028	3,532	1,188
1992 Jun	185	722	422	447	398	203	929	3,521	1,174
1993 Jun	188	681	381	425	353	203	844	3,500	1,139
1994 Jun	198	690	377	440	328	207	844	3,583	1,143
1995 Feb	217	695	386	459	339	221			
Mar	219	696	389	471	340	218	813	3,624	1,206
Apr	218	693	391	465	343	219			
May	220	693	393	468	347	222			
Jun	218	690	391	477	348	220	818	3,631	1,204
Jul	220	689	394	474	349	220			
Aug	219	688	395	476	352	217			
Sep	220	691	395	481	353	214	802	3,621	1,202
Oct	221	695	397	482	354	215			
Nov	222	694	399	482	356	211			
Dec	221	693	400	485	359	218	806	3,662	1,203
1996 Jan	221	691	403	486	360	212			
Feb	220	695	405	486	359	211			
Mar	220	690	401	493	357	214	802	3,654	1,216
Apr	221	689	400	491	357	202			
May	221	687	399	492	355	200			
Jun	222	683	401	489	360	200	798	3,690	1,255
Jul	219	689	399	496	358	202			
Aug	221	689	399	494	359	199			
Sep	222	686	401	494	360	202	805	3,714	1,262
Oct	221	690	399	495	363	204			
Nov	220	689	396	494	364	204			
Dec	221	688	399	493	364	204	822	3,729	1,271
1997 Jan	223	687	401	492	364	199			
Feb	223	685	400	490	363	198			
Mar	224	685	401	488	363	202	824	3,804	1,274
Apr P	222	690	401	493	363	205			
May P	221	690	400	496	361	203			
Jun P	**222**	**691**	**403**	**488**	**362**	**203**			

GREAT BRITAIN	Transport & storage	Post and telecommunication	Financial intermediation	Real estate	Renting, research, computer & other business activities	Public administration and defence; compulsory social security	Education	Health activities	Social work activities	Other community, social & personal activities
SIC 1992 Section, subsection, group	I 60-63	I 64	J 65-67	K 70	K 71-74	L+ 75	M 80	N 85.1-85.2	N 85.3	O - Q * 90-93
1983 Jun	881	446	811	140	1,562	1,468	1,522	1,247	568	751
1984 Jun	876	447	837	147	1,643	1,453	1,544	1,250	613	787
1985 Jun	868	442	858	152	1,719	1,424	1,570	1,296	654	831
1986 Jun	846	435	881	157	1,777	1,418	1,617	1,307	707	841
1987 Jun	832	436	920	165	1,846	1,436	1,680	1,332	767	852
1988 Jun	849	453	996	176	1,964	1,419	1,742	1,381	848	874
1989 Jun	878	463	1,038	183	2,083	1,341	1,784	1,409	812	884
1990 Jun	910	462	1,047	190	2,202	1,383	1,805	1,445	794	880
1991 Jun	897	455	1,024	186	2,167	1,403	1,791	1,493	800	865
1992 Jun	887	446	991	205	2,158	1,406	1,774	1,513	846	894
1993 Jun	873	420	959	237	2,209	1,401	1,752	1,470	899	923
1994 Jun	867	422	967	250	2,209	1,384	1,772	1,481	900	917
1995 Feb										
Mar	860	420	980	259	2,328	1,362	1,766	1,501	905	926
Apr										
May										
Jun	856	423	985	260	2,348	1,347	1,781	1,519	903	928
Jul										
Aug										
Sep	850	424	985	267	2,392	1,345	1,774	1,534	903	922
Oct										
Nov										
Dec	847	427	1,000	259	2,444	1,339	1,772	1,534	907	922
1996 Jan										
Feb										
Mar	842	425	992	265	2,449	1,335	1,771	1,526	905	928
Apr										
May										
Jun	856	430	985	267	2,487	1,329	1,771	1,527	915	928
Jul										
Aug										
Sep	866	431	990	266	2,500	1,330	1,802	1,535	917	943
Oct										
Nov										
Dec	872	439	994	271	2,527	1,309	1,765	1,543	926	940
1997 Jan										
Feb										
Mar	**869**	**470**	**1,010**	**288**	**2,516**	**1,303**	**1,768**	**1,549**	**905**	**921**
Apr										
May										
Jun										

Note: Estimates for groups of industry classes are now seasonally adjusted from June 1978 for quarterly data and from September 1984 for monthly data. For unadjusted figures, please see *Tables 1.3* and *1.4*.
+ These figures do not cover all employees in national and local government. They exclude those engaged in, for example, building, education and health. Members of HM forces are excluded.
* Excludes private domestic service.

EMPLOYMENT
Employees in employment: industry: production industries: unadjusted

THOUSANDS

GREAT BRITAIN SIC 1992	Section, sub-section or group	Mar 1996 Male	Female	All	Mar 1997 Male	Female	All	1997 Jan All	Feb	Mar	Apr	May	June
PRODUCTION INDUSTRIES	C-E	2,966.2	1,182.3	4,148.5	2,955.4	1,148.3	4,103.8	4,133.4	4,135.5	4,148.5	4,088.7	4,084.6	4,101.7
MINING AND QUARRYING	C	55.6	7.8	63.4	53.9	9.2	63.1	63.7	63.5	63.4	63.4	62.3	63.3
Mining and quarrying of energy Producing materials	CA (10-12)	29.6	4.6	34.2	31.6	5.7	37.3	34.8	35.2	34.2	34.3	33.4	35.1
Mining	10/12	9.6	0.6	10.2	9.1	0.6	9.7	10.9	10.9	10.2	10.7	10.6	10.3
Oil & natural gas extraction & incidental services	11	20.0	4.0	24.0	22.4	5.2	27.6	23.9	24.3	24.0	23.6	22.8	24.8
Mining and quarrying except of energy producing materials	CB (13/14)	26.1	3.2	29.2	22.4	3.5	25.8	28.8	28.3	29.2	29.1	28.9	28.2
MANUFACTURING	D	2,793.2	1,138.5	3,931.7	2,802.8	1,110.5	3,913.3	3,915.1	3,917.8	3,931.7	3,903.5	3,901.5	3,912.6
Manufacture of food products, beverages and tobacco	DA	266.7	160.1	426.8	265.8	163.3	429.1	431.6	432.5	426.8	431.6	430.7	432.3
of food	15.1-15.8	227.7	145.9	373.5	231.1	146.0	377.1	378.2	379.5	373.5	377.3	376.5	378.4
of beverages & tobacco	15.9/16	39.0	14.3	53.3	34.7	17.3	52.1	53.4	53.0	53.3	54.4	54.2	54.0
Manufacture of textiles & textile products	DB	132.2	181.3	313.5	135.5	189.5	325.0	314.3	311.8	313.5	313.2	313.1	312.0
of textiles	17	94.6	76.9	171.5	93.3	80.5	173.8	172.5	171.1	171.5	170.5	170.0	167.7
of made-up textile articles, except apparel	17.4	14.2	19.5	33.7	12.3	21.3	33.6	34.1	33.5	33.7	34.3	33.9	32.7
of textiles, excluding made-up textiles	Rest of 17	80.4	57.3	137.8	81.0	59.2	140.2	138.4	137.6	137.8	136.2	136.1	135.0
of wearing apparel; dressing & dyeing of fur	18	37.6	104.5	142.0	42.2	109.0	151.2	141.9	140.7	142.0	142.7	143.1	144.3
Manufacture of leather & leather products including footwear	DC	19.6	15.7	35.3	20.2	14.8	35.0	36.3	36.0	35.3	35.4	35.0	35.6
of leather and leather goods	19.1/19.2	8.0	4.9	13.0	7.7	4.6	12.3	13.0	13.1	13.0	12.8	12.4	12.9
of footwear	19.3	11.6	10.8	22.4	12.5	10.1	22.6	23.3	23.0	22.4	22.5	22.6	22.7
Manufacture of wood & wood products	DD (20)	61.5	25.4	87.0	64.6	15.0	79.7	73.6	72.8	87.0	82.7	82.9	78.4
Manufacture of pulp, paper & paper products; publishing & printing	DE	283.4	164.9	448.3	280.0	162.4	442.4	447.2	449.2	448.3	444.1	444.6	446.3
of pulp, paper & paper products	21	81.8	34.8	116.7	80.4	36.7	117.1	115.5	117.6	116.7	116.7	117.3	116.9
of corrugated paper & paperboard, sacks & bags, cartons, boxes, cases and other containers	21.21	30.4	11.5	41.9	32.7	10.3	43.0	..	..	41.9	41.4	41.6	42.1
of pulp, paper, sanitary goods, stationery, wallpaper and paper products nec	Rest of 21	51.4	23.4	74.8	47.7	26.3	74.1	..	..	74.8	75.3	75.7	74.8
Publishing, printing & reproduction of recorded media	22	201.6	130.1	331.6	199.6	125.8	325.3	331.8	331.6	331.6	327.4	327.2	329.4
printing & service activities related to printing	22.2	138.1	61.9	200.0	135.9	58.7	194.5	..	..	200.0	196.5	196.8	198.4
publishing & reproduction of recorded media	Rest of 22	63.5	68.2	131.6	63.7	67.1	130.8	..	..	131.6	130.9	130.4	131.0
Manufacture of coke, refined petroleum products & nuclear fuel	DF (23)	24.2	5.2	29.4	26.5	5.2	31.7	28.9	28.8	29.4	29.0	29.1	28.9
of refined petroleum products	23.2	14.2	3.2	17.4	16.8	3.4	20.2	16.9	16.8	17.4	17.2	17.3	17.1
Manufacture of chemicals, chemical products & man-made fibres	DG (24)	174.1	76.5	250.6	173.4	71.9	245.3	248.0	248.1	250.6	250.2	251.4	252.2
Manufacture of rubber and plastic products	DH (25)	163.3	55.5	218.8	171.1	51.7	222.8	221.2	219.9	218.8	219.8	219.0	221.0
Manufacture of other non-metallic mineral products	DI (26)	105.9	31.0	136.9	102.1	29.0	131.2	136.8	135.7	136.9	134.7	134.1	133.5
Manufacture of basic metals and fabricated metal products	DJ	465.3	87.8	553.0	470.8	82.6	553.4	550.7	556.9	553.0	551.8	551.5	550.2
of basic metals	27	116.5	15.0	131.5	113.8	13.6	127.5	133.2	133.0	131.5	130.5	130.7	130.1
of fabricated metal products, except machinery	28	348.8	72.8	421.6	357.0	68.9	425.9	417.5	423.9	421.6	421.3	420.8	420.1
Manufacture of machinery & eqpt. nec	DK (29)	323.7	74.1	397.8	324.5	74.0	398.5	403.3	404.3	397.8	398.5	398.5	400.6
Manufacture of electrical & optical equipment	DL	327.9	165.0	492.9	322.8	163.7	486.5	481.8	481.6	492.9	487.1	488.2	490.4
of office machinery & computers	30	36.1	16.8	52.9	35.7	13.0	48.7	52.2	52.3	52.9	51.0	51.2	50.6
of electrical machinery & apparatus nec	31	116.9	56.8	173.7	119.9	59.1	179.0	167.6	166.3	173.7	174.7	175.1	176.9
of electric motors, etc; control apparatus & insulated cable	31.1-31.3	69.5	33.6	103.1	72.9	35.4	108.3	97.8	96.6	103.1	103.1	103.4	103.9
of accumulators, primary cells, batteries, lighting eqpt., lamps & electrical eqpt. nec	31.4-31.6	47.4	23.2	70.6	46.9	23.7	70.6	69.8	69.6	70.6	71.6	71.7	73.0
of radio, television & communication eqpt.	32	76.9	44.4	121.2	70.8	42.7	113.5	120.1	120.5	121.2	117.5	118.7	118.9
of electronic components	32.1	34.0	19.8	53.8	32.4	19.0	51.4	53.4	53.8	53.8	51.1	51.9	51.5
of radio & TV and telephone apparatus; sound & video recorders etc.	32.2-32.3	42.9	24.6	67.4	38.3	23.7	62.1	66.7	66.7	67.4	66.4	66.7	67.4
of medical, precision & optical eqpt; watches	33	98.0	47.1	145.1	96.5	48.8	145.3	141.9	142.6	145.1	144.0	143.3	144.1
Manufacture of transport equipment	DM	313.8	44.2	357.9	318.9	44.7	363.6	359.0	358.4	357.9	355.7	354.4	360.8
of motor vehicles, trailers	34	179.2	26.5	205.7	178.5	28.3	206.8	207.1	207.5	205.7	208.9	208.3	208.4
of other transport equipment	35	134.5	17.7	152.2	140.3	16.5	156.8	151.8	150.9	152.2	146.8	146.0	152.3
of aircraft and spacecraft	35.3	84.8	11.7	96.6	88.1	11.2	99.3	..	..	96.6	93.7	93.2	96.2
of other transport equipment except aircraft & spacecraft	Rest of 35	49.7	5.9	55.6	52.3	5.2	57.5	..	..	55.6	53.1	52.9	56.1
Manufacturing nec	DN	131.8	51.7	183.5	126.6	42.6	169.2	182.2	181.8	183.5	169.6	169.0	170.3
of furniture	36.1	82.7	24.8	107.4	83.3	22.8	106.1	109.5	109.4	107.4	104.7	103.9	104.6
ELECTRICITY, GAS AND WATER SUPPLY	E	117.4	36.0	153.4	98.7	28.7	127.3	154.6	154.1	153.4	121.8	120.8	125.7
Electricity, gas, steam and hot water supply	40	86.0	25.2	111.2	67.3	18.0	85.3	112.6	112.3	111.2	81.1	79.1	83.9
Collection, purification and distribution of water	41	31.3	10.8	42.2	31.4	10.7	42.0	42.0	41.9	42.2	40.7	41.7	41.9

P Provisional
R Revised

GREAT BRITAIN SIC 1992	Section, sub-section or group	1996 Jul	Aug	Sep	Oct	Nov	Dec	1997 Jan	Feb	Mar	Apr P	May P	June P
PRODUCTION INDUSTRIES	C-E	4,128.5	4,133.1	4,135.9	4,146.4	4,138.4	4,140.8	4,111.4	4,095.6	4,103.8	4,105.8	4,106.9	4,125.2
MINING AND QUARRYING	C	62.2	62.0	62.5	63.0	63.1	62.7	64.2	63.3	63.1	63.8	64.7	64.9
Mining and quarrying of energy Producing materials	CA (10-12)	33.4	34.0	36.1	36.4	36.4	35.9	37.6	37.0	37.3	37.8	38.3	38.7
Mining	10/12	10.7	10.7	10.0	10.1	10.1	9.5	9.5	9.5	9.7	10.1	10.0	10.1
Oil & natural gas extraction & incidental services	11	22.7	23.3	26.1	26.3	26.3	26.4	28.1	27.5	27.6	27.7	28.2	28.6
Mining and quarrying except of energy producing materials	CB (13/14)	28.8	28.0	26.4	26.7	26.7	26.8	26.6	26.3	25.8	25.9	26.5	26.2
MANUFACTURING	D	3,949.8	3,955.2	3,950.0	3,958.5	3,952.3	3,954.8	3,920.2	3,904.9	3,913.3	3,914.9	3,916.2	3,933.7
Manufacture of food products, beverages and tobacco	DA	443.3	445.8	446.1	446.7	449.7	445.8	432.5	430.4	429.1	427.2	429.7	433.2
of food	15.1-15.8	387.1	389.2	390.0	389.6	393.7	390.2	379.1	377.2	377.1	375.0	377.2	379.7
of beverages & tobacco	15.9/16	56.2	56.6	56.1	57.1	56.1	55.6	53.4	53.2	52.1	52.2	52.4	53.5
Manufacture of textiles & textile products	DB	319.3	319.7	320.1	322.6	321.7	320.9	327.3	326.4	325.0	327.5	324.5	327.8
of textiles	17	173.3	173.2	172.6	173.2	172.9	173.7	177.1	175.4	173.8	174.7	172.8	176.7
of made-up textile articles, except apparel	17.4	37.9	37.7	35.2	36.1	35.7	35.9	37.2	35.9	33.6	33.4	33.1	36.1
of textiles, excluding made-up textiles	Rest of 17	135.4	135.5	137.4	137.0	137.3	137.8	139.9	139.5	140.2	141.2	139.8	140.6
of wearing apparel; dressing & dyeing of fur	18	146.0	146.5	147.5	149.4	148.8	147.2	150.2	151.1	151.2	152.8	151.6	151.2
Manufacture of leather & leather products including footwear	DC	35.7	35.4	34.0	33.6	33.3	32.9	34.0	33.6	35.0	34.5	34.3	35.1
of leather and leather goods	19.1/19.2	12.9	12.4	11.8	12.2	12.7	12.3	12.2	12.0	12.3	11.6	11.7	12.4
of footwear	19.3	22.8	23.0	22.1	21.4	20.7	20.6	21.8	21.6	22.6	22.9	22.7	22.7
Manufacture of wood & wood products	DD (20)	85.2	85.2	79.6	82.7	83.2	82.9	80.0	77.9	79.7	79.9	81.3	80.3
Manufacture of pulp, paper & paper products; publishing & printing	DE	451.0	449.0	444.3	444.2	442.5	445.2	443.3	443.0	442.4	440.5	441.5	442.9
of pulp, paper & paper products	21	117.9	117.9	117.0	116.5	117.3	117.3	118.5	118.7	117.1	115.8	115.7	115.8
of corrugated paper & paperboard, sacks & bags, cartons, boxes, cases and other containers	21.21	41.9	41.9	41.7	42.3	42.9	43.2	42.8	43.4	43.0	42.6	41.7	42.0
of pulp, paper, sanitary goods, stationery, wallpaper and paper products nec	Rest of 21	76.1	76.0	75.3	74.2	74.4	74.1	75.6	75.3	74.1	73.3	74.0	73.8
Publishing, printing & reproduction of recorded media	22	333.1	331.0	327.3	327.7	325.2	327.9	324.9	324.3	325.3	324.7	325.8	327.2
printing & service activities related to printing	22.2	200.3	198.4	196.4	195.7	193.3	193.5	192.0	192.8	194.5	194.2	194.5	194.9
publishing & reproduction of recorded media	Rest of 22	132.8	132.6	130.9	132.0	131.8	134.4	132.9	131.5	130.8	130.5	131.3	132.3
Manufacture of coke, refined petroleum products & nuclear fuel	DF (23)	28.8	28.9	28.7	28.7	28.2	28.3	28.7	28.5	31.7	31.4	31.2	31.6
of refined petroleum products	23.2	17.1	17.1	17.0	17.1	16.5	16.7	17.1	17.0	20.2	20.1	19.9	20.3
Manufacture of chemicals, chemical products & man-made fibres	DG (24)	251.1	250.2	249.1	246.6	246.2	246.2	246.6	245.7	245.3	246.7	246.7	246.9
Manufacture of rubber and plastic products	DH (25)	218.6	222.0	222.8	221.4	221.0	221.6	222.9	222.5	222.8	220.8	219.8	220.9
Manufacture of other non-metallic mineral products	DI (26)	134.9	134.3	132.7	133.1	133.7	133.6	132.7	132.2	131.2	128.5	128.1	128.1
Manufacture of basic metals and fabricated metal products	DJ	556.1	559.1	555.6	558.2	556.1	556.8	550.7	551.1	553.4	558.8	559.4	563.0
of basic metals	27	130.1	129.9	129.4	128.4	128.8	129.3	127.3	126.7	127.5	127.0	127.3	127.3
of fabricated metal products, except machinery	28	426.1	429.2	426.2	429.8	427.4	427.5	423.4	424.3	425.9	431.8	432.1	435.7
Manufacture of machinery & eqpt. nec	DK (29)	399.2	400.1	401.3	400.5	397.5	400.2	401.8	398.7	398.5	399.9	399.4	401.7
Manufacture of electrical & optical equipment	DL	495.6	496.5	499.5	497.9	495.4	495.9	488.1	484.4	486.5	488.5	490.8	489.7
of office machinery & computers	30	50.9	50.6	50.9	50.6	50.1	51.1	49.1	48.7	48.7	52.5	53.3	53.1
of electrical machinery & apparatus nec	31	177.8	178.0	182.1	181.3	181.1	181.1	180.5	178.1	179.0	179.4	179.1	177.7
of electric motors, etc; control apparatus & insulated cable	31.1-31.3	105.6	105.7	109.5	108.8	107.9	107.9	108.7	106.8	108.3	108.5	108.4	106.9
of accumulators, primary cells, batteries, lighting eqpt., lamps & electrical eqpt. nec	31.4-31.6	72.3	72.3	72.5	72.5	73.2	73.1	71.8	71.3	70.6	70.9	70.7	70.7
of radio, television & communication eqpt.	32	121.9	121.8	120.7	122.1	120.1	118.7	113.6	112.3	113.5	113.0	113.9	113.3
of electronic components	32.1	52.6	52.1	52.3	52.9	51.7	51.8	50.2	50.2	51.4	51.4	52.2	52.3
of radio & TV and telephone apparatus; sound & video recorders etc.	32.2-32.3	69.3	69.7	68.4	69.2	68.5	67.0	63.4	62.2	62.1	61.5	61.7	61.0
of medical, precision & optical eqpt; watches	33	144.9	146.1	145.9	143.9	144.0	144.9	144.9	145.2	145.3	143.7	144.4	145.6
Manufacture of transport equipment	DM	357.5	357.5	361.3	364.5	364.8	365.5	363.3	362.1	363.6	361.3	360.3	363.2
of motor vehicles, trailers	34	210.2	207.0	208.3	209.1	208.7	209.3	207.3	206.5	206.8	205.5	204.7	205.6
of other transport equipment	35	147.3	150.6	153.1	155.4	156.2	156.2	156.0	155.6	156.8	155.8	155.6	157.6
of aircraft and spacecraft	35.3	94.1	94.9	94.9	97.8	98.1	99.3	98.1	98.3	99.3	99.2	99.2	99.1
of other transport equipment except aircraft & spacecraft	Rest of 35	53.2	55.7	58.2	57.6	58.1	56.9	57.9	57.3	57.5	56.6	56.4	58.5
Manufacturing nec	DN	173.6	171.3	174.8	177.8	178.8	179.0	168.3	168.3	169.2	169.5	169.3	169.3
of furniture	36.1	106.5	105.4	108.9	111.3	111.9	113.3	106.1	105.6	106.1	106.5	107.6	107.3
ELECTRICITY, GAS AND WATER SUPPLY	E	116.5	115.9	123.3	124.9	123.0	123.2	127.1	127.5	127.3	127.1	125.9	126.6
Electricity, gas, steam and hot water supply	40	75.2	74.7	82.4	83.5	81.9	82.0	85.3	85.6	85.3	85.6	84.8	85.4
Collection, purification and distribution of water	41	41.4	41.2	40.9	41.4	41.1	41.2	41.7	41.8	42.0	41.5	41.1	41.2

P Provisional
R Revised

Index 1990=100

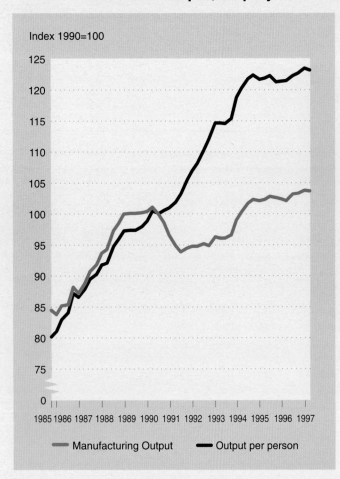

Manufacturing Output — Output per person

Index 1990=100

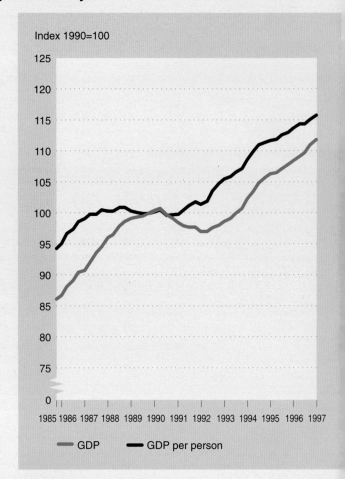

GDP — GDP per person

Seasonally adjusted (1990=100)

UNITED KINGDOM	Whole economy			Production industries			Manufacturing industries		
SIC 1992	Output *	Workforce in employment +	Output per person employed	Output	Workforce in employment +	Output per person employed	Output	Workforce in employment +	Output per person employed
1989	99.4	99.4	100.0	100.3	102.9	97.5	100.1	102.7	97.5
1990	100.0	100.0	100.0	100.0	100.0	100.0	100.0	100.0	100.0
1991	97.9	97.1	100.8	96.6	92.5	104.6	95.0	92.3	102.9
1992	97.4	94.6	102.9	97.0	86.8	111.8	94.9	86.8	109.4
1993	99.6	93.6	106.3	99.1	83.1	119.3	96.3	83.8	114.9
1994	104.0	94.4	110.2	104.4	82.2	127.1	100.8	83.4	120.8
1995	106.9	95.2	112.3	106.7	82.3	129.5	102.5	84.1	121.8
1996	109.5	95.8	114.4	106.8	82.4	129.7	102.8	84.2	122.0
1989 Q1	99.1	98.7	100.3	99.9	103.2	96.9	100.0	102.8	97.3
Q2	99.3	99.3	100.1	99.9	103.0	97.0	100.1	102.8	97.4
Q3	99.5	99.6	99.9	100.5	102.9	97.7	100.1	102.8	97.4
Q4	99.9	100.0	99.9	100.8	102.4	98.5	100.2	102.3	98.0
1990 Q1	100.4	100.1	100.2	100.0	101.6	98.4	100.4	101.5	98.9
Q2	100.7	100.3	100.5	101.4	100.7	100.7	101.1	100.6	100.5
Q3	99.7	100.1	99.6	99.7	99.7	100.0	99.9	99.8	100.1
Q4	99.2	99.5	99.7	98.8	98.0	100.9	98.6	98.0	100.6
1991 Q1	98.4	98.5	99.8	97.7	95.6	102.1	96.6	95.6	101.0
Q2	97.9	97.4	100.5	96.5	93.2	103.6	94.9	93.1	101.9
Q3	97.7	96.6	101.2	95.7	91.3	104.8	93.9	91.0	103.2
Q4	97.7	95.9	101.8	96.7	89.8	107.6	94.5	89.6	105.5
1992 Q1	97.0	95.7	101.4	96.7	88.7	109.0	94.8	88.6	107.0
Q2	97.0	95.2	101.9	96.2	87.7	109.7	94.8	87.6	108.2
Q3	97.6	94.2	103.6	97.2	86.2	112.8	95.2	86.3	110.3
Q4	98.0	93.5	104.8	97.7	84.5	115.7	94.9	84.6	112.1
1993 Q1	98.6	93.5	105.5	98.0	83.7	117.2	96.3	84.0	114.7
Q2	99.1	93.5	105.9	98.3	83.3	118.1	96.1	83.8	114.7
Q3	99.9	93.7	106.6	99.4	82.9	119.9	96.1	83.8	114.6
Q4	100.7	93.9	107.2	100.7	82.5	122.0	96.6	83.7	115.4
1994 Q1	102.2	94.0	108.6	102.3	82.3	124.3	99.0	83.3	118.8
Q2	103.5	94.1	110.0	104.1	82.1	126.8	100.3	83.4	120.3
Q3	104.8	94.5	111.0	105.6	82.1	128.7	101.7	83.5	121.8
Q4	105.7	94.9	111.4	105.7	82.1	128.6	102.3	83.5	122.4
1995 Q1	106.3	95.1	111.7	106.2	82.2	129.2	102.1	83.9	121.7
Q2	106.5	95.2	111.9	106.3	82.3	129.1	102.3	84.0	121.9
Q3	107.1	95.1	112.6	107.1	82.2	130.3	102.8	84.0	122.3
Q4	107.8	95.4	113.0	107.0	82.6	129.5	102.6	84.6	121.3
1996 Q1	108.4	95.4	113.7	107.2	82.5	129.9	102.4	84.3	121.4
Q2	109.1	95.4	114.4	107.5	81.8	131.4	102.1	84.1	121.5
Q3	109.7	95.9	114.4	108.2	81.5	132.7	103.2	84.4	122.3
Q4	110.9	96.3	115.1	108.6	81.5	133.3	103.3	84.2	122.7
1997 Q1	111.8	96.6	115.8	108.4	81.5	133.1	103.8	84.1	123.5
Q2	**NA**	**NA**	**NA**	**108.8**	**81.7**	**133.2**	**103.7**	**84.2**	**123.2**

* Gross domestic product for whole economy.
+ The workforce in employment comprises: employees in employment, the self-employed, HM Forces and participants in work-related government-supported training and employment programmes.
This series is used as a denominator for the productivity calculations for the reasons explained on page S6 of the August 1988 issue of *Employment Gazette*.
The Manufacturing index has been rebased from 1988=100 to 1990=100, in common with other economic series. Figures on a 1988=100 basis were last published in *Employment Gazette*, September 1993.

2.1 CLAIMANT COUNT
UK summary

	MALE AND FEMALE						UNEMPLOYED BY DURATION		
	UNEMPLOYED		SEASONALLY ADJUSTED #						
	Number	Per cent workforce *	Number	Per cent workforce *	Change since previous month	Average change over 3 months ended	Up to 4 weeks	Over 4 weeks aged under 60	Over 4 weeks aged 60 and over
1993)	2,919.2	10.3	2,900.6	10.3					
1994) Annual	2,636.5	9.4	2,619.3	9.3					
1995) averages	2,325.6	8.3	2,308.2	8.2					
1996)	2,122.2	7.6	2,104.0	7.5					
1995 Jul 13	2,336.2	8.3	2,311.0	8.2	-2.1	-6.9	325	1,991	21
Aug 10	2,350.2	8.4	2,290.0	8.2	-21.0	-10.1	263	2,068	20
Sep 14	2,292.2	8.2	2,264.0	8.1	-26.0	-16.4	256	2,017	20
Oct 12	2,212.3	7.9	2,264.6	8.1	0.6	-15.5	251	1,942	19
Nov 9	2,196.1	7.8	2,244.6	8.0	-20.0	-15.1	242	1,935	19
Dec 14	2,228.2	7.9	2,235.5	8.0	-9.1	-9.5	236	1,972	19
1996 Jan 11	2,310.5	8.2	2,206.8	7.9	-28.7	-19.3	252	2,037	20
Feb 8	2,303.0	8.2	2,212.3	7.9	5.5	-10.8	243	2,039	21
Mar 14	2,230.8	7.9	2,186.7	7.8	-25.6	-16.3	206	2,005	20
Apr 11	2,223.9	7.9	2,182.4	7.8	-4.3	-8.1	236	1,968	20
May 9	2,147.4	7.6	2,166.3	7.7	-16.1	-15.3	196	1,931	20
Jun 13	2,096.3	7.5	2,150.3	7.7	-16.0	-12.1	203	1,874	19
Jul 11	2,158.1	7.7	2,126.0	7.6	-24.3	-18.8	299	1,841	19
Aug 8	2,176.4	7.7	2,108.7	7.5	-17.3	-19.2	244	1,914	19
Sep 12	2,103.7	7.5	2,070.8	7.4	-37.9	-26.5	226	1,860	18
Oct 10	1,977.2	7.0	2,025.2	7.2	-45.6	-33.6	213	1,747	17
Nov 14	1,871.4	6.7	1,929.8	6.9	-95.4	-59.6	208	1,648	15
Dec 12	1,868.2	6.6	1,883.1	6.7	-46.7	-62.6	204	1,649	15
1997 Jan 9	1,907.8	6.8	1,814.5	6.5	-68.6	-70.2	223	1,670	15
Feb 13	1,827.8	6.5	1,748.1	6.2	-66.4	-60.6	211	1,603	13
Mar 13	1,745.3	6.2	1,710.8	6.1	-37.3	-57.4	196	1,538	12
Apr 10	1,688.0	6.0	1,654.4	5.9	-56.4	-53.4	202	1,476	10
May 8	1,620.5	5.8	1,637.3	5.8	-17.1	-36.9	189	1,422	10
Jun 12 R	1,550.1	5.5	1,599.8	5.7	-37.5	-37.0	192	1,349	9
Jul 10 P	**1,585.3**	**5.6**	**1,550.0**	**5.5**	**-49.8**	**-34.8**	**260**	**1,316**	**9**

2.2 CLAIMANT COUNT
GB summary

	Number	Per cent workforce *	Number	Per cent workforce *	Change since previous month	Average change over 3 months ended	Up to 4 weeks	Over 4 weeks aged under 60	Over 4 weeks aged 60 and over
1993)	2,814.1	10.2	2,796.9	10.2					
1994) Annual	2,539.2	9.3	2,522.3	9.2					
1995) averages	2,237.4	8.2	2,220.1	8.1					
1996)	2,038.1	7.5	2,020.0	7.4					
1995 Jul 13	2,244.3	8.2	2,222.7	8.1	-2.8	-6.8	315	1,909	19
Aug 10	2,258.2	8.3	2,202.9	8.1	-19.8	-9.7	256	1,983	19
Sep 14	2,202.1	8.1	2,177.5	8.0	-25.4	-16.0	248	1,936	19
Oct 12	2,126.8	7.8	2,178.2	8.0	0.7	-14.8	244	1,864	19
Nov 9	2,111.9	7.7	2,158.2	7.9	-20.0	-14.9	236	1,857	18
Dec 14	2,144.1	7.8	2,149.2	7.9	-9.0	-9.4	231	1,894	19
1996 Jan 11	2,224.2	8.1	2,121.0	7.8	-28.2	-19.1	246	1,958	20
Feb 8	2,217.2	8.1	2,126.5	7.8	5.5	-10.6	237	1,960	20
Mar 14	2,146.4	7.9	2,101.4	7.7	-25.1	-15.9	200	1,926	20
Apr 11	2,138.4	7.8	2,096.4	7.7	-5.0	-8.2	230	1,889	19
May 9	2,064.7	7.6	2,080.6	7.6	-15.8	-15.3	191	1,854	19
Jun 11	2,011.7	7.4	2,063.6	7.6	-17.0	-12.6	195	1,799	19
Jul 11	2,067.3	7.6	2,039.3	7.5	-24.3	-19.0	288	1,762	18
Aug 8	2,083.9	7.6	2,021.3	7.4	-18.0	-19.8	238	1,828	18
Sep 12	2,014.9	7.4	1,985.0	7.3	-36.3	-26.2	218	1,778	17
Oct 10	1,895.7	6.9	1,942.8	7.1	-42.2	-32.2	207	1,672	16
Nov 14	1,797.5	6.6	1,853.8	6.8	-89.0	-55.8	203	1,580	15
Dec 12	1,836.9	6.6	1,808.8	6.6	0.0	-44.7	218	1,604	15
1997 Jan 9	1,836.9	6.7	1,743.5	6.4	-65.3	-36.8	218	1,604	15
Feb 13	1,760.2	6.4	1,679.9	6.1	-63.6	-43.0	206	1,541	13
Mar 13	1,679.5	6.1	1,643.8	6.0	-36.1	-55.0	191	1,477	12
Apr 10	1,624.1	5.9	1,589.6	5.8	-54.2	-51.3	197	1,417	10
May 8	1,559.2	5.7	1,573.1	5.8	-16.5	-35.6	184	1,365	9
Jun 12 R	1,489.3	5.4	1,537.2	5.6	-35.9	-35.5	185	1,295	9
Jul 10 P	**1,520.1**	**5.6**	**1,489.5**	**5.5**	**-47.7**	**-33.4**	**251**	**1,261**	**8**

P The latest national and regional seasonally-adjusted claimant count figures are provisional and subject to revision, mainly in the following month.
R Revised.
* National and regional claimant count rates are calculated by expressing the number of unemployed claimants as a percentage of the estimated total workforce (the sum of unemployed claimants, employees in employment, self-employed, HM Forces and participants on work-related government training programmes) at mid-1996 for 1996 and 1997 figures and at the corresponding mid-year estimates for earlier years.

MALE UNEMPLOYED Number	Per cent workforce *	SEASONALLY ADJUSTED # Number	Per cent workforce *	FEMALE UNEMPLOYED Number	Per cent workforce *	SEASONALLY ADJUSTED # Number	Per cent workforce *	MARRIED Number		
2,236.1	14.0	2,225.7	13.9	683.1	5.6	674.9	5.5		1993)	
2,014.4	12.7	2,004.8	12.7	622.1	5.1	614.6	5.0		1994)	Annual
1,770.0	11.2	1,760.2	11.2	555.6	4.5	548.1	4.4		1995)	averages
1,610.3	10.3	1,599.9	10.2	511.9	4.1	504.1	4.1		1996)	
1,758.6	11.2	1,759.6	11.2	577.5	4.7	551.4	4.5	143.1	1995	Jul 13
1,753.7	11.1	1,744.4	11.1	596.4	4.8	545.6	4.4	152.1		Aug 10
1,724.0	11.0	1,727.0	11.0	568.2	4.6	537.0	4.3	139.2		Sep 14
1,676.4	10.7	1,724.6	11.0	535.9	4.3	540.0	4.4	133.4		Oct 12
1,670.7	10.6	1,708.9	10.9	525.5	4.3	535.7	4.3	131.1		Nov 9
1,707.2	10.8	1,704.2	10.8	521.0	4.2	531.3	4.3	131.4		Dec 14
1,766.4	11.3	1,680.9	10.7	544.1	4.4	525.9	4.2	138.2	1996	Jan 11
1,761.0	11.2	1,687.2	10.8	541.9	4.4	525.1	4.2	136.6		Feb 8
1,707.2	10.9	1,666.3	10.6	523.6	4.2	520.4	4.2	132.0		Mar 14
1,695.5	10.8	1,659.9	10.6	528.5	4.3	522.5	4.2	138.7		Apr 11
1,643.9	10.5	1,647.5	10.5	503.5	4.1	518.8	4.2	128.4		May 9
1,599.5	10.2	1,631.4	10.4	496.8	4.0	518.9	4.2	125.0		Jun 13
1,616.5	10.3	1,613.5	10.3	541.6	4.4	512.5	4.1	133.1		Jul 11
1,614.1	10.3	1,600.0	10.2	562.4	4.5	508.7	4.1	142.9		Aug 8
1,572.4	10.0	1,572.0	10.0	531.4	4.3	498.8	4.0	128.5		Sep 12
1,492.6	9.5	1,537.5	9.8	484.6	3.9	487.7	3.9	116.5		Oct 10
1,424.1	9.1	1,469.9	9.4	447.3	3.6	459.9	3.7	105.5		Nov 14
1,430.5	9.1	1,432.9	9.1	437.7	3.5	450.2	3.6	102.5		Dec 12
1,463.5	9.3	1,384.7	8.8	444.3	3.6	429.8	3.5	104.7	1997	Jan 9
1,403.3	9.0	1,335.8	8.5	424.5	3.4	412.3	3.3	96.5		Feb 13
1,342.4	8.6	1,307.5	8.3	402.9	3.2	403.3	3.2	89.9		Mar 13
1,298.8	8.3	1,270.0	8.1	389.1	3.1	384.4	3.1	86.6		Apr 10
1,249.9	8.0	1,251.4	8.0	370.6	3.0	385.9	3.1	80.9		May 8
1,193.3	7.6	1,222.4	7.8	356.8	2.9	377.4	3.0	76.8		Jun 12 R
1,201.3	**7.7**	**1,193.7**	**7.6**	**384.0**	**3.1**	**356.3**	**2.9**	**80.4**		**Jul 10 P**

MALE UNEMPLOYED Number	Per cent workforce *	SEASONALLY ADJUSTED # Number	Per cent workforce *	FEMALE UNEMPLOYED Number	Per cent workforce *	SEASONALLY ADJUSTED # Number	Per cent workforce *	MARRIED Number		
2,155.4	13.9	2,145.7	13.8	658.8	5.5	651.2	5.5		1993)	
1,939.1	12.6	1,929.5	12.6	600.1	5.0	592.8	4.9		1994)	Annual
1,701.4	11.1	1,691.5	11.1	536.1	4.5	528.6	4.4		1995)	averages
1,545.3	10.1	1,535.0	10.1	492.8	4.1	485.1	4.0		1996)	
1,689.4	11.0	1,691.3	11.1	554.9	4.6	531.4	4.4	136.5	1995	Jul 13
1,684.7	11.0	1,676.7	11.0	573.5	4.8	526.2	4.4	145.2		Aug 10
1,655.2	10.8	1,659.6	10.9	546.9	4.5	517.9	4.3	133.5		Sep 14
1,609.8	10.5	1,657.1	10.8	517.0	4.3	521.1	4.3	128.1		Oct 12
1,604.5	10.5	1,641.5	10.7	507.4	4.2	516.7	4.3	125.9		Nov 9
1,640.7	10.7	1,636.9	10.7	503.4	4.2	512.3	4.3	126.2		Dec 14
1,698.4	11.2	1,614.0	10.6	525.9	4.3	507.0	4.2	132.9	1996	Jan 11
1,693.3	11.1	1,620.3	10.6	524.0	4.3	506.2	4.2	131.3		Feb 8
1,640.5	10.8	1,599.9	10.5	505.8	4.2	501.5	4.1	126.7		Mar 14
1,628.6	10.7	1,593.3	10.5	509.7	4.2	503.1	4.2	132.6		Apr 11
1,578.7	10.4	1,581.0	10.4	486.0	4.0	499.6	4.1	123.1		May 9
1,534.0	10.1	1,564.6	10.3	477.7	3.9	499.0	4.1	119.6		Jun 13
1,549.0	10.2	1,547.0	10.2	518.3	4.3	492.3	4.1	125.9		Jul 11
1,545.8	10.2	1,533.2	10.1	538.1	4.4	488.1	4.0	135.3		Aug 8
1,505.0	9.9	1,506.1	9.9	509.1	4.2	478.9	4.0	122.2		Sep 12
1,429.8	9.4	1,474.0	9.7	465.8	3.8	468.8	3.9	111.1		Oct 10
1,366.3	9.0	1,410.9	9.3	431.2	3.6	442.9	3.7	100.9		Nov 14
1,373.9	9.0	1,375.3	9.0	422.4	3.5	433.5	3.6	98.3		Dec 12
1,407.4	9.2	1,329.5	8.7	429.5	3.5	414.0	3.4	100.7	1997	Jan 9
1,349.5	8.9	1,282.6	8.4	410.8	3.4	397.3	3.3	93.1		Feb 13
1,289.8	8.5	1,255.1	8.2	389.7	3.2	388.7	3.2	86.7		Mar 13
1,247.7	8.2	1,218.7	8.0	376.4	3.1	370.9	3.1	83.6		Apr 10
1,200.7	7.9	1,200.9	7.9	358.5	3.0	372.2	3.1	78.2		May 8
1,145.1	7.5	1,173.1	7.7	344.2	2.8	364.1	3.0	74.2		Jun 12 R
1,151.4	**7.6**	**1,145.3**	**7.5**	**368.7**	**3.0**	**344.2**	**2.8**	**77.2**		**Jul 10 P**

The seasonally-adjusted series takes account of past discontinuities to be consistent with the current coverage of the count (see *Employment Gazette*, December 1990, p 608 for the list of discontinuities taken into account, and p S16 of the April 1994 issue). To maintain a consistent assessment, the seasonally-adjusted series relates only to claimants aged 18 and over.

THOUSANDS

	CLAIMANTS			PER CENT WORKFORCE *			SEASONALLY ADJUSTED #					
	All	Male	Female	All	Male	Female	Number	Per cent workforce *	Change since previous month	Average change over 3 months ended	Male	Female
NORTH EAST												
1993)	149.6	119.8	29.8	13.0	18.3	6.0	148.7	12.9			119.3	29.4
1994) Annual	141.6	113.5	28.1	12.4	17.8	5.6	141.2	12.4			113.3	27.9
1995) average	130.5	104.4	26.1	11.5	16.5	5.2	130.3	11.5			104.2	26.1
1996)	118.4	94.0	24.4	10.6	15.3	4.8	118.0	10.6			93.8	24.3
1996 Jul 11	119.3	93.7	25.6	10.7	15.3	5.1	118.9	10.7	-1.1	-1.6	94.2	24.7
Aug 8	118.6	92.2	26.4	10.6	15.0	5.2	117.4	10.5	-1.5	-1.5	93.3	24.1
Sep 12	115.5	90.2	25.3	10.3	14.7	5.0	115.0	10.3	-2.4	-1.7	91.0	24.0
Oct 10	108.9	85.9	23.1	9.8	14.0	4.6	112.1	10.0	-2.9	-2.3	88.6	23.5
Nov 14	105.2	83.9	21.3	9.4	13.7	4.2	107.3	9.6	-4.8	-3.4	85.5	21.8
Dec 12	104.7	84.1	20.7	9.4	13.7	4.1	105.5	9.5	-1.8	-3.2	83.6	21.9
1997 Jan 9	107.3	85.9	21.4	9.6	14.0	4.3	101.8	9.1	-3.7	-3.4	80.9	20.9
Feb 13	102.6	81.9	20.7	9.2	13.4	4.1	98.8	8.8	-3.0	-2.8	78.7	20.1
Mar 13	99.4	79.5	19.9	8.9	13.0	3.9	97.4	8.7	-1.4	-2.7	77.7	19.7
Apr 10	97.8	78.2	19.6	8.8	12.8	3.9	94.8	8.5	-2.6	-2.3	76.1	18.7
May 8	94.4	75.7	18.8	8.5	12.3	3.7	94.6	8.5	-0.2	-1.4	75.4	19.2
Jun 12 R	91.2	73.0	18.1	8.2	11.9	3.6	93.6	8.4	-1.0	-1.3	74.6	19.0
Jul 10 P	**93.9**	**74.2**	**19.7**	**8.4**	**12.1**	**3.9**	**92.3**	**8.3**	**-1.3**	**-0.8**	**73.9**	**18.4**
NORTH WEST												
1993)	248.1	192.7	55.4	9.5	13.1	4.9	246.2	9.5			191.6	54.6
1994) Annual	221.2	171.5	49.7	8.7	11.9	4.5	220.5	8.7			171.1	49.4
1995) average	192.2	148.8	43.4	7.6	10.5	3.9	188.6	7.4			148.4	40.2
1996)	175.8	136.1	39.7	6.9	9.5	3.5	175.3	6.8			135.9	39.5
1996 Jul 11	178.9	137.0	41.9	7.0	9.6	3.7	178.2	7.0	-2.0	-1.5	136.6	41.6
Aug 8	180.9	136.8	44.1	7.1	9.6	3.9	175.7	6.9	-2.5	-2.0	135.4	40.3
Sep 12	173.9	132.8	41.1	6.8	9.3	3.6	170.8	6.7	-4.9	-3.1	132.9	37.9
Oct 10	161.9	124.9	37.0	6.3	8.7	3.3	168.5	6.6	-2.3	-3.2	131.3	37.2
Nov 14	153.1	119.1	34.0	6.0	8.3	3.0	160.5	6.3	-8.0	-5.1	125.3	35.2
Dec 12	154.1	120.8	33.3	6.0	8.4	2.9	157.7	6.2	-2.8	-4.4	123.2	34.5
1997 Jan 9	160.9	125.7	35.2	6.3	8.8	3.1	151.2	5.9	-6.5	-5.8	118.6	32.6
Feb 13	154.0	120.6	33.4	6.0	8.4	2.9	142.7	5.6	-8.5	-5.9	112.2	30.5
Mar 13	146.6	115.0	31.5	5.7	8.0	2.8	141.4	5.5	-1.3	-5.4	111.0	30.4
Apr 10	141.7	111.3	30.4	5.5	7.8	2.7	137.2	5.4	-4.2	-4.7	107.6	29.6
May 8	135.2	106.7	28.5	5.3	7.5	2.5	135.6	5.3	-1.6	-2.4	106.0	29.6
Jun 12 R	127.6	100.3	27.3	5.0	7.0	2.4	132.0	5.1	-3.6	-3.1	102.9	29.1
Jul 10 P	**131.9**	**101.8**	**30.1**	**5.1**	**7.1**	**2.7**	**128.1**	**5.0**	**-3.9**	**-3.0**	**100.7**	**27.4**
MERSEYSIDE												
1993)	95.9	75.2	20.7	15.2	21.8	7.3	95.2	15.1			74.8	20.4
1994) Annual	88.5	69.2	19.3	14.9	21.5	7.1	88.2	14.8			69.0	19.2
1995) average	79.5	61.9	17.6	13.7	19.5	6.7	79.4	13.7			61.8	17.6
1996)	74.9	58.3	16.5	13.1	18.8	6.3	74.7	13.0			58.2	16.4
1996 Jul 11	76.6	59.1	17.5	13.4	19.0	6.7	75.3	13.1	-0.6	-0.3	58.6	16.7
Aug 8	76.8	58.8	18.0	13.4	18.9	6.8	75.2	13.1	-0.1	-0.2	58.4	16.8
Sep 12	75.5	58.1	17.4	13.2	18.7	6.6	74.0	12.9	-1.2	-0.6	57.7	16.3
Oct 10	71.3	55.5	15.8	12.4	17.9	6.0	73.0	12.7	-1.0	-0.8	56.9	16.1
Nov 14	68.0	53.4	14.7	11.9	17.2	5.6	70.3	12.3	-2.7	-1.6	55.1	15.2
Dec 12	68.1	53.6	14.5	11.9	17.2	5.5	69.3	12.1	-1.0	-1.6	54.3	15.0
1997 Jan 9	69.7	54.7	15.0	12.2	17.6	5.7	67.5	11.8	-1.8	-1.8	52.8	14.7
Feb 13	68.1	53.5	14.6	11.9	17.2	5.6	65.7	11.5	-1.8	-1.5	51.6	14.1
Mar 13	66.0	52.0	14.0	11.5	16.7	5.3	65.2	11.4	-0.5	-1.4	51.2	14.0
Apr 10	64.4	50.8	13.6	11.2	16.4	5.2	63.4	11.1	-1.8	-1.4	49.8	13.6
May 8	62.4	49.3	13.0	10.9	15.9	5.0	62.5	10.9	-0.9	-1.1	49.1	13.4
Jun 12 R	60.6	47.9	12.8	10.6	15.4	4.9	61.1	10.7	-1.4	-1.4	48.1	13.0
Jul 10 P	**61.5**	**48.0**	**13.5**	**10.7**	**15.4**	**5.2**	**59.9**	**10.4**	**-1.2**	**-1.2**	**47.2**	**12.7**
YORKSHIRE AND THE HUMBER												
1993)	245.6	190.8	54.8	10.4	14.3	5.3	244.0	10.2			189.9	54.1
1994) Annual	226.4	175.2	51.2	9.7	13.5	5.0	224.8	9.6			174.3	50.5
1995) average	207.9	160.6	47.3	8.7	12.0	4.5	206.1	8.7			159.6	46.5
1996)	191.8	147.9	43.9	8.0	11.0	4.2	190.0	8.0			146.9	43.1
1996 Jul 11	193.2	147.3	45.9	8.1	10.9	4.4	191.1	8.0	-2.3	-1.9	147.6	43.5
Aug 8	195.7	146.7	49.0	8.2	10.9	4.7	190.1	8.0	-1.0	-1.5	146.7	43.4
Sep 12	188.8	143.4	45.5	7.9	10.6	4.4	186.1	7.8	-4.0	-2.4	143.8	42.3
Oct 10	178.1	136.6	41.4	7.5	10.1	4.0	183.1	7.7	-3.0	-2.7	141.3	41.8
Nov 14	170.0	131.8	38.3	7.1	9.8	3.7	175.7	7.4	-7.4	-4.8	136.1	39.6
Dec 12	172.1	134.1	38.0	7.2	10.0	3.7	172.8	7.2	-2.9	-4.4	133.7	39.1
1997 Jan 9	176.6	137.5	39.1	7.4	10.2	3.8	166.7	7.0	-6.1	-5.5	129.1	37.6
Feb 13	169.9	132.3	37.6	7.1	9.8	3.6	161.2	6.8	-5.5	-4.8	124.9	36.3
Mar 13	162.7	126.8	35.9	6.8	9.4	3.4	158.2	6.6	-3.0	-4.9	122.6	35.6
Apr 10	158.3	123.4	34.9	6.6	9.2	3.4	153.7	6.4	-4.5	-4.3	119.8	33.9
May 8	152.0	118.6	33.4	6.4	8.8	3.2	153.3	6.4	-0.4	-2.6	118.7	34.6
Jun 12 R	146.1	113.9	32.3	6.1	8.5	3.1	150.7	6.3	-2.6	-2.5	116.9	33.8
Jul 10 P	**150.7**	**115.8**	**34.8**	**6.3**	**8.6**	**3.3**	**148.3**	**6.2**	**-2.4**	**-1.8**	**115.8**	**32.5**

		CLAIMANTS			PER CENT WORKFORCE *			SEASONALLY ADJUSTED #					
		All	Male	Female	All	Male	Female	Number	Per cent workforce *	Change since previous month	Average change over 3 months ended	Male	Female

EAST MIDLANDS

1993	)	183.8	140.8	43.0	9.6	13.0	5.1	182.5	9.5			140.1	42.4
1994	) Annual	168.8	128.7	40.1	8.8	11.7	4.9	167.6	8.7			128.0	39.6
1995	) average	148.3	112.5	35.7	7.7	10.3	4.2	147.2	7.6			111.9	35.3
1996	)	133.6	101.0	32.5	6.9	9.4	3.8	132.5	6.8			100.4	32.1
1996	Jul 11	134.8	100.5	34.3	7.0	9.4	4.0	133.4	6.9	-1.6	-1.7	101.0	32.4
	Aug 8	135.7	100.2	35.5	7.0	9.3	4.1	132.0	6.8	-1.4	-1.7	99.9	32.1
	Sep 12	130.7	97.1	33.6	6.7	9.0	3.9	129.5	6.7	-2.5	-1.8	98.0	31.5
	Oct 10	121.4	91.0	30.4	6.3	8.5	3.5	126.5	6.5	-3.0	-2.3	95.6	30.9
	Nov 14	114.3	86.5	27.7	5.9	8.1	3.2	120.1	6.2	-6.4	-4.0	91.1	29.0
	Dec 12	114.6	87.6	27.0	5.9	8.2	3.1	116.2	6.0	-3.9	-4.4	88.2	28.0
1997	Jan 9	118.8	91.2	27.7	6.1	8.5	3.2	111.4	5.8	-4.8	-5.0	84.9	26.5
	Feb 13	113.8	87.5	26.3	5.9	8.1	3.0	106.5	5.5	-4.9	-4.5	81.3	25.2
	Mar 13	108.7	83.5	25.2	5.6	7.8	2.9	105.0	5.4	-1.5	-3.7	79.9	25.1
	Apr 10	104.8	80.5	24.3	5.4	7.5	2.8	101.7	5.3	-3.3	-3.2	77.7	24.0
	May 8	99.7	76.8	22.9	5.1	7.2	2.7	100.2	5.2	-1.5	-2.1	76.4	23.8
	Jun 12 R	94.2	72.4	21.8	4.9	6.7	2.5	98.0	5.1	-2.2	-2.3	74.6	23.4
	Jul 10 P	**96.6**	**72.8**	**23.8**	**5.0**	**6.8**	**2.8**	**94.8**	**4.9**	**-3.2**	**-2.3**	**72.9**	**21.9**

WEST MIDLANDS

1993	)	281.9	215.6	66.3	10.9	14.6	6.1	280.6	10.8			214.9	65.8
1994	) Annual	246.2	186.8	59.4	9.9	13.3	5.5	244.8	9.9			186.0	58.8
1995	) average	210.3	158.6	51.7	8.4	11.0	4.8	209.0	8.3			158.0	51.1
1996	)	188.6	142.0	46.6	7.4	9.8	4.3	187.4	7.4			141.3	46.1
1996	Jul 11	193.1	143.8	49.3	7.6	10.0	4.5	189.2	7.5	-3.3	-2.0	142.6	46.6
	Aug 8	194.7	143.6	51.2	7.7	10.0	4.7	186.7	7.4	-2.5	-2.5	140.7	46.0
	Sep 12	188.6	139.8	48.8	7.4	9.7	4.5	183.3	7.2	-3.4	-3.1	138.2	45.1
	Oct 10	175.9	131.8	44.1	6.9	9.1	4.0	179.5	7.1	-3.8	-3.2	135.3	44.2
	Nov 14	164.0	123.8	40.2	6.5	8.6	3.7	170.7	6.7	-8.8	-5.3	129.0	41.7
	Dec 12	162.6	123.7	38.9	6.4	8.6	3.6	166.0	6.5	-4.7	-5.8	125.4	40.6
1997	Jan 9	165.9	126.6	39.4	6.5	8.8	3.5	160.1	6.3	-5.9	-6.5	121.2	38.9
	Feb 13	159.2	121.5	37.7	6.3	8.4	3.5	154.0	6.1	-6.1	-10.5	116.7	37.3
	Mar 13	152.1	116.2	35.9	6.0	8.1	3.3	151.2	6.0	-2.8	-4.9	114.6	36.6
	Apr 10	148.5	113.7	34.8	5.9	7.9	3.2	146.7	5.8	-4.5	-4.5	112.1	34.6
	May 8	143.9	110.5	33.4	5.7	7.7	3.1	145.4	5.7	-1.3	-2.9	110.6	34.8
	Jun 12 R	138.4	106.3	32.2	5.5	7.4	2.9	141.5	5.6	-3.9	-3.2	107.9	33.6
	Jul 10 P	**141.6**	**107.0**	**34.6**	**5.6**	**7.4**	**3.2**	**137.5**	**5.4**	**-4.0**	**-3.1**	**105.4**	**32.1**

EASTERN

1993	)	225.7	170.1	55.6	9.4	12.5	5.4	224.3	9.4			169.4	55.0
1994	) Annual	195.1	146.3	48.8	8.1	10.9	4.6	194.4	8.1			145.9	48.5
1995	) average	167.5	124.8	42.4	6.9	9.1	3.9	167.2	6.9			124.5	42.7
1996	)	148.7	110.6	38.1	6.1	8.1	3.6	148.0	6.1			110.1	37.9
1996	Jul 11	148.7	109.4	39.3	6.1	8.0	3.7	148.7	6.1	-1.7	-1.8	110.3	38.4
	Aug 8	150.1	109.2	40.9	6.2	8.0	3.8	147.3	6.1	-1.4	-1.6	109.4	37.9
	Sep 12	145.3	106.1	39.2	6.0	7.8	3.7	145.6	6.0	-1.7	-1.6	108.0	37.6
	Oct 10	135.6	99.8	35.8	5.6	7.3	3.4	142.2	5.9	-3.4	-2.2	105.6	36.6
	Nov 14	127.8	94.9	32.9	5.3	7.0	3.1	131.4	5.4	-10.8	-5.3	97.1	34.3
	Dec 12	127.2	95.2	32.0	5.2	7.0	3.0	130.3	5.4	-1.1	-5.1	96.5	33.8
1997	Jan 9	130.8	98.6	32.3	5.4	7.2	3.0	123.7	5.1	-6.6	-6.2	92.5	31.2
	Feb 13	125.1	94.2	30.9	5.1	6.9	2.9	117.4	4.8	-6.3	-4.7	88.2	29.2
	Mar 13	118.2	89.2	29.0	4.9	6.6	2.7	113.7	4.7	-3.7	-5.5	85.0	28.7
	Apr 10	113.1	85.4	27.7	4.7	6.3	2.6	109.5	4.5	-4.2	-4.7	82.3	27.2
	May 8	107.8	81.7	26.2	4.4	6.0	2.4	107.8	4.4	-1.7	-3.2	81.1	26.7
	Jun 12 R	101.6	76.8	24.8	4.2	5.6	2.3	105.4	4.3	-2.4	-2.8	79.2	26.2
	Jul 10 P	**102.7**	**76.4**	**26.3**	**4.2**	**5.6**	**2.5**	**102.1**	**4.2**	**-3.3**	**-2.5**	**77.1**	**25.0**

LONDON

1993	)	469.6	348.6	121.0	11.6	14.9	7.1	467.9	11.6			347.8	120.2
1994	) Annual	434.6	322.7	111.9	10.7	14.1	6.3	432.8	10.7			321.8	111.0
1995	) average	394.7	292.1	102.6	9.8	12.9	5.8	392.8	9.7			291.2	101.7
1996	)	360.1	265.2	95.0	8.9	11.7	5.3	358.2	8.9			264.2	94.0
1996	Jul 11	364.9	267.3	97.6	9.0	11.8	5.5	360.6	8.9	-3.2	-2.7	265.6	95.0
	Aug 8	368.9	267.8	101.0	9.1	11.8	5.7	358.5	8.9	-2.1	-2.4	264.1	94.4
	Sep 12	362.8	263.5	99.3	9.0	11.6	5.6	353.4	8.7	-5.1	-3.5	260.1	93.3
	Oct 10	343.7	251.5	92.2	8.5	11.1	5.2	344.8	8.5	-8.6	-5.3	254.2	90.6
	Nov 14	324.6	238.5	86.1	8.0	10.5	4.8	330.4	8.2	-14.4	-9.4	243.5	86.9
	Dec 12	320.8	236.5	84.3	7.9	10.4	4.7	323.1	8.0	-7.3	-10.1	237.6	85.5
1997	Jan 9	315.8	233.8	82.0	7.8	10.3	4.6	313.0	7.7	-10.1	-10.6	230.8	82.2
	Feb 13	304.3	225.4	78.9	7.5	10.0	4.4	301.9	7.5	-11.1	-9.5	222.6	79.3
	Mar 13	293.1	217.3	75.9	7.2	9.6	4.3	294.7	7.3	-7.2	-9.5	216.9	77.8
	Apr 10	285.2	211.0	74.1	7.1	9.3	4.2	282.8	7.0	-11.9	-10.1	208.9	73.9
	May 8	278.7	206.4	72.3	6.9	9.1	4.1	280.6	6.9	-2.2	-7.1	206.4	74.2
	Jun 12 R	269.4	199.3	70.1	6.7	8.8	3.9	272.6	6.7	-8.0	-7.4	200.4	72.2
	Jul 10 P	**268.2**	**196.7**	**71.5**	**6.6**	**8.7**	**4.0**	**263.4**	**6.5**	**-9.2**	**-6.5**	**194.4**	**69.0**

CLAIMANT COUNT
Government Office Regions

THOUSANDS

	CLAIMANTS			PER CENT WORKFORCE *			SEASONALLY ADJUSTED #					
	All	Male	Female	All	Male	Female	Number	Per cent workforce *	Change since previous month	Average change over 3 months ended	Male	Female

SOUTH EAST

	All	Male	Female	All	Male	Female	Number	Per cent workforce	Change since previous month	Average change over 3 months ended	Male	Female
1993)	318.6	244.7	73.9	8.7	12.1	4.5	316.8	8.7			243.7	73.2
1994) Annual	272.8	208.5	64.3	7.3	10.1	3.9	271.9	7.3			208.0	63.9
1995) average	229.0	173.8	55.1	6.2	8.4	3.4	228.6	6.2			173.5	55.2
1996)	200.2	151.3	48.9	5.4	7.4	3.0	199.6	5.4			151.0	48.6
1996 Jul 11	201.2	150.7	50.4	5.4	7.3	3.1	202.0	5.5	-2.7	-2.3	152.5	49.5
Aug 8	203.1	150.6	52.6	5.5	7.3	3.2	198.6	5.4	-3.4	-2.9	150.2	48.4
Sep 12	196.0	145.4	50.6	5.3	7.1	3.1	194.5	5.3	-4.1	-3.4	146.6	47.9
Oct 10	183.3	137.1	46.2	5.0	6.7	2.8	189.8	5.1	-4.7	-4.1	142.9	46.9
Nov 14	171.1	129.2	42.0	4.6	6.3	2.6	178.4	4.8	-11.4	-6.7	135.2	43.2
Dec 12	169.7	129.0	40.7	4.6	6.3	2.5	171.9	4.7	-6.5	-7.5	129.8	42.1
1997 Jan 9	173.2	132.3	40.9	4.7	6.4	2.5	164.0	4.4	-7.9	-8.6	124.8	39.2
Feb 13	163.5	125.2	38.4	4.4	6.1	2.3	153.3	4.2	-10.7	-8.4	116.6	36.7
Mar 13	153.7	117.8	35.9	4.2	5.7	2.2	149.7	4.1	-3.6	-7.4	113.8	35.9
Apr 10	146.2	112.1	34.1	4.0	5.4	2.1	143.4	3.9	-6.3	-6.9	109.4	34.0
May 8	138.1	106.2	32.0	3.7	5.2	2.0	140.2	3.8	-3.2	-4.4	106.6	33.6
Jun 12 R	129.4	99.5	30.0	3.5	4.8	1.8	136.3	3.7	-3.9	-4.5	103.6	32.7
Jul 10 P	**131.0**	**99.3**	**31.7**	**3.5**	**4.8**	**1.9**	**130.8**	**3.5**	**-5.5**	**-4.2**	**100.1**	**30.7**

SOUTH WEST

	All	Male	Female	All	Male	Female	Number	Per cent workforce	Change since previous month	Average change over 3 months ended	Male	Female
1993)	217.8	164.6	53.2	9.5	12.7	5.5	216.4	9.5			163.8	52.6
1994) Annual	191.7	143.9	47.8	8.2	10.9	4.6	190.4	8.1			143.2	47.2
1995) average	166.3	124.1	42.3	7.1	9.5	4.1	164.9	7.0			123.3	41.6
1996)	148.2	110.3	38.0	6.3	8.4	3.6	146.9	6.2			109.5	37.4
1996 Jul 11	146.4	108.3	38.2	6.2	8.2	3.6	148.8	6.3	-1.7	-1.5	110.6	38.2
Aug 8	147.8	108.3	39.5	6.3	8.3	3.8	146.8	6.2	-2.0	-1.9	109.4	37.4
Sep 12	143.5	105.6	37.9	6.1	8.0	3.6	143.4	6.1	-3.4	-2.4	106.9	36.5
Oct 10	135.5	100.3	35.2	5.7	7.6	3.4	139.8	5.9	-3.6	-3.0	104.3	35.5
Nov 14	130.5	96.7	33.8	5.5	7.4	3.2	133.1	5.6	-6.7	-4.6	99.3	33.8
Dec 12	131.1	97.8	33.3	5.6	7.5	3.2	129.4	5.5	-3.7	-4.7	96.4	33.0
1997 Jan 9	135.8	101.4	34.4	5.8	7.7	3.3	124.4	5.3	-5.0	-5.1	93.0	31.4
Feb 13	128.4	96.1	32.3	5.4	7.3	3.1	118.5	5.0	-5.9	-4.9	88.8	29.7
Mar 13	120.0	90.2	29.8	5.1	6.9	2.8	115.1	4.9	-3.4	-4.8	85.0	29.0
Apr 10	114.0	86.2	27.8	4.8	6.6	2.7	111.6	4.7	-3.5	-4.3	83.9	27.7
May 8	106.2	80.6	25.6	4.5	6.1	2.4	108.9	4.6	-2.7	-3.2	81.7	27.2
Jun 12 R	98.2	74.7	23.5	4.2	5.7	2.2	105.6	4.5	-3.3	-3.2	79.2	26.4
Jul 10 P	**98.7**	**74.0**	**24.7**	**4.2**	**5.6**	**2.4**	**101.1**	**4.3**	**-4.5**	**-3.5**	**76.4**	**24.7**

WALES

	All	Male	Female	All	Male	Female	Number	Per cent workforce	Change since previous month	Average change over 3 months ended	Male	Female
1993)	131.1	103.2	28.0	10.4	14.4	5.1	130.3	10.3			102.7	27.6
1994) Annual	120.7	94.1	26.6	9.4	12.7	4.9	119.9	9.3			93.6	26.3
1995) average	107.8	83.4	24.4	8.8	12.2	4.5	106.9	8.7			82.9	24.0
1996)	102.7	79.2	23.5	8.2	11.4	4.3	101.7	8.2			78.6	23.1
1996 Jul 11	104.1	79.1	25.0	8.4	11.4	4.5	102.8	8.3	-1.0	-0.9	79.2	23.6
Aug 8	105.3	79.1	26.2	8.5	11.4	4.7	102.0	8.2	-0.8	-0.9	78.5	23.5
Sep 12	102.5	77.8	24.7	8.2	11.2	4.5	100.5	8.1	-1.5	-1.1	77.6	22.9
Oct 10	96.6	74.3	22.3	7.8	10.7	4.0	99.3	8.0	-1.2	-1.2	76.7	22.6
Nov 14	92.5	71.9	20.6	7.4	10.4	3.7	95.0	7.6	-4.3	-2.3	73.7	21.3
Dec 12	93.1	72.6	20.5	7.5	10.5	3.7	92.8	7.4	-2.2	-2.6	71.9	20.9
1997 Jan 9	96.4	75.3	21.1	7.7	10.9	3.8	90.0	7.2	-2.8	-3.1	70.0	20.0
Feb 13	91.8	71.7	20.1	7.4	10.3	3.6	86.9	7.0	-3.1	-2.7	67.6	19.3
Mar. 13	87.0	68.1	18.9	7.0	9.8	3.4	85.0	6.8	-1.9	-2.6	66.2	18.8
Apr 10	83.6	65.6	18.0	6.7	9.5	3.3	82.4	6.6	-2.6	-2.5	64.7	17.7
May 8	80.3	63.1	17.2	6.4	9.1	3.1	82.1	6.6	-0.3	-1.6	64.0	18.1
Jun 12 R	76.4	60.0	16.4	6.1	8.7	3.0	80.4	6.5	-1.7	-1.5	62.5	17.9
Jul 10 P	**79.5**	**61.2**	**18.3**	**6.4**	**8.8**	**3.3**	**78.1**	**6.3**	**-2.3**	**-1.4**	**61.2**	**16.9**

SCOTLAND

	All	Male	Female	All	Male	Female	Number	Per cent workforce	Change since previous month	Average change over 3 months ended	Male	Female
1993)	246.4	189.5	56.9	9.9	13.7	5.1	243.3	9.7			187.7	55.6
1994) Annual	231.5	178.6	52.8	9.4	13.0	4.8	228.4	9.3			176.8	51.5
1995) average	203.5	156.3	47.2	8.2	11.6	4.2	200.3	8.1			154.5	45.9
1996)	195.1	149.3	45.7	8.0	11.3	4.1	191.9	7.9			147.5	44.4
1996 Jul 11	206.1	152.8	53.3	8.4	11.6	4.7	194.7	8.0	-1.7	-0.9	148.7	46.0
Aug 8	206.4	152.5	53.9	8.4	11.6	4.8	194.0	7.9	-0.7	-0.9	148.2	45.8
Sep 12	191.1	145.3	45.8	7.8	11.0	4.1	191.3	7.8	-2.7	-1.7	146.4	44.9
Oct 10	183.4	141.2	42.2	7.5	10.7	3.7	188.9	7.7	-2.4	-1.9	145.0	43.9
Nov 14	176.4	136.7	39.7	7.2	10.4	3.5	181.4	7.4	-7.5	-4.2	140.1	41.3
Dec 12	178.1	138.8	39.2	7.3	10.5	3.5	178.7	7.3	-2.7	-4.2	138.3	40.4
1997 Jan 9	185.6	144.5	41.1	7.6	11.0	3.6	173.3	7.1	-5.4	-5.2	134.5	38.8
Feb 13	179.6	139.6	39.9	7.3	10.6	3.5	169.7	6.9	-3.6	-3.9	132.0	37.7
Mar 13	172.1	134.1	38.0	7.0	10.2	3.4	167.6	6.9	-2.1	-3.7	130.3	37.3
Apr 10	166.2	129.4	36.8	6.8	9.8	3.3	162.5	6.6	-5.1	-3.6	126.6	35.9
May 8	160.3	125.1	35.3	6.6	9.5	3.1	161.6	6.6	-0.9	-2.7	125.0	36.6
Jun 12 R	156.2	121.2	35.0	6.4	9.2	3.1	160.1	6.5	-1.5	-2.5	123.3	36.8
Jul 10 P	**164.0**	**124.3**	**39.7**	**6.7**	**9.4**	**3.5**	**153.3**	**6.3**	**-6.8**	**-3.1**	**120.4**	**32.9**

		CLAIMANTS			PER CENT WORKFORCE *			SEASONALLY ADJUSTED #					
		All	Male	Female	All	Male	Female	Number	Per cent workforce *	Change since previous month	Average change over 3 months ended	Male	Female
NORTHERN IRELAND													
1993	)	105.1	80.7	24.5	14.1	18.6	7.8	103.7	13.8			80.1	23.6
1994	) Annual	97.3	75.3	21.9	12.7	16.6	6.9	97.1	12.6			75.2	21.8
1995	) average	88.2	68.7	19.5	11.4	15.3	6.0	88.1	11.4			68.6	19.5
1996	)	84.2	65.0	19.1	10.9	14.7	5.8	84.0	10.9			65.0	19.0
1996	Jul 11	90.8	67.5	23.3	11.8	15.3	7.1	86.7	11.3	0.0	0.2	66.5	20.2
	Aug 8	92.6	68.3	24.3	12.0	15.5	7.4	87.4	11.4	0.7	0.6	66.8	20.6
	Sep 12	89.7	67.4	22.3	11.7	15.2	6.8	85.8	11.2	-1.6	-0.3	65.9	19.9
	Oct 10	81.6	62.8	18.8	10.6	14.2	5.8	82.4	10.7	-3.4	-1.4	63.5	18.9
	Nov 14	73.9	57.8	16.2	9.6	13.1	4.9	76.0	9.9	-6.4	-3.8	59.0	17.0
	Dec 12	71.9	56.7	15.3	9.4	12.8	4.7	74.3	9.7	-1.7	-3.8	57.6	16.7
1997	Jan 9	70.8	56.0	14.8	9.2	12.7	4.5	71.0	9.2	-3.3	-3.8	55.2	15.8
	Feb 13	67.5	53.8	13.8	8.8	12.2	4.2	68.2	8.9	-2.8	-2.6	53.2	15.0
	Mar 13	65.7	52.5	13.2	8.6	11.9	4.0	67.0	8.7	-1.2	-2.4	52.4	14.6
	Apr 10	63.8	51.1	12.7	8.3	11.6	3.9	64.8	8.4	-2.2	-2.1	51.3	13.5
	May 8	61.3	49.2	12.1	8.0	11.1	3.7	64.2	8.4	-0.6	-1.3	50.5	13.7
	Jun 12 R	60.8	48.2	12.6	7.9	10.9	3.8	62.6	8.1	-1.6	-1.5	49.3	13.3
	Jul 10 P	**65.1**	**49.9**	**15.2**	**8.5**	**11.3**	**4.7**	**60.5**	**7.9**	**-2.1**	**-1.4**	**48.4**	**12.1**

* #   See footnotes to *Tables 2.1* and *2.2*.
Note: Due to production difficulties, data for standard statistical regions have been withdrawn from this table. Figures for specific regions are available on request from the Labour Market Statistics Helpline on 0171 533 6176.

Claimant count by Travel-to-Work Areas+ as at July 10 1997

	Male	Female	All	Rate # per cent employees and unemployed	per cent workforce

TRAVEL TO WORK AREAS

England

Area	Male	Female	All	per cent employees and unemployed	per cent workforce
Accrington and Rossendale	1,659	576	2,235	4.8	4.1
Alfreton and Ashfield	2,902	830	3,732	6.2	5.5
Alnwick and Amble	740	245	985	8.5	6.8
Andover	493	212	705	2.2	1.9
Ashford	1,411	442	1,853	5.0	4.1
Aylesbury and Wycombe	3,542	1,144	4,686	2.7	2.3
Banbury	714	269	983	3.2	2.6
Barnsley	4,807	1,329	6,136	9.2	8.1
Barnstaple and Ilfracombe	1,170	373	1,543	5.5	4.2
Barrow-in-Furness	2,240	565	2,805	8.4	7.2
Basingstoke and Alton	1,419	491	1,910	2.5	2.2
Bath	2,258	812	3,070	4.4	3.8
Beccles and Halesworth	786	291	1,077	7.0	5.3
Bedford	2,555	908	3,463	4.9	4.3
Berwick-on-Tweed	356	103	459	4.7	3.9
Bicester	309	117	426	2.1	1.7
Bideford	707	235	942	9.6	7.2
Birmingham	41,104	13,107	54,211	7.6	6.9
Bishop Auckland	2,640	696	3,336	8.1	7.2
Blackburn	2,888	761	3,649	5.3	4.7
Blackpool	4,917	1,269	6,186	5.3	4.3
Blandford	177	95	272	2.7	2.1
Bodmin and Liskeard	1,178	364	1,542	6.6	4.7
Bolton and Bury	7,368	2,161	9,529	5.6	4.9
Boston	748	306	1,054	5.2	4.0
Bournemouth	4,566	1,300	5,866	5.6	4.4
Bradford	11,713	3,506	15,219	7.3	6.5
Bridgwater	1,471	478	1,949	6.3	5.1
Bridlington and Driffield	1,367	412	1,779	9.1	7.1
Bridport	337	142	479	6.3	4.2
Brighton	9,844	3,566	13,410	8.4	7.0
Bristol	12,794	4,083	16,877	5.1	4.5
Bude	430	163	593	9.4	6.1
Burnley	1,249	369	1,618	4.2	3.7
Burton-on-Trent	2,617	875	3,492	5.9	5.2
Bury St.Edmunds	722	309	1,031	2.9	2.5
Buxton	622	210	832	4.3	3.2
Calderdale	4,041	1,185	5,226	6.3	5.5
Cambridge	3,112	1,214	4,326	2.8	2.4
Canterbury	2,264	685	2,949	5.7	4.8
Carlisle	2,109	634	2,743	5.2	4.5
Castleford and Pontefract	2,967	887	3,854	6.9	6.1
Chard	290	125	415	4.6	3.6
Chelmsford and Braintree	3,249	1,218	4,467	4.3	3.6
Cheltenham	2,303	800	3,103	4.3	3.7
Chesterfield	4,110	1,182	5,292	7.8	6.8
Chichester	1,447	485	1,932	3.3	2.6
Chippenham	821	332	1,153	3.5	2.7
Cinderford and Ross-on-Wye	961	397	1,358	5.3	4.2
Cirencester	238	90	328	2.4	1.9
Clacton	1,573	417	1,990	10.2	7.7
Clitheroe	162	65	227	2.2	1.8
Colchester	2,517	899	3,416	4.1	3.5
Corby	995	293	1,288	4.4	4.0
Coventry and Hinckley	10,093	3,249	13,342	5.8	5.2
Crawley	3,155	1,100	4,255	2.0	1.8
Crewe	1,847	618	2,465	5.5	4.8
Cromer and North Walsham	977	320	1,297	7.3	5.5
Darlington	2,986	842	3,828	7.4	6.5
Dartmouth and Kingsbridge	271	99	370	4.8	3.0
Derby	7,224	2,290	9,514	6.4	5.7
Devizes	349	139	488	3.6	2.8
Diss	432	195	627	4.6	3.4
Doncaster	7,608	2,020	9,628	10.1	8.9
Dorchester and Weymouth	1,490	444	1,934	5.2	4.3
Dover and Deal	2,490	667	3,157	8.8	7.3
Dudley and Sandwell	14,411	4,505	18,916	7.1	6.5
Durham	3,173	966	4,139	6.9	6.3
Eastbourne	1,908	672	2,580	4.5	3.6
Evesham	679	293	972	3.4	2.5
Exeter	3,218	1,083	4,301	4.3	3.6
Fakenham	558	212	770	7.2	5.3
Falmouth	886	296	1,182	11.4	8.5
Folkestone	2,651	680	3,331	9.8	8.1
Gainsborough	704	246	950	8.1	6.6
Gloucester	2,610	836	3,446	4.7	4.2
Goole and Selby	1,642	618	2,260	8.9	7.4
Gosport and Fareham	1,824	691	2,515	5.0	4.1
Grantham	792	314	1,106	4.6	3.8
Great Yarmouth	2,825	826	3,651	10.2	8.2
Grimsby	5,354	1,468	6,822	9.3	8.1
Guildford and Aldershot	3,256	1,122	4,378	2.5	2.0
Harrogate	1,056	431	1,487	3.6	2.9
Hartlepool	3,631	891	4,522	12.7	11.6
Harwich	540	149	689	12.1	9.9

Area	Male	Female	All	Rates # per cent employees and unemployed	per cent workforce
Hastings	3,406	942	4,348	8.8	6.9
Haverhill	431	195	626	4.9	4.1
Heathrow	21,671	7,872	29,543	4.3	3.7
Helston	470	214	684	11.0	7.4
Hereford and Leominster	1,747	691	2,438	5.3	4.3
Hertford and Harlow	6,020	2,139	8,159	3.5	3.1
Hexham	591	202	793	5.4	4.0
Hitchin and Letchworth	1,573	602	2,175	4.1	3.5
Honiton and Axminster	473	175	648	4.1	2.8
Horncastle and Market Rasen	479	231	710	6.9	4.8
Huddersfield	4,537	1,536	6,073	5.5	4.9
Hull	11,507	3,565	15,072	8.1	7.2
Huntingdon and St.Neots	1,250	531	1,781	3.3	2.8
Ipswich	4,068	1,299	5,367	5.1	4.5
Isle of Wight	2,886	910	3,796	9.0	7.8
Keighley	1,430	549	1,979	6.7	5.7
Kendal	467	173	640	2.9	2.3
Keswick	72	20	92	2.5	1.7
Kettering and Market Harboro'	1,132	425	1,557	3.8	3.3
Kidderminster	1,384	507	1,891	4.6	3.9
King's Lynn and Hunstanton	1,837	649	2,486	6.2	5.1
Lancaster and Morecambe	2,798	948	3,746	8.2	6.9
Launceston	315	126	441	7.0	4.2
Leeds	16,225	4,820	21,045	5.7	5.2
Leek	344	118	462	3.8	3.2
Leicester	10,253	3,435	13,688	5.3	4.6
Lincoln	3,511	1,112	4,623	6.4	5.5
Liverpool	35,899	9,992	45,891	11.7	10.5
London	182,561	66,257	248,818	7.7	6.8
Loughborough and Coalville	2,003	771	2,774	4.1	3.6
Louth and Mablethorpe	784	252	1,036	8.1	6.0
Lowestoft	2,405	756	3,161	10.8	9.1
Ludlow	432	132	564	5.7	3.8
Macclesfield	1,342	414	1,756	2.9	2.4
Malton	204	81	285	2.9	2.4
Malvern and Ledbury	759	257	1,016	4.9	3.8
Manchester	34,774	9,995	44,769	6.3	5.7
Mansfield	3,571	1,000	4,571	9.8	8.4
Matlock	448	179	627	2.9	2.5
Medway and Maidstone	9,632	3,209	12,841	6.3	5.3
Melton Mowbray	461	203	664	2.7	2.3
Middlesbrough	10,619	2,700	13,319	11.5	10.5
Milton Keynes	2,858	1,033	3,891	3.5	3.2
Minehead	469	150	619	7.1	5.1
Morpeth and Ashington	3,603	968	4,571	10.0	8.8
Newark	1,024	359	1,383	6.2	5.1
Newbury	620	193	813	1.8	1.5
Newcastle upon Tyne	22,980	6,225	29,205	8.5	7.8
Newmarket	769	310	1,079	4.2	3.4
Newquay	540	165	705	7.4	5.4
Newton Abbot	1,087	388	1,475	5.7	4.4
Northallerton	375	182	557	3.1	2.5
Northampton	3,860	1,342	5,202	4.3	3.8
Northwich	1,823	620	2,443	4.3	3.8
Norwich	6,057	2,028	8,085	5.7	4.9
Nottingham	17,788	5,389	23,177	7.0	6.2
Okehampton	182	83	265	5.6	3.7
Oldham	3,832	1,100	4,932	6.4	5.6
Oswestry	674	266	940	7.0	5.5
Oxford	3,910	1,428	5,338	2.8	2.4
Pendle	1,157	354	1,511	4.7	4.1
Penrith	295	135	430	2.9	2.2
Penzance and St.Ives	1,226	403	1,629	9.8	6.9
Peterborough	3,911	1,376	5,287	5.3	4.6
Pickering and Helmsley	175	77	252	4.0	2.6
Plymouth	8,042	2,536	10,578	7.9	6.7
Poole	2,131	642	2,773	3.6	3.0
Portsmouth	7,321	2,020	9,341	7.2	5.9
Preston	5,490	1,680	7,170	4.6	4.1
Reading	3,020	866	3,886	2.6	2.2
Redruth and Camborne	1,762	500	2,262	11.3	8.8
Retford	955	368	1,323	7.4	6.1
Richmondshire	371	187	558	4.8	3.4
Ripon	252	112	364	3.6	2.6
Rochdale	3,670	981	4,651	7.9	6.8
Rotherham and Mexborough	8,841	2,252	11,093	12.6	11.2
Rugby and Daventry	1,477	553	2,030	3.5	3.1
Salisbury	1,016	385	1,401	3.1	2.4
Scarborough and Filey	1,701	512	2,213	6.7	5.3
Scunthorpe	2,968	956	3,924	6.2	5.4
Settle	145	66	211	3.9	2.4
Shaftesbury	402	160	562	3.9	2.7
Sheffield	17,142	5,304	22,446	8.8	7.9
Shrewsbury	1,283	448	1,731	4.0	3.3
Sittingbourne and Sheerness	2,444	772	3,216	8.2	6.9
Skegness	391	111	502	4.4	3.3
Skipton	261	78	339	2.6	2.0
Sleaford	366	137	503	4.0	3.1
Slough	4,331	1,342	5,673	3.1	2.7
South Molton	158	70	228	6.2	3.6

Claimant count by Travel-to-Work Areas+ as at July 10 1997

	Male	Female	All	Rate # per cent employees and unemployed	per cent workforce		Male	Female	All	Rates # per cent employees and unemployed	per cent workforce
South Tyneside	5,446	1,419	6,865	14.4	12.9	South Pembrokeshire	1,313	323	1,636	13.5	10.1
Southampton	7,054	1,902	8,956	5.0	4.2	Swansea	5,916	1,650	7,566	7.9	7.0
Southend	14,070	4,566	18,636	7.6	6.3	Welshpool	214	109	323	4.8	3.3
Spalding and Holbeach	512	254	766	3.8	2.8	Wrexham	2,192	719	2,911	5.6	4.9
St.Austell	1,169	372	1,541	6.7	5.1						
						Scotland					
Stafford	1,723	633	2,356	3.9	3.3						
Stamford	417	213	630	3.7	2.9	Aberdeen	4,188	1,585	5,773	2.8	2.6
Stockton-on-Tees	5,904	1,611	7,515	9.9	9.2	Alloa	1,379	471	1,850	12.6	11.0
Stoke	7,403	2,219	9,622	5.3	4.7	Annan	374	124	498	6.2	5.1
Stroud	1,202	480	1,682	4.7	3.7	Arbroath	878	404	1,282	15.3	12.4
						Ayr	2,567	953	3,520	7.6	6.7
Sudbury	644	239	883	5.0	3.9						
Sunderland	11,791	2,906	14,697	9.6	8.8	Badenoch	199	69	268	6.5	5.0
Swindon	2,800	939	3,739	3.1	2.6	Banff	292	125	417	4.1	3.2
Taunton	1,633	516	2,149	4.6	3.8	Bathgate	2,537	794	3,331	6.3	5.8
Telford and Bridgnorth	2,501	827	3,328	4.0	3.5	Berwickshire	227	90	317	6.9	5.0
						Blairgowrie and Pitlochry	433	154	587	6.0	4.6
Thanet	3,626	996	4,622	12.3	9.7						
Thetford	789	314	1,103	5.4	4.4	Brechin and Montrose	862	322	1,184	10.5	8.0
Thirsk	133	64	197	3.4	2.6	Buckie	253	115	368	8.8	7.3
Tiverton	342	133	475	4.7	3.5	Campbeltown	282	73	355	10.6	7.6
Torbay	2,742	790	3,532	7.1	5.4	Crieff	150	75	225	5.5	4.4
						Cumnock and Sanquhar	1,405	358	1,763	15.5	12.8
Torrington	224	96	320	7.2	4.5						
Totnes	342	177	519	6.8	4.7	Dumbarton	2,269	634	2,903	9.8	8.8
Trowbridge and Frome	1,614	593	2,207	4.7	3.8	Dumfries	1,311	432	1,743	6.3	5.7
Truro	1,051	353	1,404	5.5	4.4	Dundee	6,011	1,898	7,909	8.9	8.1
Tunbridge Wells	2,074	691	2,765	2.9	2.3	Dunfermline	3,234	1,075	4,309	9.4	8.2
						Dunoon and Bute	634	203	837	10.7	7.7
Uttoxeter and Ashbourne	262	114	376	2.9	2.5						
Wakefield and Dewsbury	6,019	1,673	7,692	7.2	6.4	Edinburgh	12,308	3,885	16,193	5.2	4.8
Walsall	8,314	2,680	10,994	7.6	6.8	Elgin	791	351	1,142	6.4	5.6
Wareham and Swanage	251	83	334	2.9	2.3	Falkirk	3,459	1,145	4,604	8.0	7.2
Warminster	244	130	374	4.6	3.6	Forfar	493	220	713	6.2	5.3
						Forres	296	99	395	11.7	9.4
Warrington	2,791	917	3,708	4.1	3.8						
Warwick	1,971	733	2,704	3.2	2.7	Fraserburgh	225	102	327	5.4	4.1
Watford and Luton	9,759	3,261	13,020	3.9	3.4	Galashiels	387	145	532	3.4	2.9
Wellingborough and Rushden	1,555	540	2,095	4.4	3.8	Girvan	302	103	405	14.5	10.9
Wells	951	347	1,298	5.2	4.0	Glasgow	37,578	11,200	48,778	8.4	7.7
						Greenock	2,210	683	2,893	8.1	7.2
Weston-super-Mare	1,839	625	2,464	6.2	4.9						
Whitby	408	146	554	8.5	5.5	Haddington	397	149	546	5.0	4.1
Whitchurch and Market Drayton	366	155	521	3.6	2.7	Hawick	329	104	433	5.6	4.8
Whitehaven	2,001	554	2,555	9.2	8.2	Huntly	178	78	256	5.5	4.4
Widnes and Runcorn	3,704	1,125	4,829	8.4	7.7	Invergordon and Dingwall	1,260	319	1,579	13.6	11.7
						Inverness	2,162	662	2,824	6.8	6.0
Wigan and St.Helens	10,034	3,030	13,064	8.3	7.3						
Winchester and Eastleigh	1,045	363	1,408	1.9	1.6	Irvine	4,083	1,422	5,505	11.5	10.2
Windermere	66	36	102	1.2	0.9	Islay/Mid Argyll	251	101	352	7.7	6.3
Wirral and Chester	13,057	3,966	17,023	8.7	7.7	Keith	232	90	322	5.5	4.5
Wisbech	889	351	1,240	8.8	6.5	Kelso and Jedburgh	146	52	198	3.6	2.9
						Kilmarnock	2,400	842	3,242	10.9	9.6
Wolverhampton	7,660	2,357	10,017	8.1	7.2						
Woodbridge and Leiston	754	229	983	4.5	3.7	Kirkcaldy	4,692	1,555	6,247	9.9	8.6
Worcester	1,917	688	2,605	4.0	3.5	Lanarkshire	11,120	3,247	14,367	10.2	9.1
Workington	2,273	589	2,862	11.4	9.5	Lochaber	306	92	398	5.2	4.3
Worksop	1,433	410	1,843	7.8	7.0	Lockerbie	207	95	302	8.4	6.2
						Newton Stewart	282	94	376	15.8	10.2
Worthing	2,114	657	2,771	3.8	3.1						
Yeovil	1,195	480	1,675	3.7	3.0	North East Fife	764	308	1,072	6.4	5.1
York	3,287	1,103	4,390	4.2	3.6	Oban	281	79	360	4.9	3.7
						Orkney Islands	248	102	350	4.8	3.8
Wales						Peebles	163	63	226	5.2	4.3
						Perth	1,494	506	2,000	6.7	5.8
Aberdare	1,385	363	1,748	12.8	10.7						
Aberystwyth	574	264	838	8.5	6.5	Peterhead	495	180	675	5.1	4.3
Bangor and Caernarfon	2,281	663	2,944	9.7	8.3	Shetland Islands	287	112	399	3.7	3.3
Blaenau,Gwent & Abergavenny	2,502	730	3,232	9.7	8.4	Skye and Wester Ross	417	108	525	7.1	5.7
Brecon	247	112	359	4.3	3.2	Stewartry	358	146	504	8.1	5.8
						Stirling	1,598	512	2,110	5.8	5.1
Bridgend	2,769	1,020	3,789	6.7	5.9						
Cardiff	10,702	3,048	13,750	6.4	5.8	Stranraer	539	151	690	9.7	8.0
Cardigan	469	190	659	9.0	5.7	Sutherland	377	109	486	13.1	9.9
Carmarthen	719	227	946	4.9	3.8	Thurso	380	102	482	7.9	6.6
Conwy and Colwyn	1,910	490	2,400	8.2	6.4	Western Isles	971	301	1,272	13.0	9.2
						Wick	386	101	487	11.6	9.1
Denbigh	444	162	606	7.1	4.9						
Dolgellau and Barmouth	276	70	346	7.8	5.8	**Northern Ireland**					
Fishguard	216	63	279	11.3	6.3						
Haverfordwest	1,616	427	2,043	13.4	10.3	Ballymena	1,210	468	1,678	6.9	5.8
Holyhead	1,541	482	2,023	13.9	11.0	Belfast	23,835	7,433	31,268	8.5	7.4
						Coleraine	3,110	966	4,076	12.0	10.0
Lampeter and Aberaeron	365	138	503	10.3	6.5	Cookstown	904	296	1,200	13.1	10.6
Llandeilo	208	70	278	9.8	5.6	Craigavon	3,697	1,346	5,043	8.2	6.9
Llandrindod Wells	334	145	479	6.0	4.0						
Llanelli	2,241	675	2,916	9.8	8.4	Dungannon	1,526	508	2,034	11.7	9.7
Machynlleth	273	79	352	11.2	7.2	Enniskillen	2,025	616	2,641	12.8	10.4
						Londonderry	6,020	1,481	7,501	14.3	12.3
Merthyr and Rhymney	3,736	950	4,686	10.4	9.1	Magherafelt	995	354	1,349	10.5	8.7
Monmouth	185	71	256	6.6	4.6	Newry	3,223	866	4,089	14.0	11.7
Neath and Port Talbot	2,386	717	3,103	8.0	7.3						
Newport	4,189	1,365	5,554	7.1	6.4	Omagh	1,698	519	2,217	12.6	10.3
Newtown	211	74	285	2.8	2.1	Strabane	1,661	378	2,039	17.1	14.1
Pontypool and Cwmbran	1,811	596	2,407	6.0	5.4						
Pontypridd and Rhondda	3,800	1,044	4,844	8.0	7.2						
Porthmadoc and Ffestiniog	384	155	539	8.8	6.8						
Pwllheli	366	125	491	8.5	6.1						
Shotton, Flint and Rhyl	3,392	993	4,385	5.6	4.8						

+ Travel-to-Work Areas (TTWA's) are defined in the supplement to the September 1984 *Employment Gazette*, with slight amendments as given in the October 1984 (p 467), March 1985 (p 126), February 1986 (p 86) and December 1987 (p S25) issues.

Claimant count rates are calculated as a percentage of the estimated total workforce (the sum of employees in employment, unemployment claimants, self-employed, HM Forces and participants on work-related government-supported training programmes) and as a percentage of estimates of employees in employment and the unemployed only.
Data on claimant unemployment for Assisted Areas, which were redefined on 1 August 1993, are available from the Office for National Statistics Nomis® database. Claimant count rates are available only for those Assisted Areas which map precisely to Travel-to-Work Areas. All the TTWA rates shown are calculated using mid-1996 based denominators.

THOUSANDS

UNITED KINGDOM		18-24				25-49				50 and over				All ages *			
		Up to 26 weeks	Over 26 and up to 52 weeks	Over 52 weeks	All	Up to 26 weeks	Over 26 and up to 52 weeks	Over 52 weeks	All	Up to 26 weeks	Over 26 and up to 52 weeks	Over 52 weeks	All	Up to 26 weeks	Over 26 and up to 52 weeks	Over 52 weeks	All
MALE AND FEMALE																	
1995	Jul	368.2	132.4	153.3	653.8	525.3	243.9	542.8	1312.1	124.0	62.2	165.9	352.1	1033.9	440.0	862.3	2336.2
	Oct	345.6	107.6	141.5	594.7	504.9	228.8	522.0	1255.8	119.2	64.1	161.9	345.2	984.7	401.9	825.7	2212.3
1996	Jan	346.0	120.6	135.6	602.1	571.9	236.6	518.4	1326.9	139.0	62.9	161.8	363.6	1072.9	421.6	816.0	2310.5
	Apr	292.4	135.9	130.0	558.3	525.3	245.4	513.9	1284.6	138.3	62.4	162.2	363.0	972.1	445.5	806.3	2223.9
	Jul	331.3	120.7	127.3	579.4	489.9	234.8	499.3	1224.1	122.9	61.4	152.1	336.4	960.6	418.5	779.0	2158.1
	Oct	296.2	94.0	118.3	508.5	446.0	209.0	476.3	1131.2	111.2	62.4	147.6	321.2	868.1	366.6	742.4	1977.2
1997	Jan	281.6	92.4	105.9	479.9	469.2	186.7	445.4	1101.3	117.5	52.4	139.7	309.5	884.1	332.6	691.1	1907.8
	Apr	243.3	87.7	90.7	421.7	417.7	158.6	397.1	973.3	105.8	40.2	128.6	274.6	784.0	287.5	616.5	1688.0
	Jul	**272.7**	**72.6**	**77.6**	**422.9**	**417.0**	**138.6**	**343.0**	**898.7**	**101.1**	**35.0**	**110.2**	**246.3**	**807.1**	**247.1**	**531.0**	**1585.3**
MALE																	
1995	Jul	237.4	92.7	115.4	445.4	383.7	187.1	463.5	1034.4	91.4	47.0	130.2	268.5	721.8	327.7	709.2	1758.6
	Oct	226.7	76.9	106.1	409.7	372.7	176.3	444.9	993.9	88.3	48.4	126.8	263.5	696.1	302.4	678.0	1676.4
1996	Jan	235.5	84.7	102.1	422.3	430.9	182.2	442.6	1055.6	104.2	47.0	127.0	278.2	779.8	314.8	671.9	1766.4
	Apr	200.7	94.6	98.0	393.3	389.7	188.0	438.0	1015.7	102.3	46.3	127.4	276.0	702.1	329.9	663.5	1695.5
	Jul	213.3	85.6	94.8	393.8	353.6	180.5	424.7	958.8	88.7	45.5	119.2	253.5	665.0	312.6	638.9	1616.5
	Oct	195.0	67.4	88.1	350.5	326.6	159.8	404.4	890.8	80.7	46.1	115.3	242.1	610.6	274.1	607.9	1492.6
1997	Jan	194.0	64.9	79.7	338.6	355.7	144.6	379.6	880.0	86.7	38.6	109.7	235.0	645.5	248.8	569.1	1463.5
	Apr	169.6	61.3	68.1	299.0	317.3	125.6	338.4	781.3	77.0	29.8	101.1	207.9	573.9	217.2	507.6	1298.8
	Jul	**180.4**	**52.0**	**57.5**	**289.9**	**312.0**	**111.6**	**292.7**	**716.3**	**72.2**	**25.9**	**87.2**	**185.3**	**573.8**	**190.0**	**437.5**	**1201.3**
FEMALE																	
1995	Jul	130.8	39.7	38.0	208.4	141.6	56.8	79.3	277.7	32.7	15.2	35.7	83.6	312.1	112.3	153.1	577.5
	Oct	118.9	30.7	35.4	185.0	132.3	52.5	77.1	261.9	30.9	15.8	35.1	81.7	288.7	99.5	147.7	535.9
1996	Jan	110.5	35.9	33.5	179.8	141.0	54.4	75.8	271.2	34.8	15.8	34.7	85.4	293.1	106.8	144.2	544.1
	Apr	91.7	41.3	32.0	165.0	135.6	57.5	75.9	268.9	36.1	16.1	34.9	87.0	270.0	115.6	142.8	528.5
	Jul	118.0	35.1	32.5	185.6	136.4	54.3	74.6	265.2	34.2	15.8	32.9	82.9	295.6	105.9	140.1	541.6
	Oct	101.2	26.6	30.1	157.9	119.3	49.2	71.9	240.5	30.5	16.3	32.3	79.1	257.6	92.6	134.5	484.6
1997	Jan	87.6	27.5	26.2	141.3	113.5	42.1	65.7	221.3	30.7	13.7	30.0	74.5	238.6	83.7	122.0	444.3
	Apr	73.6	26.4	22.6	122.6	100.4	33.0	58.7	192.1	28.8	10.4	27.5	66.7	210.0	70.2	108.9	389.1
	Jul	**92.2**	**20.6**	**20.2**	**132.9**	**105.1**	**27.0**	**50.4**	**182.4**	**28.9**	**9.1**	**23.0**	**61.0**	**233.3**	**57.1**	**93.5**	**384.0**

See footnotes to *Tables 2.1* and *2.2*.
* Including some aged under 18.

New From the Office for National Statistics

PACSTAT
Production and Construction Statistics

PACSTAT contains statistical data from over 100 former ACOP Business Monitors* on a single CD-ROM.

Providing a range of industry specific statistics including:

- employment;
- wages & salaries; and
- capital expenditure.

With Windows compatible software, accessibility and manipulation of PACSTAT multi-dimensional data is simple. PACSTAT uses the Standard Industrial Classification (SIC) 1992 codes, and the 1996 version contains data from the 1994 annual sample inquiry into production and construction. Also included is comparative data from 1993, together with selected back data from 1986.

For further information on PACSTAT or details on how to order your copy please call the:

ONS Sales Desk on 0171 533 5678

---

* Formerly published as the Annual Census of Production/ACOP and Annual Census of Construction/ACOC Business Monitor Series.

2.6 CLAIMANT COUNT
Age and duration: July 10 1997
Government Office Regions

Duration of unemployment in weeks	Male 18-24	Male 25-49	Male 50 and over	Male All ages *	Female 18-24	Female 25-49	Female 50 and over	Female All ages *
NORTH EAST								
2 or less	2,275	2,922	681	6,011	1,318	955	195	2,581
Over 2 and up to 4	1,769	2,237	491	4,618	992	620	140	1,833
4 8	2,041	3,254	756	6,224	781	886	243	2,035
8 13	1,971	3,111	838	6,055	681	798	275	1,841
13 26	3,521	6,103	1,599	11,333	1,179	1,644	565	3,462
26 52	3,621	6,359	1,443	11,456	1,259	1,282	481	3,041
52 104	2,538	6,263	1,523	10,325	799	1,087	410	2,298
104 156	807	3,315	917	5,039	208	461	191	860
156 208	394	2,071	644	3,109	95	286	110	491
208 260	198	1,556	489	2,243	52	197	89	338
Over 260	172	5,557	2,040	7,769	31	537	336	904
All	19,307	42,748	11,421	74,182	7,395	8,753	3,035	19,684
NORTH WEST								
2 or less	4,051	4,697	1,018	9,978	2,447	1,869	444	4,909
Over 2 and up to 4	3,055	3,640	726	7,585	1,623	1,203	274	3,230
4 8	3,305	5,506	1,130	10,157	1,425	1,649	459	3,711
8 13	3,037	5,364	1,275	9,862	1,191	1,434	430	3,195
13 26	5,004	9,489	2,271	16,945	1,854	2,482	812	5,285
26 52	4,831	9,841	2,153	16,884	1,661	1,968	670	4,341
52 104	2,790	8,356	1,926	13,076	949	1,372	482	2,807
104 156	830	3,685	890	5,405	226	566	221	1,013
156 208	320	2,014	578	2,912	72	281	120	473
208 260	169	1,413	436	2,018	37	169	75	281
Over 260	142	4,970	1,877	6,989	22	515	316	853
All	27,534	58,975	14,280	101,811	11,507	13,508	4,303	30,098
MERSEYSIDE								
2 or less	1,242	1,441	278	3,030	781	523	107	1,460
Over 2 and up to 4	943	1,079	208	2,287	541	381	70	1,035
4 8	1,349	1,940	362	3,746	592	628	153	1,427
8 13	1,084	1,889	408	3,441	460	501	158	1,164
13 26	2,185	3,770	781	6,793	890	930	278	2,131
26 52	2,658	4,480	871	8,028	957	956	296	2,224
52 104	2,122	4,717	898	7,739	752	954	265	1,972
104 156	677	2,253	459	3,389	220	382	136	738
156 208	322	1,377	297	1,996	93	209	77	379
208 260	214	991	235	1,440	42	143	66	251
Over 260	180	4,514	1,388	6,082	30	472	252	754
All	12,976	28,451	6,185	47,971	5,358	6,079	1,858	13,535
YORKSHIRE AND THE HUMBER								
2 or less	3,770	4,691	1,099	9,782	2,366	1,783	431	4,744
Over 2 and up to 4	2,970	3,920	805	7,859	1,677	1,201	254	3,261
4 8	3,416	5,763	1,376	10,788	1,503	1,768	529	3,968
8 13	3,088	5,755	1,356	10,370	1,237	1,552	501	3,452
13 26	5,403	10,626	2,771	18,965	2,170	2,934	1,026	6,274
26 52	5,494	11,074	2,588	19,187	2,086	2,436	814	5,401
52 104	3,713	9,841	2,552	16,110	1,336	1,812	739	3,889
104 156	1,105	4,796	1,360	7,261	314	735	354	1,403
156 208	412	2,426	814	3,652	136	381	212	729
208 260	245	1,630	593	2,468	60	218	122	400
Over 260	230	6,450	2,721	9,401	41	730	547	1,318
All	29,846	66,972	18,035	115,843	12,926	15,550	5,529	34,839
EAST MIDLANDS								
2 or less	2,604	2,877	650	6,244	1,830	1,292	310	3,537
Over 2 and up to 4	1,916	2,318	515	4,841	1,166	832	210	2,279
4 8	2,069	3,461	812	6,485	925	1,213	367	2,615
8 13	1,774	3,375	959	6,221	784	1,157	337	2,379
13 26	3,289	6,589	1,778	11,761	1,396	2,178	655	4,296
26 52	3,435	6,843	1,693	12,014	1,281	1,587	605	3,494
52 104	2,026	6,090	1,650	9,769	742	1,235	480	2,461
104 156	633	2,968	837	4,438	247	485	249	981
156 208	259	1,736	594	2,589	69	274	139	482
208 260	147	1,255	448	1,850	33	184	98	315
Over 260	143	4,573	1,830	6,546	31	584	361	976
All	18,295	42,085	11,766	72,758	8,504	11,021	3,811	23,815
WEST MIDLANDS								
2 or less	3,362	3,964	906	8,382	2,411	1,625	355	4,490
Over 2 and up to 4	2,563	3,201	615	6,492	1,631	1,096	262	3,065
4 8	3,047	4,901	1,170	9,277	1,394	1,566	490	3,555
8 13	2,855	5,273	1,278	9,530	1,182	1,549	520	3,363
13 26	5,141	9,748	2,436	17,464	2,258	2,812	931	6,104
26 52	4,587	9,547	2,353	16,524	2,146	2,189	811	5,173
52 104	3,287	9,112	2,395	14,799	1,360	1,797	760	3,918
104 156	481	2,519	768	3,768	452	796	414	1,662
156 208	287	1,966	654	2,907	206	446	230	882
208 260	308	7,832	3,057	11,197	85	320	191	596
Over 260	133	3,556	1,557	5,246	80	1,017	664	1,761
All	26,949	62,423	16,908	107,007	13,205	15,213	5,628	34,569

Duration of unemployment in weeks	Male 18-24	Male 25-49	Male 50 and over	Male All ages *	Female 18-24	Female 25-49	Female 50 and over	Female All ages *
EASTERN								
2 or less	2,729	3,240	853	6,938	1,826	1,291	409	3,630
Over 2 and up to 4	1,672	2,416	616	4,790	971	932	273	2,254
4 8	2,036	3,852	1,069	7,090	956	1,316	416	2,807
8 13	1,877	3,846	1,119	6,955	844	1,347	423	2,702
13 26	3,234	7,073	2,037	12,446	1,483	2,417	874	4,854
26 52	3,120	7,310	2,057	12,517	1,268	1,870	760	3,925
52 104	1,880	6,605	1,944	10,432	797	1,464	662	2,924
104 156	655	3,324	1,117	5,096	214	666	356	1,236
156 208	255	1,842	676	2,773	90	361	199	650
208 260	144	1,351	587	2,082	30	249	154	433
Over 260	133	3,556	1,557	5,246	32	503	363	898
All	17,735	44,415	13,632	76,365	8,511	12,416	4,889	26,313
LONDON								
2 or less	3,894	6,701	1,097	11,835	2,992	3,285	533	6,950
Over 2 and up to 4	2,804	5,570	863	9,360	1,909	2,352	416	4,816
4 8	3,861	9,430	1,624	15,100	2,403	3,686	748	7,020
8 13	3,760	10,393	1,805	16,124	2,110	3,653	846	6,748
13 26	6,934	18,764	3,458	29,333	3,740	6,626	1,520	12,052
26 52	6,984	19,634	3,700	30,391	3,861	6,298	1,530	11,747
52 104	5,684	21,606	4,157	31,459	2,923	6,032	1,694	10,656
104 156	2,182	12,205	2,582	16,969	963	2,931	893	4,787
156 208	1,014	7,782	1,841	10,637	391	1,587	578	2,556
208 260	534	5,370	1,470	7,374	157	899	387	1,443
Over 260	372	13,432	4,312	18,116	57	1,722	965	2,744
All	38,023	130,887	26,909	196,698	21,506	39,071	10,110	71,519
SOUTH EAST								
2 or less	3,425	4,710	1,159	9,442	2,160	1,863	513	4,666
Over 2 and up to 4	2,199	3,363	793	6,450	1,185	1,147	259	2,675
4 8	2,644	5,468	1,406	9,662	1,176	1,739	561	3,602
8 13	2,316	5,340	1,476	9,263	947	1,609	620	3,280
13 26	3,867	9,407	2,743	16,114	1,556	2,807	1,018	5,478
26 52	3,448	9,194	2,360	15,038	1,288	2,202	870	4,382
52 104	2,313	8,553	2,543	13,413	904	1,879	868	3,655
104 156	788	4,483	1,556	6,827	272	833	479	1,584
156 208	296	2,481	905	3,682	105	424	263	792
208 260	167	1,704	728	2,599	47	295	189	531
Over 260	134	4,517	2,145	6,796	27	592	418	1,037
All	21,597	59,220	17,814	99,286	9,667	15,390	6,058	31,682
SOUTH WEST								
2 or less	2,644	3,392	761	6,922	1,741	1,454	342	3,642
Over 2 and up to 4	1,689	2,534	529	4,844	904	951	224	2,148
4 8	2,037	3,975	945	7,078	938	1,284	426	2,727
8 13	1,740	3,665	1,024	6,518	711	1,188	355	2,318
13 26	2,948	6,651	1,905	11,581	1,271	2,105	762	4,189
26 52	2,924	6,986	1,941	11,858	1,118	1,767	733	3,632
52 104	1,946	6,625	2,045	10,619	747	1,587	646	2,980
104 156	611	3,145	1,140	4,896	199	654	374	1,227
156 208	215	1,699	676	2,590	79	296	192	567
208 260	126	1,166	507	1,799	34	209	124	367
Over 260	119	3,550	1,615	5,284	25	502	367	894
All	16,999	43,388	13,088	73,989	7,767	11,997	4,545	24,691
WALES								
2 or less	2,300	2,497	545	5,449	1,618	1,070	243	3,012
Over 2 and up to 4	1,715	2,074	452	4,337	944	708	170	1,894
4 8	1,904	2,971	681	5,689	885	942	249	2,150
8 13	1,726	2,839	692	5,359	602	826	261	1,764
13 26	2,857	5,229	1,368	9,561	1,042	1,496	503	3,110
26 52	3,164	5,703	1,281	10,174	1,020	1,207	393	2,635
52 104	2,039	5,518	1,436	8,995	594	885	398	1,878
104 156	656	2,655	641	3,952	157	366	156	679
156 208	246	1,229	373	1,848	70	191	89	350
208 260	124	924	290	1,338	26	129	77	232
Over 260	115	3,216	1,134	4,465	16	356	233	605
All	16,846	34,855	8,893	61,167	6,974	8,176	2,772	18,309
SCOTLAND								
2 or less	3,785	5,290	1,141	10,571	2,412	2,975	611	6,228
Over 2 and up to 4	3,655	4,990	985	9,916	2,141	1,932	353	4,651
4 8	4,105	6,820	1,529	12,944	1,953	2,151	607	5,061
8 13	3,382	6,301	1,522	11,628	1,244	1,903	620	4,044
13 26	5,788	11,410	2,902	20,566	2,108	3,375	1,212	7,011
26 52	5,764	11,534	2,828	20,252	1,820	2,541	932	5,416
52 104	3,560	10,273	2,705	16,559	1,054	1,910	802	3,776
104 156	981	4,198	1,153	6,332	245	645	358	1,248
156 208	404	2,569	821	3,794	82	326	180	588
208 260	221	1,764	666	2,651	46	212	148	406
Over 260	178	6,130	2,816	9,124	34	660	546	1,240
All	31,823	71,279	19,068	124,337	13,139	18,630	6,369	39,669
NORTHERN IRELAND								
2 or less	1,137	1,153	217	2,515	1,111	991	196	2,309
Over 2 and up to 4	1,348	1,146	190	2,690	1,273	568	91	1,942
4 8	1,647	1,881	335	3,871	1,155	674	152	1,990
8 13	1,017	1,720	330	3,073	475	474	133	1,089
13 26	1,661	2,954	634	5,256	747	870	213	1,838
26 52	1,967	3,138	618	5,726	789	660	230	1,680
52 104	1,784	4,328	771	6,883	570	783	272	1,625
104 156	427	1,192	221	1,840	195	375	155	725
156 208	677	1,889	322	2,888	79	258	117	454
208 260	724	2,582	485	3,791	43	199	103	345
Over 260	348	1,789	388	2,525	26	742	466	1,234
All	11,633	20,691	3,968	36,330	6,463	6,594	2,128	15,231

* Include some aged under 18. These figures have been affected by the change in benefit regulations for under 18-year-olds introduced in September 1988. See also note + to *Tables 2.1* and *2.2*.

GREAT BRITAIN

Duration of unemployment in weeks	Under 18	18	19	20-24	25-29	30-34	35-39	40-44	45-49	50-54	55-59	60 and over	All ages
MALE													
One or less	1,049	2,351	2,386	12,407	7,210	5,316	3,704	2,918	2,617	2,411	1,752	526	44,647
Over 1 and up to 2	844	2,357	2,540	14,040	8,103	5,908	4,345	3,315	2,986	2,838	1,981	680	49,937
2 – 4	1,489	3,748	3,539	19,663	12,652	9,074	6,355	4,966	4,295	4,039	2,780	779	73,379
4 – 6	1,238	2,990	2,517	13,218	10,196	7,864	5,556	4,327	3,827	3,710	2,687	788	58,918
6 – 8	987	2,228	1,999	8,862	7,997	6,253	4,723	3,505	3,093	2,840	2,264	571	45,322
8 – 13	1,813	5,193	4,213	19,204	17,851	14,039	10,175	8,007	7,079	6,916	5,427	1,409	101,326
13 – 26	1,783	8,628	7,706	33,837	31,811	25,916	19,057	14,601	13,474	12,959	10,322	2,768	182,862
26 – 39	401	4,227	4,514	20,890	19,618	15,813	11,622	8,987	8,059	7,477	6,339	1,090	109,037
39 – 52	119	2,340	3,728	14,331	13,867	10,977	8,027	6,030	5,505	5,527	4,530	305	75,286
52 – 65	51	367	2,925	10,421	10,279	8,300	6,323	4,898	4,434	4,193	3,402	206	55,799
65 – 78	8	180	1,719	6,318	7,279	6,570	5,217	4,104	3,696	3,977	3,242	144	42,454
78 – 104	5	106	1,953	9,909	11,727	10,510	7,923	6,494	5,805	5,687	4,714	209	65,042
104 – 156	0	43	313	10,600	13,312	12,519	9,950	8,136	7,470	7,277	6,417	234	76,271
156 – 208	0	0	12	4,606	7,125	7,460	5,920	4,798	4,442	4,624	4,235	128	43,350
208 – 260	0	0	0	2,576	4,676	5,041	4,381	3,674	3,318	3,499	3,493	111	30,769
Over 260	0	0	0	2,226	11,092	15,918	14,823	13,145	13,319	12,998	13,107	387	97,015
All	9,787	34,758	40,064	203,108	194,795	167,478	128,101	101,905	93,419	90,972	76,692	10,335	1,151,414
FEMALE													
One or less	827	1,540	1,588	7,976	3,041	1,752	1,322	1,319	1,448	1,235	721	0	22,769
Over 1 and up to 2	642	1,529	1,783	9,486	3,695	2,212	1,749	1,679	1,768	1,546	991	0	27,080
2 – 4	1,197	2,235	2,181	11,268	4,665	2,677	2,052	1,938	2,023	1,789	1,115	1	33,141
4 – 6	930	1,688	1,390	6,149	3,470	2,225	1,691	1,657	1,855	1,799	1,172	1	24,027
6 – 8	741	1,262	1,015	3,427	2,431	1,634	1,267	1,247	1,351	1,303	971	2	16,651
8 – 13	1,394	2,867	2,157	6,969	5,247	3,544	2,863	2,764	3,099	3,161	2,177	8	36,250
13 – 26	1,337	4,953	3,997	11,997	9,131	6,558	5,093	5,218	5,806	5,849	4,293	14	64,246
26 – 39	351	2,168	2,325	6,770	4,645	2,928	2,391	2,631	2,927	2,997	2,367	14	32,514
39 – 52	97	1,184	2,207	5,111	3,313	2,059	1,515	1,874	2,020	1,936	1,572	9	22,897
52 – 65	25	211	1,364	4,009	2,392	1,440	1,190	1,418	1,472	1,395	1,126	4	16,046
65 – 78	8	98	884	2,180	1,556	1,083	911	1,095	1,240	1,315	1,077	5	11,452
78 – 104	4	57	894	3,260	2,299	1,629	1,268	1,374	1,647	1,807	1,469	8	15,716
104 – 156	0	13	127	3,577	2,590	1,919	1,406	1,579	2,026	2,187	1,979	15	17,418
156 – 208	0	0	13	1,475	1,409	1,061	727	787	1,078	1,205	1,175	9	8,939
208 – 260	0	0	0	649	775	662	486	534	767	844	871	5	5,593
Over 260	0	0	0	426	1,694	1,799	1,394	1,402	1,901	2,535	2,814	19	13,984
All	7,553	19,805	21,925	84,729	52,353	35,182	27,325	28,516	32,428	32,903	25,890	114	368,723

UNITED KINGDOM

Duration of unemployment in weeks	Under 18	18	19	20-24	25-29	30-34	35-39	40-44	45-49	50-54	55-59	60 and over	All ages
MALE													
One or less	1,051	2,406	2,470	12,737	7,412	5,432	3,788	2,974	2,667	2,454	1,788	533	45,712
Over 1 and up to 2	850	2,433	2,670	14,502	8,344	6,039	4,462	3,405	3,052	2,905	2,035	690	51,387
2 – 4	1,495	3,882	3,740	20,676	13,085	9,367	6,530	5,102	4,404	4,130	2,855	803	76,069
4 – 6	1,240	3,084	2,641	14,085	10,616	8,116	5,742	4,467	3,917	3,793	2,769	803	61,273
6 – 8	993	2,323	2,072	9,256	8,236	6,450	4,888	3,615	3,175	2,921	2,325	584	46,838
8 – 13	1,819	5,364	4,371	19,892	18,403	14,433	10,510	8,261	7,264	7,100	5,547	1,435	104,399
13 – 26	1,790	8,909	7,975	34,948	32,740	26,654	19,613	14,997	13,809	13,267	10,590	2,826	188,118
26 – 39	403	4,388	4,695	21,607	20,201	16,264	11,939	9,221	8,237	7,652	6,481	1,103	112,191
39 – 52	120	2,436	4,009	14,862	14,324	11,320	8,266	6,205	5,666	5,688	4,649	313	77,858
52 – 65	51	371	3,091	10,931	10,645	8,636	6,567	5,066	4,567	4,322	3,494	213	57,954
65 – 78	8	182	1,798	6,664	7,636	6,869	5,450	4,256	3,847	4,103	3,331	150	44,294
78 – 104	5	107	2,029	10,509	12,331	11,009	8,270	6,741	5,997	5,868	4,847	217	67,930
104 – 156	0	43	316	11,321	13,990	13,228	10,459	8,540	7,752	7,536	6,633	244	80,062
156 – 208	0	0	12	4,954	7,596	7,954	6,256	5,051	4,677	4,834	4,409	132	45,875
208 – 260	0	0	0	2,772	5,026	5,424	4,760	3,939	3,543	3,717	3,666	121	32,968
Over 260	0	0	0	2,397	12,015	17,640	16,668	15,071	15,198	14,611	14,352	438	108,390
All	9,825	35,928	41,889	212,113	202,600	174,835	134,168	106,911	97,772	94,901	79,771	10,605	1,201,318
FEMALE													
One or less	834	1,572	1,672	8,269	3,141	1,807	1,360	1,355	1,488	1,266	742	0	23,506
Over 1 and up to 2	646	1,585	1,907	10,008	3,929	2,341	1,883	1,796	1,876	1,639	1,042	0	28,652
2 – 4	1,207	2,319	2,378	12,260	4,887	2,790	2,133	2,034	2,079	1,845	1,150	1	35,083
4 – 6	933	1,747	1,472	6,915	3,661	2,316	1,747	1,714	1,895	1,855	1,208	1	25,464
6 – 8	747	1,296	1,063	3,593	2,506	1,684	1,311	1,288	1,380	1,334	1,000	2	17,204
8 – 13	1,401	2,966	2,246	7,256	5,400	3,654	2,945	2,831	3,161	3,240	2,231	8	37,339
13 – 26	1,345	5,117	4,175	12,402	9,427	6,740	5,221	5,356	5,932	5,967	4,387	15	66,084
26 – 39	352	2,252	2,417	6,973	4,754	3,007	2,440	2,695	2,996	3,062	2,430	14	33,392
39 – 52	97	1,230	2,388	5,294	3,399	2,108	1,566	1,920	2,078	1,996	1,613	10	23,699
52 – 65	25	213	1,426	4,212	2,478	1,483	1,228	1,464	1,518	1,454	1,159	4	16,664
65 – 78	8	98	914	2,258	1,616	1,124	940	1,139	1,276	1,356	1,104	5	11,838
78 – 104	4	58	919	3,429	2,392	1,679	1,315	1,430	1,715	1,861	1,527	8	16,337
104 – 156	0	13	128	3,771	2,708	1,980	1,459	1,635	2,113	2,269	2,052	15	18,143
156 – 208	0	0	13	1,554	1,464	1,105	767	839	1,145	1,262	1,235	9	9,393
208 – 260	0	0	0	692	821	699	515	572	816	895	923	5	5,938
Over 260	0	0	0	452	1,819	1,964	1,525	1,546	2,078	2,777	3,036	21	15,218
All	7,599	20,466	23,118	89,338	54,402	36,481	28,355	29,614	33,546	34,078	26,839	118	383,954

2.7 CLAIMANT COUNT
Age

UNITED KINGDOM	All 18 and over	18 to 19	20 to 24	25 to 29	30 to 39	40 to 49	50 to 59	60 and over	All ages *
MALE AND FEMALE									
1996 Jul	2139.8	149.7	429.6	353.9	503.7	366.4	315.1	21.3	2158.1
Oct	1960.9	140.7	367.7	324.6	466.6	340.0	301.5	19.7	1907.8
1997 Jan	1890.7	136.1	343.8	314.0	456.9	330.4	291.3	18.2	1907.8
Apr	1669.6	125.5	296.2	275.6	404.9	292.8	261.7	12.9	1688.0
Jul	**1567.8**	**121.4**	**301.5**	**257.0**	**373.8**	**267.8**	**235.6**	**10.7**	**1585.3**
MALE									
1996 Jul	1606.1	94.8	299.0	274.6	408.9	275.3	232.5	20.9	1616.5
Oct	1483.4	88.6	261.9	252.7	380.6	257.5	222.7	19.4	1463.5
1997 Jan	1453.6	87.7	251.0	248.5	378.4	253.1	217.0	18.0	1463.5
Apr	1288.2	81.3	217.8	219.5	336.8	224.9	195.2	12.7	1298.8
Jul	**1191.5**	**77.8**	**212.1**	**202.6**	**309.0**	**204.7**	**174.7**	**10.6**	**1201.3**
FEMALE									
1996 Jul	533.7	54.9	130.6	79.3	94.8	91.1	82.6	0.3	541.6
Oct	477.5	52.1	105.8	71.9	86.0	82.5	78.8	0.3	444.3
1997 Jan	437.1	48.4	92.9	65.5	78.6	77.2	74.3	0.2	444.3
Apr	381.4	44.2	78.4	56.0	68.2	67.9	66.5	0.1	389.1
Jul	**376.4**	**43.6**	**89.3**	**54.4**	**64.8**	**63.2**	**60.9**	**0.1**	**384.0**

* Including some aged under 18.

2.8 CLAIMANT COUNT
Duration

UNITED KINGDOM	Up to 4 weeks	Over 4 and up to 26 weeks	Over 26 and up to 52 weeks	Over 52 and up to 104 weeks	Over 104 and up to 156 weeks	Over 156 weeks	All unemployed	Total over 52 weeks
MALE AND FEMALE								Thousand
1996 Jul	298.7	661.9	418.5	336.5	136.4	306.1	2158.1	779.0
Oct	213.4	654.8	366.6	319.7	130.8	291.9	1977.2	742.4
1997 Jan	222.7	661.4	332.6	296.3	122.8	271.9	1907.8	691.1
Apr	201.8	582.2	287.5	256.9	112.8	246.8	1688.0	616.5
Jul	**260.4**	**546.7**	**247.1**	**215.0**	**98.2**	**217.8**	**1585.3**	**531.0**
	Proportion of number unemployed						Per cent	
1996 Jul	13.8	30.7	19.4	15.6	6.3	14.2	100.0	36.1
Oct	10.8	33.1	18.5	16.2	6.6	14.8	100.0	37.5
1997 Jan	11.7	34.7	17.4	15.5	6.4	14.3	100.0	36.2
Apr	12.0	34.5	17.0	15.2	6.7	14.6	100.0	36.5
Jul	**16.4**	**34.5**	**15.6**	**13.6**	**6.2**	**13.7**	**100.0**	**33.5**
MALE								Thousand
1996 Jul	189.9	475.1	312.6	264.2	111.2	263.5	1616.5	638.9
Oct	149.7	460.9	274.1	250.8	106.2	250.9	1492.6	607.9
1997 Jan	159.4	486.2	248.8	234.6	100.4	234.1	1463.5	569.1
Apr	144.1	429.9	217.2	203.2	92.2	212.3	1298.8	507.6
Jul	**173.2**	**400.6**	**190.0**	**170.2**	**80.1**	**187.2**	**1201.3**	**437.5**
	Proportion of number unemployed						Per cent	
1996 Jul	11.7	29.4	19.3	16.3	6.9	16.3	100.0	39.5
Oct	10.0	30.9	18.4	16.8	7.1	16.8	100.0	40.7
1997 Jan	10.9	33.2	17.0	16.0	6.9	16.0	100.0	38.9
Apr	11.1	33.1	16.7	15.6	7.1	16.3	100.0	39.1
Jul	**14.4**	**33.3**	**15.8**	**14.2**	**6.7**	**15.6**	**100.0**	**36.4**
FEMALE Thousand								
1996 Jul	108.8	186.8	105.9	72.3	25.2	42.6	541.6	140.1
Oct	63.6	193.9	92.6	68.9	24.6	41.0	484.6	134.5
1997 Jan	63.3	175.2	83.7	61.8	22.4	37.9	444.3	122.0
Apr	57.7	152.3	70.2	53.7	20.7	34.5	389.1	108.9
Jul	**87.2**	**146.1**	**57.1**	**44.8**	**18.1**	**30.5**	**384.0**	**93.5**
	Proportion of number unemployed						Per cent	
1996 Jul	20.1	34.5	19.6	13.3	4.7	7.9	100.0	25.9
Oct	13.1	40.0	19.1	14.2	5.1	8.5	100.0	27.7
1997 Jan	14.3	39.4	18.8	13.9	5.0	8.5	100.0	27.5
Apr	14.8	39.1	18.0	13.8	5.3	8.9	100.0	28.0
Jul	**22.7**	**38.0**	**14.9**	**11.7**	**4.7**	**8.0**	**100.0**	**24.4**

Claimant count in counties and local authority districts as at July 10 1997

	Male	Female	All	Rate + Per cent employees and unemployed	Rate + Per cent workforce
SOUTH EAST					
Berkshire	**7,556**	**2,234**	**9,790**	**2.8**	**2.4**
Bracknell	833	257	1,090		
Newbury	858	275	1,133		
Reading	2,028	530	2,558		
Slough	2,060	598	2,658		
Windsor and Maidenhead	1,137	362	1,499		
Wokingham	640	212	852		
Buckinghamshire (former county)					
Milton Keynes	2,621	919	3,540	3.6	3.2
Rest of Buckinghamshire	**3,893**	**1,311**	**5,204**	**2.8**	**2.3**
Aylesbury Vale	1,377	502	1,879		
Chiltern	532	167	699		
South Buckinghamshire	414	180	594		
Wycombe	1,570	462	2,032		
East Sussex (former county)					
Brighton and Hove	8,112	2,948	11,060	10.4	8.9
Rest of East Sussex	**6,709**	**2,101**	**8,810**	**6.0**	**4.6**
Eastbourne	1,331	421	1,752		
Hastings	2,419	626	3,045		
Lewes	1,112	382	1,494		
Rother	1,034	335	1,369		
Wealden	813	337	1,150		
Hampshire (former county)					
Portsmouth	4,720	1,305	6,025	7.1	6.2
Southampton	5,086	1,282	6,368	5.8	5.0
Rest of Hampshire	**10,986**	**3,639**	**14,625**	**3.6**	**2.9**
Basingstoke and Deane	1,238	420	1,658		
East Hampshire	883	313	1,196		
Eastleigh	848	281	1,129		
Fareham	798	309	1,107		
Gosport	1,105	414	1,519		
Hart	382	143	525		
Havant	2,072	508	2,580		
New Forest	1,504	478	1,982		
Rushmoor	720	257	977		
Test Valley	731	264	995		
Winchester	705	252	957		
Isle of Wight	**2,886**	**910**	**3,796**	**9.0**	**7.8**
Kent	**28,298**	**8,688**	**36,986**	**6.4**	**5.4**
Ashford	1,458	451	1,909		
Canterbury	2,264	685	2,949		
Dartford	1,567	478	2,045		
Dover	2,490	667	3,157		
Gillingham	1,635	610	2,245		
Gravesham	1,985	593	2,578		
Maidstone	1,774	656	2,430		
Rochester-upon-Medway	3,181	999	4,180		
Sevenoaks	1,108	410	1,518		
Shepway	2,651	680	3,331		
Swale	2,444	772	3,216		
Thanet	3,626	996	4,622		
Tonbridge and Malling	1,093	379	1,472		
Tunbridge Wells	1,022	312	1,334		
Oxfordshire	**5,079**	**1,850**	**6,929**	**2.6**	**2.2**
Cherwell	967	347	1,314		
Oxford	2,188	736	2,924		
South Oxfordshire	764	295	1,059		
Vale of White Horse	652	241	893		
West Oxfordshire	508	231	739		
Surrey	**7,062**	**2,364**	**9,426**	**2.3**	**1.9**
Elmbridge	873	315	1,188		
Epsom and Ewell	532	182	714		
Guildford	885	287	1,172		
Mole Valley	419	124	543		
Reigate and Banstead	861	285	1,146		
Runnymede	555	183	738		
Spelthorne	838	281	1,119		
Surrey Heath	360	140	500		
Tandridge	550	189	739		
Waverley	650	212	862		
Woking	539	166	705		
West Sussex	**6,278**	**2,131**	**8,409**	**2.8**	**2.4**
Adur	601	234	835		
Arun	1,197	392	1,589		
Chichester	830	293	1,123		
Crawley	1,013	334	1,347		
Horsham	717	282	999		
MidSussex	771	278	1,049		
Worthing	1,149	318	1,467		
LONDON					
Greater London	**196,698**	**71,519**	**268,217**	**7.5**	**6.6**
Barking and Dagenham	3,635	1,187	4,822		
Barnet	5,494	2,252	7,746		
Bexley	3,916	1,473	5,389		
Brent	9,426	3,313	12,739		
Bromley	4,316	1,454	5,770		
Camden	6,668	2,859	9,527		
City of London	94	29	123		
City of Westminster	4,514	1,902	6,416		
Croydon	7,458	2,557	10,015		
Ealing	6,722	2,407	9,129		

	Male	Female	All	Rate + Per cent employees and unemployed	Rate + Per cent workforce
Enfield	6,604	2,332	8,936		
Greenwich	7,455	2,507	9,962		
Hackney	11,142	4,007	15,149		
Hammersmith and Fulham	5,436	2,284	7,720		
Haringey	9,798	3,575	13,373		
Harrow	3,199	1,329	4,528		
Havering	3,160	1,085	4,245		
Hillingdon	3,462	1,220	4,682		
Hounslow	4,205	1,557	5,762		
Islington	8,170	3,219	11,389		
Kensington and Chelsea	3,481	1,695	5,176		
Kingston-upon-Thames	1,735	671	2,406		
Lambeth	12,115	4,478	16,593		
Lewisham	9,623	3,270	12,893		
Merton	3,503	1,260	4,763		
Newham	9,396	2,945	12,341		
Redbridge	5,107	1,872	6,979		
Richmond-upon-Thames	2,050	857	2,907		
Southwark	10,019	3,668	13,687		
Sutton	2,258	812	3,070		
Tower Hamlets	8,212	2,264	10,476		
Waltham Forest	7,104	2,407	9,511		
Wandsworth	7,221	2,772	9,993		
EASTERN					
Bedfordshire (former county)					
Luton	3,961	1,221	5,182	6.5	5.8
Rest of Bedfordshire	**4,359**	**1,669**	**6,028**	**4.4**	**3.6**
Mid Bedfordshire	823	400	1,223		
North Bedfordshire	2,372	813	3,185		
South Bedfordshire	1,164	456	1,620		
Cambridgeshire	**8,647**	**3,241**	**11,888**	**3.9**	**3.3**
Cambridge	1,677	601	2,278		
East Cambridgeshire	515	248	763		
Fenland	1,298	498	1,796		
Huntingdon	1,310	572	1,882		
Peterborough	3,036	999	4,035		
South Cambridgeshire	811	323	1,134		
Essex	**25,075**	**8,450**	**33,525**	**6.2**	**5.1**
Basildon	2,975	979	3,954		
Braintree	1,557	623	2,180		
Brentwood	649	215	864		
Castle Point	1,305	477	1,782		
Chelmsford	1,777	624	2,401		
Colchester	1,885	699	2,584		
Epping Forest	1,469	572	2,041		
Harlow	1,375	487	1,862		
Maldon	736	216	952		
Rochford	920	346	1,266		
Southend-on-Sea	4,980	1,486	6,466		
Tendring	2,366	654	3,020		
Thurrock	2,671	873	3,544		
Uttlesford	410	199	609		
Hertfordshire	**10,234**	**3,540**	**13,774**	**3.2**	**2.8**
Broxbourne	1,100	391	1,491		
Dacorum	1,205	427	1,632		
East Hertfordshire	888	357	1,245		
Hertsmere	858	329	1,187		
North Hertfordshire	1,234	418	1,652		
St Albans	924	340	1,264		
Stevenage	1,341	444	1,785		
Three Rivers	696	226	922		
Watford	1,120	310	1,430		
Welwyn Hatfield	868	298	1,166		
Norfolk	**13,824**	**4,688**	**18,512**	**6.3**	**5.1**
Breckland	1,415	565	1,980		
Broadland	1,197	496	1,693		
Great Yarmouth	2,592	758	3,350		
North Norfolk	1,306	442	1,748		
Norwich	3,985	1,173	5,158		
South Norfolk	1,246	505	1,751		
West Norfolk	2,083	749	2,832		
Suffolk	**10,265**	**3,504**	**13,769**	**5.1**	**4.4**
Babergh	910	330	1,240		
Forest Heath	531	209	740		
Ipswich	2,716	758	3,474		
Mid Suffolk	756	337	1,093		
St Edmundsbury	1,032	442	1,474		
Suffolk Coastal	1,405	489	1,894		
Waveney	2,915	939	3,854		
SOUTH WEST					
Avon (former county)					
Bath & North East Somerset	2,421	898	3,319	4.4	3.8
Bristol	9,920	2,949	12,869	5.8	5.3
North Somerset	2,213	753	2,966	5.3	4.3
South Gloucestershire	2,259	883	3,142	3.5	3.1
Cornwall	**9,524**	**3,102**	**12,626**	**7.9**	**6.0**
Caradon	1,163	405	1,568		
Carrick	1,823	587	2,410		
Isles of Scilly	4	1	5		
Kerrier	2,048	664	2,712		
North Cornwall	1,264	397	1,661		
Penwith	1,552	520	2,072		
Restormel	1,670	528	2,198		

Claimant count in counties and local authority districts as at July 10 1997

	Male	Female	All	Rate + Per cent employees and unemployed	Rate + Per cent workforce
Devon	**18,475**	**6,101**	**24,576**	6.1	4.9
East Devon	1,079	394	1,473		
Exeter	2,024	645	2,669		
Mid Devon	673	293	966		
North Devon	1,361	458	1,819		
Plymouth	6,776	2,114	8,890		
South Hams	892	369	1,261		
Teignbridge	1,506	519	2,025		
Torbay	2,645	755	3,400		
Torridge	982	356	1,338		
West Devon	537	198	735		
Dorset (former county)					
Bournemouth	3,595	974	4,569	6.6	5.6
Poole	1,841	516	2,357	3.9	3.2
Rest of Dorset	**3,616**	**1,300**	**4,916**	4.1	3.1
Christchurch	428	134	562		
East Dorset	575	244	819		
North Dorset	314	154	468		
Purbeck	352	121	473		
West Dorset	778	329	1,107		
Weymouth and Portland	1,169	318	1,487		
Gloucestershire	**7,244**	**2,592**	**9,836**	4.4	3.6
Cheltenham	1,859	602	2,461		
Cotswold	468	194	662		
Forest of Dean	872	380	1,252		
Gloucester	2,158	664	2,822		
Stroud	1,186	477	1,663		
Tewkesbury	701	275	976		
Wiltshire (former county)					
Thamesdown	2,281	740	3,021	2.9	2.5
Rest of Wiltshire	**3,988**	**1,578**	**5,566**	3.5	2.7
Kennet	606	250	856		
North Wiltshire	1,043	422	1,465		
Salisbury	980	362	1,342		
West Wiltshire	1,359	544	1,903		
Somerset	**6,612**	**2,305**	**8,917**	4.8	3.9
Mendip	1,382	511	1,893		
Sedgemoor	1,590	517	2,107		
South Somerset	1,526	610	2,136		
Taunton Deane	1,582	491	2,073		
West Somerset	532	176	708		
WEST MIDLANDS					
Hereford and Worcester	**9,103**	**3,477**	**12,580**	4.6	3.9
Bromsgrove	1,121	478	1,599		
Hereford	968	364	1,332		
Leominster	490	166	656		
Malvern Hills	958	338	1,296		
Redditch	1,415	564	1,979		
South Herefordshire	539	240	779		
Worcester	1,419	472	1,891		
Wychavon	889	381	1,270		
Wyre Forest	1,304	474	1,778		
Shropshire	**5,165**	**1,801**	**6,966**	4.2	3.4
Bridgnorth	456	210	666		
North Shropshire	485	183	668		
Oswestry	582	237	819		
Shrewsbury and Atcham	1,132	391	1,523		
South Shropshire	423	143	566		
The Wrekin	2,087	637	2,724		
Staffordshire (former county)					
Stoke-on-Trent	4,972	1,335	6,307	5.5	5.0
Rest of Staffordshire	**10,319**	**3,802**	**14,121**	5.0	4.2
Cannock Chase	1,387	491	1,878		
East Staffordshire	1,760	595	2,355		
Lichfield	963	420	1,383		
Newcastle-under-Lyme	1,556	550	2,106		
South Staffordshire	1,318	476	1,794		
Stafford	1,319	491	1,810		
Staffordshire Moorlands	944	344	1,288		
Tamworth	1,072	435	1,507		
Warwickshire	**6,053**	**2,219**	**8,272**	4.1	3.5
North Warwickshire	659	261	920		
Nuneaton and Bedworth	1,876	638	2,514		
Rugby	1,141	402	1,543		
Stratford-on-Avon	925	401	1,326		
Warwick	1,452	517	1,969		
West Midlands	**71,395**	**21,935**	**93,330**	7.7	7.1
Birmingham	33,025	9,933	42,958		
Coventry	7,278	2,225	9,503		
Dudley	6,019	1,947	7,966		
Sandwell	8,477	2,589	11,066		
Solihull	3,074	1,088	4,162		
Walsall	6,724	2,099	8,823		
Wolverhampton	6,798	2,054	8,852		
EAST MIDLANDS					
Derbyshire (former county)					
Derby	6,028	1,813	7,841	7.5	6.9
Rest of Derbyshire	**12,083**	**3,823**	**15,906**	6.1	5.2
Amber Valley	1,652	579	2,231		
Bolsover	1,536	407	1,943		
Chesterfield	2,530	724	3,254		
Derbyshire Dales	611	262	873		
Erewash	1,787	566	2,353		
High Peak	1,176	356	1,532		
North East Derbyshire	1,778	543	2,321		
South Derbyshire	1,013	386	1,399		
Leicestershire (former county)					
Leicester	7,974	2,451	10,425	6.1	5.7
Rutland	173	72	245	2.2	1.6
Rest of Leicestershire	**5,555**	**2,296**	**7,851**	3.4	2.9
Blaby	731	303	1,034		
Charnwood	1,763	742	2,505		
Harborough	431	169	600		
Hinckley and Bosworth	708	323	1,031		
Melton	369	165	534		
North West Leicestershire	991	331	1,322		
Oadby and Wigston	562	263	825		
Lincolnshire	**8,928**	**3,270**	**12,198**	5.4	4.4
Boston	683	283	966		
East Lindsey	1,657	582	2,239		
Lincoln	2,673	747	3,420		
North Kesteven	940	377	1,317		
South Holland	536	261	797		
South Kesteven	1,249	534	1,783		
West Lindsey	1,190	486	1,676		
Northamptonshire	**8,008**	**2,826**	**10,834**	4.2	3.6
Corby	922	268	1,190		
Daventry	576	265	841		
East Northamptonshire	656	262	918		
Kettering	980	352	1,332		
Northampton	3,461	1,147	4,608		
South Northamptonshire	450	221	671		
Wellingborough	963	311	1,274		
Nottinghamshire	**24,009**	**7,264**	**31,273**	7.3	6.6
Ashfield	2,538	716	3,254		
Bassetlaw	2,235	734	2,969		
Broxtowe	1,536	563	2,099		
Gedling	1,815	644	2,459		
Mansfield	2,387	692	3,079		
Newark and Sherwood	1,733	575	2,308		
Nottingham	10,482	2,869	13,351		
Rushcliffe	1,283	471	1,754		
YORKSHIRE AND THE HUMBER					
Humberside (former county)					
East Riding of Yorkshire	4,721	1,774	6,495	6.4	5.4
Kingston-upon-Hull	9,228	2,600	11,828	9.3	8.6
North East Lincolnshire	5,078	1,364	6,442	9.6	8.7
North Lincolnshire	3,077	978	4,055	5.9	5.2
North Yorkshire (former county)					
York	2,840	908	3,748	4.2	3.6
Rest of North Yorkshire	**6,597**	**2,534**	**9,131**	4.6	3.6
Craven	435	155	590		
Hambleton	825	373	1,198		
Harrogate	1,344	556	1,900		
Richmondshire	377	189	566		
Ryedale	441	179	620		
Scarborough	2,086	647	2,733		
Selby	1,089	435	1,524		
South Yorkshire	**37,684**	**10,655**	**48,339**	9.9	8.7
Barnsley	5,427	1,512	6,939		
Doncaster	8,664	2,224	10,888		
Rotherham	7,606	2,007	9,613		
Sheffield	15,987	4,912	20,899		
West Yorkshire	**46,618**	**14,026**	**60,644**	6.4	5.7
Bradford	11,858	3,589	15,447		
Calderdale	4,041	1,185	5,226		
Kirklees	7,554	2,373	9,927		
Leeds	16,482	4,913	21,395		
Wakefield	6,683	1,966	8,649		
NORTH WEST					
Cheshire	**15,297**	**4,923**	**20,220**	4.9	4.2
Chester	1,754	578	2,332		
Congleton	848	317	1,165		
Crewe and Nantwich	1,692	538	2,230		
Ellesmere Port and Neston	1,464	453	1,917		
Halton	3,495	1,064	4,559		
Macclesfield	1,510	469	1,979		
Vale Royal	1,743	587	2,330		
Warrington	2,791	917	3,708		
Cumbria	**9,588**	**2,729**	**12,317**	6.3	5.2
Allerdale	2,422	656	3,078		
Barrow-In-Furness	1,921	445	2,366		
Carlisle	1,930	562	2,492		
Copeland	2,099	578	2,677		
Eden	359	155	514		
South Lakeland	857	333	1,190		
Greater Manchester	**54,334**	**15,725**	**70,059**	6.8	6.0
Bolton	4,720	1,246	5,966		
Bury	2,147	736	2,883		
Manchester	16,471	4,630	21,101		
Oldham	4,171	1,211	5,382		

Claimant count in counties and local authority districts as at July 10 1997

	Male	Female	All	Rate + Per cent employees and unemployed	Rate + Per cent workforce
Rochdale	4,813	1,277	6,090		
Salford	4,774	1,272	6,046		
Stockport	3,950	1,139	5,089		
Tameside	3,868	1,248	5,116		
Trafford	3,495	1,078	4,573		
Wigan	5,925	1,888	7,813		
Lancashire	**22,592**	**6,721**	**29,313**	**4.8**	**4.2**
Blackburn	2,788	715	3,503		
Blackpool	3,353	809	4,162		
Burnley	1,232	361	1,593		
Chorley	1,281	382	1,663		
Fylde	467	140	607		
Hyndburn	1,056	351	1,407		
Lancaster	2,810	957	3,767		
Pendle	1,157	354	1,511		
Preston	3,087	865	3,952		
Ribble Valley	320	138	458		
Rossendale	713	270	983		
South Ribble	1,008	367	1,375		
West Lancashire	2,113	636	2,749		
Wyre	1,207	376	1,583		
MERSEYSIDE					
Merseyside	**47,971**	**13,535**	**61,506**	**11.9**	**10.7**
Knowsley	5,948	1,527	7,475		
Liverpool	20,322	5,638	25,960		
Sefton	7,512	2,184	9,696		
St Helens	4,325	1,233	5,558		
Wirral	9,864	2,953	12,817		
NORTH EAST					
Cleveland (former county)					
Hartlepool	3,429	841	4,270	12.6	11.3
Middlesborough	5,779	1,461	7,240	11.2	10.6
Redcar and Cleveland	4,622	1,168	5,790	12.2	10.7
Stockton-on-Tees	5,904	1,611	7,515	9.8	8.9
Durham (former county)					
Darlington	2,762	753	3,515	7.5	7.1
Rest of Durham	**10,848**	**2,978**	**13,826**	**8.5**	**7.6**
Chester-le-Street	1,166	336	1,502		
Derwentside	2,124	555	2,679		
Durham	1,615	545	2,160		
Easington	2,039	465	2,504		
Sedgefield	1,863	546	2,409		
Teesdale	361	146	507		
Wear Valley	1,680	385	2,065		
Northumberland	**6,342**	**1,911**	**8,253**	**7.7**	**6.6**
Alnwick	606	211	817		
Berwick-upon-Tweed	388	110	498		
Blyth Valley	1,946	603	2,549		
Castle Morpeth	823	270	1,093		
Tynedale	760	259	1,019		
Wansbeck	1,819	458	2,277		
Tyne and Wear	**34,496**	**8,961**	**43,457**	**9.2**	**8.4**
Gateshead	5,272	1,309	6,581		
Newcastle upon Tyne	9,589	2,586	12,175		
North Tyneside	5,373	1,509	6,882		
South Tyneside	5,446	1,419	6,865		
Sunderland	8,816	2,138	10,954		
WALES	**61,167**	**18,309**	**79,476**	**5.3**	**4.6**
Blaenau Gwent	1,988	553	2,541	12.0	10.6
Bridgend	2,408	829	3,237	9.2	7.9
Caerphilly	3,781	1,033	4,814	9.8	8.7
Cardiff	7,597	2,120	9,717	5.6	5.2
Carmarthenshire	3,415	1,056	4,471	8.1	6.6
Ceredigion	1,122	470	1,592	8.3	5.8
Conwy	2,115	558	2,673	8.3	6.3
Denbighshire	1,681	472	2,153	6.9	5.9
Flintshire	2,105	675	2,780	4.9	4.4
Gwynedd	3,186	938	4,124	9.0	7.0
Isle of Anglesey	1,846	607	2,453	13.4	10.4
Merthyr Tydfil	1,550	381	1,931	9.7	8.2
Monmouthshire	1,118	457	1,575	5.5	4.7
Neath Port Talbot	2,835	851	3,686	8.4	7.4
Newport	3,366	1,039	4,405	7.1	6.5
Pembrokeshire	3,258	863	4,121	13.1	9.2
Powys	1,428	574	2,002	4.9	3.6
Rhondda, Cynon, Taff	5,237	1,424	6,661	8.8	7.6
Swansea	5,157	1,444	6,601	7.5	6.8
The Vale of Glamorgan	2,198	758	2,956	5.9	5.1
Torfaen	1,762	556	2,318	6.2	5.3
Wrexham	2,014	651	2,665	5.3	4.6
SCOTLAND	**124,337**	**39,669**	**164,006**	**13.0**	**9.2**
Aberdeen, City of	3,375	1,203	4,578	2.7	2.5
Aberdeenshire	2,137	956	3,093	4.5	3.9
Angus	2,496	1,031	3,527	10.7	9.4
Argyll and Bute	1,953	613	2,566	8.0	6.2
Borders, The Scottish	1,252	454	1,706	4.6	3.7
Clackmannanshire, The	1,267	431	1,698	12.8	8.5
Dumfries and Galloway	3,251	1,092	4,343	7.9	6.4
Dundee, City of	5,472	1,643	7,115	8.9	8.4
East Ayrshire	3,756	1,177	4,933	12.3	10.2
East Dunbartonshire	1,788	703	2,491	10.4	8.8
East Lothian	1,387	422	1,809	8.2	4.4
East Renfrewshire	1,224	513	1,737	10.7	8.4

	Male	Female	All	Rate + Per cent employees and unemployed	Rate + Per cent workforce
Edinburgh, City of	10,042	3,244	13,286	4.9	4.6
Falkirk	3,337	1,087	4,424	8.3	7.0
Fife	8,799	2,993	11,792	9.5	7.8
Glasgow, City of	23,840	6,657	30,497	8.7	8.3
Highland	5,487	1,562	7,049	8.3	7.2
Inverclyde	2,079	632	2,711	8.5	7.9
Midlothian	1,276	368	1,644	8.1	6.7
Moray	1,572	655	2,227	7.2	6.1
North Ayrshire	4,060	1,423	5,483	11.6	10.4
North Lanarkshire	8,935	2,718	11,653	10.5	9.4
Orkney Islands	248	102	350	4.8	3.8
Perthshire and Kinross	2,222	801	3,023	6.5	5.4
Renfrewshire	4,383	1,375	5,758	6.5	6.0
Shetland Islands	287	112	399	3.7	3.3
South Ayrshire	2,738	1,029	3,767	7.9	7.0
South Lanarkshire	6,954	2,156	9,110	8.6	7.5
Stirling	1,638	527	2,165	6.0	5.1
West Dunbartonshire	3,452	837	4,289	11.8	10.6
West Lothian	2,659	852	3,511	6.3	5.7
Western Isles	971	301	1,272	13.0	9.2
NORTHERN IRELAND	**49,904**	**15,231**	**65,135**	**9.9**	**8.4**
Antrim	869	327	1,196		
Ards	1,470	525	1,995		
Armagh	1,401	525	1,926		
Ballymena	1,210	468	1,678		
Ballymoney	728	184	912		
Banbridge	585	235	820		
Belfast	12,021	3,154	15,175		
Carrickfergus	843	317	1,160		
Castlereagh	1,109	369	1,478		
Coleraine	1,765	638	2,403		
Cookstown	904	296	1,200		
Craigavon	1,711	586	2,297		
Derry	4,882	1,184	6,066		
Down	1,674	657	2,331		
Dungannon	1,526	508	2,034		
Fermanagh	2,025	616	2,641		
Larne	671	221	892		
Limavady	1,138	297	1,435		
Lisburn	2,263	715	2,978		
Magherafelt	995	354	1,349		
Moyle	617	144	761		
Newry and Mourne	3,223	866	4,089		
Newtown abbey	1,512	528	2,040		
North Down	1,403	620	2,023		
Omagh	1,698	519	2,217		
Strabane	1,661	378	2,039		

+ Claimant count rates are calculated as a percentage of the estimated total workforce (the sum of employees in employment, unemployed claimants, self-employed, HM Forces and participants on work-related government-training programmes) and as a percentage of estimates of employees in employment and the unemployed only. All the county rates shown are calculated using mid-1996 based denominators.

2.10 CLAIMANT COUNT
Area statistics
Claimant count in Parliamentary constituencies as at July 10 1997

	Male	Female	All
SOUTH EAST			
Berkshire			
Bracknell	800	260	1,060
Maidenhead	725	206	931
Newbury	627	197	824
Reading East	1,231	332	1,563
Reading West	1,112	294	1,406
Slough	1,930	551	2,481
Windsor	736	257	993
Wokingham	395	137	532
Isle of Wight			
Isle of Wight	2,886	910	3,796
Kent			
Ashford	1,458	451	1,909
Canterbury	1,595	513	2,108
Chatham and Aylesford	1,687	491	2,178
Dartford	1,675	525	2,200
Dover	2,310	626	2,936
Faversham and Mid Kent	1,229	432	1,661
Folkestone and Hythe	2,651	680	3,331
Gillingham	1,635	610	2,245
Gravesham	1,985	593	2,578
Maidstone and The Weald	1,182	409	1,591
Medway	1,840	631	2,471
North Thanet	2,419	631	3,050
Sevenoaks	858	309	1,167
Sittingbourne and Sheppey	1,946	630	2,576
South Thanet	2,056	578	2,634
Tonbridge and Malling	889	310	1,199
Tunbridge Wells	883	269	1,152
Oxfordshire			
Banbury	847	307	1,154
Henley	490	185	675
Oxford East	1,866	588	2,454
Oxford West and Abingdon	713	301	1,014
Wantage	623	226	849
Witney	540	243	783
Buckinghamshire			
Aylesbury	1,051	366	1,417
Beaconsfield	577	255	832
Buckingham	497	186	683
Chesham and Amersham	525	169	694
Milton Keynes South West	1,426	509	1,935
North East Milton Keynes	1,195	410	1,605
Wycombe	1,243	335	1,578
East Sussex			
Bexhill and Battle	876	309	1,185
Brighton Kemptown	2,734	881	3,615
Brighton Pavilion	3,381	1,307	4,688
Eastbourne	1,369	440	1,809
Hastings and Rye	2,649	689	3,338
Hove	2,329	857	3,186
Lewes	851	328	1,179
Wealden	632	238	870
Hampshire			
Aldershot	854	297	1,151
Basingstoke	984	316	1,300
East Hampshire	1,000	315	1,315
Eastleigh	775	244	1,019
Fareham	710	270	980
Gosport	1,193	453	1,646
Havant	1,630	394	2,024
New Forest East	757	250	1,007
New Forest West	747	228	975
North East Hampshire	573	215	788
North West Hampshire	595	248	843
Portsmouth North	1,655	459	2,114
Portsmouth South	3,065	846	3,911
Romsey	693	234	927
Southampton Itchen	2,365	555	2,920
Southampton Test	2,491	650	3,141
Winchester	705	252	957
Surrey			
East Surrey	660	224	884
Epsom and Ewell	714	239	953
Esher and Walton	719	258	977
Guildford	710	233	943
Mole Valley	479	143	622
Reigate	616	208	824
Runnymede and Weybridge	709	240	949
South West Surrey	556	179	735
Spelthorne	838	281	1,119
Surrey Heath	495	179	674
Woking	566	180	746
West Sussex			
Arundel and South Downs	507	191	698
Bognor Regis and Littlehampton	897	279	1,176
Chichester	804	281	1,085
Crawley	1,013	334	1,347
East Worthing and Shoreham	967	338	1,305
Horsham	597	230	827
Mid Sussex	598	217	815
Worthing West	895	261	1,156
LONDON			
Barking	1,975	671	2,646
Battersea	2,610	1,012	3,622

	Male	Female	All
Beckenham	1,884	616	2,500
Bethnal Green and Bow	5,031	1,394	6,425
Bexleyheath and Crayford	1,287	515	1,802
Brent East	3,616	1,262	4,878
Brent North	1,641	677	2,318
Brent South	4,169	1,374	5,543
Brentford and Isleworth	2,131	884	3,015
Bromley and Chislehurst	1,225	416	1,641
Camberwell and Peckham	4,082	1,477	5,559
Carshalton and Wallington	1,339	466	1,805
Chingford and Woodford Green	1,333	507	1,840
Chipping Barnet	1,368	562	1,930
Cities of London and Westminster	2,368	931	3,299
Croydon Central	2,692	859	3,551
Croydon North	3,615	1,293	4,908
Croydon South	1,151	405	1,556
Dagenham	1,660	516	2,176
Dulwich and West Norwood	3,523	1,392	4,915
Ealing, Acton and Shepherd's Bush	3,787	1,389	5,176
Ealing North	2,234	803	3,037
Ealing Southall	2,828	988	3,816
East Ham	3,867	1,189	5,056
Edmonton	2,741	944	3,685
Eltham	2,002	623	2,625
Enfield North	2,137	706	2,843
Enfield, Southgate	1,726	682	2,408
Erith and Thamesmead	3,321	1,117	4,438
Feltham and Heston	2,074	673	2,747
Finchley and Golders Green	1,902	842	2,744
Greenwich and Woolwich	3,631	1,263	4,894
Hackney North and Stoke Newington	5,426	2,072	7,498
Hackney South and Shoreditch	5,716	1,935	7,651
Hammersmith and Fulham	3,309	1,511	4,820
Hampstead and Highgate	2,766	1,383	4,149
Harrow East	1,832	788	2,620
Harrow West	1,367	541	1,908
Hayes and Harlington	1,527	520	2,047
Hendon	2,224	848	3,072
Holborn and St Pancras	3,902	1,476	5,378
Hornchurch	1,053	382	1,435
Hornsey and Wood Green	3,676	1,484	5,160
Ilford North	1,576	617	2,193
Ilford South	2,995	1,015	4,010
Islington North	4,507	1,796	6,303
Islington South and Finsbury	3,663	1,423	5,086
Kensington and Chelsea	1,770	963	2,733
Kingston and Surbiton	1,362	506	1,868
Lewisham, Deptford	4,087	1,457	5,544
Lewisham East	2,394	818	3,212
Lewisham West	3,142	995	4,137
Leyton and Wanstead	3,128	1,027	4,155
Mitcham and Morden	2,290	768	3,058
North Southwark and Bermondsey	4,250	1,464	5,714
Old Bexley and Sidcup	1,130	462	1,592
Orpington	1,207	422	1,629
Poplar and Canning Town	4,536	1,305	5,841
Putney	1,673	665	2,338
Regent's Park and Kensington North	3,951	1,732	5,683
Richmond Park	1,240	566	1,806
Romford	1,023	349	1,372
Ruislip - Northwood	852	289	1,141
Streatham	4,664	1,788	6,452
Sutton and Cheam	919	346	1,265
Tooting	2,938	1,095	4,033
Tottenham	6,122	2,091	8,213
Twickenham	1,183	456	1,639
Upminster	1,084	354	1,438
Uxbridge	1,083	411	1,494
Vauxhall	5,615	2,025	7,640
Walthamstow	3,179	1,113	4,292
West Ham	4,174	1,321	5,495
Wimbledon	1,213	492	1,705
EASTERN			
Cambridgeshire			
Cambridge	1,543	534	2,077
Huntingdon	964	418	1,382
North East Cambridgeshire	1,499	578	2,077
North West Cambridgeshire	1,116	409	1,525
Peterborough	2,181	710	2,891
South Cambridgeshire	611	263	874
South East Cambridgeshire	733	329	1,062
Essex			
Basildon	1,973	672	2,645
Billericay	1,454	482	1,936
Braintree	1,244	485	1,729
Brentwood and Ongar	808	277	1,085
Castle Point	1,305	477	1,782
Colchester	1,509	543	2,052
Epping Forest	1,212	480	1,692
Harlow	1,473	517	1,990
Harwich	1,986	534	2,520
Maldon and East Chelmsford	1,066	340	1,406
North Essex	756	276	1,032
Rayleigh	900	355	1,255
Rochford and Southend East	3,294	939	4,233
Saffron Walden	723	337	1,060
Southend West	1,958	635	2,593
Thurrock	2,219	698	2,917
West Chelmsford	1,195	403	1,598
Hertfordshire			
Broxbourne	1,129	405	1,534
Hemel Hempstead	945	324	1,269
Hertford and Stortford	704	278	982

Claimant count in Parliamentary constituencies as at July 10 1997

	Male	Female	All
Hertsmere	858	329	1,187
Hitchin and Harpenden	775	254	1,029
North East Hertfordshire	798	284	1,082
South West Hertfordshire	751	252	1,003
St Albans	710	277	987
Stevenage	1,432	479	1,911
Watford	1,293	374	1,667
Welwyn Hatfield	839	284	1,123
Norfolk			
Great Yarmouth	2,592	758	3,350
Mid Norfolk	1,217	457	1,674
North Norfolk	1,306	442	1,748
North West Norfolk	1,699	567	2,266
Norwich North	1,826	634	2,460
Norwich South	2,747	795	3,542
South Norfolk	1,172	484	1,656
South West Norfolk	1,265	551	1,816
Bedfordshire			
Bedford	1,973	670	2,643
Luton North	1,669	540	2,209
Luton South	2,352	702	3,054
Mid Bedfordshire	605	290	895
North East Bedfordshire	719	291	1,010
South West Bedfordshire	1,002	397	1,399
Suffolk			
Bury St Edmunds	947	403	1,350
Central Suffolk and North Ipswich	1,089	375	1,464
Ipswich	2,180	603	2,783
South Suffolk	948	345	1,293
Suffolk Coastal	1,342	471	1,813
Waveney	2,726	864	3,590
West Suffolk	1,033	443	1,476

SOUTH WEST

	Male	Female	All
Avon (former county)			
Bath	1,780	615	2,395
Bristol East	2,668	780	3,448
Bristol North West	1,958	537	2,495
Bristol South	2,807	705	3,512
Bristol West	2,547	976	3,523
Kingswood	1,332	440	1,772
Northavon	743	332	1,075
Wansdyke	765	345	1,110
Weston-Super-Mare	1,542	504	2,046
Woodspring	671	249	920
Cornwall			
Falmouth and Camborne	2,362	699	3,061
North Cornwall	1,821	562	2,383
South East Cornwall	1,463	498	1,961
St Ives	2,081	749	2,830
Truro and St Austell	1,797	594	2,391
Devon			
East Devon	784	278	1,062
Exeter	2,024	645	2,669
North Devon	1,407	479	1,886
Plymouth Devonport	2,539	735	3,274
Plymouth Sutton	3,642	1,132	4,774
South West Devon	993	385	1,378
Teignbridge	1,356	458	1,814
Tiverton and Honiton	922	388	1,310
Torbay	2,118	588	2,706
Torridge and West Devon	1,487	539	2,026
Totnes	1,203	474	1,677
Gloucestershire			
Cheltenham	1,721	540	2,261
Cotswold	550	220	770
Forest of Dean	904	398	1,302
Gloucester	2,158	664	2,822
Stroud	1,104	451	1,555
Tewkesbury	807	319	1,126
Dorset			
Bournemouth East	1,612	449	2,061
Bournemouth West	1,983	525	2,508
Christchurch	692	254	946
Mid Dorset and North Poole	866	297	1,163
North Dorset	552	240	792
Poole	1,216	323	1,539
South Dorset	1,391	387	1,778
West Dorset	740	315	1,055
Wiltshire			
Devizes	925	359	1,284
North Swindon	919	304	1,223
North Wiltshire	827	344	1,171
Salisbury	946	349	1,295
South Swindon	1,397	451	1,848
Westbury	1,255	511	1,766
Somerset			
Bridgwater	1,671	522	2,193
Somerton and Frome	1,004	418	1,422
Taunton	1,609	521	2,130
Wells	1,211	450	1,661
Yeovil	1,117	394	1,511

WEST MIDLANDS

	Male	Female	All
Hereford and Worcester			
Bromsgrove	1,121	478	1,599
Hereford	1,390	538	1,928
Leominster	886	338	1,224
Mid Worcestershire	739	315	1,054
Redditch	1,439	576	2,015
West Worcestershire	821	297	1,118
Worcester	1,419	472	1,891
Wyre Forest	1,288	463	1,751
Staffordshire			
Burton	1,737	573	2,310
Cannock Chase	1,460	513	1,973
Lichfield	837	373	1,210
Newcastle-under-Lyme	1,176	402	1,578
South Staffordshire	1,143	403	1,546
Stafford	1,075	389	1,464
Staffordshire Moorlands	984	350	1,334
Stoke-on-Trent Central	2,149	536	2,685
Stoke-on-Trent North	1,396	393	1,789
Stoke-on-Trent South	1,477	423	1,900
Stone	636	278	914
Tamworth	1,221	504	1,725
Shropshire			
Ludlow	767	299	1,066
North Shropshire	1,067	420	1,487
Shrewsbury and Atcham	1,132	391	1,523
Telford	1,375	384	1,759
The Wrekin	824	307	1,131
Warwickshire			
North Warwickshire	1,226	493	1,719
Nuneaton	1,399	439	1,838
Rugby and Kenilworth	1,242	446	1,688
Stratford-on-Avon	877	380	1,257
Warwick and Leamington	1,309	461	1,770
West Midlands			
Aldridge - Brownhills	1,239	441	1,680
Birmingham Edgbaston	2,612	819	3,431
Birmingham Erdington	3,153	865	4,018
Birmingham Hall Green	2,001	623	2,624
Birmingham Hodge Hill	2,847	744	3,591
Birmingham Ladywood	6,331	1,780	8,111
Birmingham Northfield	1,921	597	2,518
Birmingham Perry Barr	3,207	996	4,203
Birmingham Selly Oak	2,605	881	3,486
Birmingham Sparkbrook and Small	5,454	1,626	7,080
Birmingham Yardley	1,836	541	2,377
Coventry North East	2,950	850	3,800
Coventry North West	2,050	710	2,760
Coventry South	2,278	665	2,943
Dudley North	2,212	678	2,890
Dudley South	1,660	562	2,222
Halesowen and Rowley Regis	1,649	508	2,157
Meriden	2,070	676	2,746
Solihull	1,004	412	1,416
Stourbridge	1,453	464	1,917
Sutton Coldfield	1,058	461	1,519
Walsall North	2,735	752	3,487
Walsall South	2,750	906	3,656
Warley	2,421	752	3,173
West Bromwich East	2,459	767	3,226
West Bromwich West	2,642	805	3,447
Wolverhampton North East	2,357	654	3,011
Wolverhampton South East	2,289	625	2,914
Wolverhampton South West	2,152	775	2,927

EAST MIDLANDS

	Male	Female	All
Lincolnshire			
Boston and Skegness	1,062	389	1,451
Gainsborough	1,230	509	1,739
Grantham and Stamford	1,055	456	1,511
Lincoln	2,708	771	3,479
Louth and Horncastle	1,238	453	1,691
Sleaford and North Hykeham	990	379	1,369
South Holland and The Deepings	645	313	958
Northamptonshire			
Corby	1,247	403	1,650
Daventry	816	376	1,192
Kettering	1,102	410	1,512
Northampton North	1,897	618	2,515
Northampton South	1,652	581	2,233
Wellingborough	1,294	438	1,732
Nottinghamshire			
Ashfield	2,118	613	2,731
Bassetlaw	1,976	581	2,557
Broxtowe	1,308	466	1,774
Gedling	1,470	537	2,007
Mansfield	2,094	617	2,711
Newark	1,527	573	2,100
Nottingham East	4,395	1,246	5,641
Nottingham North	3,092	786	3,878
Nottingham South	2,995	837	3,832
Rushcliffe	1,283	471	1,754
Sherwood	1,751	537	2,288
Derbyshire			
Amber Valley	1,440	496	1,936
Bolsover	1,803	480	2,283
Chesterfield	2,290	669	2,959
Derby North	2,188	675	2,863
Derby South	3,502	1,032	4,534
Erewash	1,723	526	2,249
High Peak	1,204	375	1,579

Claimant count in Parliamentary constituencies as at July 10 1997

	Male	Female	All		Male	Female	All
North East Derbyshire	1,751	525	2,276	Ashton under Lyne	1,980	556	2,536
South Derbyshire	1,351	492	1,843	Bolton North East	1,894	431	2,325
West Derbyshire	859	366	1,225	Bolton South East	1,921	502	2,423
				Bolton West	905	313	1,218
Leicestershire				Bury North	946	326	1,272
Blaby	679	280	959	Bury South	1,201	410	1,611
Bosworth	633	292	925	Cheadle	710	258	968
Charnwood	769	326	1,095	Denton and Reddish	1,496	481	1,977
Harborough	795	365	1,160	Eccles	1,680	465	2,145
Leicester East	1,999	745	2,744	Hazel Grove	889	278	1,167
Leicester South	3,122	914	4,036	Heywood and Middleton	2,137	614	2,751
Leicester West	2,853	792	3,645	Leigh	1,625	522	2,147
Loughborough	1,235	513	1,748	Makerfield	1,625	536	2,161
North West Leicestershire	991	331	1,322	Manchester Blackley	2,940	669	3,609
Rutland and Melton	626	261	887	Manchester Central	4,891	1,288	6,179
				Manchester Gorton	3,613	1,097	4,710
YORKSHIRE AND THE HUMBER				Manchester Withington	2,805	1,050	3,855
				Oldham East and Saddleworth	1,668	495	2,163
Humberside (former county)				Oldham West and Royton	2,016	577	2,593
Beverley and Holderness	1,393	564	1,957	Rochdale	2,516	632	3,148
Brigg and Goole	1,517	487	2,004	Salford	2,345	566	2,911
Cleethorpes	2,137	699	2,836	Stalybridge and Hyde	1,651	549	2,200
East Yorkshire	1,564	509	2,073	Stockport	1,739	435	2,174
Great Grimsby	3,355	816	4,171	Stretford and Urmston	2,050	599	2,649
Haltemprice and Howden	837	383	1,220	Wigan	1,939	616	2,555
Kingston upon Hull East	2,959	788	3,747	Worsley	1,485	455	1,940
Kingston upon Hull North	3,490	1,048	4,538	Wythenshawe and Sale East	2,585	644	3,229
Kingston upon Hull West and Hessle	2,961	843	3,804				
Scunthorpe	1,891	579	2,470	**Lancashire**			
				Blackburn	2,318	551	2,869
North Yorkshire				Blackpool North and Fleetwood	1,769	457	2,226
Harrogate and Knaresborough	928	364	1,292	Blackpool South	2,393	563	2,956
Richmond	902	392	1,294	Burnley	1,232	361	1,593
Ryedale	742	283	1,025	Chorley	1,281	382	1,663
Scarborough and Whitby	1,932	601	2,533	Fylde	723	225	948
Selby	1,271	516	1,787	Hyndburn	1,185	395	1,580
Skipton and Ripon	721	296	1,017	Lancaster and Wyre	1,236	537	1,773
Vale of York	662	305	967	Morecambe and Lunesdale	1,955	577	2,532
York, City of	2,279	685	2,964	Pendle	1,157	354	1,511
				Preston	2,716	738	3,454
South Yorkshire				Ribble Valley	636	254	890
Barnsley Central	2,182	550	2,732	Rossendale and Darwen	1,054	390	1,444
Barnsley East and Mexborough	2,332	624	2,956	South Ribble	948	353	1,301
Barnsley West and Penistone	1,697	539	2,236	West Lancashire	1,989	584	2,573
Don Valley	2,112	568	2,680				
Doncaster Central	3,268	867	4,135	**MERSEYSIDE**			
Doncaster North	2,500	588	3,088				
Rother Valley	2,136	668	2,804	**Merseyside**			
Rotherham	2,981	717	3,698	Birkenhead	3,844	975	4,819
Sheffield Attercliffe	2,179	658	2,837	Bootle	3,495	797	4,292
Sheffield Brightside	3,286	806	4,092	Crosby	1,653	556	2,209
Sheffield Central	4,663	1,421	6,084	Knowsley North and Sefton East	2,969	865	3,834
Sheffield Hallam	1,171	513	1,684	Knowsley South	3,642	923	4,565
Sheffield Heeley	2,708	771	3,479	Liverpool Garston	2,844	788	3,632
Sheffield Hillsborough	1,980	743	2,723	Liverpool Riverside	5,263	1,585	6,848
Wentworth	2,489	622	3,111	Liverpool Walton	4,111	1,092	5,203
				Liverpool Wavertree	3,881	1,091	4,972
West Yorkshire				Liverpool West Derby	4,223	1,082	5,305
Batley and Spen	1,672	458	2,130	Southport	1,701	570	2,271
Bradford North	3,077	831	3,908	St Helens North	1,992	600	2,592
Bradford South	2,310	614	2,924	St Helens South	2,333	633	2,966
Bradford West	3,692	1,116	4,808	Wallasey	3,068	882	3,950
Calder Valley	1,493	531	2,024	Wirral South	1,398	520	1,918
Colne Valley	1,486	520	2,006	Wirral West	1,554	576	2,130
Dewsbury	1,502	431	1,933				
Elmet	1,185	407	1,592	**NORTH EAST**			
Halifax	2,548	654	3,202				
Hemsworth	1,848	547	2,395	**Cleveland (former county)**			
Huddersfield	2,562	822	3,384	Hartlepool	3,429	841	4,270
Keighley	1,469	564	2,033	Middlesbrough	4,460	1,113	5,573
Leeds Central	4,191	1,054	5,245	Middlesbrough South and East	2,687	754	3,441
Leeds East	3,094	784	3,878	Redcar	3,254	762	4,016
Leeds North East	1,951	681	2,632	Stockton North	3,388	873	4,261
Leeds North West	1,372	592	1,964	Stockton South	2,516	738	3,254
Leeds West	2,323	622	2,945				
Morley and Rothwell	1,509	444	1,953	**Northumberland**			
Normanton	1,265	431	1,696	Berwick-upon-Tweed	1,332	411	1,743
Pontefract and Castleford	1,833	498	2,331	Blyth Valley	1,946	603	2,549
Pudsey	857	329	1,186	Hexham	889	318	1,207
Shipley	1,310	464	1,774	Wansbeck	2,175	579	2,754
Wakefield	2,069	632	2,701				
				Durham			
NORTH WEST				Bishop Auckland	1,977	497	2,474
				Darlington	2,620	708	3,328
Cheshire				Durham City of	1,615	545	2,160
Chester, City of	1,550	485	2,035	Easington	1,811	409	2,220
Congleton	848	317	1,165	North Durham	2,026	526	2,552
Crewe and Nantwich	1,577	492	2,069	North West Durham	1,983	563	2,546
Eddisbury	1,004	361	1,365	Sedgefield	1,578	483	2,061
Ellesmere Port and Neston	1,532	479	2,011				
Halton	2,305	691	2,996	**Tyne and Wear**			
Macclesfield	957	294	1,251	Blaydon	1,811	521	2,332
Tatton	796	247	1,043	Gateshead East and Washington West	2,007	551	2,558
Warrington North	1,537	463	2,000	Houghton and Washington East	2,100	557	2,657
Warrington South	1,254	454	1,708	Jarrow	2,426	639	3,065
Weaver Vale	1,937	640	2,577	Newcastle upon Tyne Central	2,857	888	3,745
				Newcastle upon Tyne East and Wallsen	3,120	840	3,960
Cumbria				Newcastle upon Tyne North	2,119	539	2,658
Barrow and Furness	2,206	546	2,752	North Tyneside	2,619	697	3,316
Carlisle	1,678	461	2,139	South Shields	3,263	835	4,098
Copeland	2,099	578	2,677	Sunderland North	2,620	573	3,193
Penrith and The Border	774	314	1,088	Sunderland South	3,402	783	4,185
Westmorland and Lonsdale	572	232	804	Tyne Bridge	4,019	904	4,923
Workington	2,259	598	2,857	Tynemouth	2,133	634	2,767
Greater Manchester							
Altrincham and Sale West	1,082	361	1,443				

Claimant count in Parliamentary constituencies as at July 10 1997

	Male	Female	All		Male	Female	All
WALES				Paisley South	2,083	575	2,658
				Perth	1,537	523	2,060
Aberavon	1,356	403	1,759	Ross Skye and Inverness West	2,046	568	2,614
Alyn and Deeside	1,102	357	1,459	Roxburgh and Berwickshire	744	271	1,015
Blaenau Gwent	1,988	553	2,541	Stirling	1,309	425	1,734
Brecon and Radnorshire	891	354	1,245	Strathkelvin and Bearsden	1,481	558	2,039
Bridgend	1,344	503	1,847	Tweeddale Ettrick and Lauderdale	713	261	974
Caernarfon	1,595	460	2,055	West Aberdeenshire and Kincardine	626	313	939
Caerphilly	2,132	559	2,691	West Renfrewshire	1,104	374	1,478
Cardiff Central	2,135	729	2,864	Western Isles	971	301	1,272
Cardiff North	910	297	1,207				
Cardiff South and Penarth	2,516	593	3,109	**NORTHERN IRELAND**			
Cardiff West	2,301	589	2,890				
Carmarthen East and Dinefwr	1,147	369	1,516	Belfast East	2,300	628	2,928
Carmarthen West and South	1,822	479	2,301	Belfast North	3,466	754	4,220
Ceredigion	1,122	470	1,592	Belfast South	2,941	1,396	4,337
Clwyd South	1,008	333	1,341	Belfast West	4,918	770	5,688
Clwyd West	1,104	302	1,406	East Antrim	2,216	738	2,954
Conwy	1,866	510	2,376	East Londonderry	2,903	935	3,838
Cynon Valley	1,629	422	2,051	Fermanagh and South Tyrone	2,935	964	3,899
Delyn	1,003	318	1,321	Foyle	4,882	1,184	6,066
Gower	1,219	424	1,643	Lagan Valley	1,490	617	2,107
Islwyn	1,140	367	1,507	Mid Ulster	2,515	810	3,325
Llanelli	1,759	531	2,290	Newry and Armagh	3,571	1,027	4,598
Meirionnydd Nant Conwy	886	277	1,163	North Antrim	2,555	796	3,351
Merthyr Tydfil and Rhymney	2,059	488	2,547	North Down	1,622	715	2,337
Monmouth	1,031	425	1,456	South Antrim	1,679	655	2,334
Montgomeryshire	514	212	726	South Down	2,658	979	3,637
Neath	1,479	448	1,927	Strangford	1,837	638	2,475
Newport East	1,614	512	2,126	Upper Bann	2,057	728	2,785
Newport West	1,963	604	2,567	West Tyrone	3,359	897	4,256
Ogmore	1,365	432	1,797				
Pontypridd	1,592	486	2,078				
Preseli Pembrokeshire	1,945	540	2,485				
Rhondda	1,857	470	2,327				
Swansea East	1,907	429	2,336				
Swansea West	2,031	591	2,622				
Torfaen	1,638	511	2,149				
Vale of Clwyd	1,356	353	1,709				
Vale of Glamorgan	1,791	610	2,401				
Wrexham	1,204	392	1,596				
Ynys-Mon	1,846	607	2,453				
SCOTLAND							
Aberdeen Central	1,528	528	2,056				
Aberdeen North	869	289	1,158				
Aberdeen South	978	386	1,364				
Airdrie and Shotts	2,291	697	2,988				
Angus	1,798	755	2,553				
Argyll and Bute	1,398	432	1,830				
Ayr	1,783	656	2,439				
Banff and Buchan	925	358	1,283				
Caithness Sutherland and Easter Ros	1,728	448	2,176				
Carrick Cumnock and Doon Valley	2,311	708	3,019				
Central Fife	2,206	735	2,941				
Clydebank and Milngavie	1,983	501	2,484				
Clydesdale	1,787	510	2,297				
Coatbridge and Chryston	1,804	581	2,385				
Cumbernauld and Kilsyth	1,426	504	1,930				
Cunninghame North	1,892	637	2,529				
Cunninghame South	2,168	786	2,954				
Dumbarton	2,269	634	2,903				
Dumfries	1,750	604	2,354				
Dundee East	2,911	878	3,789				
Dundee West	2,561	765	3,326				
Dunfermline East	1,908	599	2,507				
Dunfermline West	1,471	492	1,963				
East Kilbride	1,652	621	2,273				
East Lothian	1,169	354	1,523				
Eastwood	1,224	513	1,737				
Edinburgh Central	1,976	723	2,699				
Edinburgh East and Musselburgh	1,636	390	2,026				
Edinburgh North and Leith	2,409	773	3,182				
Edinburgh Pentlands	1,478	495	1,973				
Edinburgh South	1,507	572	2,079				
Edinburgh West	1,254	359	1,613				
Falkirk East	1,602	519	2,121				
Falkirk West	1,735	568	2,303				
Galloway and Upper Nithsdale	1,501	488	1,989				
Glasgow Anniesland	2,112	521	2,633				
Glasgow Baillieston	2,661	640	3,301				
Glasgow Cathcart	1,717	545	2,262				
Glasgow Govan	2,725	741	3,466				
Glasgow Kelvin	2,743	987	3,730				
Glasgow Maryhill	3,416	1,067	4,483				
Glasgow Pollok	2,478	649	3,127				
Glasgow Rutherglen	1,707	485	2,192				
Glasgow Shettleston	2,590	583	3,173				
Glasgow Springburn	2,992	805	3,797				
Gordon	695	338	1,033				
Greenock and Inverclyde	1,504	477	1,981				
Hamilton North and Bellshill	2,151	651	2,802				
Hamilton South	1,616	457	2,073				
Inverness East Nairn and Lochab	1,713	546	2,259				
Kilmarnock and Loudoun	2,400	842	3,242				
Kirkcaldy	2,217	743	2,960				
Linlithgow	1,294	377	1,671				
Livingston	1,365	475	1,840				
Midlothian	1,071	290	1,361				
Moray	1,463	602	2,065				
Motherwell and Wishaw	1,923	515	2,438				
North East Fife	997	424	1,421				
North Tayside	1,220	482	1,702				
Ochil	1,759	605	2,364				
Orkney and Shetland	535	214	749				
Paisley North	1,771	581	2,352				

UNITED KINGDOM		18-19	20-24	25-29	30-39	40-49	50-59	60 and over	All ages *
MALE AND FEMALE									
1994	Jul	20.0	17.2	11.4	8.5	6.6	8.7	2.3	9.4
	Oct	18.7	15.3	10.6	8.0	6.2	8.3	2.1	8.8
1995	Jan	18.6	15.3	10.9	8.3	6.3	8.4	2.1	8.9
	Apr	17.3	14.2	10.3	7.9	6.1	8.1	1.9	8.5
	Jul	17.3	15.2	10.0	7.7	5.9	7.6	1.7	8.3
	Oct	16.6	13.5	9.5	7.4	5.6	7.4	1.6	7.9
1996	Jan	16.8	13.7	10.0	7.8	6.0	7.8	1.8	8.3
	Apr	15.7	12.7	9.5	7.6	5.9	7.8	1.7	7.9
	Jul	15.9	14.2	9.4	7.0	5.5	7.1	1.6	7.7
	Oct	14.5	11.4	8.3	6.3	5.0	6.6	1.3	6.8
1997	Jan	14.5	11.4	8.3	6.3	5.0	6.6	1.3	6.8
	Apr	13.3	9.8	7.3	5.6	4.4	5.9	0.9	6.0
	Jul	**11.7**	**10.2**	**7.0**	**5.1**	**4.1**	**5.2**	**1.0**	**5.6**
MALE									
1994	Jul	23.7	21.6	15.2	11.9	9.3	11.8	3.7	12.6
	Oct	22.1	19.5	14.3	11.3	8.8	11.3	3.2	11.8
1995	Jan	22.3	19.8	14.7	11.7	9.0	11.5	3.2	12.1
	Apr	20.8	18.4	13.8	11.2	8.7	11.0	2.9	11.5
	Jul	20.5	18.9	13.4	10.8	8.2	10.2	2.6	11.1
	Oct	19.5	17.2	12.7	10.4	8.0	10.0	2.6	10.6
1996	Jan	20.2	17.7	13.5	11.1	8.5	10.5	2.8	11.2
	Apr	18.9	16.4	12.8	10.6	8.2	10.5	2.7	10.7
	Jul	19.4	17.6	12.6	9.8	7.8	9.6	2.4	10.3
	Oct	18.1	15.4	11.6	9.1	7.3	9.2	2.2	9.5
1997	Jan	18.0	14.8	11.4	9.1	7.1	9.0	2.1	9.3
	Apr	16.6	12.8	10.1	8.1	6.3	8.1	1.5	8.3
	Jul	**13.8**	**13.0**	**9.6**	**7.4**	**5.8**	**7.0**	**1.5**	**7.7**
FEMALE									
1994	Jul	15.7	11.6	6.1	3.7	3.4	4.9	0.1	5.3
	Oct	14.9	9.9	5.6	3.4	3.1	4.6	0.1	4.8
1995	Jan	14.5	9.6	5.6	3.4	3.2	4.6	0.1	4.8
	Apr	13.3	8.8	5.3	3.4	3.1	4.5	0.1	4.6
	Jul	13.7	10.4	5.3	3.4	3.1	4.3	0.1	4.7
	Oct	13.3	8.9	5.0	3.2	2.9	4.2	0.1	4.4
1996	Jan	13.0	8.6	5.1	3.3	3.0	4.4	0.1	4.5
	Apr	12.0	7.8	4.9	3.3	3.1	4.5	0.1	4.3
	Jul	12.1	9.8	5.0	3.1	3.0	4.2	0.1	4.4
	Oct	11.5	8.0	4.5	2.8	2.7	4.0	0.1	3.9
1997	Jan	10.7	7.0	4.1	2.6	2.5	3.7	0.0	3.6
	Apr	9.7	5.9	3.5	2.2	2.2	3.3	0.0	3.2
	Jul	**9.3**	**6.7**	**3.5**	**2.0**	**2.1**	**3.0**	**0.0**	**3.1**

* Includes those aged under 18. These figures have been affected by the benefit regulations for under 18-year olds introduced in September 1988. See also note + to *Tables 2.1* and *2.2*.

Notes: 1 Unemployment rates by age are expressed as a percentage of the estimated workforce in the corresponding age groups at mid-1995 for 1995 and 1996, and at the corresponding mid-year estimates for earlier years.

2 While the figures are presented to one decimal place, they should not be regarded as implying precision to that degree. The figures for those aged 18-19 are subject to the widest errors.

UNEMPLOYMENT
Selected countries

THOUSANDS

	EC average	Major 7 nations (G7)	United Kingdom *	Australia ##	Austria #	Belgium ++	Canada ##	Denmark ++	Finland ++	France ++	Germany # (FR)
STANDARDISED RATE: SEASONALLY ADJUSTED (2)											
1992	9.3	6.9	10.1	10.7	..	7.3	11.2	9.2	13.0	10.4	6.6
1993	10.7	7.2	10.4	10.8	4.0	8.9	11.2	10.1	17.5	11.7	7.9
1994	11.1	7.0	9.6	9.8	3.8	10.0	10.4	8.2	17.9	12.3	8.4
1995	10.8	6.8	8.7	8.6	3.9	9.9	9.5	7.2	16.6	11.7	8.2
1996	10.9	6.8	8.2	8.6	4.4	9.8	9.7	6.9	15.9	12.4	9
1996 May	10.9	6.9	8.3	8.5	4.4	9.9	9.4	7.0	18.5	12.4	8.9
Jun	10.9	6.8	8.3	8.3	4.1	9.7	10.0	6.0	16.1	12.3	8.9
Jul	10.9	6.8	8.2	8.5	4.1	9.7	9.9	6.4	15.5	12.3	8.9
Aug	10.9	6.7	8.2	8.7	4.1	9.8	9.5	6.1	15.7	12.4	8.9
Sep	10.9	6.8	8.4	8.7	4.1	9.7	10.0	5.7	15.1	12.5	9.1
Oct	10.9	6.8	8.1	8.8	4.4	9.6	10.0	5.6	15.1	12.6	9.2
Nov	10.8	6.8	7.8	8.4	4.3	9.5	10.0	6.4	15.3	12.6	9.3
Dec	10.8	6.8	7.7	8.6	4.3	9.5	9.7	6.3	14.9	12.5	9.4
1997 Jan	10.9	6.8	7.6	8.6	4.4	9.5	9.7	6.6	15.3	12.5	9.6
Feb	10.8	6.8	7.4	8.8	4.4	9.5	9.7	6.4	15.1	12.5	9.6
Mar	10.8	6.7	7.2	8.8	4.4	9.6	9.3	6.3	15.7	12.5	9.7
Apr	10.8	6.6	7.0	8.8	4.4	9.6	9.6	6.2	15.9	12.5	9.6
May	10.8	6.6	6.9	..	4.4	9.6	9.5	6.2	..	12.6	9.8
NUMBERS UNEMPLOYED, NATIONAL DEFINITIONS (1) SEASONALLY ADJUSTED											
1996 Jul			2126	781	229	586	1488	252	450	3060	3938
Aug			2109	806	229	588	1432	246	446	3092	3963
Sep			2071	800	226	581	1510	235	442	3115	4009
Oct			2025	804	228	573	1526	233	440	3112	4057
Nov			1930	779	226	571	1532	229	439	3122	4118
Dec			1883	792	220	570	1485	228	439	3082	4165
1997 Jan			1815	791	229	565	1481	232	435	3100	4311
Feb			1748	811	235	576	1477	226	430	3092	4313
Mar			1711	803	231	577	1418	223	425	3088	4291
Apr			1654	802	234	579	1464	223	420	3081	4302
May			1637	810	234	574	1453	224	415	3114	4363
Jun			1601	778	..	..	1396	..	..	3191	4379
Jul			1550	801	..	..	1384	..	..	..	4396
% rate: latest month			5.5	8.7	7.1	13.5	9.0	8.1	16.4	12.6	11.5
Latest 3 months: change on previous 3 months			(0.4)	(0.1)	0.1	0.1	(0.3)	(0.2)	(0.6)	0.0	0.2
NUMBERS UNEMPLOYED, NATIONAL DEFINITIONS (1) NOT SEASONALLY ADJUSTED											
1992			2779	925	193	473	1640	315	328	2818	2993
1993			2919	939	222	550	1649	345	441	2999	3443
1994			2639	856	215	589	1541	340	453	3094	3693
1995			2326	766	216	597	1422	285	427	2976	3622
1996			2122	783	231	588	1469	242	405	3063	3980
1996 Jul			2158	732	187	599	1540	243	468	2919	3912
Aug			2176	771	190	620	1453	249	440	3039	3902
Sep			2104	800	192	608	1379	221	427	3150	3848
Oct			1977	765	214	590	1397	218	425	3179	3867
Nov			1871	737	235	579	1447	214	428	3197	3942
Dec			1868	806	261	588	1412	214	468	3189	4148
1997 Jan			1908	854	302	579	1578	259	453	3264	4658
Feb			1828	906	289	572	1566	245	438	3205	4672
Mar			1745	845	252	560	1530	237	424	3120	4477
Apr			1688	800	236	551	1493	227	410	3020	4347
May			1620	792	211	537	1469	211	395	2982	4256
Jun			1550	751	..	..	1378	..	..	..	4222
Jul			1585	751	..	..	1431	..	..	..	4354
% rate: latest month			5.6	8.2	6.5	12.6	9.0	7.6	15.5	N/A	11.4
Latest month: change on a year ago			(2.1)	0.2	0.1	(0.4)	(0.8)	(0.7)	(1.7)	N/A	1.2

Notes: 1 The figures on national definitions are not directly comparable due to differences in coverage and methods of compilation.
2 Unemployment as a percentage of the total labour force. The standardised unemployment rates are based on national statistics but have been adjusted when necessary, and as far as the available data allow, to bring them as close as possible to the internationally agreed ILO definitions. The standardised rates are therefore more suitable than the national figures for comparing the levels of unemployment between countries. The OECD are now using Eurostat unemployment rates for all EU countries. Rates for all other countries are caluclated by the OECD.
The following symbols apply only to the figures on national definitions.
* The seasonally adjusted series for the United Kingdom takes account of past discontinuities to be consistent with the current coverage (see notes to *Table 2.1*).
+ Numbers registered at employment offices. Rates are calculated as percentages of civilian labour force, except Greece, which excludes civil servants, professional people, and farmers.

		Greece +	Irish Republic +	Italy **	Japan **	Luxem-bourg #	Nether-lands ++	Norway ++	Portugal #	Spain +	Sweden ##	Switzer-land ++	United States ##
1992		7.9	15.4	9.0	2.2	2.1	5.6	5.9	4.2	18.5	5.8	2.9	7.4
1993		8.6	15.6	10.3	2.5	2.7	6.6	6.0	5.7	22.8	9.5	3.8	6.8
1994		8.9	14.3	11.4	2.9	3.2	7.1	5.5	7.0	24.1	9.8	3.6	6.1
1995		9.2	12.3	11.9	3.1	2.9	6.9	5.0	7.3	22.9	9.2	3.3	5.6
1996		9.6	11.8	12.0	3.4	3.3	6.3	..	7.3	22.1	10.0	..	5.4
1996	May	..	11.9	12.0	3.5	3.2	6.3	4.9	7.4	22.2	10.3	..	5.3
	Jun	..	12.5	12.0	3.5	3.1	6.5	..	7.3	22.3	9.9	..	5.4
	Jul	..	12.5	12.0	3.4	3.1	6.7	..	7.3	22.1	10.0	..	5.2
	Aug	..	12.5	12.1	3.3	3.1	6.7	4.8	7.3	22.0	10.1	..	5.2
	Sep	..	11.8	11.9	3.3	3.3	6.3	..	7.2	22.1	10.2	..	5.2
	Oct	..	11.5	11.9	3.3	3.4	6.2	..	7.1	21.7	10.0	..	5.3
	Nov	..	11.3	12.0	3.3	3.5	6.2	4.7	7.1	21.6	10.2	..	5.3
	Dec	..	11.2	12.0	3.3	3.6	6.1	..	7.2	21.4	10.6	..	5.4
1997	Jan	..	11.2	12.2	3.3	3.6	5.9	..	7.2	21.2	10.4	..	5.3
	Feb	..	11.0	12.2	3.3	3.6	5.7	4.1	7.3	21.2	10.9	..	5.2
	Mar	..	11.1	12.3	3.2	3.6	5.5	..	7.2	21.0	10.9	..	4.9
	Apr	..	10.9	12.4	3.3	3.7	5.4	..	7.3	20.9	10.7	..	4.8
	May	..	10.8	..	3.6	3.7	..	..	7.2	20.8	10.9	..	5.0

NUMBERS UNEMPLOYED, NATIONAL DEFINITIONS (1) SEASONALLY ADJUSTED

		Greece +	Irish Republic +	Italy **	Japan **	Luxem-bourg #	Nether-lands ++	Norway ++	Portugal #	Spain +	Sweden ##	Switzer-land ++	United States ##
1996	Jul	185	284	2754	2310	5.7	441	91	..	2252	..	167.3	7276
	Aug	178	283	..	2220	5.7	441	90	..	2236	..	170.3	6910
	Sep	183	281	2210	2210	5.7	441	89	..	2233	..	173.7	7043
	Oct	183	274	2729	2270	5.9	433	88	..	2232	..	179.7	7019
	Nov	180	269	..	2180	6.0	431	87	..	2220	..	184	7187
	Dec	181	267	..	2220	6.3	428	84	..	2208	..	188	7167
1997	Jan	191	263	2817	2220	6.2	417	82	..	2198	..	194	7268
	Feb	191	260	..	2280	6.2	398	81	..	2190	..	195	7205
	Mar	212	261	..	2190	6.1	387	81	..	2167	..	196	7144
	Apr	204	257	2864	2250	6.4	385	78	..	2160	..	195	6714
	May	..	256	..	2380	6.5	395	..	..	2142	..	194	6534
	Jun	..	256	..	..	..	..	..	..	..	..	..	..
	Jul	..	255	..	..	..	..	..	..	..	..	..	..
% rate: latest month		N/A	N/A	12.4	3.6	N/A	..	3.4	..	13.4	..	5.3	4.8
Latest 3 months: change on previous 3 months		N/A	N/A	0	0	N/A	..	0	..	0	..	0	0

NUMBERS UNEMPLOYED, NATIONAL DEFINITIONS (1) NOT SEASONALLY ADJUSTED

		Greece +	Irish Republic +	Italy **	Japan **	Luxem-bourg #	Nether-lands ++	Norway ++	Portugal #	Spain +	Sweden ##	Switzer-land ++	United States ##
1992		185	283	2549	1421	2.7	337	114	317	2260	232	92	9384
1993		176	294	2335	1656	3.5	417	118	347	2538	356	163	8734
1994		180	282	2561	1920	4.6	485	110	396	2647	340	171	7997
1995		184	278	2724	2098	5.1	462	102	430	2449	332	153	7404
1996		185	279	2763	2250	5.7	441	91	468	2275	346	169	7236
1996	Jul	164	288	2690	2210	5.1	433	103	455	2171	466	162	7693
	Aug	152	288	..	2240	5.1	441	98	453	2144	431	164	6868
	Sep	156	279	..	2240	5.7	438	85	452	2195	369	166	6700
	Oct	173	268	2790	2270	6.0	431	79	457	2235	349	174	6577
	Nov	197	263	..	2120	6.4	432	77	463	2251	343	183	6816
	Dec	211	270	..	2080	6.5	437	79	460	2216	385	192	6680
1997	Jan	226	269	2809	2220	6.9	429	90	471	2257	383	206	7933
	Feb	226	264	..	2300	6.8	415	84	481	2263	357	206	7647
	Mar	227	262	..	2340	6.4	399	81	472	2228	339	202	7399
	Apr	210	256	2875	2310	6.4	381	76	467	2182	318	198	6551
	May	..	248	..	2440	6.1	376	..	..	2124	321	192	6398
	Jun	..	255	..	..	..	..	..	..	2092	413	..	..
	Jul	..	259	..	..	..	..	..	..	2009	486	..	..
% rate: latest month		N/A	N/A	12.5	3.5	N/A	5.6	3.4	..	12.5	10.8	5.3	4.7
Latest month: change on a year ago		N/A	N/A	0.2	N/C	N/A	(0.7)	(0.8)	..	(1.2)	0.3	0.8	(0.7)

Numbers registered at employment offices. Rates are calculated as percentages of total employees.
++ Insured unemployed. Rates are calculated as percentages of total insured labour force.
** Labour force sample survey. Rates are calculated as a percentage of total labour force.
Labour force sample survey. Rates are calculated as a percentage of the civilian labour force.
N/C No change.
N/A Not available.

THOUSANDS

UNITED KINGDOM
Month ending

INFLOW +

		Male and Female		Male		Female		
		All	Change since previous year	All	Change since previous year	All	Change since previous year	Married
1996	Jul 11	364.4	-14.4	232.9	-14.1	131.4	-0.4	30.6
	Aug 8	308.7	-27.5	199.8	-19.4	108.9	-8.1	31.6
	Sep 12	280.7	-38.4	188.9	-26.9	91.8	-11.5	23.5
	Oct 10	279.0	-41.8	194.7	-29.1	84.3	-12.6	21.1
	Nov 14	268.7	-43.1	190.3	-28.7	78.3	-14.6	21.2
	Dec 12	257.7	-30.6	189.9	-22.9	67.8	-7.7	17.9
1997	Jan 9	303.3	-19.0	215.0	-8.6	88.3	-10.4	25.3
	Feb 13	292.3	-16.9	206.6	-13.1	85.7	-3.8	23.0
	Mar 13	263.4	-6.1	188.3	-1.8	75.1	-4.3	21.4
	Apr 10	270.4	-21.0	190.2	-10.4	80.2	-10.6	25.2
	May 8	257.0	3.9	185.0	5.7	71.9	-1.8	20.8
	Jun 12	261.9	6.4	186.6	9.0	75.3	-2.7	20.5
	Jul 10	**338.0**	**-26.4**	**223.7**	**-9.3**	**114.3**	**-17.1**	**26.3**

UNITED KINGDOM
Month ending

OUTFLOW +

		Male and Female		Male		Female		
		All	Change since previous year	All	Change since previous year	All	Change since previous year	Married
1996	Jul 11	297.5	-10.5	214.5	-6.7	82.9	-3.9	21.8
	Aug 8	288.8	-32.3	202.5	-22.0	86.3	-10.3	21.0
	Sep 12	343.7	-25.6	225.1	-16.5	118.6	-9.1	36.0
	Oct 10	416.0	8.8	281.1	5.7	134.9	3.0	34.1
	Nov 14	360.4	31.0	249.7	24.5	110.7	6.5	30.8
	Dec 12	261.1	0.7	182.9	1.8	78.2	-1.2	21.2
1997	Jan 9	260.5	27.3	179.4	19.9	81.1	7.4	23.0
	Feb 13	361.6	44.3	258.8	33.3	102.8	11.0	30.1
	Mar 13	352.8	-20.8	254.3	-17.5	98.5	-3.3	28.5
	Apr 10	326.0	27.2	232.6	19.3	93.4	7.9	28.5
	May 8	330.0	-6.0	238.1	2.9	92.0	-8.8	26.9
	Jun 12	322.9	23.1	235.6	19.6	87.3	3.5	24.0
	Jul 10	**299.9**	**2.5**	**215.0**	**0.5**	**84.9**	**2.0**	**22.3**

* The unemployment flow statistics are described in *Employment Gazette*, August 1983, pp 351-358. Flow figures are collected for four or five-week periods between count dates; the figures in the table are converted to a standard $4^1/_3$ week month.

+ The flows in this table are not on quite the same basis as those in *Table 2.20*. While *Table 2.20* relates to computerised records only for GB, this table gives estimates of total flows for the UK. It is assumed that computerised inflows are the best estimates of total inflows, while outflows are calculated by subtracting the changes in stocks from the inflows.

INFLOW Month ending	Age group									
	Under 18	18-19	20-24	25-29	30-34	35-44	45-54	55-59	60 and over	All ages
MALE										
1997 Feb 13	6.2	20.2	42.7	33.9	25.9	33.9	26.4	9.4	3.1	201.7
Mar 13	5.0	17.3	37.7	31.0	24.0	32.1	24.9	8.9	2.7	183.6
Apr 10	4.8	16.2	36.0	30.6	24.2	33.1	27.9	10.1	3.1	186.0
May 8	5.2	16.7	35.7	30.7	23.6	31.7	25.1	9.0	2.7	180.4
Jun 12	4.9	16.9	38.5	30.8	23.8	31.2	23.9	8.4	2.6	181.1
Jul 10	**4.8**	**21.8**	**59.0**	**35.8**	**26.1**	**33.2**	**25.3**	**8.6**	**2.7**	**217.3**
FEMALE										
1997 Feb 13	4.5	12.3	19.4	12.1	7.7	11.9	12.0	3.5	0.0	83.4
Mar 13	3.7	10.3	15.9	10.5	7.1	10.9	11.5	3.4	0.0	73.2
Apr 10	3.5	9.3	15.7	11.0	7.6	12.7	13.9	4.2	0.0	77.9
May 8	3.9	9.1	14.5	10.3	6.6	10.7	11.4	3.4	0.0	69.8
Jun 12	3.6	9.4	17.1	10.5	6.8	10.5	11.1	3.4	0.0	72.4
Jul 10	**3.7**	**14.1**	**37.1**	**14.8**	**8.6**	**13.6**	**13.3**	**3.7**	**0.0**	**108.9**
Changes on a year earlier **MALE**										
1997 Feb 13	0.6	0.7	-2.1	-1.9	-2.2	-3.3	-3.0	-1.0	-0.5	-12.7
Mar 13	0.6	0.8	0.0	0.2	-0.2	-0.5	-1.6	-0.4	-0.7	-1.8
Apr 10	1.2	0.9	-1.1	-0.4	-0.7	-1.1	-5.5	-1.8	-1.3	-9.7
May 8	1.0	1.2	-0.1	1.7	0.8	1.3	0.1	0.0	-0.6	5.5
Jun 12	1.3	1.9	0.4	1.7	1.8	1.6	0.7	0.2	-0.3	9.2
Jul 10	**0.9**	**-0.4**	**-8.4**	**-0.4**	**0.3**	**0.4**	**-1.0**	**-0.1**	**-0.4**	**-9.1**
FEMALE										
1997 Feb 13	0.7	-0.1	-1.4	-0.8	-0.9	-0.7	-0.6	0.2	0.0	-3.7
Mar 13	0.6	0.3	-1.2	-0.9	-0.5	-1.2	-0.8	0.0	0.0	-3.9
Apr 10	0.8	0.2	-1.8	-1.5	-1.1	-2.7	-3.0	-0.7	0.0	-9.9
May 8	0.7	0.2	-1.3	-0.7	-0.6	-0.2	0.2	0.1	0.0	-1.7
Jun 12	0.8	0.6	-1.5	-0.3	-0.3	-0.9	-0.5	0.2	0.0	-1.9
Jul 10	**0.9**	**-1.2**	**-9.3**	**-1.6**	**-1.2**	**-1.9**	**-1.4**	**-0.1**	**0.0**	**-15.9**

OUTFLOW Month ending	Age group									
	Under 18	18-19	20-24	25-29	30-34	35-44	45-54 +	55-59 +	60 and over +	All ages
MALE										
1997 Feb 13	4.4	16.7	49.1	42.1	33.9	45.0	35.3	12.7	5.8	244.9
Mar 13	4.3	17.4	49.1	41.0	32.6	43.2	34.6	12.8	5.5	240.4
Apr 10	4.3	16.3	45.1	37.2	29.3	39.2	31.9	12.7	5.0	221.0
May 8	4.3	16.3	44.0	36.8	29.0	38.7	31.6	13.6	4.8	219.1
Jun 12	4.5	16.9	44.8	37.0	29.2	38.6	30.7	11.8	4.2	217.6
Jul 10	**4.1**	**15.6**	**43.4**	**34.4**	**27.1**	**35.8**	**27.9**	**10.4**	**3.5**	**202.3**
FEMALE										
1997 Feb 13	3.4	10.6	22.9	15.2	10.1	14.4	15.2	4.8	0.2	96.8
Mar 13	3.1	10.8	21.7	14.0	9.3	13.9	15.0	4.9	0.2	92.9
Apr 10	3.1	10.0	20.0	13.2	8.8	13.2	14.5	5.2	0.2	88.1
May 8	3.2	9.8	19.0	12.6	8.2	12.6	13.9	5.3	0.2	84.9
Jun 12	3.5	9.6	18.5	12.0	7.9	12.0	13.1	4.5	0.2	81.1
Jul 10	**3.0**	**9.4**	**20.1**	**11.8**	**7.3**	**11.7**	**12.2**	**4.0**	**0.1**	**79.5**
Changes on a year earlier **MALE**										
1997 Feb 13	1.3	2.0	3.0	4.2	4.0	5.4	4.4	1.6	0.6	26.4
Mar 13	0.7	1.2	0.0	1.0	1.1	2.5	2.9	1.3	0.3	10.9
Apr 10	1.2	1.8	1.7	2.1	1.5	2.8	3.0	0.5	0.2	14.8
May 8	0.9	0.9	-2.0	-1.6	-1.0	-1.3	-1.6	-2.2	-0.8	-8.6
Jun 12	1.5	2.2	1.1	1.6	1.2	1.4	0.6	-0.6	-0.7	8.3
Jul 10	**1.2**	**0.8**	**-2.9**	**-1.5**	**-0.7**	**-0.8**	**-0.8**	**-0.6**	**-1.0**	**-6.3**
FEMALE										
1997 Feb 13	0.9	0.6	0.0	1.2	0.9	1.6	2.4	0.9	0.0	8.5
Mar 13	0.4	0.4	-1.5	-0.1	0.0	0.1	1.2	0.8	-0.1	1.2
Apr 10	0.8	0.4	-0.8	0.2	0.8	1.5	2.1	0.9	-0.1	5.8
May 8	0.7	0.0	-3.4	-1.8	-1.3	-2.7	-2.4	-0.4	-0.1	-11.6
Jun 12	1.2	0.8	-0.7	-0.2	-0.2	-0.6	0.0	0.1	-0.1	0.2
Jul 10	**0.8**	**0.6**	**-1.6**	**-0.7**	**-0.7**	**0.4**	**0.6**	**0.3**	**-0.1**	**-0.5**

* Flows figures are collected for four or five-week periods between count dates; the figures in the table are converted to a standard 4 $\frac{1}{3}$ week month.
+ The outflows, for older age groups in particular, are affected by the exclusion of non-computerised records from this table. Those who attend benefit offices only quarterly, who are mainly aged 50 and over, cease to be part of the computerised records.

2.23 CLAIMANT UNEMPLOYMENT
Claim history: interval between claims
Claims starting during the quarter ending April 1997 by the interval between the latest and previous claim

Interval (weeks)	Onflows (per cent)			Onflows (thousands)		
	Female	Male	All	Female	Male	All
4 or less	14	18	17	30.2	94.5	124.7
Over 4 and up to 13	13	17	16	28.8	91.4	120.2
Over 13 and up to 26	11	14	13	23.9	73.9	97.8
Over 26 and up to 39	5	7	7	11.5	37.6	49.1
Over 39 and up to 52	4	5	5	9.0	27.5	36.5
Over 52 and up to 104	8	9	9	17.1	49.0	66.1
Over 104	14	13	13	31.7	67.6	99.3
No previous Claims	31	17	21	68.5	90.3	158.8
Total	100	100	100	220.7	531.7	752.4

ONFLOWS **REGIONS**

Interval (weeks)	North East	Noth West (GOR)	Merseyside	Yorkshire & Humber	East Midlands	West Midlands	Eastern	London	South East (GOR)	South West	Wales	Scotland	Great Britain
PER CENT													
4 or less	19	17	19	19	17	15	16	15	15	17	17	16	17
Over 4 and up to 13	17	16	16	16	16	16	15	17	16	16	15	15	16
Over 13 and up to 26	13	14	14	13	12	13	13	14	11	13	14	13	13
Over 26 and up to 39	7	6	6	7	7	7	7	6	6	6	7	6	7
Over 39 and up to 52	5	5	4	5	6	5	5	5	5	4	5	5	5
Over 52 and up to 104	8	9	8	9	8	8	9	9	10	9	8	9	9
Over 104	12	13	14	13	13	14	13	13	14	13	13	14	13
No previous Claims	19	21	18	19	21`	22	23	22	23	21	21	21	21
Total	100	100	100	100	100	100	100	100	100	100	100	100	100
THOUSANDS													
4 or less	8.1	12.7	4.3	14.5	8.3	10.2	9.2	15.4	11.5	10.1	6.8	13.5	124.7
Over 4 and up to 13	7.6	12.1	3.5	11.8	7.8	10.6	8.9	17.3	11.8	9.6	6.0	13.2	120.2
Over 13 and up to 26	5.8	10.3	3.2	9.6	6.1	8.8	7.5	13.9	8.5	7.3	5.4	11.2	97.8
Over 26 and up to 39	3.1	4.5	1.3	5.4	3.5	4.3	3.9	6.4	4.7	3.5	2.9	5.5	49.1
Over 39 and up to 52	2.1	3.6	1.0	3.5	3.0	3.3	2.6	4.7	3.5	2.6	2.1	4.7	36.5
Over 52 and up to 104	3.6	6.7	1.9	6.6	4.1	5.2	5.0	9.3	7.8	5.1	3.1	7.6	66.1
Over 104	5.2	9.6	3.2	10.1	6.7	8.9	7.5	12.8	10.8	7.5	5.2	11.8	99.3
No previous Claims	8.1	15.5	4.1	14.4	10.5	14.5	13.7	22.4	17.1	12.4	8.3	17.8	158.8
Total	43.6	75.0	22.6	75.8	50.0	65.8	58.3	102.1	75.7	58.2	39.8	85.3	752.36

Notes 1: JUVOS cohort is a 5% sample of computerised claims.
2: 'Latest' claims in this table started between 10 January 1997 and 10 April 1997 inclusive.
3: 'Previous' claims in this table must have started after 8 January 1987.
4: The widest 95% Confidence Interval for the regional percentages is +/- 2.3 percentage points (Merseyside).
5: The widest 95% Confidence Interval for the male/female percentages is +/-0.9 percentage points.
6: All claims have been grossed by a factor of 20 to represent the population.

2.24 CLAIMANT UNEMPLOYMENT
By sought and usual occupation
United Kingdom as at July 10 1997

UNITED KINGDOM	SOC Sub-major groups	Usual occupation						Sought occupation					
		Men		Women		All		Men		Women		All	
Description		Thousand	Per cent	Thousand	Per cent	Thousand	Per cent	Thousand	Per cent	Thousand	Per cent	Thousand	Per cent
Corporate managers and administrators	10-15&19	33.4	2.8	9.1	2.4	42.5	2.7	36.2	3.0	10.7	2.8	46.9	3.0
Managers/proprietors in agriculture and services	16-17	17.3	1.4	5.0	1.3	22.3	1.4	17.6	1.5	5.6	1.5	23.2	1.5
Science and engineering professionals	20-21	13.5	1.1	1.9	0.5	15.5	1.0	16.6	1.4	3.0	0.8	19.6	1.2
Health professionals	22	0.6	0.0	0.3	0.1	0.9	0.1	0.7	0.1	0.5	0.1	1.2	0.1
Teaching professionals	23	11.9	1.0	11.6	3.1	23.5	1.5	13.5	1.1	13.4	3.5	26.9	1.7
Other professional occupations	24-29	9.1	0.8	3.8	1.0	12.8	0.8	11.4	1.0	5.4	1.4	16.8	1.1
Science and engineering associate professionals	30-32	13.6	1.1	1.9	0.5	15.5	1.0	17.5	1.5	2.6	0.7	20.1	1.3
Health associate professionals	34	1.3	0.1	2.9	0.8	4.2	0.3	1.6	0.1	3.5	0.9	5.1	0.3
Other associate professional occupations	33&35-39	37.5	3.1	16.8	4.4	54.3	3.5	48.0	4.0	23.2	6.1	71.1	4.5
Clerical occupations	40-44&49	108.4	9.1	63.7	16.7	172.0	10.9	137.6	11.5	78.3	20.6	215.8	13.7
Secretarial occupations	45-46	1.7	0.1	16.2	4.3	17.9	1.1	1.9	0.2	18.1	4.8	20.0	1.3
Skilled construction trades	50	72.5	6.1	0.5	0.1	73.0	4.6	75.5	6.3	0.6	0.2	76.1	4.8
Skilled engineering trades	51-52	38.8	3.3	0.7	0.2	39.5	2.5	41.0	3.4	0.8	0.2	41.8	2.7
Other skilled trades	53-59	101.8	8.5	8.3	2.2	110.0	7.0	108.0	9.1	8.4	2.2	116.4	7.4
Protective service occupations	60-61	15.7	1.3	0.8	0.2	16.5	1.0	16.5	1.4	1.1	0.3	17.6	1.1
Personal service occupations	62-69	43.8	3.7	46.9	12.3	90.7	5.8	47.7	4.0	56.8	14.9	104.5	6.6
Buyers, brokers and sales representatives	70-71	12.9	1.1	2.2	0.6	15.1	1.0	13.7	1.1	2.5	0.7	16.2	1.0
Other sales occupations	72-73&79	45.9	3.9	49.4	13.0	95.4	6.1	56.2	4.7	64.9	17.1	121.1	7.7
Industrial plant and machine operators, assemblers	80-86&89	52.3	4.4	14.8	3.9	67.1	4.3	52.8	4.4	14.5	3.8	67.3	4.3
Drivers and mobile machine operators	87-88	81.0	6.8	2.1	0.5	83.0	5.3	97.4	8.2	2.8	0.7	100.1	6.4
Other occupations in agriculture, forestry&fishing	90	12.5	1.0	2.2	0.6	14.7	0.9	13.2	1.1	2.9	0.8	16.1	1.0
Other elementary occupations	91-99	337.0	28.2	54.2	14.2	391.2	24.9	353.3	29.6	55.1	14.5	408.4	26.0
No previous occupation/ sought occupation unknown		130.9	11.0	65.1	17.1	196.0	12.5	15.6	1.3	5.8	1.5	21.3	1.4
Total		**1,193.3**		**380.4**		**1,573.7**		**1,193.3**		**380.4**		**1,573.7**	

Note: Excludes clerically operated claims.
Not seasonally adjusted.

REDUNDANCIES IN GREAT BRITAIN 2.32
THOUSANDS

		1994 Summer	1994 Autumn	1994 Winter	1995 Spring	1995 Summer	1995 Autumn	1995 Winter	1996 Spring	1996 Summer	1996 Autumn	1996 Winter
Now in employment (found new job since redundancy)	All	49	61	53	87	80	82	77	74	84	76	67
Not in employment	All	145	129	66	133	130	131	148	133	124	109	119
All people	All	194	190	119	220	210	213	225	207	208	185	186
	Men	132	129	80	137	132	135	149	143	136	116	123
	Women	62	61	39	82	78	78	75	64	72	69	63

Note: Figures are based on estimates from the Labour Force Survey, and show the numbers of people who were made redundant in the three months prior to their interview.

REDUNDANCIES BY REGION 2.33

	Great Britain	Northern	Yorkshire and Humberside	East Midlands	East Anglia	South East	South East excluding Greater London	Greater London	South West	West Midlands	North West	Wales	Scotland
Redundancies (thousands) All													
Winter 1995	225	16	19	16	13	70	40	30	16	17	23	10	25
Spring 1996	207	11	16	13	*	61	39	22	17	22	26	11	21
Summer 1996	208	13	19	17	*	55	39	16	16	19	25	13	23
Autumn 1996	185	*	20	15	*	58	37	21	15	15	19	*	22
Winter 1996	186	*	13	18	*	54	40	15	12	19	25	*	23
Redundancy rates (redundancies per 1,000 employees) All													
Winter 1995	10	14	10	10	15	10	9	11	9	8	10	10	13
Spring 1996	9	10	8	8	*	9	9	8	10	11	11	11	11
Summer 1996	9	11	10	10	*	8	9	6	9	9	11	13	11
Autumn 1996	8	*	11	9	*	8	8	8	8	7	8	*	11
Winter 1996	8	*	7	10	*	8	9	6	6	9	10	*	11

* Less than 10,000 in cell: estimate not shown.

REDUNDANCIES BY AGE 2.34

Ages	16 to 24	25 to 34	35 to 44	45 to 54	55 and over	All ages
Redundancies (thousands)						
Winter 1995	56	59	43	33	34	225
Spring 1996	41	49	46	44	27	207
Summer 1996	47	48	45	42	25	208
Autumn 1996	41	52	31	38	22	185
Winter 1996	39	48	39	38	22	186
Redundancy rates (redundancies per 1,000 employees)						
Winter 1995	16	10	8	7	14	10
Spring 1996	12	8	9	9	11	9
Summer 1996	13	8	9	9	11	9
Autumn 1996	11	9	6	8	9	8
Winter 1996	11	8	7	8	9	8

REDUNDANCIES BY INDUSTRY 2.35

SIC 1992	Agriculture & fishing (A,B)	Energy and water (C,E)	Manufacturing (D)	Construction (F)	Distribution, hotels & restaurants (G,H)	Transport (I)	Banking, finance & insurance (J,K)	Public admin, education & health (L,M,N)	Other services (O,P,Q)
Redundancies (thousands)									
Winter 1995	*	*	66	30	44	15	34	16	*
Spring 1996	*	*	64	24	42	14	27	14	10
Summer 1996	*	*	64	20	43	12	31	20	11
Autumn 1996	*	*	44	20	44	12	28	19	*
Winter 1996	*	*	56	23	37	15	26	17	*
Redundancy rates (redundancies per 1,000 employees)									
Winter 1995	*	*	14	30	10	11	11	3	*
Spring 1996	*	*	14	26	10	10	9	3	8
Summer 1996	*	*	14	21	10	8	10	3	10
Autumn 1996	*	*	9	20	10	8	9	3	*
Winter 1996	*	*	12	23	8	10	8	3	*

Note: Table 2.35 assumes that people do not change industry when starting employment after having been made redundant.
* Less than 10,000 in cell: estimate not shown.

REDUNDANCIES BY OCCUPATION 2.36

SOC	Managers and administrators	Professional	Associate professional and technical	Clerical and secretarial	Craft and related	Personal and protective services	Sales	Plant and machine operatives	Other
Redundancies (thousands)									
Winter 1995	32	*	12	33	36	14	24	41	23
Spring 1996	27	15	10	33	30	16	20	30	23
Summer 1996	33	11	12	28	37	17	23	30	16
Autumn 1996	26	11	11	28	30	15	19	22	20
Winter 1996	22	*	11	30	31	16	17	32	19
Redundancy rates (redundancies per 1,000 employees)									
Winter 1995	10	*	6	9	16	6	13	18	12
Spring 1996	8	7	5	9	14	6	11	14	12
Summer 1996	10	5	6	8	17	7	12	14	9
Autumn 1996	8	5	6	8	14	6	10	10	11
Winter 1996	7	*	5	8	14	6	9	15	10

Note: Table 2.36 assumes that people do not change occupation when starting employment after having been made redundant.
* Less than 10,000 in cell: estimate not shown.

3.1 VACANCIES
UK vacancies at Jobcentres:* seasonally adjusted

THOUSANDS

UNITED KINGDOM		UNFILLED VACANCIES			INFLOW		OUTFLOW		of which PLACINGS	
		Level	Change since previous month	Average change over 3 months ended	Level	Average change over 3 months ended	Level	Average change over 3 months ended	Level	Average change over 3 months ended
1993)		127.8			185.6		183.7		138.1	
1994) Annual		158.0			211.4		208.1		160.6	
1995) averages		182.8			223.5		222.5		170.9	
1996)		225.8			203.0		196.9		139.0	
1995	Jul	180.8	0.7	-0.4	223.9	2.0	222.5	2.0	172.9	2.3
	Aug	183.0	2.2	1.0	229.8	3.4	227.7	3.3	176.1	3.1
	Sep	193.1	10.1	4.3	228.0	2.8	221.2	0.6	170.0	-0.4
	Oct	190.7	-2.4	3.3	231.2	2.4	231.9	3.1	179.7	2.0
	Nov	192.0	1.3	3.0	235.1	1.8	234.0	2.1	178.9	0.7
	Dec	188.3	-3.7	-1.6	221.4	-2.2	221.4	0.1	167.3	-0.8
1996	Jan	187.3	-1.0	-1.1	217.1	-4.7	219.3	-4.2	167.0	-4.2
	Feb	187.9	0.6	-1.4	225.7	-3.1	225.4	-2.9	166.8	-3.9
	Mar	195.1	7.2	2.3	224.7	1.1	219.7	-0.6	158.5	-2.9
	Apr	197.0	1.9	3.2	228.0	3.6	222.7	1.1	157.8	-3.1
	May	205.1	8.1	5.7	228.6	1.0	222.4	-1.0	157.3	-3.2
	Jun	218.8	13.7	7.9	218.1	-2.2	206.9	-4.3	145.3	-4.4
	Jul	230.1	11.3	11.0	223.1	-1.6	212.4	-3.4	147.7	-3.4
	Aug	237.0	6.9	10.6	218.7	-3.3	212.1	-3.4	147.3	-3.3
	Sep	253.6	16.6	11.6	220.6	0.8	207.1	0.1	143.8	-0.5
	Oct	262.6	9.0	10.8	202.2	-7.0	193.6	-6.3	131.7	-5.3
	Nov	268.7	6.1	10.6	229.6	3.6	220.9	2.9	145.2	-0.7
	Dec	266.3	-2.4	4.2	225.7	1.7	234.4	9.1	160.0	5.4
1997	Jan	263.1	-3.2	0.2	204.1	0.6	213.5	6.6	150.0	6.1
	Feb	271.6	8.5	1.0	243.4	4.6	236.6	5.2	160.6	5.1
	Mar	275.3	3.7	3.0	250.4	8.2	255.6	7.1	173.1	4.4
	Apr	274.6	-0.7	3.8	238.2	11.4	240.3	8.9	163.7	4.6
	May	274.3	-0.3	0.9	239.0	-1.5	239.0	0.8	163.2	0.9
	Jun R	282.9	8.6	2.5	225.9	-8.2	217.7	-12.6	141.1	-10.7
	Jul P	**284.4**	**1.5**	**3.3**	**224.9**	**-4.4**	**226.7**	**-4.5**	**137.5**	**-8.7**

Note: Vacancies notified to and placings made by Jobcentres do not represent the total number of vacancies/engagements in the economy. Latest estimates suggest that about a third of all vacancies nationally are notified to Jobcentres; and about a quarter of all engagements are made through Jobcentres. Inflow, outflow and placings figures are collected for four or five-week periods between count dates; the figures in this table are converted to a standard 4 $1/3$ week month.
* Excluding vacancies on government programmes (except vacancies on Enterprise Ulster and Action for Community Employment (ACE) which are included in the seasonally-adjusted figures for Northern Ireland). Figures on the current basis are available back to 1980. For further details, see *Employment Gazette*, p 143, October 1985.
P The latest national and regional seasonally adjusted vacancy figures are provisional and subject to revision, mainly in the following month.
R Revised.

3.2 VACANCIES
Government Office Regions: vacancies remaining unfilled at Jobcentres:* seasonally adjusted

THOUSANDS

		North East	North West	Mersey-side	Yorkshire and the Humber	East Midlands	West Midlands	Eastern	London	South East	South West	Wales	Scotland	Great Britain	Northern Ireland	United Kingdom
1995	Jul	6.3	18.6	4.1	13.5	12.8	14.9	14.6	15.7	22.0	14.3	13.1	23.6	173.5	7.3	180.8
	Aug	6.3	18.9	4.3	13.5	13.2	15.1	14.6	15.5	21.9	14.4	13.5	24.0	175.6	7.4	183.0
	Sep	6.4	19.2	4.2	14.2	13.4	16.6	14.6	16.9	22.6	15.4	14.3	24.4	185.0	8.1	193.1
	Oct	6.4	19.5	4.2	13.9	13.3	16.7	14.6	17.5	22.0	15.9	14.0	24.2	183.2	7.5	190.7
	Nov	6.5	19.4	4.2	13.7	13.0	16.7	15.0	18.1	22.7	16.1	14.1	23.9	184.6	7.4	192.0
	Dec	6.4	18.8	4.1	13.6	12.5	15.9	14.3	18.8	23.3	15.9	13.5	23.7	180.9	7.4	188.3
1996	Jan	6.4	18.9	4.1	13.8	12.5	16.0	14.5	18.4	23.7	15.5	13.4	23.5	180.1	7.2	187.3
	Feb	6.6	18.7	4.0	13.9	12.7	16.0	14.6	19.5	24.1	15.4	13.2	23.5	180.9	7.0	187.9
	Mar	6.8	19.4	4.5	14.6	13.0	16.5	15.3	21.0	24.8	16.6	13.5	23.1	187.9	7.2	195.1
	Apr	6.6	19.0	4.8	15.0	13.0	16.5	14.6	21.6	26.4	17.0	13.3	22.9	190.0	7.0	197.0
	May	7.2	20.2	4.7	15.3	13.1	17.4	16.3	25.1	25.7	17.3	13.4	23.4	198.3	6.8	205.1
	Jun	7.9	21.5	4.6	15.7	13.7	18.5	17.3	28.3	27.7	18.9	14.0	24.4	212.0	6.8	218.8
	Jul	8.4	23.3	4.7	16.6	14.4	19.5	17.9	30.1	28.9	19.4	14.6	25.8	223.4	6.7	230.1
	Aug	8.8	22.7	5.0	17.9	14.9	19.8	18.6	31.8	29.5	20.0	15.1	26.0	230.5	6.5	237.0
	Sep	9.5	23.8	5.2	19.4	16.5	20.6	19.6	34.5	30.7	21.6	15.7	27.6	246.8	6.8	253.6
	Oct	9.9	25.3	5.3	19.6	17.4	21.5	21.1	37.0	32.2	22.0	16.0	28.6	255.8	6.8	262.6
	Nov	9.7	25.4	5.9	19.8	18.1	21.6	21.5	39.5	32.4	22.9	15.7	28.7	261.1	7.6	268.7
	Dec	9.6	25.1	5.7	19.0	18.4	21.7	22.2	38.6	32.3	23.0	15.7	28.2	259.2	7.1	266.3
1997	Jan	9.3	24.5	5.8	19.1	17.9	21.2	22.0	38.0	31.6	23.0	15.8	28.0	256.5	6.6	263.1
	Feb	9.8	25.7	6.0	20.3	18.6	21.9	23.9	36.9	33.0	24.1	17.1	28.5	265.0	6.6	271.6
	Mar	10.0	25.5	6.1	20.8	18.7	22.5	23.1	36.0	35.2	25.1	17.3	28.7	268.8	6.5	275.3
	Apr	9.9	25.1	6.2	20.9	18.7	23.1	22.1	35.9	34.1	25.8	17.6	28.8	268.3	6.3	274.6
	May	10.2	24.6	6.7	20.8	19.0	23.1	21.5	35.5	34.5	25.1	17.9	28.7	267.7	6.5	274.3
	Jun R	10.3	26.7	6.9	20.9	19.4	23.5	22.8	35.5	34.7	27.0	18.2	30.2	276.1	6.8	282.9
	Jul P	**10.4**	**27.0**	**7.1**	**21.1**	**19.6**	**24.0**	**22.9**	**35.4**	**34.3**	**26.2**	**18.2**	**31.6**	**277.7**	**6.7**	**284.4**

* See footnote to *Table 3.1*.
P The latest national and regional seasonally adjusted vacancy figures are provisional and subject to revision, mainly in the following month.
R Revised.
Note: Due to production difficulties, data for standard statistical regions have been withdrawn from this table. Figures for specific regions are available on request from the Labour Market Statistics Helpline on 0171 533 6176.

	North East	North West	Mersey-side	Yorkshire and the Humber	East Midlands	West Midlands	Eastern	London	South East	South West	Wales	Scotland	Great Britain	Northern Ireland	United Kingdom
Vacancies at Jobcentres: total +															
1993)	4.9	13.7	3.2	9.9	8.8	8.9	10.2	10.0	15.3	9.6	9.6	18.5	122.7	4.0	126.6
1994) Annual	5.6	16.8	3.6	11.8	10.8	12.2	13.0	13.1	20.8	12.4	11.2	19.8	150.3	5.0	155.4
1995) averages	6.4	18.7	4.0	13.5	12.8	15.3	14.8	16.5	22.8	14.4	13.3	23.2	175.6	5.8	181.2
1996)	8.1	22.0	4.9	16.7	14.9	18.9	17.8	28.9	28.2	19.2	14.5	25.6	219.6	5.6	225.1
1996 Jul	8.5	23.1	4.7	16.8	14.5	19.4	18.2	29.8	29.6	20.3	15.0	26.1	226.0	5.3	231.3
Aug	8.8	22.3	5.1	18.1	14.6	19.3	18.5	30.8	29.8	20.3	15.1	26.3	228.9	4.9	233.8
Sep	10.3	26.1	5.8	20.5	17.5	21.7	21.5	35.0	33.5	23.2	16.7	29.8	261.7	5.8	267.4
Oct	10.9	28.1	6.0	21.7	19.7	24.0	23.3	39.6	35.9	23.7	17.3	30.8	281.1	6.1	287.2
Nov	10.4	27.0	6.3	20.9	19.4	23.1	22.6	41.3	34.6	23.2	16.2	29.8	274.7	6.6	281.3
Dec	9.1	24.0	5.5	18.1	18.0	21.0	21.2	38.6	30.8	21.3	14.5	27.2	249.2	6.0	255.2
1997 Jan	8.6	22.3	5.3	17.3	16.2	19.3	19.6	36.5	28.0	19.9	14.2	24.9	232.1	5.4	237.5
Feb	9.0	23.5	5.6	18.7	17.1	20.3	21.7	35.1	29.3	21.9	15.9	25.9	244.1	5.5	249.5
Mar	9.4	24.2	5.7	19.6	17.7	21.4	21.7	35.0	32.5	24.1	16.8	27.2	255.3	5.6	260.8
Apr	9.6	24.6	6.1	20.8	18.3	22.6	22.0	35.4	34.0	26.3	17.6	28.7	265.9	5.4	271.3
May	10.0	24.8	6.6	20.4	18.7	23.0	21.8	34.9	34.2	25.9	18.2	28.7	267.2	5.7	272.9
Jun	10.4	27.6	7.0	21.1	19.7	23.8	23.7	35.6	36.2	28.8	19.2	31.4	284.5	5.9	290.4
Jul	**10.5**	**26.9**	**7.0**	**21.3**	**19.4**	**24.3**	**23.2**	**34.9**	**35.0**	**27.0**	**18.5**	**32.1**	**280.1**	**5.6**	**285.8**
Vacancies at careers offices															
1993)	—	—	—	0.4	0.3	0.8	—	1.7	—	0.5	0.1	0.5	6.6	0.6	7.2
1994) Annual	—	—	—	0.3	0.3	0.8	—	1.4	—	0.7	0.1	0.6	6.5	0.8	7.2
1995) averages	—	—	—	0.4	0.4	0.6	—	0.8	—	0.8	0.2	0.6	6.8	0.7	7.5
1996)	0.2	1.0	0.1	1.3	0.5	1.4	1.4	2.0	2.3	0.9	0.2	0.6	11.9	0.8	12.7
1996 Jul	0.3	1.4	0.2	1.8	0.7	1.1	1.8	1.7	8.3	1.3	0.3	0.8	19.7	0.8	20.5
Aug	0.3	1.7	0.2	1.5	0.6	1.1	1.8	2.9	2.3	1.4	0.5	0.8	15.0	0.8	15.8
Sep	0.2	1.8	0.2	1.9	0.6	1.1	1.8	2.9	2.3	1.1	0.3	0.6	14.9	0.9	15.9
Oct	0.2	1.1	0.2	2.2	0.6	1.3	1.7	3.4	2.2	1.1	0.3	0.8	14.9	1.0	15.8
Nov	0.2	1.2	0.2	1.8	0.5	1.2	1.5	2.9	2.0	1.1	0.2	0.6	13.4	1.1	14.5
Dec	0.2	1.1	0.2	1.4	0.5	0.9	1.4	3.0	1.8	0.9	0.1	0.5	11.9	1.0	12.9
1997 Jan	0.1	1.0	0.1	1.3	0.5	1.0	1.3	0.5	1.9	0.9	0.2	0.5	9.4	0.9	10.2
Feb	0.2	1.4	0.2	1.5	0.6	1.1	1.4	3.1	2.1	0.9	0.2	0.6	13.1	0.9	14.0
Mar	0.2	1.6	0.2	1.7	0.6	1.3	1.2	3.2	0.8	1.1	0.2	0.7	12.8	0.9	13.6
Apr	0.2	2.0	0.2	1.9	0.7	1.2	1.7	3.0	2.8	1.2	0.3	0.7	15.9	0.8	16.7
May	0.2	2.0	0.2	1.9	0.7	1.2	1.7	3.0	2.1	1.2	0.3	0.7	15.2	0.9	16.0
Jun	0.2	1.3	0.2	1.6	0.6	1.0	1.7	2.6	2.2	1.1	0.4	1.1	14.1	0.9	15.0
Jul	**0.3**	**2.0**	**0.4**	**1.6**	**1.0**	**1.4**	**1.7**	**4.4**	**3.8**	**1.7**	**0.4**	**1.0**	**19.7**	**0.9**	**20.6**

Note: 1 About one third of all vacancies nationally are notified to Jobcentres. These could include some that are suitable for young people and similarly vacancies notified to careers offices could include some for adults. The figures represent only the number of vacancies notified by employers and remaining unfilled on the day of the count. Because of possible duplication and also due to a difference between the timing of the two counts, the two series should not be added together.

2 Due to production difficulties, data for standard statistical regions have been withdrawn from this table. Figures for specific regions are available on request from the Labour Market Statistics Helpline on 0171 533 6176.

3 Annual averages for vacancies at careers offices for GORs are unavailable prior to 1996.

+ Excluding vacancies on government programmes. See note to *Table 3.1.*

4.1 LABOUR DISPUTES
Stoppages of work

Stoppages in progress: industry

United Kingdom	12 months to June1996			12 months to June 1997(P)		
SIC 1992	Stop-pages	Workers involved	Working days lost	Stop-pages	Workers involved	Working days lost
Agriculture, hunting, forestry and fishing	1	100	100	-	-	-
Mining and quarrying	5	600	1,600	4	900	2,600
Manufacturing of:						
food,beverages and tobacco;	12	2,100	10,000	7	3,000	7,600
textiles and textile products;	10	9,300	4,800	3	300	900
leather and leather products;	-	-	-	-	-	-
wood and wood products;	-	-	-	-	-	-
pulp, paper and paper products; printing and publishing;	1	100	2,800	1	100	1,700
coke,refined petroleum products, nuclear fuels;	2	2500	8,400	1	3,000	9,000
chemicals, chemical products and man-made fibres;	4	1,900	5,100	-	-	#
rubber and plastics;	3	200	1,000	1	+	#
other non-metallic mineral products;	1	100	400	1	700	6,300
basic metals and fabricated metal products;	13	1,300	7,400	7	500	4,900
machinery and equipment nec;	9	1,900	5,900	8	2,000	8,800
electrical and optical equipment;	8	3,300	3,600	6	600	3,000
transport equipment;	14	17,900	18,200	25	20,400	73,500
manufacturing nec.	1	200	200	4	1,600	21,400
Electricity, gas and water supply	-	-	-	-	-	-
Construction	13	4,000	11,300	4	1,900	2,800
Wholesale and retail trade; repairs	-	-	-	-	-	-
Hotels and restaurants	4	500	10,100	-	-	-
Transport, storage and communication	61	158,300	303,500	74	138,700	666,700
Financial intermediation	1	100	100	2	30,000	19,000
Real estate, renting and business activities	6	1,100	1,300	4	100	200
Public administration and defence	23	31,300	160,800	24	39,100	114,000
Education	27	3,300	24,000	47	133,300	147,100
Health and social work	14	3,000	15,400	11	8,700	14,300
Other community,social and personal service activities	14	1,800	11,200	10	1,700	5,200
All industries and services	246 *	244,900	607,100	240 *	386,600	1,109,200

* Some stoppages which affected more than one industry group have been counted under each of the industries but only once in the total for all industries and services.
\+ Less than 50 workers involved.
\# Less then 50 working days lost.

Stoppages: June 1997 (P)

United Kingdom	Number of stoppages	Workers involved	Working days lost
Stoppages in progress	32	13,200	41,900
of which, stoppages:			
Beginning in month	24	12,100 *	36,600
Continuing from earlier months	8	1,100	5,400

* All directly involved

The monthly figures are provisional and subject to revision, normally upwards, to take account of additional or revised information received after going to press. For notes on coverage, see *Definitions* page at the end of the *Labour Market Data* section. The figures for 1996 are provisional.

Stoppages in progress: cause

United Kingdom	12 months to June 1997		
	Stoppages	Workers involved	Working days lost
Pay: wage-rates and earnings levels	78	247,500	826,200
extra wage and fringe benefits	13	41,800	36,600
Duration and pattern of hours worked	17	8,900	43,600
Redundancy questions	44	41,200	75,000
Trade union matters	13	2,200	5,100
Working conditions and supervision	14	19,200	79,900
Manning and work allocation	36	18,100	31,500
Dismissal and other disciplinary measures	27	7,700	11,200
All causes	240	386,600	1,109,200

Prominent stoppages in the 6 month period January 1 1997 to June 30 1997

Industry and location	Date when stoppage		Number of workers involved *		Number of working days lost in period	Cause or object
	Began	Ended	Directly	Indirectly		
Education						
Various areas of GB	28.11.96	27.03.97	600	-	800	Over procedural agreements or practices about the deployment of staff (total days lost 5,400)
Strathclyde	05.03.97	05.03.97	5,000	-	5,000	Over privatisation, market testing, cuts in service
London	13.03.97	contin'g	200	-	5,800	Over a particular case or threat of redundancy
London	22.04.97	contin'g	100	-	6,700	Over a particular case or threat of redundancy
Financial intermediation						
Various areas of Scotland	02.01.97	02.01.97	10,000	-	9,000	Over workers' entitlement to annual & occasional holidays
Manufacturing industries						
West Midlands Met County	03.01.97	28.02.97	700	-	6,300	Over pay increases to accompany and compensate for a basic pay change
Northern Ireland	09.04.97	23.06.97	300	-	6,400	Over straight pay increase
Tyne & Wear Met County	01.04.97	08.05.97	2,400	-	26,200	Over straight pay increase
Humberside	16.05.97	18.05.97	3,000	-	9,000	Over personal cash allowances which are ancillary to the job and over work breaks
Public administration and defence; compulsory social security						
Essex	19.04.97	06.05.97	1,000	+	6,800	Over privatisation, market testing, cuts in service
Transport, storage and communication						
Various areas of GB	05.03.97	24.04.97	2,700	400	5,900	Over straight pay increase
Other community, social & personal service activities						
Strathclyde	30.01.97	07.03.97	12,200	-	20,500	Over market testing, privatisation, cuts in services

* The figures shown are the highest number of workers involved during the six month period.
\+ Less than 50 workers involved.

United Kingdom	Number of stoppages		Number of workers (000)		Working days lost in all stoppages in progress in period (000)	
	Beginning in period	In progress in period	Beginning involvement in period in any dispute	All involvement in period	All industries and services	All manufacturing industries
1994	203	205	107	107	278	58
1995	232	235	170	174	415	65
1996	230	244	353	364	1303	97
1994 Jun	29	36	29.0	42.4	70.5	10.0
Jul	22	28	8.1	14.6	31.7	8.1
Aug	12	18	10.9	15.1	39.0	8.3
Sep	12	19	5.4	9.6	19.6	2.6
Oct	16	19	6.9	9.9	14.5	1.1
Nov	17	19	5.5	6.9	17.0	3.8
Dec	15	21	8.4	10.4	22.6	4.8
1995 Jan	12	15	14.7	17.9	24.3	4.5
Feb	16	19	20.9	22.1	18.0	0.3
Mar	16	17	7.0	19.0	28.3	1.3
Apr	22	26	18.1	20.4	33.9	5.4
May	24	29	26.1	29.8	51.3	11.1
Jun	16	23	2.5	4.3	16.0	5.4
Jul	25	29	16.5	16.9	32.2	1.6
Aug	24	31	9.9	10.5	18.5	3.0
Sep	24	35	4.7	13.4	24.5	1.6
Oct	13	25	4.0	10.4	30.6	7.3
Nov	21	34	21.7	30.4	77.2	13.5
Dec	19	32	24.4	29.0	59.6	9.9
1996 Jan	10	24	5.6	17.1	51.3	5.9
Feb	26	36	6.3	9.8	36.0	2.7
Mar	16	27	4.2	5.1	15.2	9.3
Apr	18	27	6.1	8.3	13.2	3.5
May	14	23	2.5	4.1	7.6	0.6
Jun	32	43	138.6	140.4	241.0	8.7
Jul	14	28	6.5	127.2	148.6	7.6
Aug	25	33	22.4	135.7	442.2	3.5
Sep	19	29	5.4	120.7	121.9	8.4
Oct	20	26	3.8	16.5	39.3	13.7
Nov	24	34	124.4	127.1	162.1	23.0
Dec	12	23	27.1	28.8	24.9	9.8
1997 Jan	20	30	18.2	19.5	23.4	10.4
Feb	12	27	5.8	8.1	13.9	3.7
Mar	22	35r	25.6	32.1	36.2	4.2
Apr	26	35r	13.1r	14.6r	47.4r	27.4r
May	18r	31r	10.0r	14.7r	36.3r	19.1r
June	**14**	**20**	**3.5**	**4.9**	**12.9**	**6.4**

Working days lost in all stoppages in progress in period by industry

United Kingdom	Agriculture, hunting, forestry & fishing	Mining, quarrying, electricity, gas and water	Manufacturing	Construction	Wholesale & retail trade; repairs; hotels and restaurants	Transport, storage & communication	Finance, real estate, renting & business activities	Public administration and defence	Education	Health and social work	Other community, social and personal service activities
SIC 1992	A,B	C,E	D	F	G,H	I	J,K	L	M	N	O,P,Q
1994	-	1	58	5	1	110	7	11	70	5	11
1995	-	1	65	10	6	120	10	95	67	16	23
1996	-	2	97	8	5	884	11	158	129	8	3
1994 Jun	-	-	10.0	4.3	0.7	27.9	0.1	0.8	23.9	0.4	2.3
Jul	-	-	8.1	-	-	15.9	-	2.3	4.4	-	0.9
Aug	-	-	8.3	-	-	18.2	-	6.2	4.6	1.6	-
Sep	-	-	2.6	-	-	13.0	1.1	0.3	1.8	0.1	0.6
Oct	-	-	1.1	0.3	-	3.5	-	-	9.5	-	0.1
Nov	-	0.3	3.8	-	-	1.4	-	0.1	9.8	0.5	1.0
Dec	-	0.3	4.8	-	-	6.4	-	0.5	10.2	0.4	-
1995 Jan	-	-	4.5	-	-	13.6	-	1.0	5.3	-	-
Feb	-	0.1	0.3	-	-	1.0	2.5	0.9	6.9	-	6.2
Mar	-	0.1	1.3	5.0	-	1.7	-	-	20.1	-	0.2
Apr	-	-	5.4	0.9	0.2	11.8	-	0.6	13.9	0.3	0.8
May	-	1.0	11.1	0.2	0.1	24.0	6.5	2.8	4.5	0.9	0.1
Jun	-	-	5.4	0.7	0.1	0.8	0.1	1.1	0.6	0.8	6.4
Jul	-	-	1.6	0.1	-	18.5	0.7	0.6	1.5	0.1	9.1
Aug	-	0.2	3.0	-	-	4.9	-	7.7	-	2.6	0.1
Sep	-	0.1	1.6	0.3	-	4.4	0.1	8.0	5.5	4.4	0.1
Oct	-	-	7.3	-	1.3	7.8	0.1	9.0	1.6	3.7	-
Nov	-	-	13.5	2.4	2.2	27.9	-	26.4	4.3	0.1	0.4
Dec	-	9.9	0.5	2.0	4.1	-	36.7	2.8	3.4	0.1	-
1996 Jan	-	-	5.9	-	2.2	9.2	-	33.0	0.9	-	0.2
Feb	0.1	-	2.7	5.2	2.2	2.8	0.2	21.8	0.4	0.1	0.5
Mar	-	1.3	9.3	0.1	0.3	0.2	0.2	1.8	1.0	0.5	0.5
Apr	-	-	3.5	2.5	-	1.8	-	3.7	1.1	0.5	-
May	-	-	0.6	0.1	-	0.9	-	3.9	2.1	-	-
Jun	-	-	8.7	0.2	-	221.0	-	8.1	2.9	-	0.2
Jul	-	-	7.6	-	-	135.7	-	4.0	1.1	-	0.2
Aug	-	-	3.5	-	-	394.0	0.1	44.6	-	-	-
Sep	-	-	8.4	-	-	98.9	-	13.0	0.3	1.3	-
Oct	-	0.3	13.7	0.1	-	1.6	-	23.0	0.1	0.5	-
Nov	-	-	23.0	-	-	16.1	-	0.6	117.1	3.8	1.4
Dec	-	0.2	9.8	-	-	1.5	10.0	0.1	1.5	1.7	-
1997 Jan	-	-	10.4	-	-	0.5	9.0	-	2.6	0.3	0.6
Feb	-	-	3.7	-	-	1.9	-	0.3	0.7	4.5	2.8
Mar	-	-	4.2	-	-	3.8	-	19.4	6.9	1.8	0.1
Apr	-	2.1	27.4r	1.1r	-	4.6	-	4.0	7.8r	0.5	-
May	-	-	19.1r	1.6r	-	5.4	-	4.9	5.2	-	-
June	**-**	**-**	**6.4**	**-**	**-**	**2.7**	**-**	**-**	**3.8**	**-**	**-**

* See 'Definitions' page at the end of 'Labour Market Data' section for notes of coverage. The figures for 1996 are provisional.

OFFICE FOR NATIONAL STATISTICS

MONEY MATTERS

Do you need a comprehensive picture of financial statistics?

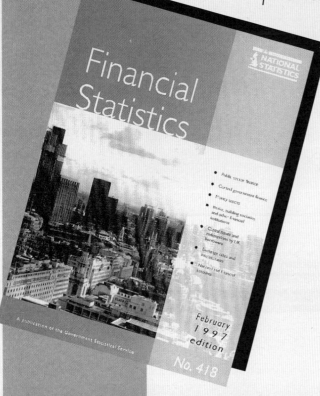

If so, you can't afford to be without *Financial Statistics*, monthly from National Statistics

Data in *Financial Statistics* include

- financial accounts and balance sheets for individual sectors of the economy

- government income and expenditure

- public sector borrowing

- banking statistics

- institutional investment

- company finance and liquidity

- security prices

- exchange and interest rates

Financial Statistics

Subscriptions available from The Stationery Office at £270 per year (including postage).
ISSN 0015 203X
Single issues available at £22.50 from the National Statistics Sales Office on 0171 533 5678.

Financial Statistics is also available from National Statistics on diskette or via the internet - call the National Statistics Sales Office on 0171 533 5678 for further information.

Average Earnings Index: all employees: main industrial sectors

GREAT BRITAIN SIC 1992	Whole economy (Divisions 01-93)				Manufacturing industries (Divisions 15-37)				Production industries (Divisions 10-41)				Service industries (Divisions 50-93)			
	Actual	Seasonally adjusted			Actual	Seasonally adjusted			Actual	Seasonally adjusted			Actual	Seasonally adjusted		
			Per cent change over previous 12 months				Per cent change over previous 12 months				Per cent change over previous 12 months				Per cent change over previous 12 months	
1990=100				Underlying *				Underlying *				Underlying *				Underlying *
1993)	118.5				120.5				121.0				117.5			
1994) Annual	123.2				126.2				126.9				121.7			
1995) averages	127.4				131.9				132.4				125.1			
1996)	**132.3**				**137.8**				**138.1**				**129.7**			
1993 Jan	116.1	117.0	4.5	4 3/4	117.1	118.2	4.9	5 1/4	117.6	118.6	4.9	5 1/4	115.6	116.3	4.3	4 1/2
Feb	116.7	117.2	4.0	4 1/2	118.3	118.7	4.9	5	118.7	119.1	4.8	5	116.1	116.5	3.7	4 1/4
Mar	119.6	117.2	2.8	4	121.9	118.8	3.9	5	122.1	119.5	3.8	5	118.5	115.8	2.4	3 3/4
Apr	117.5	117.6	4.0	4	119.0	119.2	5.4	5	119.7	119.5	5.3	5	116.5	116.8	3.3	3 1/4
May	118.0	117.9	3.5	3 3/4	120.4	120.1	4.9	5	120.8	120.4	4.8	5	116.9	116.9	3.1	3
Jun	118.5	118.3	3.6	3 3/4	120.9	120.4	5.0	5	121.3	120.7	4.8	5	117.0	117.2	3.0	2 3/4
Jul	119.5	118.8	3.8	3 1/2	121.8	121.0	4.9	4 3/4	122.4	121.6	5.0	4 3/4	118.3	117.7	3.3	2 3/4
Aug	118.2	118.9	3.3	3 1/4	119.5	121.2	3.8	4 1/2	119.9	121.5	4.0	4 1/2	117.3	117.7	2.8	2 3/4
Sep	118.0	119.2	3.1	3	120.1	121.9	4.6	4 1/4	120.6	122.3	4.8	4 1/2	116.8	118.0	2.4	2 1/4
Oct	118.4	119.7	2.1	3	121.3	122.1	3.8	4 1/4	121.7	122.6	3.8	4 1/4	116.9	118.5	1.4	2 1/4
Nov	120.0	120.4	3.3	3	122.4	122.6	4.1	4	123.1	123.3	4.3	4 1/4	118.7	119.0	2.6	2 1/2
Dec	121.6	120.5	3.2	3 1/4	123.5	122.5	3.9	4 1/4	124.1	123.3	4.0	4 1/4	120.8	119.5	2.9	2 3/4
1994 Jan	120.3	121.2	3.6	3 3/4	122.6	123.7	4.7	4 1/2	123.3	124.3	4.8	4 1/2	119.2	119.8	3.1	3 1/4
Feb	122.0	122.2	4.3	3 3/4	123.5	123.6	4.2	4 3/4	123.9	124.1	4.2	4 3/4	121.7	121.8	4.6	3 1/2
Mar	124.9	121.8	3.9	4	128.4	124.7	5.0	4 3/4	128.4	125.2	4.8	4 3/4	123.6	120.4	3.9	4
Apr	121.6	121.7	3.5	3 3/4	124.6	124.7	4.6	4 3/4	125.1	124.9	4.5	4 3/4	120.3	120.6	3.2	3 1/2
May	123.5	123.3	4.6	4	125.6	125.4	4.4	4 1/2	129.3	129.0	7.2	4 1/2	121.0	120.9	3.4	3 3/4
Jun	123.0	123.0	3.9	3 3/4	126.2	125.8	4.5	4 1/4	126.4	125.9	4.3	4 1/4	121.3	121.6	3.8	3 1/2
Jul	124.0	123.3	3.8	3 3/4	126.9	126.1	4.2	4 1/4	127.3	126.5	4.0	4 1/4	122.5	121.9	3.6	3 1/2
Aug	122.8	123.7	4.1	3 3/4	125.0	126.9	4.8	4 1/2	125.5	127.4	4.9	4 1/4	121.4	122.1	3.7	3 1/2
Sep	122.7	124.1	4.1	3 3/4	125.6	127.6	4.7	4 3/4	126.1	128.1	4.7	4 1/2	121.0	122.4	3.7	3 1/2
Oct	122.9	124.4	3.9	3 3/4	127.2	128.2	5.0	4 3/4	127.5	128.6	4.9	4 1/2	120.9	122.6	3.5	3 1/4
Nov	124.0	124.6	3.5	3 3/4	128.5	128.9	5.1	5	128.7	129.1	4.7	4 3/4	121.8	122.3	2.7	3
Dec	127.0	125.8	4.4	3 3/4	130.8	129.5	5.7	5	131.2	130.1	5.5	5	125.5	124.2	3.9	2 3/4
1995 Jan	124.8	125.7	3.8	3 3/4	128.4	129.6	4.8	5 1/4	129.2	130.3	4.8	5 1/4	123.1	123.7	3.2	2 3/4
Feb	125.9	125.9	3.0	3 1/2	130.4	130.2	5.3	5	131.1	130.9	5.5	5	123.8	123.8	1.6	2 3/4
Mar	130.3	126.5	3.8	3 1/2	134.5	130.4	4.5	5 1/4	134.6	130.9	4.5	5 1/4	128.9	125.2	4.0	2 3/4
Apr	126.2	126.3	3.8	3 3/4	131.1	131.1	5.1	4 3/4	131.4	131.2	5.0	4 3/4	123.8	124.0	2.8	3
May	127.0	126.8	2.8	3 1/2	131.1	131.2	4.6	4 3/4	131.6	131.5	2.0	4 3/4	125.0	124.8	3.2	2 3/4
Jun	126.8	127.0	3.2	3 1/2	131.8	131.5	4.5	4 1/2	132.6	132.2	5.0	4 3/4	123.9	124.4	2.3	2 3/4
Jul	127.9	127.2	3.2	3 1/4	133.2	132.2	4.9	4 1/2	133.6	132.7	4.9	4 3/4	125.3	124.7	2.3	2 1/2
Aug	126.6	127.8	3.3	3 1/4	130.2	132.4	4.3	4 1/4	130.8	133.0	4.4	4 1/2	124.5	125.4	2.7	2 1/2
Sep	126.6	128.1	3.2	3 1/4	130.5	132.7	4.0	4	131.3	133.4	4.2	4 1/2	124.0	125.5	2.6	2 1/2
Oct	127.2	128.8	3.6	3 1/4	132.3	133.6	4.2	4	132.9	134.2	4.4	4 1/4	124.4	126.2	2.9	2 3/4
Nov	128.3	129.0	3.6	3 1/4	133.2	133.7	3.8	4	133.7	134.2	4.0	4	125.9	126.5	3.5	2 3/4
Dec	130.6	129.4	2.8	3 1/4	136.1	134.6	3.9	4	136.2	135.0	3.7	4	128.3	127.0	2.2	3
1996 Jan	128.9	129.9	3.3	3 1/2	133.6	134.9	4.1	4 1/4	134.1	135.3	3.8	4	126.9	127.5	3.1	3
Feb	130.8	130.6	3.7	3 3/4	136.4	135.8	4.4	4 1/4	136.8	136.2	4.1	4	128.2	128.1	3.5	3 1/2
Mar	135.5	131.1	3.7	3 3/4	140.7	136.2	4.4	4 1/4	140.9	136.7	4.5	4 1/4	133.3	129.2	3.2	3 1/2
Apr	131.4	131.6	4.1	3 3/4	136.7	136.5	4.2	4 1/4	137.2	136.9	4.4	4 1/4	128.9	129.0	4.0	3 1/2
May	131.0	130.8	3.2	3 3/4	136.4	136.7	4.2	4 1/4	136.8	137.0	4.1	4	128.3	128.1	2.6	3 1/2
Jun	131.6	131.9	3.9	3 3/4	137.5	137.3	4.4	4 1/4	137.7	137.4	4.0	4	128.7	129.4	4.0	3 1/2
Jul	133.1	132.4	4.1	4	139.0	137.9	4.3	4 1/2	139.2	138.2	4.2	4	130.3	129.8	4.0	3 3/4
Aug	131.3	132.7	3.9	4	136.1	138.4	4.6	4 1/2	136.3	138.6	4.2	4 1/4	128.8	129.9	3.6	3 3/4
Sep	131.9	133.4	4.2	4	136.6	139.0	4.7	4 1/2	137.0	139.2	4.4	4 1/4	129.0	130.6	4.0	3 3/4
Oct	131.9	133.6	3.7	4	137.6	139.2	4.2	4 1/2	138.0	139.5	3.9	4 1/4	129.0	130.9	3.7	4
Nov	133.5	134.2	4.0	4 1/4	139.5	139.9	4.7	4 3/4	139.9	140.3	4.5	4 1/2	130.4	131.1	3.6	4
Dec	137.1	135.7	4.9	4 3/4	143.1	141.3	5.0	4 3/4	143.4	142.0	5.2	4 3/4	134.2	132.9	4.6	4 1/2
1997 Jan	135.2	136.3	4.9	4 3/4	139.2	140.6	4.2	4 3/4	139.8	141.1	4.3	4 3/4	133.6	134.1	5.2	4 3/4
Feb	136.3	136.0	4.1	4 1/2	142.9	142.0	4.6	4 1/2	142.9	142.0	4.3	4 1/4	133.6	133.5	4.2	5
Mar	141.7	136.9	4.4	4 1/2	146.7	141.9	4.2	4 1/2	146.5	142.0	3.9	4 1/4	140.1	135.6	5.0	4 3/4
Apr	136.9	137.0	4.2	4 1/2	142.2	141.9	4.0	4 1/4	142.7	142.4	4.0	4 1/4	134.6	134.6	4.3	4 3/4
May	136.4	136.3	4.2	4 1/4	142.3	142.7	4.4	4 1/4	142.9	143.2	4.5	4 1/4	133.3	133.0	3.9	4 1/2
Jun P	**137.0**	**137.4**	**4.2**	**4 1/4**	**143.4**	**143.3**	**4.3**	**4 1/4**	**143.4**	**143.3**	**4.2**	**4 1/4**	**134.0**	**134.8**	**4.2**	**4 1/2**

Notes: 1 Figures for years 1984-89 on a 1985=100 basis were published in *Employment Gazette,* October 1989; the 1985=100 series was discontinued after July 1989.
2 Figures on a 1988=100 basis were last published in *Employment Gazette,* September 1993.
3 The Index has been reclassified from SIC 1980 to SIC 1992, in common with other economic series in the national accounts. Figures on a SIC 1980 basis were last published in *Employment Gazette,* May 1995.
4 For enquiries, see telephone numbers on final pink page.
* The underlying rate of change is provisional for the latest two months and is not seasonally adjusted. For a note on the underlying rate of change see Statistical Update, *Employment Gazette,* p 291, July 1995.

5.3 EARNINGS
Average Earnings Index: all employees: by industry (unadjusted)

GREAT BRITAIN SIC 1992	Agriculture and forestry (E&W)	Mining and quarrys	Food products; beverages and tobacco	Textiles	Clothing leather and footwear	Wood, wood products and other manu'ing n.e.c.	Pulp, paper products printing and publishing	Chemicals and chemical products	Rubber and plastic products	Other non-metallic mineral products	Basic metals	Fabric'd metal products (excl. machinery)	Machinery and equipment n.e.c.
1990=100	(01,02)	(10-14)	(15,16)	(17)	(18,19)	(20,23,36,37)	(21,22)	(24)	(25)	(26)	(27)	(28)	(29)
1993) annual	117.7	126.1	125.0	123.2	117.7	114.5	118.9	121.2	122.6	115.3	115.6	119.2	122.7
1994) averages	121.5	136.2	130.6	128.7	123.6	120.0	123.6	125.6	128.4	120.6	123.7	127.4	128.2
1995)	126.4	139.0	136.2	132.7	129.3	123.9	128.5	131.7	133.7	124.8	131.8	133.4	134.3
1996)	**133.7**	**142.2**	**140.9**	**138.8**	**134.1**	**131.2**	**133.9**	**137.1**	**137.7**	**128.7**	**137.8**	**139.0**	**139.8**
1993 Jan	109.7	122.5	120.4	119.0	115.2	110.7	114.5	119.4	118.1	112.2	117.8	114.9	120.3
Feb	108.9	122.2	123.9	119.3	117.1	114.0	115.4	119.2	120.8	114.3	108.9	115.6	121.5
Mar	113.0	125.9	129.2	121.2	116.0	114.9	118.8	130.4	124.1	114.1	111.0	118.3	124.5
Apr	114.4	126.3	123.3	121.5	116.9	112.2	117.3	118.6	120.2	114.2	116.0	120.3	121.0
May	114.7	125.0	125.9	123.4	117.1	116.6	118.5	118.9	122.5	114.8	113.5	120.1	121.5
June	118.6	126.1	123.7	125.8	118.7	114.2	119.5	120.9	123.8	117.4	112.4	120.4	123.5
July	124.1	128.1	123.9	123.8	120.5	115.5	119.0	120.2	124.0	115.9	123.8	120.3	124.0
Aug	134.7	123.2	123.5	124.0	117.4	113.2	119.4	118.5	120.9	115.9	110.5	119.1	121.1
Sep	126.0	125.3	123.2	124.4	118.8	114.4	120.8	118.6	123.3	115.8	114.8	118.9	122.6
Oct	121.2	126.8	123.6	125.4	118.0	114.2	120.6	119.2	123.4	115.3	124.4	120.0	123.6
Nov	117.8	128.5	129.0	125.3	117.5	116.1	121.1	124.4	123.3	116.0	113.8	120.9	124.9
Dec	108.7	133.5	130.3	125.4	119.1	118.3	122.1	126.5	126.2	118.1	117.8	121.1	124.4
1994 Jan	112.6	131.5	126.0	124.8	119.6	114.9	120.2	123.2	124.4	116.9	122.4	121.4	125.2
Feb	112.5	129.4	126.2	125.4	122.9	120.4	119.9	124.1	125.0	118.4	114.8	125.3	126.7
Mar	121.6	132.2	137.4	129.0	125.4	118.9	124.5	134.4	129.4	120.2	118.9	126.5	130.3
Apr	117.1	132.9	127.8	127.1	123.8	116.6	120.8	123.1	126.4	120.6	126.8	124.0	127.7
May	119.4	189.4	129.6	127.8	123.1	121.1	123.4	123.0	130.2	121.2	119.4	126.9	128.3
June	121.3	131.1	129.3	130.7	123.5	118.4	125.0	126.4	128.9	122.5	118.2	128.3	127.1
July	127.7	133.2	129.9	130.9	121.8	119.5	122.9	123.8	129.8	123.1	138.7	127.3	127.9
Aug	134.9	126.9	130.1	128.1	122.3	120.2	123.3	122.0	126.6	119.5	120.5	126.3	126.3
Sep	130.6	129.4	129.1	128.2	123.3	119.5	125.2	123.7	128.6	120.0	121.2	129.0	127.8
Oct	124.7	129.6	129.7	130.2	124.9	119.7	124.8	123.7	129.3	120.4	133.1	130.3	129.0
Nov	119.4	131.1	135.7	130.3	124.7	123.9	125.9	126.7	130.7	121.3	122.6	131.1	130.3
Dec	115.9	137.5	136.5	132.2	128.0	127.1	127.1	133.6	131.6	123.6	128.1	132.4	131.2
1995 Jan	118.1	139.7	132.7	129.3	126.8	119.1	124.7	128.5	130.3	121.5	133.8	128.4	129.9
Feb	114.7	142.2	132.4	131.0	128.2	124.5	125.8	134.0	132.2	124.3	124.7	132.3	131.7
Mar	122.4	141.0	142.7	134.0	130.9	122.7	129.3	141.8	135.0	125.0	128.0	137.0	135.2
Apr	129.5	135.7	133.3	130.7	128.0	121.6	128.6	129.4	132.8	124.6	139.9	132.4	131.7
May	124.9	137.6	135.4	133.6	129.5	124.6	127.9	129.0	134.5	124.6	126.6	133.6	133.0
June	120.7	144.3	134.3	134.1	128.8	122.4	131.4	131.5	133.5	125.6	127.2	133.6	134.8
July	123.0	134.5	136.1	133.4	127.8	123.7	128.9	129.7	135.4	127.5	148.7	134.0	136.2
Aug	141.0	135.8	135.8	132.3	128.6	122.8	127.5	127.2	132.4	123.0	124.4	131.4	133.0
Sep	143.5	138.2	133.8	131.5	129.5	123.0	129.5	128.0	133.4	124.0	125.3	133.6	134.6
Oct	135.1	140.9	134.0	132.6	129.7	123.9	129.2	128.2	133.5	124.7	143.2	134.1	136.5
Nov	122.9	141.0	140.6	134.1	130.9	125.9	128.8	131.1	134.6	124.9	126.7	135.8	136.6
Dec	121.2	137.1	142.7	135.2	132.3	132.1	129.8	141.9	136.8	127.5	133.4	135.0	138.8
1996 Jan	116.0	142.1	136.5	132.5	131.6	126.8	129.8	133.2	133.5	125.1	137.2	134.7	136.2
Feb	123.1	144.8	137.0	133.9	134.8	132.4	131.3	134.5	137.8	126.9	133.1	137.4	140.6
Mar	133.1	148.9	145.9	136.9	134.3	129.7	135.9	149.2	139.1	129.3	132.8	142.3	142.1
Apr	129.6	144.2	138.0	135.7	132.9	128.9	132.0	135.8	136.9	129.8	146.0	137.8	138.8
May	133.8	140.5	139.6	137.9	133.3	131.5	132.6	134.4	137.1	128.8	132.5	136.6	139.0
June	126.8	136.5	139.0	144.1	134.9	131.1	136.7	136.7	138.0	128.6	132.8	138.6	139.5
July	134.1	139.3	142.9	140.3	133.6	131.7	133.2	136.8	137.4	131.1	151.8	138.6	141.1
Aug	151.4	134.4	140.3	138.3	132.8	128.4	133.1	133.0	136.7	127.7	132.9	138.1	137.8
Sep	153.1	140.4	138.9	139.2	135.1	130.7	134.6	134.2	137.4	128.1	133.6	140.1	138.7
Oct	136.4	140.8	138.3	141.7	135.1	131.5	134.4	134.3	137.9	128.8	144.3	139.9	138.7
Nov	130.5	146.3	146.9	141.7	134.9	132.3	135.2	137.2	139.5	129.9	135.7	142.1	141.8
Dec	135.9	148.4	147.4	143.8	136.4	138.8	137.9	145.6	141.3	130.8	141.3	142.4	143.1
1997 Jan	123.1	147.6	140.2	139.9	137.1	132.0	136.4	138.0	139.7	129.2	144.8	140.6	139.5
Feb	128.6	147.1	142.7	141.1	141.8	138.9	137.3	141.2	141.9	130.4	137.0	144.2	145.0
Mar	137.7	152.6	155.4	143.5	143.2	137.4	140.3	155.4	145.2	133.8	141.4	148.3	145.1
Apr	136.0	150.7	146.0	142.1	140.1	133.7	138.3	140.8	140.5	133.1	147.1	142.3	143.6
May	136.4	149.5	144.4	142.5	138.9	138.8	139.6	139.6	142.2	133.2	140.1	142.6	143.8
Jun P	**134.6**	**143.2**	**143.6**	**145.1**	**140.6**	**138.0**	**140.7**	**143.3**	**142.7**	**135.2**	**137.4**	**142.7**	**145.8**

Notes: 1 Figures for the years 1985 to 1989 on a 1985=100 basis were published in *Employment Gazette* in October 1989; the 1985=100 series was discontinued after July 1989.
2 Figures on a 1988=100 basis were last published in *Employment Gazette* in September 1993.
3 The Index has been reclassified from SIC 1980 to SIC 1992, in common with other economic series in the national accounts. Figures on an SIC 1980 basis were last published in *Employment Gazette*, May 1995.
4 Industrial groupings which have not changed are; agriculture and forestry, chemical and man-made fibres (now called chemicals and chemical products); mechanical engineering (machinery and equipment nes); electrical, electronic and instrument engineering (electrical and optical equipment); food, drink and tobacco (food products, beverages and tobacco); paper products, printing and publishing (pulp, paper products, printing and publishing); construction; hotels and catering (hotels and restaurants); transport and communication (transport, storage and communication); public administration; education and health services (education, health and social work).
5 For enquiries, see telephone numbers on p S84.

EARNINGS 5.3
Average Earnings Index: all employees: by industry (unadjusted)

Electrical and optical equipment	Transport equipment	Electricity, gas and water supply	Construction	Wholesale trade	Retail trade and repairs	Hotels and restaurants	Transport, storage and communication +	Financial intermediation	Real estate renting and business activities	Public administration services	Education health and social work	Other services #	GREAT BRITAIN SIC 1992	
(30-33)	(34,35)	(40,41)	(45)	(51)	(50,52)	(55)	(60-64)	(65-67)	(70-74)	(75)	(80-85)	(90-93)	1990=100	
121.7	119.2	123.1	116.5	114.9	112.3	118.0	119.9	119.1	113.2	119.3	120.2	117.3	1993)	Annual
127.2	126.4	127.1	120.0	119.1	115.9	119.9	124.3	128.1	115.8	123.5	122.9	122.5	1994)	Averages
132.9	133.2	133.6	123.5	124.4	118.3	122.3	128.2	133.4	119.3	126.0	124.6	129.5	1995)	
140.2	**140.4**	**138.7**	**127.8**	**130.2**	**123.2**	**125.3**	**132.5**	**140.5**	**124.3**	**128.7**	**128.5**	**136.1**	**1996)**	
117.8	114.9	120.5	114.9	113.5	110.9	115.7	119.1	113.8	111.0	117.2	118.7	118.6	1993	Jan
119.1	117.3	121.1	114.6	114.3	110.4	117.4	116.7	119.1	111.2	118.4	118.5	118.1		Feb
122.7	120.4	121.9	119.0	117.4	113.8	117.7	118.7	127.6	116.6	117.8	118.7	117.8		Mar
120.1	117.7	122.9	116.5	115.9	111.6	116.8	117.5	117.5	114.6	117.6	118.5	118.5		Apr
123.4	118.4	121.7	115.9	113.3	111.2	118.1	119.2	118.3	112.7	119.5	119.3	118.1		May
122.2	120.7	121.5	119.0	112.8	113.8	118.1	120.6	116.5	111.2	120.1	119.7	114.3		June
122.8	122.1	125.2	116.5	119.6	113.2	117.3	120.9	118.5	112.8	119.5	122.3	114.4		July
120.9	118.8	122.7	115.2	113.6	111.3	117.2	118.2	116.5	112.3	120.3	124.4	114.1		Aug
120.5	118.6	122.5	114.9	111.5	112.3	119.6	118.7	117.3	110.8	119.5	121.8	114.9		Sept
122.5	119.9	124.1	115.3	113.4	111.8	116.4	119.3	117.5	112.6	120.2	120.2	115.8		Oct
123.7	120.5	127.3	117.3	115.2	111.6	116.8	122.1	124.0	113.7	121.1	120.4	119.5		Nov
124.1	121.2	125.2	118.8	117.8	115.5	124.4	127.2	123.1	118.5	120.4	119.9	123.9		Dec
124.2	121.6	124.4	116.9	115.4	115.1	116.1	123.5	123.5	113.9	120.6	120.1	121.5	1994	Jan
124.6	122.5	124.9	117.9	118.5	115.1	117.4	120.7	143.8	114.2	123.1	119.7	119.7		Feb
130.1	126.7	125.0	120.6	124.2	117.7	119.6	124.3	144.8	115.5	123.3	120.2	121.6		Mar
124.9	124.6	125.6	118.2	119.9	116.5	118.8	123.1	123.9	115.6	121.5	120.8	119.3		Apr
127.1	125.2	124.4	119.0	119.0	115.8	120.9	122.7	126.6	115.5	123.2	121.8	121.4		May
127.9	127.3	125.3	122.2	117.7	118.1	119.5	122.0	126.2	116.1	122.9	123.6	121.7		June
128.0	127.6	126.3	121.5	120.3	116.7	120.0	128.1	125.3	116.9	122.9	125.4	122.0		July
126.7	125.4	131.9	119.2	118.2	115.9	119.2	122.8	122.0	116.2	124.3	126.2	122.0		Aug
126.1	125.4	129.7	119.9	117.5	115.5	119.2	124.1	120.8	114.7	124.5	124.9	121.6		Sept
127.4	129.1	128.9	119.3	118.1	113.7	119.0	124.9	123.0	115.2	123.5	123.3	124.2		Oct
128.8	129.5	128.5	122.1	118.3	113.8	122.2	125.2	127.3	115.4	125.9	121.7	126.8		Nov
131.0	131.9	130.5	122.8	122.2	117.1	127.0	130.6	129.7	120.7	126.8	127.1	128.3		Dec
129.6	129.7	129.8	120.7	119.2	117.5	121.0	126.3	131.4	117.7	125.3	121.8	126.7	1995	Jan
133.6	131.8	130.1	120.8	121.8	115.6	123.5	124.5	137.3	118.0	126.9	121.9	125.3		Feb
135.7	136.7	130.6	123.7	129.3	121.2	119.7	129.5	163.4	120.4	127.5	121.5	126.0		Mar
131.3	135.4	132.6	122.0	123.7	116.6	123.7	127.8	129.9	119.6	124.3	123.3	126.0		Apr
133.3	131.8	132.1	122.9	122.0	118.2	122.8	126.2	129.9	119.0	124.7	122.9	155.4		May
132.4	133.3	133.3	126.4	124.3	119.3	119.9	126.3	130.3	118.5	125.5	124.1	123.2		June
133.8	133.7	138.4	125.6	124.1	118.3	121.8	130.9	131.3	118.3	125.7	126.8	127.1		July
131.8	131.1	135.8	122.1	125.1	119.4	121.7	127.1	126.1	117.6	125.5	128.0	126.9		Aug
131.0	130.9	134.8	123.6	122.8	117.8	120.8	127.5	125.5	117.0	126.9	126.4	127.8		Sept
132.1	133.5	134.0	123.2	122.8	117.1	121.6	128.8	128.1	119.2	126.7	125.7	127.6		Oct
134.2	134.4	134.7	125.4	127.5	117.9	121.8	130.3	131.8	120.1	126.1	126.3	131.7		Nov
136.5	135.7	136.8	126.1	130.1	120.7	128.7	133.5	136.0	125.9	126.5	126.4	130.8		Dec
136.0	133.8	134.2	124.6	126.7	119.5	122.5	130.4	137.4	121.7	126.7	125.6	132.2	1996	Jan
141.9	136.5	134.6	125.8	129.8	119.1	124.6	129.2	141.5	124.3	127.8	127.4	131.8		Feb
140.6	149.2	135.4	129.7	134.8	125.7	123.8	132.5	172.9	125.3	129.0	125.5	131.1		Mar
138.5	139.2	137.3	126.4	127.8	122.3	122.8	131.3	143.1	125.1	127.6	126.9	134.5		Apr
139.3	138.2	139.2	126.1	128.7	122.2	124.8	130.9	133.9	123.5	128.4	128.5	135.8		May
138.7	140.4	140.6	128.5	129.6	125.5	123.7	131.4	135.2	124.6	127.1	128.5	132.9		June
140.1	141.9	141.4	128.3	130.6	125.5	126.6	134.7	137.5	124.0	128.6	130.3	136.6		July
138.9	139.4	141.2	125.3	129.4	122.9	125.1	130.3	132.1	123.8	128.3	131.5	137.5		Aug
138.8	138.1	138.9	128.4	127.4	124.1	123.3	133.4	131.6	121.3	129.7	130.6	139.3		Sep
138.9	141.7	140.2	127.3	129.3	121.6	125.3	132.3	134.6	123.7	130.1	128.9	137.9		Oct
141.0	142.0	138.9	130.5	130.0	123.2	126.3	135.4	138.1	124.2	130.7	128.5	140.8		Nov
149.1	144.4	142.4	132.1	137.9	126.9	134.4	138.3	147.6	130.4	130.5	129.7	142.4		Dec
142.5	142.1	141.2	129.6	133.6	124.5	127.4	136.9	152.5	129.7	130.4	129.5	143.4	1997	Jan
151.0	145.2	138.8	130.1	136.0	123.8	129.4	133.8	152.6	129.7	131.3	130.1	143.4		Feb
149.9	150.4	138.0	133.2	140.5	130.8	129.6	135.9	187.0	139.6	131.2	130.2	145.1		Mar
145.1	144.9	141.9	129.8	133.7	126.7	126.3	136.7	157.5	131.3	130.3	131.0	140.2		Apr
146.2	144.9	145.7	132.2	133.7	127.3	130.1	136.8	140.0	130.8	130.9	131.2	147.0		May
147.8	**146.2**	**142.6**	**134.1**	**134.7**	**131.0**	**129.7**	**136.6**	**143.4**	**131.2**	**130.2**	**131.4**	**143.4**		**Jun P**

+ Excluding sea transport.
# Excluding private domestic and personal services.

UNITED KINGDOM		Manufacturing	Per cent change from a year earlier	Energy and water supply	Production industries	Construction	Whole economy	Per cent change from a year earlier
1985		82.2	5.0	80.9	72.5	67.3	69.8	5.4
1986		85.5	3.9	76.2	75.0	70.2	73.0	4.6
1987		87.4	2.2	84.9	79.4	71.7	76.7	5.1
1988		89.5	2.4	95.2	84.6	77.6	82.3	7.2
1989		93.8	4.8	96.2	93.7	90.7	90.6	10.2
1990		100.0	6.6	100.0	100.0	100.0	100.0	10.4
1991		105.2	5.2	111.3	101.3	107.7	106.8	6.8
1992		105.5	0.3	113.0	105.2	104.1	110.4	3.4
1993		105.0	-0.5	105.6	103.8	99.2	110.2	-0.1
1994		104.5	-0.4	97.8	100.6	98.9	109.5	-0.7
1995		108.3	3.6	..	..	..	111.3	1.7
1996		113.0	4.3	..	..	..	113.1	1.7
1992	Q2	105.5	-0.1	..	..	..	111.0	4.7
	Q3	105.4	-0.6	..	..	..	110.4	2.6
	Q4	105.0	-0.5	..	..	..	110.1	1.3
1993	Q1	103.4	-2.4	..	..	..	109.6	-0.5
	Q2	104.5	-1.0	..	..	..	110.4	-0.6
	Q3	105.9	0.5	..	..	..	110.6	0.2
	Q4	106.1	1.0	..	..	..	110.3	0.3
1994	Q1	104.4	1.0	..	..	..	110.2	0.5
	Q2	104.2	-0.3	..	..	..	109.1	-1.2
	Q3	104.2	-1.6	..	..	..	109.0	-1.4
	Q4	105.3	-0.8	..	..	..	109.6	-0.7
1995	Q1	106.8	2.3	..	..	..	110.5	0.3
	Q2	107.7	3.4	..	..	..	111.0	1.7
	Q3	108.3	3.9	..	..	..	111.1	1.9
	Q4	110.4	4.9	..	..	..	112.4	2.6
1996	Q1	111.7	4.6	..	..	..	112.3	1.6
	Q2	112.6	4.6	..	..	..	112.2	1.1
	Q3	113.2	4.6	..	..	..	113.6	2.2
	Q4	114.2	3.5	..	..	..	114.3	1.7
1997	Q1	114.6	2.6	..	..	..	115.4	2.8
	Q2	**115.8**	**2.8**	**..**	**..**	**..**	**NA**	**NA**
1994	Nov	104.8	-1.5	..	..	..	..	..
	Dec	106.4	1.4	..	..	..	..	..
1995	Jan	106.8	2.3	..	..	..	..	..
	Feb	106.4	2.2	..	..	..	..	..
	Mar	107.3	2.5	..	..	..	..	..
	Apr	107.8	3.3	..	..	..	..	..
	May	107.6	3.5	..	..	..	..	..
	Jun	107.8	3.3	..	..	..	..	..
	Jul	108.6	4.6	..	..	..	..	..
	Aug	107.8	3.7	..	..	..	..	..
	Sep	108.4	3.4	..	..	..	..	..
	Oct	109.5	4.7	..	..	..	..	..
	Nov	109.8	4.8	..	..	..	..	..
	Dec	111.9	5.2	..	..	..	..	..
1996	Jan	111.3	4.2	..	..	..	..	..
	Feb	111.8	5.1	..	..	..	..	..
	Mar	112.1	4.4	..	..	..	..	..
	Apr	112.9	4.8	..	..	..	..	..
	May	112.4	4.5	..	..	..	..	..
	Jun	112.6	4.4	..	..	..	..	..
	Jul	112.9	4.0	..	..	..	..	..
	Aug	113.4	5.3	..	..	..	..	..
	Sep	113.3	4.6	..	..	..	..	..
	Oct	113.4	3.6	..	..	..	..	..
	Nov	114.2	4.0	..	..	..	..	..
	Dec	115.1	2.8	..	..	..	..	..
1997	Jan	114.3	2.7	..	..	..	..	..
	Feb	114.7	2.6	..	..	..	..	..
	Mar	114.7	2.4	..	..	..	..	..
	Apr	114.6	1.5	..	..	..	..	..
	May	116.3	3.4	..	..	..	..	..
	Jun	**116.3**	**3.3**	**..**	**..**	**..**	**..**	**..**
Three months ending: 1994	Oct	104.4	-1.7	..	..	..	..	..
	Nov	104.7	-1.6	..	..	..	..	..
	Dec	105.3	-0.8	..	..	..	..	..
1995	Jan	106.0	0.7	..	..	..	..	..
	Feb	106.5	2.0	..	..	..	..	..
	Mar	106.8	2.3	..	..	..	..	..
	Apr	107.1	2.7	..	..	..	..	..
	May	107.5	3.1	..	..	..	..	..
	Jun	107.7	3.4	..	..	..	..	..
	Jul	108.0	3.8	..	..	..	..	..
	Aug	108.1	3.9	..	..	..	..	..
	Sep	108.3	3.9	..	..	..	..	..
	Oct	108.6	3.9	..	..	..	..	..
	Nov	109.2	4.3	..	..	..	..	..
	Dec	110.4	4.9	..	..	..	..	..
1996	Jan	111.0	4.7	..	..	..	..	..
	Feb	111.7	4.8	..	..	..	..	..
	Mar	111.7	4.6	..	..	..	..	..
	Apr	112.3	4.8	..	..	..	..	..
	May	112.5	4.6	..	..	..	..	..
	Jun	112.6	4.6	..	..	..	..	..
	Jul	112.6	4.3	..	..	..	..	..
	Aug	113.0	4.5	..	..	..	..	..
	Sep	113.2	4.6	..	..	..	..	..
	Oct	113.4	4.5	..	..	..	..	..
	Nov	113.7	4.0	..	..	..	..	..
	Dec	114.2	3.5	..	..	..	..	..
1997	Jan	114.5	3.2	..	..	..	..	..
	Feb	114.7	2.7	..	..	..	..	..
	Mar	114.6	2.6	..	..	..	..	..
	Apr	114.7	2.2	..	..	..	..	..
	May	115.2	2.5	..	..	..	..	..
	Jun	**115.8**	**2.8**	**..**	**..**	**..**	**..**	**..**

Note: Manufacturing is based on seasonally adjusted monthly statistics of average earnings, employed labour force and output. Other sectors are based on national accounts data of wages and salaries, employment and output.
* Wages and salaries per unit of output.
  The indices have been rebased from 1988=100 to 1990=100, in common with other economic series. Figures on a 1985=100 basis were last published in *Employment Gazette*, September 1993.

5.9 EARNINGS
Selected countries: index of wages per head: manufacturing (manual workers)

1990=100	Great Britain (1,2)	Belgium (7,8)	Canada (8)	Denmark (6,8)	France (4)	Germany (FR) (8)	Greece (8)	Irish Republic (8)	Italy (4)	Japan (2,5)	Netherlands (4)	Spain (2,8,9)	Sweden (6,8)	United States (8,10)
Annual averages														
1990	100.0	100	100.0	100.0	100.0	100.0	100	100	100.0	100.0	100.0	100.0	100.0	100.0
1991	108.2	105	104.8	104.5	104.6	106.6	117	105	109.8	103.5	104.0	108.2	105.5	103.0
1992	115.4	110	108.4	107.9	108.7	114.2	133	110	115.7	104.6	108.3	116.5	110.3	106.0
1993	120.5	114	110.7	110.6	111.1	120.4	147	117	120.0	104.7	111.8	124.4	113.9	108.0
1994	126.2	117	112.5	113.2	113.4	123.9	166	118	124.0	106.9	113.7	130.0	118.6	111.0
1995	131.9	118	114.1	117.6	116.1	128.0	188	123	127.8	110.4	115.0	136.4	124.9	114.0
1996	**137.8**	**120**	**117.7**	**122.4**	**119.0**	**134.7**	**..**	**..**	**130.1**	**113.1**	**117.2**	**143.6**	**133.1**	**118.0**
Quarterly averages														
1995 Q1	130.1	118.0	113.4	115.5	114.5	125.2	179.0	119.0	126.4	110.3	114.5	133.4	121.2	113.0
Q2	131.3	118.0	113.5	119.1	115.5	126.3	186.0	119.0	126.7	111.4	114.9	135.4	124.5	114.0
Q3	132.4	118.0	114.1	117.6	116.3	129.3	190.0	120.0	128.7	108.5	115.3	137.0	126.0	115.0
Q4	134.0	118.0	115.3	118.2	116.8	131.4	196.0	123.0	129.5	111.0	115.3	139.2	127.9	115.0
1996 Q1	135.6	120.0	115.4	120.4	117.1	134.1	198.0	122.0	128.8	112.2	116.3	140.7	129.6	116.0
Q2	136.8	120.0	116.9	124.3	118.1	134.7	202.0	124.0	129.3	113.2	116.7	143.0	135.1	118.0
Q3	138.4	121.0	118.4	122.3	119.3	134.9	..	124.0	130.9	113.8	117.4	144.4	133.0	118.0
Q4	140.1	121.0	120.0	122.7	119.8	135.2	..	..	131.6	113.5	118.2	145.9	134.8	120.0
1997 Q1	141.5	121.0	119.2	..	120.6	135.2	..	..	133.9	118.0	119.1	147.2	136.6	120.0
Q2	**142.6**	..	..	..	..	..	..	..	..	..	..	..	..	..
Monthly														
1995 Jan	129.6	..	113.5	..	115.3	125.2	..	..	126.4	111.0	115.0	..	121.1	113.0
Feb	130.2	..	113.6	115.5	..	..	..	..	126.4	110.6	115.0	..	121.2	113.0
Mar	130.4	..	113.2	..	..	..	..	119.0	126.5	110.9	115.0	..	121.4	113.0
Apr	131.1	..	113.4	..	115.7	126.3	..	..	126.6	111.1	115.1	..	124.4	113.0
May	131.2	..	113.5	118.6	..	..	..	..	126.7	110.5	115.1	..	122.2	113.0
Jun	131.5	118.0	113.5	..	..	..	..	119.0	126.7	116.8	115.1	..	125.1	114.0
Jul	132.2	..	113.0	..	116.3	129.3	..	..	128.5	106.1	115.5	..	127.2	114.0
Aug	132.4	..	114.3	117.6	..	..	..	..	128.5	106.2	115.5	..	123.8	114.0
Sep	132.7	118.0	114.7	..	..	..	..	120.0	129.2	111.0	115.5	..	126.8	115.0
Oct	133.6	..	114.8	..	116.8	131.4	..	..	129.4	111.4	115.5	..	126.8	115.0
Nov	133.7	..	114.9	118.2	..	..	..	..	129.5	110.8	115.4	..	127.1	115.0
Dec	134.6	118.0	116.3	..	..	..	..	123.0	129.5	110.5	115.5	..	129.7	116.0
1996 Jan	134.9	..	115.2	..	117.1	134.1	..	..	128.8	110.2	116.2	..	129.3	117.0
Feb	135.8	..	115.7	120.4	..	..	..	..	128.8	112.9	116.4	..	129.3	116.0
Mar	136.2	120.0	115.4	..	..	..	..	122.0	128.8	113.0	116.4	..	130.4	116.0
Apr	136.5	..	115.2	..	118.1	134.7	..	..	129.1	112.8	116.7	..	134.5	118.0
May	136.7	..	116.8	124.3	..	..	..	..	129.2	112.7	116.7	..	136.1	117.0
Jun	137.3	120.0	118.7	..	..	..	..	124.0	129.5	114.2	116.8	..	134.7	118.0
Jul	137.9	..	117.2	..	119.3	134.9	..	..	130.9	112.6	117.4	..	134.3	118.0
Aug	138.4	..	118.5	122.3	..	..	..	..	130.9	114.7	117.4	..	131.6	118.0
Sep	139.0	121.0	119.5	..	..	..	..	124.0	130.9	114.0	117.4	..	133.2	119.0
Oct	139.2	..	119.3	..	119.8	135.2	..	..	131.4	114.2	118.1	..	132.8	118.0
Nov	139.9	..	120.5	122.7	..	..	..	..	131.5	113.6	118.2	..	134.5	119.0
Dec	141.3	121.0	120.1	..	..	..	..	..	131.8	112.7	118.2	..	137.0	121.0
1997 Jan	140.6	..	118.7	..	120.6	135.2	..	..	133.8	121.6	119.0	..	135.4	120.0
Feb	142.0	..	119.7	..	..	..	..	..	133.8	116.3	119.2	..	135.8	120.0
Mar	141.9	121.0	119.2	..	..	..	..	..	134.0	116.0	119.2	..	138.5	121.0
Apr	141.9	..	118.0	..	121.3	..	..	..	134.1	115.8	..	..	..	121.0
May	142.7	..	..	..	..	..	..	..	..	115.9	..	..	..	121.0
Jun P	**143.3**	..	..	..	..	..	..	..	..	..	..	..	..	..
Increases on a year earlier														
Annual averages														
1990	9	5	5	5	4	5	19	6	7	5	3	9	9	3
1991	8	5	5	4	5	7	17	5	10	4	4	8	6	3
1992	7	5	3	3	4	7	13	4	5	1	4	8	5	3
1993	5	3	2	2	2	5	11	6	4	0	3	7	3	2
1994	5	3	2	2	2	3	13	1	3	2	2	5	4	3
1995	5	1	1	4	2	3	13	4	3	3	1	5	5	3
1996	**4**	**2**	**3**	**4**	**2**	**5**	..	..	**2**	**2**	**2**	**5**	**7**	**4**
Quarterly averages														
1995 Q1	5	2	0	3	2	2	13	2	2	4	1	4	4	2
Q2	5	2	1	4	2	3	15	2	2	3	1	5	5	3
Q3	4	3	2	4	2	4	13	3	3	3	1	5	6	4
Q4	4	0	2	4	2	5	13	4	4	2	1	6	6	2
1996 Q1	4	2	2	4	2	7	11	3	2	2	2	5	7	3
Q2	4	2	3	4	2	7	9	4	2	2	2	6	9	4
Q3	5	3	4	4	3	4	..	3	2	5	2	5	6	3
Q4	5	3	4	4	3	3	..	..	2	2	3	5	5	4
1997 Q1	4	1	3	..	3	1	..	..	4	5	2	5	5	3
Q2	**4**	..	..	..	..	..	..	..	..	..	..	..	..	..
Monthly														
1995 Feb	6	..	1	3	..	..	..	..	2	3	1	..	5	2
Mar	5	..	0	..	..	..	..	3	2	3	1	..	4	2
Apr	5	..	1	..	2	2	..	..	2	4	1	..	5	2
May	4	..	1	4	..	..	..	..	2	3	1	..	2	2
Jun	4	..	1	..	..	..	..	2	2	1	1	..	6	3
Jul	5	..	1	..	2	4	..	1	3	8	1	..	6	3
Aug	4	..	3	4	..	..	..	1	3	1	1	..	6	3
Sep	4	..	3	..	..	..	..	3	4	2	1	..	7	3
Oct	4	..	2	..	2	5	..	..	4	2	1	..	6	3
Nov	4	..	1	4	..	..	..	..	4	1	1	..	6	3
Dec	4	..	2	..	..	..	..	4	4	5	1	..	7	3
1996 Jan	4	..	1	..	2	7	..	..	2	-1	1	..	7	4
Feb	4	..	2	4	..	..	..	..	2	2	1	..	7	3
Mar	4	..	2	..	..	..	..	3	2	2	1	..	7	3
Apr	4	..	2	..	2	7	..	..	2	2	1	..	8	4
May	4	..	3	5	..	..	..	..	2	2	1	..	11	4
Jun	4	2	5	..	..	..	..	4	2	-2	1	..	8	4
Jul	4	..	4	..	3	4	..	..	2	6	2	..	6	4
Aug	5	..	4	4	..	..	..	..	2	8	2	..	6	4
Sep	5	3	4	..	..	..	..	3	1	3	2	..	5	3
Oct	4	..	4	..	3	3	..	..	2	3	2	..	5	3
Nov	5	..	5	4	..	..	..	..	2	3	2	..	6	3
Dec	5	3	3	..	..	..	..	..	2	2	2	..	6	4
1997 Jan	4	..	3	..	3	1	..	..	4	10	2	..	5	3
Feb	5	..	3	..	..	..	..	..	4	3	2	..	5	3
Mar	4	1	3	..	..	..	..	..	4	3	2	..	6	4
Apr	4	..	2	..	3	..	..	..	4	3	..	..	..	3
May	4	..	..	..	..	..	..	..	..	3	..	..	..	3
Jun P	**4**	..	..	..	..	..	..	..	..	..	..	..	..	..

Source: OECD - Main Economic Indicators.

Notes: 1 Wages and salaries on a weekly basis (all employees).
2 Seasonally adjusted.
3 Males only.
4 Hourly wage rates.
5 Monthly earnings.
6 Including mining.
7 Including mining and transport.
8 Hourly earnings.
9 All industries.
10 Production workers.

6.1 RETAIL PRICES
Summary of recent movements

| | | All items (RPI) | All items excluding | | | | | |
| | | | Mortgage interest payments (RPIX) | | Mortgage interest payments and indirect taxes (RPIY) | | Housing | |
		Index Jan 13, 1987=100	Percentage change over 12 months	Index Jan 13, 1987=100	Percentage change over 12 months	Index Jan 13, 1987=100	Percentage change over 12 months	Index Jan 13, 1987=100	Percentage change over 12 months
1996	Jul	152.4	2.2	151.9	2.8	147.7	2.4	148.8	2.6
	Aug	153.1	2.1	152.8	2.8	148.7	2.4	149.7	2.6
	Sep	153.8	2.1	153.6	2.9	149.6	2.5	150.5	2.6
	Oct	153.8	2.7	153.6	3.3	149.6	3.0	150.5	2.9
	Nov	153.9	2.7	153.7	3.3	149.7	3.0	150.6	3.0
	Dec	154.4	2.5	154.2	3.1	149.5	2.7	151.6	2.6
1997	Jan	154.4	2.8	153.9	3.1	149.3	2.8	150.7	2.7
	Feb	155.0	2.7	154.5	2.9	149.9	2.5	151.3	2.5
	Mar	155.4	2.6	154.9	2.7	150.3	2.3	151.7	2.2
	Apr	156.3	2.4	155.8	2.5	150.8	2.0	152.2	2.1
	May	156.9	2.6	156.3	2.5	151.3	2.0	152.7	2.1
	Jun	157.5	2.9	156.7	2.7	151.8	2.2	153.0	2.2
	Jul	**157.5**	**3.3**	**156.4**	**3.0**	**151.0**	**2.2**	**152.6**	**2.6**

6.2 RETAIL PRICES
Detailed figures for various groups, sub-groups and sections for July 15 1997

	Index Jan 1987=100	Percentage change over 1 month	Percentage change over 12 months
ALL ITEMS	157.5	0.0	3.3
Food and catering	151.0	-0.2	1.4
Alcohol and tobacco	183.9	0.4	4.0
Housing and household expenditure	158.6	0.3	3.7
Personal expenditure	134.5	-2.7	2.0
Travel and leisure	159.5	0.6	4.7
Consumer durables	114.4	-3.0	0.3
Seasonal food	119.3	-2.9	-0.7
Food excluding seasonal	146.3	0.0	0.9
All items excluding seasonal food	158.4	0.0	3.4
All items excluding food	160.4	0.1	3.8
Other indices			
All items excluding:			
mortgage interest payments(RPIX)	156.4	-0.2	3.0
housing	152.6	-0.3	2.6
mortgage interest payments and indirect taxes (RPIY)[1]	151.0	-0.5	2.2
mortgage interest payments and council tax	156.3	-0.2	2.8
mortgage interest payments and depreciation	156.3	-0.3	2.8
Food	142.2	-0.4	0.6
Bread	137.7		0
Cereals	141.8		0
Biscuits and cakes	153.8		0
Beef	131.3		-1
Lamb	154.3		3
of which, home-killed lamb	154.9		-1
Pork	150.8		-5
Bacon	163.9		2
Poultry	114.2		0
Other meat	133.6		0
Fish	124.1		-1
of which, fresh fish	124.9		-3
Butter	165.6		-1
Oil and fats	140.0		3
Cheese	168.1		4
Eggs	143.5		-6
Milk fresh	153.2		0
Milk products	144.4		-2
Tea	149.9		-1
Coffee and other hot drinks	132.6		11
Soft drinks	181.1		4
Sugar and preserves	155.9		-1
Sweets and chocolates	148.3		2
Potatoes	125.0		-10
of which, unprocessed potatoes	83.1		-18
Vegetables	120.4		1
of which, other fresh vegetables	108.8		0
Fruit	132.2		4
of which, fresh fruit	129.5		4
Other foods	147.5		2
Catering	182.7	0.3	3.6
Restaurant meals	180.4		4
Canteen meals	199.5		5
Take-aways and snacks	179.2		3
Alcoholic drink	175.0	0.5	2.6
Beer	185.8		4
on sales	191.2		4
off sales	153.5		2
Wines and spirits	160.0		1
on sales	179.8		4
off sales	148.7		0
Tobacco	205.2	0.1	7.0
Cigarettes	207.9		7
Tobacco	183.1		4
Housing	180.9	1.1	6.8
Rent	217.2		3
Mortgage interest payments	183.3		15
Depreciation (Jan 1995 = 100)	109.2		6
Community charge and rates/council tax	154.5		7
Water and other payments	257.8		4
Repairs and maintenance charges	178.4		8
Do-it yourself materials	154.7		3
Dwelling insurance & ground rent	186.2		2
Fuel and light	131.2	-0.4	-3.0
Coal and solid fuels	126.6		2
Electricity	140.7		-5
Gas	124.2		0
Oil and other fuels	114.8		-2
Household goods	137.3	-1.5	0.9
Furniture	139.7		2
Furnishings	140.3		2
Electrical appliances	98.6		-5
Other household equipment	139.4		0
Household consumables	157.5		0
Pet care	145.5		3
Household services	143.8	0.2	1.6
Postage	153.0		0
Telephones, telemessages, etc	103.5		-3
Domestic services	182.2		4
Fees and subscriptions	164.1		4
Clothing and footwear	115.9	-4.7	1.1
Men's outerwear	113.2		0
Women's outerwear	99.4		2
Children's outerwear	116.5		0
Other clothing	153.1		4
Footwear	118.1		-1
Personal goods and services	169.8	0.1	3.2
Personal articles	118.9		0
Chemists goods	179.3		4
Personal services	222.2		5
Motoring expenditure	165.9	1.0	6.4
Purchase of motor vehicles	142.0		2
Maintenance of motor vehicles	187.4		6
Petrol and oil	183.0		15
Vehicles tax and insurance	191.2		3
Fares and other travel costs	170.9	0.5	3.8
Rail fares	187.7		3
Bus and coach fares	184.2		4
Other travel costs	151.1		4
Leisure goods	123.9	-0.2	0.3
Audio-visual equipment	65.1		-6
Tapes and discs	119.9		2
Toys, photographic and sport goods	120.8		0
Books and newspapers	182.3		4
Gardening products	144.1		1
Leisure services	182.5	0.5	4.9
Television licences and rentals	125.7		2
Entertainment and other recreation	221.7		5
Foreign holidays (Jan 1993 = 100)	118.0		6
UK holidays (Jan 1994 = 100)	109.2		4

Note: Indices are given to one decimal place to provide as much information as is available although accuracy is reduced at lower levels of aggregation.
For this reason, annual percentage changes for individual sections are given rounded to the nearest whole number.

[1] The taxes excluded are council tax, VAT, duties, vehicle excise duty, insurance tax and airport tax.

Average retail prices on July 15 for a number of important items derived from prices collected by the Office for National Statistics for the purpose of the General Index of Retail Prices in more than 146 areas in the United Kingdom are given below.

It is only possible to calculate a meaningful average price for fairly standard items; that is, those which do not vary between retail outlets.

The averages given are subject to uncertainty, an indication of which is given in the ranges within which at least four-fifths of the recorded prices fell, given in the final column below.

Average prices on July 15 1997

Item	Number of quotations	Average price (pence)	Price range within which 80 per cent of quotations fell (pence)
Beef: home-killed, per kg			
Best beef mince	663	373	218-537
Topside	651	636	479-689
Brisket (without bone)	502	418	369-506
Rump steak *	671	887	769-1003
Stewing steak	650	451	284-678
Lamb: home-killed, per kg			
Loin (with bone)	542	882	659-1029
Shoulder (with bone)	504	361	268-439
Lamb: imported (frozen), per kg			
Loin (with bone)	158	512	399-615
Leg (with bone)	167	456	428-499
Pork: home-killed, per kg			
Loin (with bone)	673	512	399-664
Shoulder (without bone)	540	340	218-449
Bacon, per kg			
Streaky *	563	449	299-621
Gammon *	606	608	481-744
Back *	602	601	438-803
Ham			
Ham (not shoulder), 113g/per 4oz	573	91	59-109
Sausages, 454g/per lb			
Pork	538	138	109-164
Canned meats			
Corned beef, 340g	255	90	65-117
Chicken: roasting, oven ready, per kg			
Frozen	197	176	140-215
Fresh or chilled	662	260	196-375
Fresh and smoked fish, per kg			
Cod fillets	425	570	419-750
Rainbow trout	382	459	352-549
Bread			
White loaf, sliced, 800g	240	53	39-81
White loaf, unwrapped, 800g	222	70	55-89
Brown loaf, sliced, 400g	233	52	29-69
Brown loaf, unsliced, 800g	226	72	55-90
Flour			
Self raising, per 1.5kg	235	60	39-79
Butter			
Home produced, per 250g	235	83	78-92
Imported, per 250g	249	85	75-99
Margarine			
Margarine/Low fat spread per 500g	249	73	41- 99
Cheese, per kg			
Cheddar type	239	533	417- 685
Eggs			
Size 2 (65-70g), per dozen	237	154	118- 175
Size 4 (55-60g), per dozen	235	137	95- 167
Milk			
Pasteurised, per pint +	282	35	27- 35
Tea			
Loose, per 125g	233	64	46- 79
Tea bags, per 250g	254	133	94- 165
Coffee			
Pure, instant per 100g	277	208	189- 255
Ground (filter fine), 227g/per 8oz	236	231	163- 299
Sugar			
Granulated, per kg	257	76	61- 79
Fresh vegetables			
Potatoes, old loose, 454g/per lb	356	27	12- 35
Potatoes, new loose, 454g/per lb	396	16	9- 25
Tomatoes, 454g/per lb	611	58	45- 79
Cabbage, hearted, 454g/per lb	569	30	19- 39
Cauliflower, each	574	64	49- 79
Brussels sprouts, 454g/per lb	-	-	-
Carrots, 454g/per lb	610	26	19- 29
Onions, 454g/per lb	609	31	25- 39
Mushrooms, 113g/per 4oz	582	34	28- 40
Cucumber, each	600	50	39- 60
Lettuce - iceberg, each	603	65	45- 79
Leeks, 454g/per lb	508	83	68- 89
Fresh fruit			
Apples, cooking, 454g/per lb	567	56	45- 59
Apples, dessert, 454g/per lb	605	55	48- 65
Pears, dessert, 454g/per lb	589	48	39- 59
Oranges, each	573	22	15- 26
Bananas, 454g/per lb	596	46	39- 50
Grapes, 454g/per lb	528	112	95- 149
Avocado pear, each	448	54	39- 68
Grapefruit, each	593	28	24- 35
Items other than food			
Draught bitter, per pint	565	165	141- 190
Draught lager, per pint	568	183	164- 207
Whisky per nip	573	129	110- 149
Cigarettes 20 king size filter	854	294	253- 318
Coal, per 50kg	213	654	535- 890
Smokeless fuel per 50kg	248	937	795-1230
4-star petrol per litre	553	69	65- 71
Derv per litre	550	63	60- 66
Unleaded petrol ord. per litre	553	63	60- 65

* Or Scottish equivalent.

+ Average price estimates include prices of delivered milk and shop-bought milk. However, 80 per cent price range includes only shop-bought milk.

General Notes - Retail Prices

The responsibility for the Retail Prices Index was transferred in July 1989 from the Employment Department to the Office for National Statistics (formerly Central Statistical Office). The RPI is now being published in full in the ONS' *Business Monitor MM23*.

Structure

With effect from February 1987 the structure of the published components was recast. In some cases, therefore, no direct comparison of the new component with the old is possible. The relationship between the old and the new index structure is shown in *Employment Gazette*, p 379, September 1986.

Definitions

Seasonal food: items of food the prices of which show significant seasonal variations. These are fresh fruit and vegetables, fresh fish, eggs and home-killed lamb.

Consumer durables: Furniture, furnishings, electrical appliances and other household equipment, men's, women's and children's outerwear and footwear, audio-visual equipment, records and tapes, toys, photographic and sports goods.

6.4 RETAIL PRICES
General index of retail prices

UNITED KINGDOM January 13 1987 = 100	ALL ITEMS	All items except food	All items except seasonal food +	All items except housing	All items except mortgage interest	National-ised industries**	Consumer durables	Food All	Food Seasonal +	Food Non-seasonal + food	Catering	Alcoholic drink
1987 Weights	1,000	833	974	843	956	57	139	167	26	141	46	76
1988	1,000	837	975	840	958	54	141	163	25	138	50	78
1989	1,000	846	977	825	940	46	135	154	23	131	49	83
1990	1,000	842	976	815	925	—	132	158	24	134	47	77
1991	1,000	849	976	808	924	—	128	151	24	127	47	77
1992	1,000	848	978	828	936	—	127	152	22	130	47	80
1993	1,000	856	979	836	952	—	127	144	21	123	45	78
1994	1,000	858	980	842	956	—	127	142	20	122	45	76
1995	1,000	861	978	813	958	—	123	139	22	117	45	77
1996	1,000	857	978	810	958	—	116	143	22	121	48	78
1997	1,000	864	981	814	961	—	122	136	19	117	49	80
1987 Annual averages	101.9	102.0	101.9	101.6	101.9	100.9	101.2	101.1	101.6	101.0	102.8	101.7
1988	106.9	107.3	107.0	105.8	106.6	106.7	103.7	104.6	102.4	105.0	109.6	106.9
1989	115.2	116.1	115.5	111.5	112.9	—	107.2	110.5	105.0	111.6	116.5	112.9
1990	126.1	127.4	126.4	119.2	122.1	—	111.3	119.4	116.4	119.9	126.4	123.8
1991	133.5	135.1	133.8	128.3	130.3	—	114.8	125.6	121.6	126.3	139.1	139.2
1992	138.5	140.5	139.1	134.3	136.4	—	115.5	128.3	114.7	130.6	147.9	148.1
1993	140.7	142.6	141.4	138.4	140.5	—	115.9	130.6	111.4	134.0	155.6	154.7
1994	144.1	146.5	144.8	141.6	143.8	—	115.5	131.9	117.7	134.3	162.1	158.5
1995	149.1	151.4	149.6	145.4	147.9	—	116.2	137.0	127.2	138.5	169.0	164.5
1996	152.7	154.9	153.4	149.3	152.3	—	117.1	141.4	125.4	144.2	175.7	169.2
1987 Jan 13	100.0	100.0	100.0	100.0	100.0	100.0	100.0	100.0	100.0	100.0	100.0	100.0
1988 Jan 12	103.3	103.4	103.3	103.2	103.7	102.8	101.2	102.9	103.7	102.7	106.4	103.7
1989 Jan 17	111.0	111.7	111.2	108.5	109.4	110.9	104.5	107.4	103.2	108.2	113.1	109.9
1990 Jan 16	119.5	120.2	119.6	114.6	116.1	—	108.0	116.0	116.3	116.0	121.2	116.3
1991 Jan 15	130.2	131.6	130.4	122.7	126.0	—	110.7	122.9	121.2	123.1	132.2	129.7
1992 Jan 14	135.6	137.1	135.9	131.6	133.1	—	113.2	128.4	125.2	129.0	144.3	143.9
1993 Jan 12	137.9	139.7	138.6	135.0	137.4	—	112.8	128.8	112.2	131.7	151.7	151.0
1994 Jan 18	141.3	143.5	142.1	139.3	141.3	—	113.0	130.0	110.3	133.5	159.1	156.9
1995 Jan 17	146.0	148.3	146.5	142.9	145.2	—	113.2	134.1	126.3	135.3	165.7	161.3
Jul 18	149.1	151.6	149.9	145.0	147.7	—	113.4	135.9	116.9	139.3	169.2	165.6
Aug 15	149.9	152.1	150.3	145.9	148.6	—	114.9	138.7	132.2	139.6	169.8	165.6
Sep 12	150.6	152.8	151.0	146.7	149.2	—	117.5	139.1	132.0	140.1	170.4	166.0
Oct 17	149.8	152.1	150.5	146.2	148.7	—	117.2	137.5	122.0	140.2	171.0	166.8
Nov 14	149.8	152.2	150.5	146.2	148.8	—	118.1	137.6	121.2	140.5	171.5	165.9
Dec 12	150.7	152.9	151.3	147.2	149.6	—	119.0	138.8	126.2	140.9	171.9	164.6
1996 Jan 16	150.2	152.3	150.7	146.8	149.3	—	113.8	139.6	128.5	141.4	172.5	166.0
Feb 13	150.9	152.8	151.3	147.6	150.2	—	115.5	141.1	131.8	142.5	172.9	167.1
Mar 12	151.5	153.3	151.9	148.4	150.9	—	117.4	142.3	134.9	143.3	173.3	167.4
Apr 16	152.6	154.6	153.0	149.0	152.0	—	117.5	142.3	132.3	143.8	174.0	168.0
May 14	152.9	154.8	153.3	149.5	152.5	—	118.0	143.3	134.9	144.5	174.6	168.6
Jun 11	153.0	154.9	153.5	149.7	152.6	—	118.0	143.2	132.1	144.9	175.5	169.7
Jul 16	152.4	154.5	153.2	148.8	151.9	—	114.1	141.3	120.1	145.0	176.3	170.5
Aug 13	153.1	155.1	153.7	149.7	152.8	—	115.6	142.9	126.5	145.8	176.9	170.5
Sep 10	153.8	156.2	154.7	150.5	153.6	—	118.5	141.4	119.2	145.5	177.5	170.7
Oct 15	153.8	156.4	154.8	150.5	153.6	—	118.1	140.3	114.4	145.0	177.9	171.0
Nov 12	153.9	156.6	154.9	150.6	153.7	—	119.3	139.7	113.7	144.5	178.3	170.7
Dec 16	154.4	157.2	155.4	151.1	154.2	—	120.0	139.9	116.0	144.2	178.8	170.1
1997 Jan 14	154.4	157.0	155.3	150.7	153.9	—	114.2	141.0	120.3	144.7	179.2	171.1
Feb 11	155.0	157.7	156.0	151.3	154.5	—	115.5	140.8	116.9	145.1	179.7	172.2
Mar 11	155.4	158.4	156.5	151.7	154.9	—	117.9	140.0	113.9	144.7	180.0	172.1'
Apr 15	156.3	159.3	157.4	152.2	155.8	—	117.8	140.4	114.4	145.2	181.2	172.7
May 13	156.9	159.8	157.9	152.7	156.3	—	118.3	141.5	117.0	146.0	181.7	173.8'
Jun 10	157.5	160.3	158.4	153.0	156.7	—	117.9	142.8	122.9	146.3	182.2	174.1
Jul 15	**157.5**	**160.4**	**158.4**	**152.6**	**156.4**	**—**	**114.4**	**142.2**	**119.3**	**146.3**	**182.7**	**175.0**

+ For the February, March and April 1988 indices the weights used for seasonal and non-seasonal food were 24 and 139 respectively. Thereafter the weight for home-killed lamb (a seasonal item) was increased by 1 and that for imported lamb (a non-seasonal item) correspondingly reduced by 1, in the light of new information about the relative shares of household expenditure.

** The nationalised industries index is no longer published from December 1989, see also General Notes under *Table 6.3*.

Tobacco	Housing	Fuel and light	Household goods	Household services	Clothing and footwear	Personal goods and services	Motoring expenditure	Fares and other travel	Leisure goods	Leisure services		
38	157	61	73	44	74	38	127	22	47	30	1987	Weights
36	160	55	74	41	72	37	132	23	50	29	1988	
36	175	54	71	41	73	37	128	23	47	29	1989	
34	185	50	71	40	69	39	131	21	48	30	1990	
32	192	46	70	45	63	38	141	20	48	30	1991	
36	172	47	77	48	59	40	143	20	47	32	1992	
35	164	46	79	47	58	39	136	21	46	62	1993	
35	158	45	76	47	58	37	142	20	48	71	1994	
34	187	45	77	47	54	39	125	19	46	66	1995	
35	190	43	72	48	54	38	124	17	45	65	1996	
34	186	41	72	52	56	40	128	20	47	59	1997	
100.1	103.3	99.1	102.1	101.9	101.1	101.9	103.4	101.5	101.6	101.6	1987	Annual averages
103.4	112.5	101.6	105.9	106.8	104.4	106.8	108.1	107.5	104.2	108.1	1988	
106.4	135.3	107.3	110.1	112.5	109.9	114.1	114.0	115.2	107.4	115.1	1989	
113.6	163.7	115.9	115.4	119.6	115.0	122.7	120.9	123.4	112.4	124.5	1990	
129.9	160.8	125.1	122.5	129.5	118.5	133.4	129.9	135.5	117.7	138.8	1991	
144.2	159.6	127.8	126.5	137.0	118.8	142.2	138.7	143.9	120.8	150.0	1992	
156.4	151.0	126.2	128.0	141.9	119.8	147.9	144.7	151.4	122.5	156.7	1993	
168.2	156.0	131.7	128.4	142.0	120.4	153.3	149.7	155.4	121.8	162.5	1994	
179.5	166.4	134.5	133.1	141.6	120.6	158.2	152.4	159.3	121.7	167.7	1995	
191.5	168.6	134.8	137.5	141.7	119.7	164.1	157.0	164.1	123.6	173.8	1996	
100.0	100.0	100.0	100.0	100.0	100.0	100.0	100.0	100.0	100.0	100.0	1987	Jan 13
101.4	103.9	98.3	103.3	105.0	101.1	104.3	105.1	105.1	102.8	103.6	1988	Jan 12
105.6	124.6	104.2	107.5	110.3	105.9	110.4	110.6	112.9	105.1	112.1	1989	Jan 17
108.3	145.8	110.6	112.0	116.3	110.8	118.6	115.0	117.5	110.1	119.6	1990	Jan 16
118.2	170.6	121.6	116.7	125.5	114.2	127.2	122.8	130.8	114.9	130.7	1991	Jan 15
137.4	156.0	127.7	123.9	135.3	115.7	138.4	134.0	140.9	119.3	145.5	1992	Jan 14
150.0	151.6	127.1	125.8	139.8	114.9	144.7	137.9	148.6	121.3	153.6	1993	Jan 12
166.5	150.2	125.4	126.1	142.4	116.2	149.5	147.5	154.0	122.3	160.1	1994	Jan 18
175.6	160.6	134.1	128.3	141.9	117.1	154.9	150.9	157.5	121.2	165.0	1995	Jan 17
180.2	168.3	134.4	132.0	140.7	116.2	158.3	153.9	159.9	121.3	167.9		Jul 18
180.1	168.8	134.4	133.5	140.8	118.0	159.1	153.4	160.2	121.6	168.7		Aug 15
180.1	169.1	134.7	134.9	140.9	122.6	160.0	153.0	160.0	121.8	170.1		Sep 12
180.0	167.0	134.6	134.7	140.5	122.4	160.5	151.0	159.7	122.1	169.9		Oct 17
180.0	167.3	134.6	135.8	140.6	123.0	160.9	149.8	159.8	122.1	170.2		Nov 14
184.4	167.2	134.8	137.4	140.6	123.2	161.1	153.0	159.7	122.7	170.5		Dec 12
188.1	166.4	134.9	133.3	141.6	116.3	159.9	154.0	161.1	122.4	171.0	1996	Jan 16
188.8	166.3	134.9	135.5	141.7	117.4	161.6	153.8	161.4	123.1	171.1		Feb 13
189.0	166.2	135.0	137.8	141.8	119.1	162.1	154.0	161.4	123.6	171.4		Mar 12
190.6	169.6	135.1	137.1	141.3	120.3	163.8	155.3	163.5	124.1	172.7		Apr 16
191.9	168.9	134.9	138.0	141.4	120.6	164.0	155.7	164.7	124.0	173.4		May 14
192.1	168.8	135.1	138.2	141.5	120.5	163.9	155.8	164.7	123.8	173.6		Jun 11
191.8	169.4	135.2	136.1	141.5	114.6	164.5	155.9	164.7	123.5	174.0		Jul 16
192.1	169.4	135.0	137.6	141.7	116.3	164.3	157.4	165.4	123.7	174.3		Aug 13
192.5	169.2	135.0	138.3	142.6	122.3	165.2	159.7	165.8	123.7	175.2		Sep 10
192.7	169.5	134.8	137.8	141.9	122.3	166.3	160.7	165.7	123.5	175.9		Oct 15
192.4	169.9	134.1	139.2	141.9	123.7	166.6	160.0	165.4	124.2	176.3		Nov 12
196.2	170.1	133.9	140.6	142.1	123.5	167.2	161.5	165.4	124.1	177.2		Dec 16
200.1	172.1	133.2	135.6	142.7	116.3	166.7	162.9	166.6	123.7	177.8	1997	Jan 14
200.9	172.8	133.2	136.7	143.0	118.0	167.0	163.7	167.3	124.2	178.1		Feb 11
201.5	172.9	133.2	140.1	142.8	120.4	168.2	163.6	167.6	124.3	178.4		Mar 11
203.9	176.1	132.8	139.0	143.4	121.6	169.6	163.3	168.6	124.2	180.2		Apr 15
204.7	176.7	132.3	139.6	143.6	122.1	169.8	163.4	169.5	124.3	180.9		May 13
205.0	178.9	131.7	139.4	143.5	121.6	169.7	164.2	170.1	124.2	181.6		Jun 10
205.2	**180.9**	**131.2**	**137.3**	**143.8**	**115.9**	**169.8**	**165.9**	**170.9**	**123.9**	**182.5**		**Jul 15**

Note: The structures of the published components of the index were recast in February 1987. (See General Notes under *Table 6.3*).

RETAIL PRICES
General index of retail prices: percentage changes on a year earlier 6.5

	All Items	Food	Catering	Alcoholic drink	Tobacco	Housing	Fuel and light	House-hold goods	House-hold services	Clothing and footwear	Personal goods and services	Motoring expendi-ture	Fares and other travel costs	Leisure goods	Leisure services
1988 Jan 12	3.3	2.9	6.4	3.7	1.4	3.9	-1.7	3.3	5.0	1.1	4.3	5.1	5.1	2.8	3.6
1989 Jan 17	7.5	4.4	6.3	6.0	4.1	19.9	6.0	4.1	5.0	4.7	5.8	5.2	7.4	2.2	8.2
1990 Jan 16	7.7	8.0	7.2	5.8	2.6	17.0	6.1	4.2	5.4	4.6	7.4	4.0	4.8	4.8	6.7
1991 Jan 15	9.0	5.9	9.1	11.5	9.1	17.0	9.9	4.2	7.9	3.1	7.3	6.8	11.3	4.4	9.3
1992 Jan 14	4.1	4.5	9.2	10.9	16.2	-8.6	5.0	6.2	7.8	1.3	8.8	9.1	7.7	3.8	11.3
1993 Jan 12	1.7	0.3	5.1	4.9	9.2	-2.8	-0.5	1.5	3.3	-0.7	4.6	2.9	5.5	1.7	5.6
1994 Jan 18	2.5	0.9	4.9	3.9	11.0	-0.9	-1.3	0.2	1.9	1.1	3.3	7.0	3.6	0.8	4.2
1995 Jan 17	3.3	3.2	4.1	2.8	5.5	6.9	6.9	1.7	-0.4	0.8	3.6	2.3	2.3	-0.9	3.1
Jul 18	3.5	2.7	4.3	4.1	6.9	7.3	0.4	4.5	-1.1	0.2	3.9	2.6	2.8	0.5	3.3
Aug 15	3.6	4.5	4.3	4.0	6.9	7.5	0.1	4.1	-1.1	-0.5	2.6	1.8	2.6	0.6	3.6
Sep 12	3.9	5.7	4.3	3.9	6.9	7.5	0.4	4.6	-1.1	0.3	3.1	1.7	2.6	0.5	3.8
Oct 17	3.2	4.6	4.1	4.4	6.9	4.5	0.4	4.4	-0.4	0.2	4.0	0.9	2.4	0.8	3.3
Nov 14	3.1	4.4	4.2	4.1	7.1	4.5	0.6	4.2	-0.2	0.2	4.2	0.5	2.4	0.7	3.5
Dec 12	3.2	4.6	4.1	3.6	7.9	4.2	0.7	4.8	-0.4	0.3	2.9	1.7	2.3	1.1	3.5
1996 Jan 16	2.9	4.1	4.1	2.9	7.1	3.6	0.6	3.9	-0.2	-0.1	3.2	2.1	2.3	1.0	3.6
Feb 13	2.7	4.5	3.9	2.9	6.5	2.7	0.4	4.2	-0.2	-0.9	4.3	1.6	1.7	1.3	3.7
Mar 12	2.7	4.7	3.7	2.6	6.5	2.8	0.4	4.4	-0.4	-0.9	4.0	0.9	2.0	1.6	3.9
Apr 16	2.4	4.8	3.7	2.9	6.4	0.9	0.3	3.8	-1.1	-1.2	4.5	1.6	2.9	2.1	4.0
May 14	2.2	3.8	3.6	2.7	6.6	0.7	0.4	3.4	-1.0	-1.2	3.8	1.7	3.5	2.2	4.1
Jun 11	2.1	4.5	4.0	3.0	6.6	0.0	0.6	3.6	-0.8	-1.1	3.9	1.2	3.4	1.8	3.8
Jul 16	2.2	4.0	4.2	3.0	6.4	0.7	0.6	3.1	0.6	-1.4	3.9	1.3	3.0	1.8	3.6
Aug 13	2.1	3.0	4.2	3.0	6.7	0.4	0.4	3.1	0.6	-1.4	3.3	2.6	3.2	1.7	3.3
Sep 10	2.1	1.7	4.2	2.8	6.9	0.1	0.2	2.5	1.2	-1.2	3.3	4.4	3.6	1.6	3.0
Oct 15	2.7	2.0	4.0	2.5	7.1	1.5	0.1	2.3	1.0	-0.1	3.6	6.4	3.8	1.1	3.5
Nov 12	2.7	1.5	4.0	2.9	6.9	1.6	-0.4	2.5	0.9	0.6	3.5	6.8	3.5	1.7	3.6
Dec 16	2.5	0.8	4.0	3.3	6.4	1.7	-0.7	2.3	1.1	0.2	3.8	5.6	3.6	1.1	3.9
1997 Jan 14	2.8	1.0	3.9	3.1	6.4	3.4	-1.3	1.7	0.8	0.0	4.3	5.8	3.4	1.1	4.0
Feb 11	2.7	-0.2	3.9	3.1	6.4	3.9	-1.3	0.9	0.9	0.5	4.3	6.4	3.7	0.9	4.1
Mar 11	2.6	-1.6	3.9	2.8	6.6	4.0	-1.3	1.7	0.7	1.1	3.8	6.2	3.8	0.6	4.1
Apr 15	2.4	-1.3	4.1	2.8	7.0	3.8	-1.7	1.4	1.5	1.1	3.5	5.2	3.1	0.1	4.3
May 13	2.6	-1.3	4.1	3.1	6.7	4.6	-1.9	1.2	1.6	1.2	3.5	4.9	2.9	0.2	4.3
Jun 10	2.9	-0.3	3.8	2.6	6.7	6.0	-2.5	0.9	1.4	0.9	3.5	5.4	3.3	0.3	4.6
Jul 15	**3.3**	**0.6**	**3.6**	**2.6**	**7.0**	**6.8**	**-3.0**	**0.9**	**1.6**	**1.1**	**3.2**	**6.4**	**3.8**	**0.3**	**4.9**

Note: See notes under *Table 6.3*.

6.8 RETAIL PRICES
EU countries - Harmonised Indices of Consumer Prices (HICPs)[1]

1985=100	European Comm (15)[3]	United Kingdom	Austria	Belgium	Denmark	Finland	France	Germany			
Annual averages											
1995	97.7 e	N/A	98.3	98.3	98.1	98.5	98.0	98.8			
1996	100.0	100.0	100.0	100.0	100.0	100.0	100.0	100.0			
Monthly											
1995 Apr	97.4 e	N/A	98.1	98.0	98.2	98.4	97.7	98.6			
May	97.6 e	N/A	98.2	98.1	98.5	98.5	97.8	98.7			
Jun	97.8 e	N/A	98.4	98.1	98.3	98.7	97.8	99.0			
Jul	97.7 e	N/A	98.4	98.4	97.7	98.7	97.6	99.2			
Aug	97.9 e	N/A	98.4	98.7	97.9	98.5	98.1	99.1			
Sep	98.2 e	N/A	98.5	98.6	98.5	98.7	98.5	99.0			
Oct	98.3 e	N/A	98.4	98.4	98.5	98.8	98.6	98.9			
Nov	98.4 e	N/A	98.4	98.5	98.7	98.6	98.7	98.8			
Dec	98.6 e	N/A	98.4	98.7	98.6	98.5	98.8	99.1			
1996 Jan	98.8 p	98.5	99.1 r	99.1	98.4	99.2	98.9	99.2			
Feb	99.2	98.9	99.4 r	99.2	99.0	99.5	99.3	99.7			
Mar	99.6 p	99.3	99.6 r	99.5	99.6	99.7	100.0	99.8			
Apr	99.9 p	99.9	99.7 r	100.0	99.9	99.9	100.1	99.8			
May	100.1	100.2	99.5 r	100.1	100.1	100.3	100.3	100.0			
Jun	100.2 p	100.3	100.0 r	100.0	100.1	100.3	100.2	100.1			
Jul	100.1 p	99.7	100.3 r	99.9	99.9	100.1	100.0	100.4			
Aug	100.1	100.2	100.3 r	99.9	100.1	99.9	99.8	100.3			
Sep	100.4 p	100.7	100.5 r	100.1	100.6	100.2	100.1	100.1			
Oct	100.5 p	100.7	100.5 r	100.6	100.8	100.4	100.4	100.1			
Nov	100.5	100.7	100.6 r	100.6	100.8	100.2	100.3	100.1			
Dec	100.7 p	101.0	100.6 r	100.8	100.7	100.2	100.5	100.3			
1997 Jan	100.9	100.6	100.7 r	101.3	101.0	99.9	100.7	100.9			
Feb	101.1	100.9	100.9 r	101.2	101.0	100.2	101.0	101.3			
Mar	101.3	101.1	100.8 r	101.0	101.1	100.6	101.1	101.1			
Apr	101.4 p	101.5	101.1 r	100.9	101.4	100.9	101.1	101.0			
May	101.6 p	101.8	101.1 r	101.6	102.0	101.2	101.2	101.4			
Jun	101.7 p	102.0	101.1 p	101.6	102.3	101.4	101.2	101.6			
Increases on a year earlier											Per cent
Annual averages											
1996	2.4 p	N/A	1.8	1.8	1.9	1.5	2.1	1.2			
Monthly											
1996 Apr	2.6 p	N/A	1.6 r	2.0	1.7	1.5	2.5	1.2			
May	2.6 p	N/A	1.3 r	2.0	1.6	1.8	2.6	1.3			
Jun	2.4 p	N/A	1.6 r	1.9	1.8	1.6	2.5	1.1			
Jul	2.4 p	N/A	1.8 r	1.5	2.3	1.4	2.5	1.2			
Aug	2.2 p	N/A	1.5 r	1.2	2.2	1.4	1.7	1.2			
Sep	2.2 p	N/A	1.4 r	1.5	2.1	1.5	1.6	1.1			
Oct	2.3 p	N/A	1.7 r	2.2	2.3	1.6	1.8	1.2			
Nov	2.2 p	N/A	2.0 r	2.1	2.1	1.6	1.6	1.3			
Dec	2.1 p	N/A	2.3 r	2.1	2.1	1.7	1.7	1.2			
1997 Jan	2.2 p	2.1	1.2 r	2.2	2.6	0.7	1.8	1.7			
Feb	2.0	2.0	1.4 r	2.0	2.0	0.6	1.7	1.6			
Mar	1.7 p	1.8	1.2 r	1.3	1.5	0.8	1.1	1.3			
Apr	1.5 p	1.6	1.2 r	0.9	1.5	0.9	1.0	1.2			
May	1.5 p	1.6	1.3 r	1.5	1.9	0.9	0.9	1.4			
Jun	1.6 p	1.7	1.0p	1.6	2.2	1.1	1.0	1.5			

Notes: 1 Harmonised Indices of Consumer Prices (HICPs) are being calculated in each member state of the European Union for the purpose of international comparisons. This is in the context of one of the convergence criteria for monetary union as required by the Maastricht treaty . The rules underlying the construction of the HICPs for EU member states were published in a Commission Regulation of 9 September 1996. The HICPs replace the Interim Indices of Consumer Prices which were published by Eurostat in a monthly news release.
2 Figures for Irish Republic for 1996 are only available on a quarterly basis.
3 Percentage change figures for 1996 are estimated.

Greece	Irish Republic[2]	Italy[3]	Luxembourg	Netherlands	Portugal	Spain	Sweden				1985=100
											Annual averages
92.7	NA	96.2 e	98.8 p	98.6	97.2	96.6	99.2			1995	
100.0	100.0	100.0	100.0	100.0	100.0	100.0	100.0			1996	
											Monthly
92.1	N/A	95.3 e	98.6 p	99.1	97.3	96.4	99.4				Apr
93.0	98.0	95.9 e	98.7 p	98.9	97.2	96.4	99.5				May
93.5	N/A	96.5 e	98.8 p	98.7	96.9	96.5	99.3				Jun
91.8	N/A	96.7 e	98.8 p	98.0	96.9	96.5	99.0				Jul
91.9	98.0	96.9 e	98.8 p	98.1	97.3	96.8	99.0				Aug
94.1	N/A	97.2 e	98.9 p	99.0	97.5	97.2	99.9				Sep
94.8	N/A	97.5 e	99.1 p	99.0	97.8	97.3	100.0				Oct
95.2	98.4	98.1 e	99.2 p	99.0	97.9	97.6	100.0				Nov
96.7	N/A	98.2 e	99.3 p	98.5	97.9	97.9	99.7				Dec
96.3	N/A	98.6	99.4	98.9	98.3	98.5	99.1			1996	Jan
96.1	99.1	99.0	99.5	99.3	98.8	98.7	99.3				Feb
98.9	N/A	99.3	99.6	100.3	99.0	99.1	100.0				Mar
99.9	N/A	99.7	99.8	100.5	99.8	99.7	100.4				Apr
100.7	100.0	100.1	99.9	100.2	100.2	100.1	100.5				May
100.9	N/A	100.3	99.9	99.7	100.2	100.0	100.1				Jun
99.1	N/A	100.2	100.0	99.5	100.4	100.1	99.9				Jul
99.0	100.2	100.3	100.1	99.4	100.7	100.4	99.6				Aug
101.3	N/A	100.4	100.1	100.4	100.7	100.7	100.4				Sep
102.1	N/A	100.5	100.3	100.8	100.5	100.8	100.4				Oct
102.2	100.7	100.9	100.6	100.7	100.7	100.8	100.2				Nov
103.4	N/A	101.0	100.6	100.5	100.7	101.1	100.2				Dec
102.7	100.3	101.2	100.7	100.7	101.1	101.3	100.4			1997	Jan
102.3	100.9	101.3	101.0	100.9	101.2	101.2	100.4				Feb
104.7	101.0	101.5	100.9	101.6	101.3	101.3	101.0				Mar
105.6	101.0	101.6	100.9	101.7	101.4	101.3	101.6				Apr
106.1	101.1	101.8	101.0	101.9	102.1	101.4	101.7				May
106.5	**101.4**	**101.9**	**101.1**	**101.4**	**101.8**	**101.4**	**101.8**				**Jun**
											Increases on a year earlier
Per cent											**Annual averages**
7.9	N/A	4.0	1.2	1.5	2.9	3.6 p	0.8			1996	
Monthly											**Monthly**
8.5	N/A	4.6	1.2	1.4	2.6	3.4	1.0			1996	Apr
8.3	2.0	4.4	1.2	1.3	3.1	3.8	1.0				May
7.9	N/A	3.9	1.1	1.0	3.4	3.6	0.8				Jun
8.0	N/A	3.6	1.2	1.5	3.6	3.7	0.9				Jul
7.7	2.2	3.5	1.3	1.3	3.5	3.7	0.6				Aug
7.7	N/A	3.3	1.2	1.4	3.3	3.6	0.5				Sep
7.7	N/A	3.1	1.2	1.8	2.8	3.6	0.4				Oct
7.4	2.3	2.9	1.4	1.7	2.9	3.3	0.2				Nov
6.9	N/A	2.9	1.3	2.0	2.9	3.3	0.5				Dec
6.6	N/A	2.6	1.3	1.8	2.8	2.8	1.3			1997	Jan
6.5	1.7	2.3	1.5	1.6	2.4	2.5	1.1				Feb
5.9	N/A	2.2	1.3	1.3	2.3	2.2	1.0				Mar
5.7	N/A	1.9	1.1	1.2	1.6	1.6	1.2				Apr
5.4 r	1.4	1.7	1.1	1.7	1.9	1.3	1.2				May
5.6	**NA**	**1.6**	**1.2**	**1.7**	**1.6**	**1.4**	**1.7**				**Jun**

Source: Office for National Statistics/Eurostat

1990=100	United Kingdom[1]	Germany (West)[1]	France[1]	Italy[1]
Annual averages				
1993	116.1	111.0	107.5	116.7
1994	118.8	113.9	109.2	121.4
1995	122.0	115.7 P	111.1	127.7
1996	125.3	117.1 P	113.3 P	132.6 P
Monthly				
1996 Jan	123.2	116.2 P	112.1	130.7 P
Feb	123.8	116.4 P	112.5	131.1 P
Mar	124.5	116.7 P	113.2	131.5 P
Apr	125.0	117.2 P	113.4	132.2 P
May	125.4	117.7 P	113.6	132.7 P
Jun	125.6	117.8 P	113.5	133.0 P
Jul	124.8	117.8 P	113.3	132.8 P
Aug	125.6	117.1 P	113.0	132.9 P
Sep	126.3	117.1 P	113.4	133.3 P
Oct	126.3	117.2 P	113.7	133.4 P
Nov	126.3	117.1 P	113.7 P	133.8 P
Dec	126.8	117.2 P	113.7 P	133.9 P
1997 Jan	126.4	118.4 P	113.7 P	133.9 P
Feb	126.9	118.4 P	113.7 P	133.9 P
Mar	127.3	118.5 P	113.9 P	133.9 P
Apr	127.7	118.7 P	113.9 P	133.9 P
May	128.1	119.2 P	113.9 P	133.9 P
Jun	128.4	119.8 P	..	..
Increases on a year earlier					Per cent
Annual averages				
1993	3.0	3.6	2.2	4.4
1994	2.3	2.6	1.6	4.0
1995	2.7	1.6 P	1.7	5.2
1996	2.7	1.2 P	2.0	3.8 P
Monthly				
1996 Jan	2.7	0.9 P	1.9	5.4 P
Feb	2.7	0.9 P	1.9	4.9 P
Mar	2.7	1.0 P	2.3	4.5 P
Apr	2.8	1.2 P	2.3	4.6 P
May	2.5	1.5 P	2.3	4.4 P
Jun	2.7	1.2 P	2.3	3.9 P
Jul	2.6	1.3 P	2.3	3.6 P
Aug	2.6	1.4 P	1.6	3.4 P
Sep	2.6	1.4 P	1.6	3.4 P
Oct	2.9	1.5 P	1.8	3.1 P
Nov	3.0	1.5 P	1.7 P	2.7 P
Dec	2.6	1.4 P	1.6 P	2.6 P
1997 Jan	2.7	1.9 P	1.4 P	2.4 P
Feb	2.5	1.7 P	1.1 P	2.1 P
Mar	2.2	1.6 P	0.6 P	1.8 P
Apr	2.1	1.3 P	0.4 P	1.3 P
May	2.1	1.3 P	0.4 P	1.3 P
Jun	2.2	1.7 P	..	..

Notes: 1 Comparisons of consumer price indices are affected by differences in national concepts and definitions especially in the treatment of housing costs. Consumer price indices excluding housing costs are therefore given as the best available basis for comparison for non-EU countries. This is in accordance with a resolution adopted by the 14th International Conference of Labour Statisticians that countries should "provide for the dissemination at the international level of an index which excludes shelter, in addition to the all-items index." Figures are given for each country on the nearest basis to the UK series "All items excluding housing." Where necessary the figures in this table have been estimated by the ONS using data kindly supplied by other countries.

2 The definition of housing costs varies between countries. The figures shown for most countries exclude owner-occupiers' costs, rents, repairs and maintenance. For Canada, fuel and lighting are also excluded.

3 Figures for the four EU member states have been provided in this table for comparison with non-EU countries only. The best measure of comparison between these four countries are the Harmonised Indices of Consumer Prices shown in *Table 6.8*.

United States	Japan	Canada		1990=100
				Annual averages
110.3	105.9	109.5		1993
112.9	106.3	109.6		1994
115.9	105.8	112.5		1995
119.2	105.8	114.9		1996
Monthly				**Monthly**
117.2	105.4	113.2	1996	Jan
117.6	105.2	113.4		Feb
118.3	105.4	114.0		Mar
118.9	106.2	114.6		Apr
119.2	106.4	115.0		May
119.2	105.9	114.9		Jun
119.2	105.6	114.9		Jul
119.3	105.5	115.0		Aug
119.8	105.9	115.2		Sep
120.3	106.1	115.4		Oct
120.6	105.8	116.3		Nov
120.7	105.9	116.2		Dec
120.9	105.1 P	116.5	1997	Jan
121.1	104.8 P	116.7		Feb
121.1	104.9 P	117.0		Mar
121.5	107.6 P	117.0		Apr
121.5	107.6 P	117.2		May
121.5	..	117.6		Jun
				Increases on a year earlier
				Annual averages
Per cent				
3.0	1.0	2.0		1993
2.4	0.4	0.2		1994
2.6	-0.5	2.6		1995
2.8	0.0	2.1		1996
Monthly				
2.4	-0.8	2.0	1996	Jan
2.4	-0.5	1.6		Feb
2.6	-0.2	1.9		Mar
2.8	0.2	1.9		Apr
2.8	0.1	2.0		May
2.7	-0.3	1.9		Jun
2.8	0.3	1.7		Jul
2.7	0.2	2.0		Aug
2.8	0.0	1.9		Sep
2.9	0.5	2.3		Oct
3.3	0.5	2.8		Nov
3.4	0.6	3.1		Dec
3.1	-0.3 P	2.9	1997	Jan
3.0	-0.4 P	2.9		Feb
2.4	-0.6 P	2.4		Mar
2.2	1.3 P	2.1		Apr
1.9	1.1 P	1.9		May
1.9	..	2.4		Jun

Source: Office for National Statistics/National Statistical Offices/OECD

LABOUR FORCE SURVEY
Economic activity,+ seasonally adjusted §§

THOUSANDS

GREAT BRITAIN	In employment # Employees	Self-employed	Govt-supported training and employment programmes §	Unpaid family workers **	In employment ++	ILO unemployed	Total economically active	Economically inactive	All aged 16 and over
ALL									
Spr 1979	22,600	1,769	..	..	24,369	1,466 X	25,836 X	15,310 X	41,146
Spr 1981	21,574	2,191	..	..	23,765	2,521 X	26,286 X	15,654 X	41,940
Spr 1983	20,446	2,292	366	..	23,103	2,891 X	25,994 X	16,399 X	42,394
Spr 1984	20,673	2,606	321	..	23,626	2,964 X	26,590 X	16,130 X	42,720
Spr 1984	20,673	2,606	321	..	23,626	3,143	26,768	15,951	42,720
Spr 1985	20,890	2,703	402	..	23,995	3,026	27,021	15,990	43,011
Spr 1986	20,982	2,718	414	..	24,117	3,031	27,148	16,100	43,246
Spr 1987	21,010	2,957	513	..	24,489	2,946	27,435	16,053	43,487
Spr 1988	21,708	3,136	541	..	25,389	2,424	27,813	15,852	43,665
Spr 1989	22,269	3,429	490	..	26,195	2,021	28,216	15,623	43,839
Spr 1990	22,488	3,471	458	..	26,421	1,925	28,346	15,616	43,962
Spr 1991	22,132	3,318	418	..	25,883	2,361	28,243	15,835	44,078
Spr 1992	21,577	3,147	356	176	25,255	2,745	28,000	16,159	44,159
Spr 1993	21,371	3,109	333	145	24,959	2,909	27,868	16,349	44,217
Sum 1993	21,363	3,111	329	151	24,953	2,879	27,832	16,398	44,230
Aut 1993	21,404	3,140	323	140	25,007	2,851	27,858	16,388	44,246
Win 1993/4	21,404	3,193	323	135	25,055	2,798	27,853	16,409	44,262
Spr 1994	21,475	3,219	315	140	25,150	2,716	27,865	16,412	44,277
Sum 1994	21,557	3,220	296	138	25,211	2,667	27,878	16,415	44,293
Aut 1994	21,597	3,263	291	142	25,293	2,523	27,816	16,507	44,322
Win 1994/5	21,644	3,289	277	128	25,338	2,457	27,795	16,557	44,352
Spr 1995	21,737	3,274	267	133	25,412	2,435	27,846	16,534	44,381
Sum 1995	21,894	3,242	254	125	25,515	2,408	27,923	16,487	44,410
Aut 1995	21,945	3,238	246	131	25,560	2,383	27,944	16,504	44,447
Win 1995/6	22,062	3,219	235	118	25,634	2,334	27,968	16,517	44,485
Spr 1996	22,085	3,213	225	122	25,645	2,321	27,966	16,556	44,522
Sum 1996	22,096	3,289	225	114	25,724	2,255	27,978	16,582	44,560
Aut 1996	22,252	3,283	200	115	25,851	2,221	28,072	16,527	44,599
Win 1996/7	22,401	3,277	199	108	25,985	2,111	28,096	16,542	44,638
Spring 1997	**22,507**	**3,260**	**197**	**111**	**26,076**	**2,037**	**28,113**	**16,564**	**44,677**
Changes									
Win 96/7 - Spr 97	106	-17	-1	3	91	-74	17	22	39
Per cent	*0.5*	*-0.5*	*-0.6*	*2.7*	*0.4*	*-3.5*	*0.1*	*0.1*	*0.1*
MEN									
Spr 1979	13,381	1,449	..	..	14,830	787 X	15,617 X	4,067 X	19,684
Spr 1981	12,427	1,753	..	..	14,180	1,583 X	15,763 X	4,324 X	20,087
Spr 1983	11,672	1,759	221	..	13,651	1,838 X	15,490 X	4,842 X	20,332
Spr 1984	11,643	1,988	201	..	13,845	1,802 X	15,647 X	4,872 X	20,519
Spr 1984	11,643	1,988	201	..	13,845	1,861	15,707	4,813	20,519
Spr 1985	11,683	2,039	255	..	13,977	1,818	15,795	4,886	20,681
Spr 1986	11,583	2,057	278	..	13,920	1,817	15,736	5,071	20,806
Spr 1987	11,487	2,231	329	..	14,052	1,755	15,807	5,138	20,945
Spr 1988	11,836	2,375	339	..	14,552	1,425	15,978	5,074	21,052
Spr 1989	11,984	2,626	313	..	14,928	1,173	16,101	5,058	21,158
Spr 1990	12,082	2,647	296	..	15,029	1,122	16,150	5,099	21,249
Spr 1991	11,803	2,535	252	..	14,598	1,470	16,068	5,251	21,318
Spr 1992	11,363	2,374	234	54	14,025	1,835	15,860	5,509	21,369
Spr 1993	11,154	2,321	219	41	13,735	1,955	15,690	5,730	21,420
Sum 1993	11,147	2,331	219	47	13,744	1,907	15,651	5,782	21,432
Aut 1993	11,178	2,346	215	42	13,781	1,882	15,663	5,785	21,448
Win 1993/4	11,189	2,383	218	37	13,826	1,837	15,663	5,801	21,464
Spr 1994	11,209	2,414	207	47	13,877	1,797	15,673	5,806	21,479
Sum 1994	11,252	2,425	194	49	13,920	1,774	15,693	5,801	21,495
Aut 1994	11,313	2,458	192	44	14,007	1,664	15,670	5,846	21,516
Win 1994/5	11,317	2,478	187	41	14,022	1,611	15,633	5,904	21,537
Spr 1995	11,380	2,480	173	40	14,073	1,582	15,655	5,904	21,559
Sum 1995	11,447	2,447	160	44	14,098	1,566	15,664	5,916	21,580
Aut 1995	11,469	2,448	158	42	14,117	1,542	15,660	5,945	21,604
Win 1995/6	11,523	2,419	148	35	14,125	1,539	15,664	5,965	21,629
Spr 1996	11,551	2,403	142	40	14,137	1,525	15,662	5,992	21,654
Sum 1996	11,542	2,466	143	37	14,187	1,472	15,659	6,019	21,678
Aut 1996	11,637	2,459	122	40	14,258	1,432	15,690	6,014	21,703
Win 1996/7	11,743	2,454	119	37	14,353	1,326	15,679	6,050	21,728
Spr 1997	**11,817**	**2,421**	**121**	**37**	**14,395**	**1,294**	**15,689**	**6,064**	**21,753**
Changes									
Win 96/7 - Spr 97	74	-33	2	0	42	-32	11	14	25
Per cent	*0.6*	*-1.4*	*1.6*	*-1.2*	*0.3*	*-2.4*	*0.1*	*0.2*	*0.1*
WOMEN									
Spr 1979	9,220	319	..	..	9,539	679 X	10,218 X	11,243 X	21,462
Spr 1981	9,147	438	..	..	9,585	937 X	10,522 X	11,330 X	21,852
Spr 1983	8,774	533	145	..	9,452	1,053 X	10,505 X	11,557 X	22,062
Spr 1984	9,030	619	120	..	9,780	1,162 X	10,943 X	11,258 X	22,200
Spr 1984	9,030	619	120	..	9,780	1,282	11,062	11,138	22,200
Spr 1985	9,207	664	147	..	10,018	1,208	11,226	11,104	22,330
Spr 1986	9,399	661	136	..	10,197	1,214	11,411	11,029	22,440
Spr 1987	9,522	727	185	..	10,437	1,191	11,628	10,915	22,543
Spr 1988	9,872	761	202	..	10,836	999	11,835	10,778	22,613
Spr 1989	10,285	803	177	..	11,267	848	12,116	10,565	22,681
Spr 1990	10,406	824	162	..	11,393	803	12,196	10,517	22,713
Spr 1991	10,329	784	166	..	11,285	891	12,176	10,584	22,760
Spr 1992	10,214	773	122	122	11,230	910	12,140	10,650	22,790
Spr 1993	10,217	788	114	104	11,224	954	12,178	10,619	22,797
Sum 1993	10,215	780	110	104	11,210	972	12,182	10,616	22,798
Aut 1993	10,226	794	108	98	11,226	969	12,195	10,603	22,798
Win 1993/4	10,216	810	105	98	11,229	961	12,190	10,608	22,798
Spr 1994	10,265	806	108	93	11,273	919	12,192	10,606	22,798
Sum 1994	10,305	794	103	89	11,291	893	12,185	10,613	22,798
Aut 1994	10,284	805	99	98	11,286	859	12,146	10,661	22,806
Win 1994/5	10,327	810	90	88	11,316	845	12,161	10,653	22,814
Spr 1995	10,357	795	93	93	11,339	853	12,191	10,631	22,822
Sum 1995	10,447	795	94	81	11,417	842	12,259	10,571	22,830
Aut 1995	10,476	789	89	88	11,443	841	12,284	10,559	22,843
Win 1995/6	10,539	800	87	83	11,509	796	12,305	10,551	22,856
Spr 1996	10,534	810	83	82	11,509	796	12,305	10,564	22,869
Sum 1996	10,554	823	82	77	11,537	782	12,319	10,562	22,881
Aut 1996	10,615	824	79	75	11,593	789	12,382	10,513	22,895
Win 1996/7	10,658	824	79	71	11,632	785	12,417	10,492	22,909
Spr 1997	**10,690**	**840**	**76**	**75**	**11,681**	**743**	**12,424**	**10,500**	**22,923**
Changes									
Win 96/7 - Spr 97	32	16	-3	3	49	-42	7	7	14
Per cent	*0.3*	*2.0*	*-3.8*	*4.7*	*0.4*	*-5.4*	*0.1*	*0.1*	*0.1*

+   Since 1984 the definitions used in the Labour Force Survey (LFS) have been fully in line with international recommendations. For details see 'The quarterly Labour Force Survey: a new dimension to labour market statistics', *Employment Gazette*, October 1992, pp 483-490.

People in full-time education who also did some paid work in the reference week have been classified as in employment since spring 1983.

§   Those on employment and training programmes have been classified as in employment since spring 1983. Some of those on government-supported training programmes may consider themselves to be employees or self-employed and so appear in other categories. Full information on those on government-supported training programmes is in *Table 8.1.*

X   The Labour Force (LF) definition of unemployment and inactivity applies for these years. LF unemployment is based on a <u>one</u> week job search period, rather than <u>four</u> weeks with the ILO definition.

**   Unpaid family workers have been classified as in employment since spring 1992.

++   Includes those who did not state whether they were employees or self-employed.

§§   Revised April 1997.

GREAT BRITAIN	In employment #					ILO unemployed	Total economically active	Economically inactive	All aged 16 and over
	Employees	Self-employed	Govt-supported training and employment programmes §	Unpaid family workers**	In employment ++				
ALL									
Spr 1979	22,432	1,778	..	..	24,210	1,428 X	25,638 X	15,507 X	41,146
Spr 1981	21,405	2,201	..	..	23,606	2,483 X	26,089 X	15,851 X	41,940
Spr 1983	20,288	2,301	355	..	22,944	2,853 X	25,797 X	16,596 X	42,394
Spr 1984	20,515	2,616	311	..	23,467	2,926 X	26,393 X	16,327 X	42,720
Spr 1984	20,515	2,616	311	..	23,467	3,105	26,571	16,148	42,720
Spr 1985	20,746	2,713	390	..	23,850	2,990	26,840	16,171	43,011
Spr 1986	20,852	2,729	400	..	23,984	2,996	26,979	16,267	43,246
Spr 1987	20,892	2,969	498	..	24,368	2,912	27,280	16,208	43,487
Spr 1988	21,601	3,148	527	..	25,279	2,392	27,671	15,994	43,665
Spr 1989	22,167	3,441	478	..	26,093	1,989	28,083	15,757	43,839
Spr 1990	22,388	3,482	448	..	26,324	1,894	28,218	15,745	43,962
Spr 1991	22,034	3,330	412	..	25,792	2,329	28,121	15,957	44,078
Spr 1992	21,520	3,147	364	176	25,206	2,684	27,890	16,269	44,159
Spr 1993	21,313	3,108	341	145	24,907	2,849	27,756	16,461	44,217
Sum 1993	21,507	3,115	312	151	25,085	2,942	28,027	16,203	44,230
Aut 1993	21,441	3,164	330	140	25,075	2,842	27,916	16,330	44,246
Win 1993/4	21,298	3,165	329	135	24,928	2,790	27,718	16,544	44,262
Spr 1994	21,415	3,216	322	140	25,093	2,656	27,750	16,528	44,277
Sum 1994	21,699	3,224	280	138	25,341	2,734	28,075	16,218	44,293
Aut 1994	21,632	3,289	296	142	25,359	2,517	27,876	16,446	44,322
Win 1994/5	21,550	3,259	283	128	25,221	2,435	27,656	16,695	44,352
Spr 1995	21,675	3,269	273	133	25,350	2,376	27,726	16,655	44,381
Sum 1995	22,035	3,247	238	125	25,644	2,479	28,123	16,287	44,410
Aut 1995	21,977	3,266	251	131	25,625	2,382	28,007	16,440	44,447
Win 1995/6	21,982	3,188	242	118	25,530	2,299	27,829	16,656	44,485
Spr 1996	22,020	3,205	230	122	25,578	2,265	27,843	16,679	44,522
Sum 1996	22,235	3,295	209	114	25,853	2,327	28,180	16,379	44,560
Aut 1996	22,282	3,311	204	115	25,912	2,226	28,138	16,461	44,599
Win 1996/7	22,332	3,244	206	108	25,891	2,066	27,957	16,680	44,638
Spr 1997	**22,447**	**3,247**	**203**	**111**	**26,009**	**1,980**	**27,988**	**16,688**	**44,677**
Changes									
Win 96/7 - Spr 97	115	3	-3	3	118	-87	31	8	39
Per cent	*0.5*	*0.1*	*-1.4*	*2.7*	*0.5*	*-4.2*	*0.1*	*0.0*	*0.1*
MEN									
Spr 1979	13,302	1,442	..	..	14,743	763 X	15,507 X	4,177 X	19,684
Spr 1981	12,348	1,745	..	..	14,093	1,560 X	15,653 X	4,434 X	20,087
Spr 1983	11,601	1,751	212	..	13,565	1,815 X	15,379 X	4,952 X	20,332
Spr 1984	11,572	1,980	192	..	13,759	1,778 X	15,537 X	4,982 X	20,519
Spr 1984	11,572	1,980	192	..	13,759	1,838	15,596	4,923	20,519
Spr 1985	11,621	2,032	245	..	13,898	1,796	15,694	4,987	20,681
Spr 1986	11,528	2,050	266	..	13,846	1,796	15,642	5,165	20,806
Spr 1987	11,439	2,224	315	..	13,984	1,736	15,720	5,225	20,945
Spr 1988	11,794	2,369	326	..	14,491	1,408	15,899	5,153	21,052
Spr 1989	11,943	2,621	302	..	14,870	1,156	16,026	5,132	21,158
Spr 1990	12,038	2,641	288	..	14,971	1,106	16,077	5,172	21,249
Spr 1991	11,755	2,528	249	..	14,541	1,454	15,995	5,324	21,318
Spr 1992	11,320	2,370	239	54	13,982	1,804	15,786	5,583	21,369
Spr 1993	11,112	2,316	223	41	13,691	1,924	15,615	5,805	21,420
Sum 1993	11,261	2,332	210	47	13,850	1,941	15,791	5,641	21,432
Aut 1993	11,191	2,367	218	42	13,818	1,856	15,674	5,774	21,448
Win 1993/4	11,109	2,364	220	37	13,731	1,850	15,581	5,882	21,464
Spr 1994	11,168	2,407	211	47	13,833	1,765	15,598	5,882	21,479
Sum 1994	11,364	2,427	186	49	14,025	1,812	15,837	5,658	21,495
Aut 1994	11,324	2,482	195	44	14,044	1,639	15,684	5,832	21,516
Win 1994/5	11,243	2,458	190	41	13,931	1,616	15,547	5,990	21,537
Spr 1995	11,341	2,471	177	40	14,028	1,550	15,579	5,980	21,559
Sum 1995	11,558	2,449	152	44	14,203	1,608	15,811	5,769	21,580
Aut 1995	11,478	2,475	160	42	14,156	1,522	15,677	5,927	21,604
Win 1995/6	11,457	2,397	151	35	14,041	1,534	15,574	6,055	21,629
Spr 1996	11,514	2,392	145	40	14,091	1,495	15,585	6,068	21,654
Sum 1996	11,652	2,468	135	37	14,292	1,516	15,808	5,871	21,678
Aut 1996	11,643	2,486	124	40	14,293	1,415	15,708	5,995	21,703
Win 1996/7	11,683	2,430	122	37	14,272	1,315	15,587	6,141	21,728
Spr 1997	**11,784**	**2,402**	**125**	**37**	**14,348**	**1,265**	**15,613**	**6,141**	**21,753**
Changes									
Win 96/7 - Spr 97	101	-28	2	0	75	-50	26	-1	25
Per cent	*0.9*	*-1.1*	*2.0*	*-1.2*	*0.5*	*-3.8*	*0.2*	*0.0*	*0.1*
WOMEN									
Spr 1979	9,130	337	..	..	9,467	665 X	10,132 X	11,330 X	21,462
Spr 1981	9,057	455	..	..	9,512	923 X	10,435 X	11,417 X	21,852
Spr 1983	8,687	550	143	..	9,379	1,039 X	10,418 X	11,644 X	22,062
Spr 1984	8,943	636	119	..	9,708	1,148 X	10,856 X	11,344 X	22,200
Spr 1984	8,943	636	119	..	9,708	1,267	10,975	11,225	22,200
Spr 1985	9,126	682	145	..	9,952	1,194	11,146	11,184	22,330
Spr 1986	9,324	678	134	..	10,138	1,200	11,337	11,102	22,440
Spr 1987	9,453	745	183	..	10,384	1,176	11,560	10,983	22,543
Spr 1988	9,807	779	201	..	10,788	984	11,772	10,841	22,613
Spr 1989	10,225	820	176	..	11,224	833	12,057	10,624	22,681
Spr 1990	10,350	842	160	..	11,353	787	12,141	10,572	22,713
Spr 1991	10,279	802	164	..	11,251	875	12,127	10,633	22,760
Spr 1992	10,200	777	126	122	11,224	880	12,104	10,686	22,790
Spr 1993	10,201	792	118	104	11,215	925	12,141	10,656	22,797
Sum 1993	10,246	783	101	104	11,235	1,001	12,236	10,562	22,798
Aut 1993	10,250	797	112	98	11,257	986	12,242	10,556	22,798
Win 1993/4	10,189	801	108	98	11,197	940	12,136	10,662	22,798
Spr 1994	10,246	809	112	93	11,261	891	12,152	10,646	22,798
Sum 1994	10,335	797	94	89	11,316	923	12,239	10,559	22,798
Aut 1994	10,307	807	102	98	11,315	878	12,192	10,614	22,806
Win 1994/5	10,307	801	94	88	11,290	819	12,109	10,705	22,814
Spr 1995	10,334	798	96	93	11,321	826	12,147	10,675	22,822
Sum 1995	10,477	798	85	81	11,441	871	12,313	10,518	22,830
Aut 1995	10,499	791	91	88	11,469	861	12,330	10,513	22,843
Win 1995/6	10,525	790	91	83	11,490	765	12,255	10,601	22,856
Spr 1996	10,507	813	85	82	11,487	770	12,258	10,611	22,869
Sum 1996	10,584	827	74	77	11,562	811	12,373	10,509	22,881
Aut 1996	10,639	825	80	75	11,619	811	12,429	10,466	22,895
Win 1996/7	10,650	814	84	71	11,619	752	12,370	10,539	22,909
Spr 1997	**10,663**	**845**	**78**	**75**	**11,661**	**715**	**12,376**	**10,548**	**22,923**
Changes									
Win 96/7 - Spr 97	14	31	-5	3	43	-37	6	8	14
Per cent	*0.1*	*3.8*	*-6.5*	*4.7*	*0.4*	*-4.9*	*0.0*	*0.1*	*0.1*

+ Since 1984 the definitions used in the Labour Force Survey (LFS) have been fully in line with international recommendations. For details see 'The quarterly Labour Force Survey: a new dimension to labour market statistics', *Employment Gazette*, October 1992, pp 483-490.

\# People in full-time education who also did some paid work in the reference week have been classified as in employment since spring 1983.

§ Those on employment and training programmes have been classified as in employment since spring 1983. Some of those on government-supported training programmes may consider themselves to be employees or self-employed and so appear in other categories. Full information on those on government-supported training programmes is in *Table 8.1*.

X The Labour Force (LF) definition of unemployment and inactivity applies for these years. LF unemployment is based on a <u>one</u> week job search period, rather than <u>four</u> weeks with the ILO definition.

** Unpaid family workers have been classified as in employment since spring 1992.

++ Includes those who did not state whether they were employees or self-employed.

7.3 LABOUR FORCE SURVEY
Economic activity,+ by age

THOUSANDS

GREAT BRITAIN	SEASONALLY ADJUSTED §§			NOT SEASONALLY ADJUSTED							
	All aged 16 and over				Age groups						
	All	Men	Women	All	16-17	16-19	20-24	25-34	35-49	50-64 (Men) 50-59 (Women)	65 & over (M) 60 & over (W)
In employment *											
Spr 1984	23,626	13,845	9,780	23,467	819	1,956	2,942	5,189	7,878	4,780	722
Spr 1985	23,995	13,977	10,018	23,850	854	2,023	3,099	5,318	8,043	4,693	674
Spr 1986	24,117	13,920	10,197	23,984	848	1,984	3,124	5,467	8,159	4,606	644
Spr 1987	24,489	14,052	10,437	24,368	841	2,025	3,218	5,675	8,257	4,550	642
Spr 1988	25,389	14,552	10,836	25,279	925	2,122	3,291	6,043	8,571	4,583	670
Spr 1989	26,195	14,928	11,267	26,093	903	2,128	3,366	6,359	8,795	4,678	767
Spr 1990	26,421	15,029	11,393	26,324	801	1,972	3,287	6,616	8,968	4,713	767
Spr 1991	25,883	14,598	11,285	25,792	734	1,772	3,036	6,616	8,988	4,618	762
Spr 1992	25,255	14,025	11,230	25,206	633	1,510	2,830	6,555	8,979	4,536	797
Spr 1993	24,959	13,735	11,224	24,907	538	1,303	2,714	6,642	9,014	4,478	755
Spr 1994	25,150	13,877	11,273	25,093	547	1,278	2,612	6,740	9,116	4,582	765
Sum 1994	25,211	13,920	11,291	25,341	574	1,374	2,657	6,801	9,113	4,641	756
Aut 1994	25,293	14,007	11,286	25,359	574	1,313	2,609	6,833	9,158	4,678	769
Win 1994/5	25,338	14,022	11,316	25,221	587	1,308	2,513	6,810	9,175	4,645	770
Spr 1995	25,412	14,073	11,339	25,350	570	1,293	2,512	6,831	9,247	4,694	773
Sum 1995	25,515	14,098	11,417	25,644	619	1,404	2,638	6,887	9,221	4,723	771
Aut 1995	25,560	14,117	11,443	25,625	646	1,369	2,560	6,871	9,313	4,745	766
Win 1995/6	25,634	14,125	11,509	25,530	645	1,358	2,491	6,830	9,358	4,748	746
Spr 1996	25,645	14,137	11,509	25,578	620	1,351	2,446	6,833	9,406	4,793	749
Sum 1996	25,724	14,187	11,537	25,853	666	1,459	2,515	6,879	9,414	4,833	753
Aut 1996	25,851	14,258	11,593	25,912	679	1,425	2,435	6,932	9,479	4,894	747
Win 1996/7	25,985	14,353	11,632	25,891	674	1,417	2,395	6,926	9,443	4,959	751
Spr 1997	**26,076**	**14,395**	**11,681**	**26,009**	**657**	**1,434**	**2,354**	**6,951**	**9,459**	**5,028**	**782**
ILO unemployed *											
Spr 1984	3,143	1,861	1,282	3,105	227	551	630	723	691	450	59
Spr 1985	3,026	1,818	1,208	2,990	217	495	590	756	706	414	49
Spr 1986	3,031	1,817	1,214	2,996	223	490	607	759	686	408	46
Spr 1987	2,946	1,755	1,191	2,912	203	442	526	770	684	443	43
Spr 1988	2,424	1,425	999	2,392	152	332	432	627	556	405	40
Spr 1989	2,021	1,173	848	1,989	109	244	356	534	454	349	42
Spr 1990	1,925	1,122	803	1,894	103	256	331	509	447	317	35
Spr 1991	2,361	1,470	891	2,329	129	302	447	632	556	353	40
Spr 1992	2,745	1,835	910	2,684	121	295	499	754	691	415	31
Spr 1993	2,909	1,955	954	2,849	110	307	534	775	725	475	33
Spr 1994	2,716	1,797	919	2,656	121	294	454	741	686	455	25
Sum 1994	2,667	1,774	893	2,734	178	396	517	714	660	423	24
Aut 1994	2,523	1,664	859	2,517	140	311	445	690	643	400	28
Win 1994/5	2,457	1,611	845	2,434	115	271	424	680	648	391	22
Spr 1995	2,435	1,582	853	2,376	121	272	413	667	630	377	17
Sum 1995	2,408	1,566	842	2,479	180	374	446	644	635	361	19
Aut 1995	2,383	1,542	841	2,382	157	331	381	663	618	361	28
Win 1995/6	2,334	1,539	796	2,299	125	281	375	639	621	358	25
Spr 1996	2,321	1,525	796	2,265	142	298	360	641	596	352	19
Sum 1996	2,255	1,472	782	2,327	203	392	387	611	579	332	25
Aut 1996	2,221	1,432	789	2,226	181	347	371	591	551	339	25
Win 1996/7	2,111	1,326	785	2,066	149	299	334	552	546	310	26
Spr 1997	**2,037**	**1,294**	**743**	**1,980**	**143**	**280**	**315**	**524**	**525**	**314**	**22**
Economically inactive											
Spr 1984	15,951	4,813	11,138	16,148	708	1,078	813	1,586	1,656	2,247	8,768
Spr 1985	15,990	4,886	11,104	16,171	649	1,001	807	1,541	1,632	2,269	8,922
Spr 1986	16,100	5,071	11,029	16,267	615	971	811	1,521	1,656	2,283	9,024
Spr 1987	16,053	5,138	10,915	16,208	618	924	806	1,486	1,655	2,250	9,087
Spr 1988	15,852	5,074	10,778	15,994	549	860	784	1,441	1,576	2,238	9,096
Spr 1989	15,623	5,058	10,565	15,767	520	827	727	1,426	1,565	2,188	9,030
Spr 1990	15,616	5,099	10,517	15,745	532	841	737	1,420	1,514	2,167	9,065
Spr 1991	15,835	5,251	10,584	15,957	511	840	807	1,481	1,560	2,172	9,098
Spr 1992	16,159	5,509	10,650	16,269	579	999	896	1,535	1,554	2,198	9,086
Spr 1993	16,349	5,730	10,619	16,461	632	1,059	865	1,527	1,618	2,256	9,135
Spr 1994	16,412	5,806	10,606	16,528	586	1,023	898	1,526	1,668	2,277	9,135
Sum 1994	16,415	5,801	10,613	16,218	499	811	752	1,505	1,725	2,280	9,146
Aut 1994	16,507	5,846	10,661	16,446	553	960	834	1,500	1,731	2,289	9,132
Win 1994/5	16,557	5,904	10,653	16,695	581	1,007	913	1,534	1,743	2,356	9,141
Spr 1995	16,534	5,904	10,631	16,655	609	1,025	887	1,528	1,723	2,346	9,145
Sum 1995	16,487	5,916	10,571	16,287	516	814	690	1,498	1,779	2,357	9,149
Aut 1995	16,504	5,945	10,559	16,440	533	909	787	1,488	1,746	2,360	9,151
Win 1995/6	16,517	5,965	10,551	16,656	585	985	817	1,547	1,740	2,387	9,180
Spr 1996	16,556	5,992	10,564	16,679	613	991	831	1,536	1,758	2,387	9,188
Sum 1996	16,582	6,019	10,562	16,379	526	804	690	1,514	1,808	2,375	9,184
Aut 1996	16,527	6,014	10,513	16,461	542	905	744	1,458	1,769	2,379	9,197
Win 1996/7	16,542	6,050	10,492	16,680	585	982	781	1,482	1,808	2,387	9,199
Spr 1997	**16,564**	**6,064**	**10,500**	**16,688**	**613**	**1,006**	**799**	**1,463**	**1,809**	**2,432**	**9,179**
Economic activity rate + per cent											
Spr 1984	62.7	76.5	49.8	62.2	59.6	69.9	81.5	78.8	83.8	69.9	8.2
Spr 1985	62.8	76.4	50.3	62.4	62.3	71.6	82.0	79.7	84.3	69.2	7.5
Spr 1986	62.8	75.6	50.9	62.4	63.5	71.8	82.1	80.4	84.2	68.7	7.1
Spr 1987	63.1	75.5	51.6	62.7	62.8	72.8	82.3	81.3	84.4	68.9	7.0
Spr 1988	63.7	75.9	52.3	63.4	66.2	74.0	82.6	82.2	85.3	69.0	7.2
Spr 1989	64.4	76.1	53.4	64.1	66.0	74.1	83.8	82.9	85.5	69.7	8.3
Spr 1990	64.5	76.0	53.7	64.2	62.9	72.6	83.1	83.4	86.1	69.9	8.1
Spr 1991	64.1	75.4	53.5	63.8	62.8	71.2	81.2	83.0	86.0	69.6	8.1
Spr 1992	63.4	74.2	53.4	63.2	60.6	64.4	78.8	82.6	86.2	69.3	8.3
Spr 1993	63.0	73.2	53.4	62.8	50.6	60.3	79.0	82.9	85.8	68.7	7.9
Spr 1994	62.9	73.0	53.5	62.7	53.3	60.6	80.6	83.1	85.5	69.0	7.9
Sum 1994	62.9	73.0	53.4	63.4	60.1	68.6	80.9	83.3	85.5	69.0	7.9
Aut 1994	62.8	72.8	53.3	62.9	56.4	62.8	79.6	83.4	85.0	69.0	7.9
Win 1994/5	62.7	72.6	53.3	62.4	54.7	61.1	76.3	83.0	84.9	68.8	8.0
Spr 1995	62.7	72.6	53.4	62.5	53.1	60.4	76.7	83.1	85.1	68.4	8.0
Sum 1995	62.9	72.6	53.7	63.3	60.7	68.6	81.7	83.4	84.7	68.3	7.9
Aut 1995	62.9	72.5	53.8	63.0	60.1	65.2	78.9	83.5	85.0	68.4	8.0
Win 1995/6	62.9	72.4	53.8	62.6	56.8	62.5	77.8	82.8	85.2	68.1	7.7
Spr 1996	62.8	72.3	53.8	62.5	55.4	62.4	77.2	83.0	85.0	68.4	7.7
Sum 1996	62.8	72.2	53.8	63.2	62.3	69.7	80.8	83.2	84.7	68.5	7.8
Aut 1996	62.9	72.3	54.1	63.1	61.3	66.2	79.0	83.8	85.0	68.7	7.7
Win 1996/7	62.9	72.2	54.2	62.6	58.4	63.6	77.7	83.5	84.7	68.5	7.8
Spr 1997	**62.9**	**72.1**	**54.2**	**62.6**	**56.6**	**63.0**	**77.0**	**83.6**	**84.7**	**68.7**	**8.1**
ILO unemployment rate # per cent											
Spr 1984	11.7	11.8	11.6	11.7	21.7	22.0	17.6	12.2	8.1	8.6	7.5
Spr 1985	11.2	11.5	10.8	11.1	20.3	16.0	16.0	12.5	8.1	8.1	6.8
Spr 1986	11.2	11.5	10.6	11.1	20.8	19.8	16.3	12.2	7.8	8.1	6.6
Spr 1987	10.7	11.1	10.2	10.7	19.5	17.9	14.0	11.9	7.7	8.9	6.6
Spr 1988	8.7	8.9	8.4	8.6	14.1	13.5	11.6	9.4	6.1	8.1	5.6
Spr 1989	7.2	7.3	7.0	7.1	10.8	10.3	9.6	7.8	4.9	6.9	6.3
Spr 1990	6.8	6.9	6.6	6.7	11.4	11.5	9.1	7.1	4.7	6.3	4.4
Spr 1991	8.4	9.1	7.3	8.3	15.0	14.6	12.8	8.7	5.8	7.1	5.0
Spr 1992	9.8	11.6	7.5	9.6	16.1	16.3	15.0	10.3	7.1	8.4	3.8
Spr 1993	10.4	12.5	7.8	10.3	16.9	19.1	16.4	10.4	7.4	9.6	4.1
Spr 1994	9.7	11.5	7.5	9.6	18.1	18.7	14.8	9.9	7.0	9.0	3.2
Sum 1994	9.6	11.3	7.3	9.7	23.7	22.4	16.3	9.5	6.8	8.3	3.1
Aut 1994	9.1	10.6	7.1	9.0	19.6	19.1	14.6	9.2	6.6	7.9	3.6
Win 1994/5	8.8	10.3	6.9	8.8	16.4	17.2	14.4	9.1	6.6	7.8	2.8
Spr 1995	8.7	10.1	7.0	8.6	17.5	17.4	14.1	8.9	6.4	7.4	2.2
Sum 1995	8.6	10.0	6.9	8.8	22.6	21.0	14.5	8.6	6.4	7.1	2.4
Aut 1995	8.5	9.8	6.8	8.5	19.5	19.5	13.0	8.8	6.4	7.1	3.5
Win 1995/6	8.3	9.8	6.5	8.3	16.2	17.2	13.1	8.6	6.2	7.0	3.2
Spr 1996	8.3	9.7	6.5	8.1	18.6	18.1	12.8	8.6	6.0	6.8	2.5
Sum 1996	8.1	9.4	6.4	8.3	23.4	21.2	13.3	8.2	5.8	6.4	3.3
Aut 1996	7.9	9.1	6.4	7.9	21.1	19.6	13.2	7.9	5.5	6.5	3.3
Win 1996/7	7.5	8.5	6.3	7.4	18.1	17.4	12.2	7.4	5.5	5.9	3.3
Spr 1997	**7.2**	**8.2**	**6.0**	**7.1**	**17.9**	**16.3**	**11.8**	**7.0**	**5.3**	**5.9**	**2.8**

* The economic activity rate is the percentage of people aged 16 and over who are economically active.
+ See corresponding notes to *Table 1*.
\# The ILO unemployment rate is the percentage of economically active people who are unemployed on the ILO measure.
§§ Revised April 1997.

GREAT BRITAIN	All Full-time +			All Part-time in main job +			All persons with second job #		
	Total	Men	Women	Total	Men	Women	Total	Men	Women
All - Seasonally adjusted									
Spr 1984	18,657	13,222	5,435	4,872	562	4,310			
Spr 1985	18,947	13,356	5,591	5,027	611	4,415			
Spr 1986	19,006	13,290	5,717	5,079	613	4,466			
Spr 1987	19,181	13,345	5,836	5,268	684	4,584			
Spr 1988	19,924	13,774	6,149	5,417	749	4,667			
Spr 1989	20,469	14,110	6,359	5,699	802	4,897			
Spr 1990	20,649	14,149	6,500	5,765	875	4,891			
Spr 1991	20,108	13,714	6,394	5,769	879	4,890			
Spr 1992	19,347	13,044	6,303	5,901	977	4,924			
Spr 1993	18,979	12,730	6,249	5,974	1,003	4,971			
Spr 1994	19,019	12,793	6,226	6,122	1,080	5,042			
Spr 1995	19,253	12,942	6,311	6,156	1,129	5,026			
Sum 1995	19,273	12,958	6,315	6,237	1,137	5,099			
Aut 1995	19,263	12,961	6,301	6,295	1,154	5,141			
Win 1995/6	19,272	12,950	6,322	6,354	1,169	5,184			
Spr 1996	19,259	12,927	6,331	6,385	1,208	5,176			
Sum 1996	19,287	12,913	6,373	6,434	1,272	5,162			
Aut 1996	19,410	12,992	6,419	6,438	1,265	5,173			
Win 1996/7	19,485	13,068	6,416	6,498	1,283	5,215			
Spr 1997	**19,541**	**13,099**	**6,442**	**6,529**	**1,291**	**5,238**			
All - Not seasonally adjusted									
Spr 1984	18,495	13,100	5,395	4,874	597	4,277	701	378	323
Spr 1985	18,789	13,231	5,559	5,040	657	4,382	789	402	387
Spr 1986	18,821	13,139	5,682	5,131	690	4,441	823	411	412
Spr 1987	18,976	13,180	5,796	5,352	781	4,571	845	393	452
Spr 1988	19,743	13,625	6,118	5,488	837	4,651	976	453	523
Spr 1989	20,355	14,021	6,334	5,711	832	4,879	1,058	475	584
Spr 1990	20,538	14,063	6,475	5,779	903	4,877	1,079	513	566
Spr 1991	20,009	13,635	6,374	5,777	901	4,876	1,087	509	577
Spr 1992	19,267	12,988	6,279	5,932	990	4,942	970	441	529
Spr 1993	18,897	12,674	6,223	6,004	1,016	4,989	1,037	464	573
Spr 1994	18,933	12,737	6,197	6,152	1,093	5,058	1,142	501	641
Spr 1995	19,164	12,885	6,279	6,183	1,143	5,040	1,280	536	744
Sum 1995	19,416	13,060	6,356	6,222	1,139	5,083	1,291	531	760
Aut 1995	19,341	13,011	6,331	6,280	1,143	5,137	1,305	555	751
Win 1995/6	19,168	12,870	6,297	6,354	1,164	5,190	1,271	533	738
Spr 1996	19,166	12,869	6,297	6,410	1,221	5,189	1,284	543	742
Sum 1996	19,430	13,013	6,416	6,421	1,277	5,144	1,260	569	691
Aut 1996	19,489	13,039	6,450	6,421	1,253	5,168	1,231	549	682
Win 1996/7	19,386	12,994	6,392	6,502	1,277	5,225	1,221	543	678
Spr 1997	**19,451**	**13,043**	**6,408**	**6,554**	**1,302**	**5,252**	**1,239**	**543**	**696**
Employees - Seasonally adjusted									
Spr 1984	16,291	11,218	5,073	4,369	416	3,953			
Spr 1985	16,441	11,254	5,188	4,443	426	4,017			
Spr 1986	16,437	11,132	5,305	4,531	444	4,087			
Spr 1987	16,364	10,995	5,369	4,631	485	4,146			
Spr 1988	16,931	11,280	5,651	4,773	556	4,218			
Spr 1989	17,296	11,449	5,847	4,970	534	4,436			
Spr 1990	17,476	11,497	5,979	5,010	584	4,426			
Spr 1991	17,068	11,179	5,889	5,062	622	4,440			
Spr 1992	16,523	10,713	5,811	5,051	649	4,402			
Spr 1993	16,258	10,486	5,772	5,111	667	4,443			
Spr 1994	16,229	10,482	5,747	5,240	726	4,513			
Spr 1995	16,432	10,589	5,843	5,304	790	4,513			
Sum 1995	16,499	10,649	5,850	5,393	797	4,596			
Aut 1995	16,481	10,647	5,835	5,463	821	4,641			
Win 1995/6	16,531	10,680	5,851	5,529	842	4,687			
Spr 1996	16,535	10,674	5,860	5,550	876	4,673			
Sum 1996	16,508	10,605	5,903	5,588	937	4,651			
Aut 1996	16,650	10,704	5,946	5,601	933	4,668			
Win 1996/7	16,718	10,775	5,943	5,681	966	4,714			
Spr 1997	**16,817**	**10,844**	**5,974**	**5,688**	**972**	**4,716**			
Employees - Not seasonally adjusted									
Spr 1984	16,145	11,139	5,006	4,356	424	3,932	446	212	235
Spr 1985	16,306	11,183	5,123	4,435	435	4,000	525	234	290
Spr 1986	16,312	11,069	5,242	4,527	452	4,075	536	230	306
Spr 1987	16,247	10,939	5,308	4,631	494	4,137	575	222	353
Spr 1988	16,821	11,229	5,592	4,777	564	4,213	667	263	405
Spr 1989	17,188	11,399	5,790	4,976	543	4,433	711	267	443
Spr 1990	17,368	11,444	5,924	5,018	593	4,425	727	290	437
Spr 1991	16,961	11,123	5,839	5,071	631	4,441	746	296	450
Spr 1992	16,435	10,658	5,777	5,082	660	4,422	679	251	429
Spr 1993	16,169	10,432	5,737	5,142	678	4,463	699	259	439
Win 1993/4	16,112	10,395	5,717	5,183	713	4,470	762	280	482
Spr 1994	16,139	10,429	5,710	5,270	738	4,532	795	298	497
Spr 1995	16,340	10,539	5,802	5,333	803	4,530	899	313	586
Sum 1995	16,641	10,751	5,890	5,390	806	4,585	909	312	597
Aut 1995	16,533	10,671	5,862	5,443	807	4,636	900	311	589
Win 1995/6	16,455	10,622	5,833	5,525	834	4,692	885	299	586
Spr 1996	16,441	10,624	5,817	5,579	889	4,689	903	313	591
Sum 1996	16,650	10,704	5,946	5,585	948	4,637	884	333	552
Aut 1996	16,702	10,725	5,976	5,579	917	4,662	858	317	541
Win 1996/7	16,649	10,724	5,925	5,682	958	4,724	867	322	544
Spr 1997	**16,736**	**10,801**	**5,935**	**5,710**	**982**	**4,728**	**868**	**316**	**552**
Self-employed - Seasonally adjusted									
Spr 1984	2,156	1,848	307	449	138	311			
Spr 1985	2,241	1,903	338	462	135	326			
Spr 1986	2,279	1,932	347	437	125	312			
Spr 1987	2,452	2,074	378	504	155	348			
Spr 1988	2,627	2,224	403	508	150	358			
Spr 1989	2,880	2,445	435	547	180	367			
Spr 1990	2,915	2,460	456	554	186	368			
Spr 1991	2,807	2,371	436	512	164	348			
Spr 1992	2,610	2,197	413	537	178	360			
Spr 1993	2,537	2,124	413	572	197	374			
Spr 1994	2,616	2,201	415	602	212	390			
Spr 1995	2,655	2,252	403	619	227	392			
Sum 1995	2,619	2,217	402	621	228	393			
Aut 1995	2,625	2,221	404	613	227	386			
Win 1995/6	2,586	2,183	403	633	235	397			
Spr 1996	2,574	2,168	406	639	235	404			
Sum 1996	2,632	2,224	409	655	242	414			
Aut 1996	2,620	2,212	409	662	247	415			
Win 1996/7	2,625	2,213	412	651	240	411			
Spr 1997	**2,580**	**2,169**	**411**	**679**	**251**	**428**			
Self-employed - Not seasonally adjusted									
Spr 1984	2,166	1,846	320	448	132	315	246	161	85
Spr 1985	2,253	1,902	351	461	130	331	260	165	95
Spr 1986	2,291	1,930	360	436	119	317	283	179	105
Spr 1987	2,464	2,073	391	503	150	353	270	171	99
Spr 1988	2,639	2,223	416	507	145	363	308	190	118
Spr 1989	2,892	2,445	448	547	175	372	347	207	140
Spr 1990	2,928	2,459	469	553	180	373	352	222	130
Spr 1991	2,819	2,370	449	511	158	353	340	212	127
Spr 1992	2,611	2,195	416	536	175	360	290	190	100
Spr 1993	2,537	2,121	416	569	198	375	337	205	132
Win 1993/4	2,581	2,166	415	584	198	386	319	187	132
Spr 1994	2,616	2,197	419	599	209	390	345	203	142
Spr 1995	2,654	2,247	407	614	223	391	379	221	158
Sum 1995	2,623	2,221	403	623	227	396	382	219	163
Aut 1995	2,651	2,246	405	614	228	386	405	244	161
Win 1995/6	2,556	2,160	396	631	237	394	385	234	151
Spr 1996	2,571	2,161	411	634	231	403	380	230	151
Sum 1996	2,636	2,227	409	658	240	417	376	236	139
Aut 1996	2,648	2,238	410	663	248	415	371	232	139
Win 1996/7	2,593	2,188	405	650	242	408	353	220	133
Spr 1997	**2,570**	**2,154**	**416**	**675**	**247**	**428**	**370**	**226**	**144**

+ People whose main job is full-time. The definition of full- and part-time for employees and self employed, those on employer-based schemes and unpaid family workers is based on the respondents' own assessment. Those on college-based schemes have been included with part-timers.

\# Second jobs reported in LFS in addition to person's main full-time or part-time job. Excludes those who have changed jobs within the reference week.

7.5 LABOUR FORCE SURVEY
Alternative measures of unemployment

THOUSANDS

GREAT BRITAIN	ILO unemployment measure Seasonally adjusted				Claimant unemployment measure +		Not ILO unemployed		
	Claimants	Non claimants	Total	Difference	Total #	ILO unemployed	Economically inactive	In employment	Total
ALL									
Spr 1984			3,143	369	2,774				
Spr 1985			3,026	115	2,911				
Spr 1986			3,031	38	2,993				
Spr 1987			2,946	147	2,799				
Spr 1988			2,424	154	2,270				
Spr 1989			2,021	279	1,742				
Spr 1990			1,925	422	1,502				
Spr 1991			2,361	294	2,067				
Spr 1992	1,798	947	2,745	157	2,588	1,798	496	294	790
Sum 1992	1,828	957	2,785	126	2,659	1,828	568	264	831
Aut 1992	1,883	974	2,857	94	2,763	1,883	543	337	880
Win 1992/3	1,938	1,027	2,965	104	2,861	1,938	584	339	923
Spr 1993	1,909	1,000	2,909	72	2,837	1,909	574	354	928
Sum 1993	1,862	1,017	2,879	72	2,807	1,862	633	312	945
Aut 1993	1,820	1,031	2,851	104	2,747	1,820	584	343	927
Win 1993/4	1,762	1,036	2,798	123	2,675	1,762	583	330	913
Spr 1994	1,698	1,018	2,716	119	2,597	1,698	559	340	899
Sum 1994	1,657	1,010	2,667	150	2,518	1,657	544	317	861
Aut 1994	1,551	972	2,523	105	2,417	1,551	536	330	866
Win 1994/5	1,480	977	2,457	149	2,307	1,480	544	284	828
Spr 1995	1,443	991	2,435	189	2,246	1,443	500	303	803
Sum 1995	1,399	1,009	2,408	191	2,217	1,399	519	299	818
Aut 1995	1,412	971	2,383	212	2,171	1,412	494	265	759
Win 1995/6	1,379	956	2,334	202	2,132	1,379	474	279	753
Spr 1996	1,327	994	2,321	229	2,093	1,327	468	297	766
Sum 1996	1,255	999	2,255	213	2,041	1,255	481	305	786
Aut 1996	1,147	1,075	2,221	293	1,928	1,147	470	311	781
Win 1996/7	1,060	1,050	2,111	367	1,744	1,060	412	272	684
Spr 1997	**1,036**	**1,001**	**2,037**	**435**	**1,602**	**1,036**	**299**	**267**	**566**
Changes									
Win 96/7 - Spr 97	*-24*	*-49*	*-74*		*-142*	*-24*	*-113*	*-5*	*-118*
Spr 96 - Spr 97	*-291*	*6*	*-285*		*-491*	*-291*	*-169*	*-31*	*-200*
MEN									
Spr 1984			1,861	-95	1,956				
Spr 1985			1,818	-208	2,026				
Spr 1986			1,817	-251	2,067				
Spr 1987			1,755	-188	1,943				
Spr 1988			1,425	-150	1,575				
Spr 1989			1,173	-62	1,234				
Spr 1990			1,122	22	1,100				
Spr 1991			1,470	-92	1,562				
Spr 1992	1,409	426	1,835	-146	1,981	1,409	354	218	572
Sum 1992	1,437	420	1,857	-181	2,038	1,437	404	197	601
Aut 1992	1,482	436	1,919	-202	2,120	1,482	379	259	638
Win 1992/3	1,516	467	1,983	-212	2,195	1,516	420	259	679
Spr 1993	1,481	474	1,955	-221	2,176	1,481	416	280	695
Sum 1993	1,443	464	1,907	-247	2,154	1,443	468	243	711
Aut 1993	1,403	479	1,882	-224	2,106	1,403	434	269	703
Win 1993/4	1,364	473	1,837	-217	2,053	1,364	431	259	690
Spr 1994	1,320	476	1,797	-194	1,990	1,320	396	274	670
Sum 1994	1,287	487	1,774	-149	1,923	1,287	385	251	636
Aut 1994	1,217	446	1,664	-182	1,846	1,217	372	257	628
Win 1994/5	1,147	465	1,611	-149	1,761	1,147	393	221	614
Spr 1995	1,129	452	1,582	-131	1,712	1,129	345	238	583
Sum 1995	1,084	482	1,566	-122	1,688	1,084	369	235	604
Aut 1995	1,092	451	1,542	-110	1,653	1,092	357	204	561
Win 1995/6	1,085	454	1,539	-85	1,624	1,085	330	209	539
Spr 1996	1,034	491	1,525	-66	1,591	1,034	336	221	557
Sum 1996	987	485	1,472	-76	1,548	987	335	226	561
Aut 1996	894	538	1,432	-32	1,464	894	340	230	570
Win 1996/7	814	512	1,326	-4	1,329	814	312	204	515
Spr 1997	**803**	**491**	**1,294**	**69**	**1,225**	**803**	**229**	**193**	**422**
Changes									
Win 96/7 - Spr 97	*-11*	*-20*	*-32*		*-104*	*-11*	*-83*	*-10*	*-93*
Spr 96 - Spr 97	*-232*	*1*	*-231*		*-367*	*-232*	*-108*	*-27*	*-135*
WOMEN									
Spr 1984			1,282	464	817				
Spr 1985			1,208	323	885				
Spr 1986			1,214	288	926				
Spr 1987			1,191	335	856				
Spr 1988			999	304	695				
Spr 1989			848	340	508				
Spr 1990			803	401	402				
Spr 1991			891	386	505				
Spr 1992	389	520	910	303	607	389	142	76	218
Sum 1992	391	537	928	307	622	391	164	67	231
Aut 1992	401	538	938	295	643	401	164	78	242
Win 1992/3	422	560	982	316	665	422	164	80	244
Spr 1993	428	526	954	294	661	428	158	75	232
Sum 1993	418	553	972	319	653	418	165	70	234
Aut 1993	417	552	969	328	641	417	151	74	224
Win 1993/4	398	563	961	340	621	398	152	72	223
Spr 1994	378	541	919	313	607	378	163	65	228
Sum 1994	370	524	893	299	595	370	159	66	225
Aut 1994	334	525	859	287	572	334	165	73	238
Win 1994/5	333	512	845	299	547	333	151	63	214
Spr 1995	314	539	853	319	533	314	154	65	220
Sum 1995	316	527	842	313	529	316	150	64	214
Aut 1995	320	521	841	322	519	320	137	61	198
Win 1995/6	294	502	796	287	509	294	144	71	215
Spr 1996	293	504	796	295	501	293	132	77	209
Sum 1996	268	514	782	289	493	268	146	80	225
Aut 1996	253	537	789	326	464	253	130	82	211
Win 1996/7	247	538	785	370	415	247	100	68	168
Spr 1997	**233**	**509**	**743**	**365**	**377**	**233**	**70**	**74**	**144**
Changes									
Win 96/7 - Spr 97	*-13*	*-29*	*-42*		*-49*	*131*	*133*	*2*	*-95*
Spr 96 - Spr 97	*-59*	*6*	*-53*		*-136*	*85*	*102*	*-7*	*-135*

+ The figures are derived with reference to both the claimant count and the LFS results; the total is controlled to the actual claimant count. For a full description of the method, see the technical note to the article 'Measures of unemployment: the claimant count and the LFS compared' in the October 1993 issue of the *Employment Gazette*.
\# The claimant count figures shown are the averages of the published figures for the months of each LFS quarter.
§§ Revised April 1997.

GREAT BRITAIN — ILO unemployment measure — Not seasonally adjusted — Claimant unemployment measure +

	ILO unemployment measure				Claimant unemployment measure +		Not ILO unemployed		
	Claimants	Non claimants	Total	Difference	Total #	ILO unemployed	Economically inactive	In employment	Total
ALL									
Spr 1984	2,233	872	3,105	114	2,991	2,233	574	184	758
Spr 1985	2,164	826	2,990	-149	3,139	2,164	778	197	975
Spr 1986	2,202	794	2,996	-186	3,181	2,202	783	196	980
Spr 1987	2,096	815	2,912	-41	2,952	2,096	673	183	856
Spr 1988	1,655	737	2,392	-10	2,401	1,655	568	178	746
Spr 1989	1,143	846	1,989	214	1,775	1,143	423	209	632
Spr 1990	1,034	860	1,894	373	1,520	1,034	300	186	486
Spr 1991	1,447	883	2,329	243	2,086	1,447	390	250	640
Spr 1992	1,790	894	2,684	71	2,613	1,790	517	306	823
Sum 1992	1,828	1,018	2,846	189	2,657	1,828	567	263	829
Aut 1992	1,861	987	2,847	113	2,735	1,861	540	335	874
Win 1992/3	1,970	997	2,967	45	2,922	1,970	602	350	952
Spr 1993	1,901	948	2,849	-18	2,867	1,901	598	368	966
Sum 1993	1,862	1,080	2,942	131	2,811	1,862	636	313	949
Aut 1993	1,797	1,045	2,842	120	2,721	1,797	583	342	924
Win 1993/4	1,791	999	2,790	53	2,737	1,791	604	342	946
Spr 1994	1,689	967	2,656	32	2,624	1,689	582	353	935
Sum 1994	1,658	1,077	2,734	212	2,523	1,658	547	318	865
Aut 1994	1,526	991	2,517	125	2,392	1,526	536	329	866
Win 1994/5	1,505	930	2,435	66	2,369	1,505	567	296	864
Spr 1995	1,434	942	2,376	105	2,271	1,434	521	315	837
Sum 1995	1,402	1,077	2,479	255	2,224	1,402	522	300	822
Aut 1995	1,385	998	2,382	235	2,147	1,385	496	266	762
Win 1995/6	1,400	899	2,299	104	2,195	1,400	500	295	795
Spr 1996	1,318	947	2,265	149	2,116	1,318	488	310	798
Sum 1996	1,259	1,068	2,327	273	2,054	1,259	487	309	796
Aut 1996	1,118	1,108	2,226	324	1,902	1,118	472	313	785
Win 1996/7	**1,079**	**987**	**2,066**	**269**	**1,798**	**1,079**	**433**	**286**	**718**
MEN									
Spr 1984	1,607	231	1,838	-257	2,094	1,607	367	121	488
Spr 1985	1,567	229	1,796	-377	2,173	1,567	487	118	605
Spr 1986	1,571	225	1,796	-392	2,188	1,571	492	125	617
Spr 1987	1,490	246	1,736	-311	2,047	1,490	435	122	557
Spr 1988	1,176	231	1,408	-260	1,667	1,176	373	118	491
Spr 1989	834	322	1,156	-114	1,270	834	294	142	436
Spr 1990	777	329	1,106	-14	1,120	777	206	137	344
Spr 1991	1,111	343	1,454	-129	1,583	1,111	278	194	472
Spr 1992	1,415	390	1,804	-202	2,006	1,415	366	225	591
Sum 1992	1,430	457	1,888	-136	2,024	1,430	399	195	594
Aut 1992	1,457	436	1,893	-196	2,089	1,457	375	256	632
Win 1992/3	1,546	458	2,003	-244	2,247	1,546	434	267	702
Spr 1993	1,487	437	1,924	-281	2,204	1,487	429	289	718
Sum 1993	1,437	504	1,941	-203	2,144	1,437	466	241	707
Aut 1993	1,378	478	1,856	-220	2,076	1,378	431	267	698
Win 1993/4	1,391	460	1,850	-256	2,106	1,391	447	268	716
Spr 1994	1,325	440	1,765	-252	2,017	1,325	409	283	692
Sum 1994	1,281	530	1,812	-101	1,913	1,281	382	250	632
Aut 1994	1,191	449	1,639	-176	1,815	1,191	370	255	624
Win 1994/5	1,171	445	1,616	-198	1,813	1,171	411	231	642
Spr 1995	1,134	416	1,550	-187	1,738	1,134	357	246	603
Sum 1995	1,080	528	1,608	-71	1,679	1,080	366	233	599
Aut 1995	1,064	458	1,522	-102	1,623	1,064	356	204	559
Win 1995/6	1,107	427	1,534	-144	1,677	1,107	350	221	571
Spr 1996	1,040	455	1,495	-121	1,616	1,040	348	228	576
Sum 1996	984	532	1,516	-27	1,543	984	334	225	559
Aut 1996	865	550	1,415	-19	1,434	865	339	229	569
Win 1996/7	**834**	**481**	**1,315**	**-62**	**1,377**	**834**	**329**	**215**	**543**
WOMEN									
Spr 1984	627	641	1,267	370	897	627	208	63	270
Spr 1985	597	597	1,194	228	966	597	291	78	370
Spr 1986	631	569	1,200	206	993	631	291	71	363
Spr 1987	607	569	1,176	271	905	607	238	61	299
Spr 1988	479	505	984	250	734	479	196	59	255
Spr 1989	309	524	833	328	505	309	129	67	196
Spr 1990	257	530	787	388	400	257	94	48	142
Spr 1991	336	540	875	372	503	336	112	56	167
Spr 1992	375	505	880	273	607	375	151	81	232
Sum 1992	398	561	958	325	633	398	167	68	235
Aut 1992	403	551	954	308	646	403	164	78	243
Win 1992/3	425	539	964	289	675	425	168	82	250
Spr 1993	414	511	925	263	662	414	169	80	248
Sum 1993	425	576	1,001	334	667	425	170	72	242
Aut 1993	419	567	986	340	645	419	152	75	227
Win 1993/4	400	540	940	309	631	400	157	74	231
Spr 1994	364	527	891	284	607	364	173	70	243
Sum 1994	376	547	923	313	610	376	165	68	234
Aut 1994	335	542	878	301	576	335	167	74	241
Win 1994/5	334	485	819	264	556	334	156	65	222
Spr 1995	300	526	826	293	533	300	164	69	233
Sum 1995	322	549	871	326	545	322	156	66	223
Aut 1995	321	540	861	337	524	321	141	62	203
Win 1995/6	294	471	765	248	518	294	150	74	224
Spr 1996	279	492	770	270	501	279	140	82	222
Sum 1996	275	536	811	300	511	275	153	84	236
Aut 1996	253	558	811	342	469	253	133	83	216
Win 1996/7	**246**	**506**	**752**	**331**	**421**	**246**	**104**	**71**	**175**

+ The figures are derived with reference to both the claimant count and the LFS results; the total is controlled to the actual claimant count. For a full description of the method, see the technical note to the article 'Measures of unemployment: the claimant count and the LFS compared' in the October 1993 issue of the *Employment Gazette*.

\# The claimant count figures shown are the averages of the published figures for the months of each LFS quarter.

THOUSANDS

GREAT BRITAIN — All who received job-related training in the last 4 weeks

	Seasonally adjusted	Not seasonally adjusted					
			Age groups				
	All of working age +	All of working age +	16-19	20-24	25-34	35-49	50-59/64
ALL							
Spr 1985	1,951	2,128	410	464	559	546	148
Spr 1986	2,032	2,213	374	470	613	598	159
Spr 1987	2,196	2,430	363	504	694	694	164
Spr 1988	2,585	2,833	411	565	793	849	200
Spr 1989	2,905	3,136	407	594	881	983	255
Spr 1990	3,132	3,381	421	614	973	1,067	284
Spr 1991	2,944	3,209	364	529	960	1,051	281
Spr 1992	2,829	3,064	296	504	918	1,060	286
Spr 1993	2,826	3,057	258	496	940	1,089	275
Aut 1994 $	2,702	2,782	215	405	878	1,006	278
Win 1994/5 $	2,752	2,764	238	402	859	989	275
Spr 1995 $	2,806	3,026	222	431	980	1,081	311
Sum 1995 $	2,928	2,619	176	386	844	940	272
Aut 1995 $	2,952	3,030	255	447	952	1,081	295
Win 1995/6 $	2,978	2,988	275	444	948	1,019	302
Spr 1996 $	3,003	3,208	286	463	1,024	1,136	300
Sum 1996$	3,047	2,724	226	385	879	958	276
Aut 1996 $	3,043	3,116	285	416	1,013	1,094	308
Win 1996/7 $	**3,116**	**3,137**	**310**	**428**	**978**	**1,101**	**321**
MEN							
Spr 1985	1,151	1,293	251	277	356	324	86
Spr 1986	1,170	1,308	224	267	374	348	94
Spr 1987	1,225	1,373	212	282	415	368	85
Spr 1988	1,417	1,569	236	312	455	448	103
Spr 1989	1,557	1,706	230	320	517	498	124
Spr 1990	1,669	1,825	253	324	534	542	150
Spr 1991	1,565	1,717	207	292	531	512	149
Spr 1992	1,488	1,608	167	256	505	526	153
Spr 1993	1,457	1,573	142	261	501	522	147
Aut 1994 $	1,362	1,390	117	200	468	469	137
Win 1994/95 $	1,396	1,405	131	206	468	457	143
Spr 1995 $	1,422	1,529	118	215	526	514	155
Sum 1995 $	1,495	1,353	90	195	470	463	135
Aut 1995 $	1,507	1,536	136	221	518	518	144
Win 1995/96 $	1,506	1,513	147	229	520	467	150
Spr 1996 $	1,511	1,615	157	239	555	521	143
Sum 1996$	1,544	1,395	126	192	475	462	140
Aut 1996 $	1,499	1,524	149	200	519	505	151
Win 1996/7 $	**1,531**	**1,538**	**161**	**211**	**514**	**500**	**152**
WOMEN							
Spr 1985	800	835	159	188	203	222	63
Spr 1986	863	906	150	202	239	249	65
Spr 1987	971	1,057	150	222	279	326	78
Spr 1988	1,168	1,264	176	253	338	401	96
Spr 1989	1,349	1,430	177	273	364	485	131
Spr 1990	1,463	1,556	168	290	439	524	134
Spr 1991	1,379	1,493	157	237	428	539	131
Spr 1992	1,341	1,456	129	248	413	534	132
Spr 1993	1,370	1,484	116	235	439	566	128
Aut 1994 $	1,340	1,392	97	205	411	538	141
Win 1994/95 $	1,356	1,359	107	196	392	533	132
Spr 1995 $	1,383	1,497	104	216	455	567	155
Sum 1995 $	1,433	1,266	85	192	374	478	137
Aut 1995 $	1,444	1,493	119	225	434	563	151
Win 1995/96 $	1,472	1,475	128	215	429	552	152
Spr 1996 $	1,492	1,594	129	223	470	615	157
Sum 1996$	1,503	1,329	100	193	404	496	136
Aut 1996 $	1,544	1,592	136	217	493	590	157
Win 1996/7 $	**1,585**	**1,599**	**148**	**217**	**464**	**601**	**169**

% of all employees #

PER CENT

	Seasonally adjusted	Not seasonally adjusted					
			Age groups				
	All of working age +	All of working age +	16-19	20-24	25-34	35-49	50-59/64
ALL							
Spr 1985	9.6	10.5	24.2	16.1	11.9	7.9	3.6
Spr 1986	9.9	10.9	22.3	16.3	12.6	8.6	4.0
Spr 1987	10.7	11.9	21.6	17.2	14.0	9.9	4.9
Spr 1988	12.2	13.4	23.4	18.9	15.1	11.8	6.0
Spr 1989	13.4	14.5	23.3	19.4	16.1	13.3	7.5
Spr 1990	14.3	15.5	25.5	20.6	17.0	14.2	8.3
Spr 1991	13.7	15.0	24.4	19.0	16.7	14.0	8.4
Spr 1992	13.5	14.6	23.4	19.2	16.1	14.0	7.6
Spr 1993	13.6	14.7	23.8	19.6	16.1	14.3	7.4
Aut 1994 $	12.8	13.2	19.3	16.7	14.6	13.0	7.3
Win 1994/5 $	13.0	13.2	21.4	17.2	14.2	12.8	7.3
Spr 1995 $	13.2	14.3	20.1	18.5	16.2	13.8	8.2
Sum 1995 $	13.7	12.2	14.4	15.6	13.8	12.0	7.1
Aut 1995 $	13.8	14.1	21.5	18.7	15.6	13.7	7.7
Win 1995/6 $	13.8	13.9	23.2	19.1	15.5	12.8	7.8
Spr 1996 $	13.9	14.9	23.9	20.3	16.7	14.2	7.7
Sum 1996$	14.1	12.6	17.2	16.4	14.3	12.0	7.1
Aut 1996 $	14.0	14.3	22.3	18.3	16.3	13.6	7.8
Win 1996/7 $	**14.3**	**14.4**	**24.3**	**19.0**	**15.8**	**13.7**	**8.0**
MEN							
Spr 1985	10.0	11.3	29.5	17.9	12.6	8.7	3.4
Spr 1986	10.2	11.5	26.8	17.7	13.1	9.3	3.8
Spr 1987	10.8	12.1	25.9	18.2	14.4	9.9	4.8
Spr 1988	12.1	13.5	26.6	19.9	15.1	11.8	5.6
Spr 1989	13.2	14.5	26.7	20.0	16.8	12.9	6.8
Spr 1990	14.0	15.4	30.3	20.8	16.7	13.8	8.3
Spr 1991	13.4	14.8	27.8	20.3	16.6	13.2	8.3
Spr 1992	13.3	14.4	26.8	20.3	16.6	13.6	6.9
Spr 1993	13.2	14.3	27.3	20.1	15.8	13.5	7.0
Aut 1994 $	12.2	12.4	21.5	15.7	14.2	11.8	6.4
Win 1994/5 $	12.5	12.7	24.1	16.8	14.3	11.5	6.9
Spr 1995 $	12.6	13.7	21.9	17.6	16.0	12.8	7.9
Sum 1995 $	13.2	11.8	15.2	14.9	14.1	11.5	6.3
Aut 1995 $	13.3	13.5	23.2	17.6	15.7	12.8	6.7
Win 1995/6 $	13.2	13.4	25.1	19.0	15.7	11.5	6.9
Spr 1996 $	13.2	14.2	26.2	20.3	16.6	12.8	6.5
Sum 1996$	13.5	12.1	19.0	15.8	14.2	11.3	6.4
Aut 1996 $	13.1	13.2	23.2	16.8	15.5	12.3	6.8
Win 1996/7 $	**13.2**	**13.3**	**25.5**	**17.9**	**15.2**	**12.2**	**6.7**
WOMEN							
Spr 1985	9.1	9.5	18.9	13.9	10.8	7.1	4.1
Spr 1986	9.6	10.1	17.8	14.7	11.9	7.7	4.3
Spr 1987	10.6	11.6	17.5	16.0	13.4	10.0	5.2
Spr 1988	12.3	13.4	20.2	17.9	15.0	11.8	6.4
Spr 1989	13.7	14.6	20.0	18.8	15.2	13.9	8.3
Spr 1990	14.7	15.7	20.6	20.4	17.4	14.7	8.4
Spr 1991	13.9	15.1	20.9	17.7	16.8	14.8	8.4
Spr 1992	13.7	14.9	20.2	19.1	15.9	14.4	8.5
Spr 1993	14.0	15.2	20.6	19.0	16.4	15.1	8.1
Aut 1994 $	13.5	14.0	17.1	17.7	14.9	14.3	8.1
Win 1994/5 $	13.6	13.7	18.9	17.5	14.1	14.1	8.4
Spr 1995 $	13.9	15.1	18.4	19.4	16.4	14.9	7.9
Sum 1995 $	14.3	12.6	13.5	16.3	13.4	12.6	9.3
Aut 1995 $	14.3	14.8	19.7	19.8	15.5	14.6	8.9
Win 1995/6 $	14.5	14.6	21.4	19.1	15.3	14.2	9.0
Spr 1996 $	14.7	15.8	21.6	20.2	16.9	15.7	9.2
Sum 1996$	14.8	13.0	15.4	17.0	14.5	12.7	8.0
Aut 1996 $	15.1	15.6	21.4	19.9	17.4	14.9	9.1
Win 1996/7 $	**15.5**	**15.6**	**23.2**	**20.2**	**16.4**	**15.2**	**9.6**

+ Men aged 16-64 and women aged 16-59.
# Employees receiving job-related training as a percentage of employees in the relevant age group.
$ Data for summer 1994 onwards are not comparable with earlier periods.

GREAT BRITAIN SIC 92 (Standard Industrial Classification)

	Seasonally adjusted		Not seasonally adjusted											
	Total (millions) #§	Average	Total (millions) #§	Average	Agriculture and fishing	Energy and water	Manufac-turing	Constr -uction	Distribution hotels & catering	Transport & comms	Banking, finance & insurance etc	Public admin education & health	Other services	Total Services
					A-B	C,E	D	F	G,H	I	J,K	L-N	O-Q	G-Q
ALL														
Spr 1984	782	33.1	790	33.7	47.7	28.2	36.3	38.2	32.5	37.8	34.5	29.1	30.2	31.7
Spr 1985	810	33.8	818	34.4	47.1	35.0	37.1	38.2	33.1	38.6	33.6	29.8	30.1	32.3
Spr 1986	814	33.8	823	34.4	47.4	36.9	37.2	38.3	33.2	38.9	33.9	29.2	30.6	32.3
Spr 1987	821	33.6	830	34.1	47.4	36.2	37.1	38.3	32.8	39.0	33.1	28.9	31.4	32.1
Spr 1988	872	34.4	882	34.9	47.7	37.0	38.1	39.8	33.2	39.4	34.4	29.7	31.4	32.7
Spr 1989	894	34.2	905	34.7	49.0	37.4	37.6	39.3	33.1	39.7	34.0	29.3	31.5	32.6
Spr 1990	894	33.9	905	34.4	47.5	37.2	37.5	39.4	32.7	38.4	33.9	29.0	31.8	32.2
Spr 1991	876	33.9	887	34.4	48.0	37.8	37.2	39.0	32.7	38.7	33.9	29.7	31.2	32.4
Spr 1992	832	33.1	835	33.3	45.8	37.0	36.2	37.1	32.1	37.7	33.1	28.8	30.6	33.2
Sum 1992	829	33.1	828	32.9	45.7	36.9	35.8	37.7	32.1	37.3	32.8	27.3	30.5	31.0
Aut 1992	826	33.2	853	34.1	43.7	37.6	37.4	38.5	32.3	38.3	33.8	30.0	31.1	32.3
Win 1992/3	822	33.1	795	32.2	40.4	36.2	34.5	35.0	31.0	36.8	32.3	28.6	29.6	30.9
Spr 1993	820	33.0	833	33.6	43.3	37.5	36.9	38.2	31.9	38.0	33.4	29.3	30.8	31.8
Sum 1993	823	33.1	811	32.5	43.3	37.1	35.1	37.7	31.6	37.7	32.5	27.1	30.1	30.7
Aut 1993	820	32.9	846	33.9	42.5	38.2	37.3	39.2	32.0	38.4	33.7	29.8	30.3	32.0
Win 1993/4	829	33.2	801	32.3	40.3	35.1	34.9	35.3	31.2	38.0	32.7	28.6	28.3	31.0
Spr 1994	832	33.2	845	33.8	44.4	36.9	37.2	38.5	32.0	38.4	34.4	29.5	29.2	32.0
Sum 1994	835	33.3	824	32.6	46.5	36.0	35.4	38.5	31.6	38.4	32.9	27.1	29.5	30.8
Aut 1994	840	33.3	867	34.3	45.0	38.1	37.8	39.7	32.4	39.1	34.4	30.2	30.1	32.4
Win 1994/5	845	33.5	817	32.5	41.0	36.6	35.5	36.0	31.5	37.8	32.8	28.5	28.4	31.0
Spr 1995	848	33.5	861	34.1	45.8	38.6	37.7	39.0	32.0	39.0	34.1	29.7	30.6	32.2
Sum 1995	848	33.3	836	32.7	46.4	36.4	35.7	39.3	31.2	38.0	34.1	29.7	30.6	32.2
Aut 1995	848	33.3	876	34.3	43.9	38.8	38.0	40.2	31.6	39.2	34.6	30.2	29.9	32.3
Win 1995/6	848	33.2	820	32.2	40.9	36.4	35.4	35.9	30.3	37.6	32.9	28.6	27.9	30.7
Spr 1996	851	33.3	864	33.9	45.2	38.0	37.6	39.4	31.1	39.4	34.3	29.8	30.3	31.9
Sum 1996	857	33.4	845	32.8	45.5	37.9	35.7	39.1	30.9	38.2	33.7	27.7	29.7	30.9
Aut 1996	861	33.4	890	34.4	44.3	39.1	38.3	40.5	31.3	39.4	35.0	30.6	30.2	32.4
Win 1996/7	857	33.1	828	32.0	39.4	37.0	35.0	36.5	30.2	37.4	32.7	28.4	27.9	30.6
Spr 1997	**866**	**33.3**	**869**	**33.4**	**44.7**	**38.8**	**37.1**	**39.3**	**31.2**	**38.0**	**33.9**	**29.1**	**29.8**	**31.5**
MEN														
Spr 1984	530	38.3	536	38.9	52.4	28.2	38.9	39.5	41.5	39.8	37.3	36.3	37.9	38.9
Spr 1985	545	39.1	551	39.8	52.2	35.9	39.6	39.6	41.7	40.6	38.7	37.2	37.6	39.5
Spr 1986	545	39.3	551	39.9	51.9	37.9	39.7	39.6	42.1	40.9	39.0	36.6	37.5	39.6
Spr 1987	551	39.3	557	39.9	52.1	37.2	39.7	39.7	41.8	41.6	38.2	36.6	38.3	39.5
Spr 1988	581	40.0	587	40.6	52.1	38.1	40.8	41.1	41.4	41.8	39.6	37.3	38.3	39.9
Spr 1989	595	40.0	602	40.6	53.3	38.7	40.5	40.6	41.4	42.4	39.3	37.3	38.7	40.0
Spr 1990	593	39.5	600	40.1	52.1	38.5	40.2	40.9	40.8	41.3	39.2	36.8	38.5	39.4
Spr 1991	575	39.4	582	40.1	52.0	39.1	39.7	40.3	41.3	41.5	39.1	37.2	38.0	39.6
Spr 1992	538	38.6	540	38.9	49.9	38.8	38.7	38.9	40.2	40.7	38.2	36.1	36.8	39.2
Sum 1992	536	38.6	539	38.5	50.1	38.4	38.2	39.5	40.1	40.3	37.7	34.1	37.5	38.0
Aut 1992	534	38.8	551	39.9	48.2	39.2	40.0	40.2	40.8	41.4	39.2	37.8	37.9	39.6
Win 1992/3	530	38.7	509	37.4	44.3	37.5	36.8	36.5	38.8	39.9	37.1	35.8	35.9	37.6
Spr 1993	528	38.7	536	39.4	47.9	39.2	39.6	39.9	40.2	41.0	38.3	36.5	37.8	38.8
Sum 1993	530	38.7	526	38.2	48.5	39.0	37.6	39.5	39.6	40.5	37.5	34.0	37.0	37.7
Aut 1993	529	38.6	546	39.8	47.4	40.2	39.9	41.0	40.2	41.3	39.3	37.0	36.9	39.1
Win 1993/4	535	38.9	513	37.6	44.3	36.8	37.2	36.9	38.8	40.2	38.0	35.3	34.8	34.7
Spr 1994	536	38.9	544	39.6	48.8	38.5	39.8	40.2	39.7	41.4	39.9	36.5	35.8	35.8
Sum 1994	541	39.0	537	38.5	51.7	37.7	37.9	40.2	39.2	41.0	38.3	33.8	36.2	36.2
Aut 1994	544	39.0	561	40.2	49.9	39.6	40.4	41.4	40.2	41.6	39.9	37.3	37.0	37.0
Win 1994/5	546	39.2	525	37.9	44.6	38.1	37.9	37.5	38.8	40.3	37.6	35.5	34.4	37.6
Spr 1995	549	39.2	557	39.9	50.2	40.3	40.3	40.7	39.9	41.5	39.3	36.8	37.4	39.1
Sum 1995	548	39.0	544	38.4	51.4	37.9	38.1	40.8	38.9	40.5	39.3	36.8	37.4	39.1
Aut 1995	548	39.0	566	40.1	48.1	40.8	40.7	41.9	39.7	41.7	39.7	37.4	35.8	39.1
Win 1996	547	38.9	526	37.6	45.0	38.3	37.7	37.4	37.9	40.3	37.8	35.2	33.7	37.2
Spr 1996	548	38.9	556	39.6	50.5	39.8	40.2	41.0	38.7	42.2	39.3	36.6	36.6	38.7
Sum 1996	551	39.0	547	38.4	51.2	39.9	38.1	40.8	38.2	40.7	38.2	34.5	36.2	37.5
Aut 1996	554	39.0	572	40.2	49.7	41.3	40.7	42.1	38.7	41.8	40.2	37.8	36.7	39.1
Win 1996/7	552	38.6	530	37.3	44.0	38.6	37.3	37.9	37.1	39.8	37.6	34.6	34.1	36.8
Spr 1997	**557**	**38.8**	**559**	**39.1**	**49.7**	**40.7**	**39.7**	**40.8**	**38.3**	**40.8**	**38.8**	**35.8**	**35.7**	**38.0**
WOMEN														
Spr 1984	252	25.8	254	26.2	29.5	28.5	29.9	23.9	25.0	30.2	27.1	25.0	23.7	25.4
Spr 1985	264	26.4	267	26.8	29.2	29.7	30.9	24.3	25.4	31.3	27.8	25.6	23.8	25.9
Spr 1986	269	26.4	272	26.8	31.2	33.0	33.0	27.5	27.0	33.8	30.0	28.4	25.9	28.2
Spr 1987	271	26.0	274	26.4	30.2	30.0	30.4	24.4	25.2	30.0	27.7	24.7	25.7	25.6
Spr 1988	291	26.9	295	27.3	32.6	30.7	31.2	26.5	25.9	31.2	28.7	25.7	25.9	26.5
Spr 1989	299	26.6	303	27.0	31.2	30.4	30.5	25.8	25.8	31.3	28.4	25.3	25.7	26.3
Spr 1990	301	26.5	305	26.9	32.1	30.0	30.8	26.0	25.5	29.3	28.4	25.1	26.5	26.1
Spr 1991	301	26.7	305	27.1	33.9	31.9	30.9	27.1	25.2	30.3	28.3	25.9	26.1	26.3
Spr 1992	294	26.3	295	26.3	30.9	30.2	29.8	24.6	24.8	28.8	27.5	24.1	25.1	25.2
Sum 1992	293	26.2	289	25.8	29.6	30.5	30.9	25.3	25.0	29.3	27.8	26.4	25.7	26.3
Aut 1992	292	26.2	302	26.9	27.2	30.3	28.6	23.3	24.3	27.4	27.1	25.3	24.8	25.3
Win 1992/3	292	26.2	286	25.8	29.0	30.6	30.2	24.8	24.6	28.7	28.1	25.9	25.4	26.0
Spr 1993	292	26.1	297	26.6	26.7	30.0	28.9	23.2	24.5	29.1	27.1	23.9	25.0	24.9
Sum 1993	293	26.2	285	25.5	26.1	30.2	30.7	24.7	24.6	29.0	27.8	26.5	25.5	26.2
Aut 1993	291	26.0	300	26.7	26.1	30.2	30.7	24.7	24.6	29.0	27.8	26.5	25.5	26.2
Win 1993/4	294	26.3	288	25.8	27.9	28.3	29.2	22.0	24.2	30.0	26.8	25.4	23.5	23.4
Spr 1994	295	26.3	300	26.7	31.5	29.9	30.6	24.4	24.8	30.3	28.3	26.3	24.1	24.1
Sum 1994	295	26.1	287	25.4	31.3	28.7	29.1	23.8	24.5	30.0	26.8	23.9	23.9	24.0
Aut 1994	296	26.3	306	27.1	30.7	32.1	31.2	24.6	25.1	31.2	27.9	26.8	24.1	24.1
Win 1994/5	299	26.4	292	25.9	30.4	30.4	29.5	22.5	24.7	29.6	27.1	25.3	23.2	25.4
Spr 1995	299	26.4	304	26.9	34.1	31.6	31.1	23.8	24.8	30.3	28.0	26.5	24.6	26.2
Sum 1995	300	26.3	292	25.6	33.2	30.7	29.5	25.2	24.1	29.8	28.0	26.5	24.6	26.2
Aut 1995	300	26.2	310	27.1	32.3	30.8	31.1	24.3	24.3	30.5	28.6	26.9	24.7	26.4
Win 1995/6	301	26.2	294	25.7	29.6	29.1	29.3	23.1	23.3	28.8	27.2	25.6	23.0	25.1
Spr 1996	303	26.3	307	26.8	31.4	30.3	30.8	25.3	24.0	30.1	28.4	26.6	25.1	26.2
Sum 1996	306	26.6	298	25.8	31.0	29.6	29.4	23.9	24.1	30.0	28.5	24.5	24.4	25.3
Aut 1996	307	26.5	317	27.4	28.9	28.8	32.0	26.0	24.5	31.4	28.8	27.2	24.9	26.7
Win 1996/7	305	26.3	298	25.7	26.1	29.5	28.7	22.9	23.8	30.0	27.0	25.6	22.9	25.3
Spr 1997	**308**	**26.5**	**309**	**26.6**	**30.7**	**30.5**	**30.1**	**24.8**	**24.6**	**29.4**	**28.0**	**26.2**	**24.8**	**26.1**

+ Average hours actually worked in reference week, including hours worked in second jobs.
# Includes people with workplace outside the UK and those who did not state their industry.
§ For people with two jobs, all hours are allocated to the industry sector of main job.

GOVERNMENT-SUPPORTED TRAINING
Number of people participating in Training and Enterprise Programmes

THOUSANDS

Period ending	Training For Work			Youth Training (including credits)			Modern Apprenticeships		
	England	Wales	England and Wales	England	Wales	England and Wales	England	Wales	England and Wales
1990-91*	114.7	10.3	124.9	193.2	16.4	209.5			
1991-92*	127.7	11.5	139.2	233.2	16.5	249.6			
1992-93#	133.4	12.6	145.2	231.8	14.8	246.9			
1993-94	124.4	8.7	133.1	234.1	16.1	250.2			
1994-95	94.9	8.6	103.4	224.2	15.3	239.5			
1995-96	68.2	4.7	72.8	211.0	13.2	224.2	24.8	3.0	27.8
1996-97+	55.1	3.8	58.9	199.9	14.8	214.6	74.7	6.1	80.8
1995 23 Apr	75.4	6.6	82.0	214.4	14.6	229.0	1.3	0.4	1.7
21 May	73.1	6.3	79.2	213.6	15.1	228.7	1.4	0.4	1.7
18 Jun	69.7	6.1	75.8	211.9	15.1	227.0	1.5	0.3	1.8
16 Jul	63.2	5.0	68.3	222.0	15.5	237.5	2.1	0.3	2.4
13 Aug	60.1	4.7	64.9	224.4	15.5	239.9	2.8	0.4	3.2
13 Sep	58.4	4.5	62.9	224.6	15.5	240.1	5.6	0.5	6.1
08 Oct	61.6	4.8	66.4	229.6	16.0	245.6	9.7	1.4	11.1
05 Nov	63.4	5.0	68.5	230.0	16.0	246.0	12.3	1.8	14.2
03 Dec	65.3	5.0	70.3	228.6	15.9	244.5	14.9	2.0	16.9
31 Dec	60.7	4.8	65.5	224.2	15.5	239.7	16.8	2.1	18.9
1996 28 Jan	63.4	4.8	68.7	221.7	14.6	236.4	18.9	2.1	21.0
25 Feb	66.9	4.9	71.8	218.6	13.3	232.0	21.4	2.7	24.1
24 Mar	68.1	4.7	72.8	210.9	13.2	224.1	24.8	3.0	27.8
28 Apr	62.1	4.3	66.4	201.9	12.8	214.6	27.3	3.4	30.7
26 May	61.9	4.1	66.1	198.8	12.9	211.7	29.1	3.5	32.7
23 Jun	60.9	4.0	64.9	198.5	12.8	211.3	31.1	4.0	35.1
21 Jul	58.8	3.5	62.2	208.2	13.1	221.4	35.2	3.8	38.9
18 Aug	56.4	3.4	59.8	210.1	13.6	223.7	39.2	4.0	43.2
15 Sep	56.0	3.4	59.5	211.7	13.9	225.5	47.4	4.7	52.2
13 Oct	58.1	3.8	61.8	212.9	14.4	227.3	53.7	5.3	59.0
10 Nov	58.8	3.9	62.7	212.0	14.9	226.9	58.8	5.5	64.2
08 Dec	59.3	3.9	63.2	210.9	15.2	226.1	63.3	5.8	69.0
1997 05 Jan	53.9	3.6	57.5	205.4	15.1	220.5	65.0	5.7	70.7
02 Feb	57.2	3.8	61.0	204.0	15.1	219.1	68.3	6.1	74.4
02 Mar	58.2	4.0	62.2	199.1	14.9	214.1	72.5	6.1	78.7
30 Mar	54.3	3.8	58.1	192.6	14.8	207.4	75.6	6.1	81.7
04 May	49.9	3.6	53.5	182.2	14.8	197.0	75.4	7.1	82.4
01 Jun	**48.7**	**3.9**	**52.6**	**178.5**	**13.1**	**191.5**	**75.7**	**6.4**	**82.2**

Source: TEC Management Information, the Welsh Office

Note: Modern Apprenticeships were launched in September 1995 (in England and Wales; at the end of 1995 in Scotland), following prototyping in 17 industry sectors. Accelerated Modern Apprenticeships for 18 and 19-year-old school and college leavers, also launched in September 1995, have been merged with Modern Apprenticeships from April 1996 in England (although they will continue separately in Wales). Modern Apprenticeships aim to increase significantly the number of young people trained to technician, supervisory and equivalent-level skills, at NVQ level 3 as a minimum plus the breadth and flexibility required for the relevant industry sector. Accelerated Modern Apprenticeships figures have been merged with Modern Apprenticeships.
* Employment Training.
# Employment Training and Employment Action.
+ 1996-97 starts and in training figures include Pre-Vocational Pilots (PVPs).

GOVERNMENT-SUPPORTED TRAINING
Number of starts on Training and Enterprise Programmes

THOUSANDS

Period ending	Training For Work#*			Youth Training (including credits)			Modern Apprenticeships		
	England	Wales	England and Wales	England	Wales	England and Wales	England	Wales	England and Wales
1990-91	280.2	24.4	304.6	225.9	18.2	244.1			
1991-92	253.2	24.0	277.2	227.4	17.9	245.3			
1992-93	291.2	27.0	318.4	236.4	16.7	251.7			
1993-94	290.7	19.1	309.8	238.7	17.6	256.3			
1994-95	269.7	19.3	289.1	251.8	16.7	268.5			
1995-96	212.4	12.1	224.4	251.1	17.4	268.1	25.9	2.6	28.4
1996-97	213.4	12.5	226.5	232.9	22.0	254.3	67.8	5.3	73.1
1995 23 Apr	11.2	0.7	12.0	11.3	1.0	12.3	0.1	0.0	0.1
21 May	15.0	0.8	15.7	11.7	1.1	12.8	0.1	0.0	0.1
18 Jun	14.6	0.9	15.4	13.6	1.0	14.7	0.2	0.0	0.2
16 Jul	15.2	0.9	16.1	34.7	1.9	36.6	0.6	0.0	0.6
13 Aug	13.9	0.8	14.7	25.0	1.7	26.7	0.8	0.0	0.8
13 Sep	14.5	0.8	15.2	26.1	1.9	28.0	2.8	0.1	3.0
08 Oct	20.3	1.5	21.8	32.9	2.3	35.2	4.3	0.7	5.0
05 Nov	18.2	1.2	19.4	19.4	1.6	21.0	2.8	0.3	3.0
03 Dec	18.5	1.0	19.5	17.2	1.3	18.5	2.7	0.2	3.0
31 Dec	10.2	0.6	10.8	10.2	0.7	10.9	2.1	0.2	2.3
1996 28 Jan	17.6	1.0	18.6	15.6	1.0	16.6	2.4	0.2	2.6
25 Feb	20.6	0.9	21.5	16.2	0.9	17.1	3.1	0.4	3.4
24 Mar	22.7	0.9	23.7	16.9	1.0	17.9	4.0	0.4	4.4
28 Apr	18.4	0.9	19.4	15.0	3.3	18.3	2.8	0.3	3.1
26 May	17.2	1.0	18.2	12.0	1.1	13.1	2.5	0.3	2.7
23 Jun	16.2	0.9	17.1	16.7	1.2	17.9	2.8	0.2	3.0
21 Jul	17.0	0.9	18.0	33.8	1.7	35.5	4.9	0.4	5.2
18 Aug	15.5	0.9	16.3	22.6	1.7	24.3	5.1	0.4	5.5
15 Sep	16.2	1.0	17.2	28.7	2.2	30.9	9.7	1.0	10.6
13 Oct	19.8	1.5	21.3	24.5	2.1	26.7	8.1	0.8	8.9
10 Nov	18.3	1.1	19.4	17.9	1.8	19.7	6.7	0.6	7.3
08 Dec	17.6	1.1	18.7	15.6	1.6	17.2	6.3	0.4	6.7
1997 05 Jan	7.1	0.4	7.5	7.1	0.7	7.8	3.0	0.2	3.2
02 Feb	17.9	1.1	19.0	15.1	1.2	16.4	5.4	0.3	5.8
02 Mar	18.7	1.2	19.9	12.9	1.2	14.1	6.3	0.3	6.5
30 Mar	15.5	0.6	16.1	12.0	1.5	13.5	5.3	0.3	5.6
04 May	16.9	1.0	17.9	12.3	1.2	13.6	4.8	0.2	5.0
01 Jun	**12.1**	**0.7**	**12.8**	**8.9**	**0.9**	**9.9**	**2.5**	**0.1**	**2.7**

Note: See *Table 8.1* note.   *Source:* TEC Management Information, the Welsh Office
1990-91 and 1991-92 Employment Training; 1992-93 Employment Training Action.
* 1996-97 in training includes Pre-Vocational Pilots (PVPs).

ENGLAND and WALES		All leavers Percentage of survey respondents who were:				Completers Percentage of survey respondents who were:		
Month of survey*	Month of leaving#	In a job	In a positive outcome**	Unemployed	Completers##	In a job	In a positive outcome**	Unemployed
Jul 90 to Sep 91	(1990-91)	33	36	53	49	37	40	48
Oct 91 to Sep 92	(1991-92)	31	36	55	55	35	41	51
Oct 92 to Sep 93	(1992-93)	35	41	52	60	38	44	48
Oct 93 to Sep 94	(1993-94)	36	43	48	61	40	47	45
Oct 94 to Sep 95	(1994-95)	38	42	48	66	40	45	46
Oct 95 to Sep 96	(1995-96)	39	44	47	70	41	46	45
1994 Oct	(Apr 94)	37	43	47	64	39	45	45
Nov	(May 94)	37	42	48	62	40	45	46
Dec	(Jun 94)	36	43	47	66	37	45	46
1995 Jan	(Jul 94)	36	45	45	71	38	47	43
Feb	(Aug 94)	37	43	48	66	40	46	45
Mar	(Sep 94)	38	44	46	65	40	46	45
Apr	(Oct 94)	40	43	48	61	43	47	45
May	(Nov 94)	39	41	50	62	42	45	47
Jun	(Dec 94)	41	43	48	69	44	46	46
Jul	(Jan 95)	37	40	51	63	40	43	49
Aug	(Feb 95)	37	40	50	65	40	42	48
Sept	(Mar 95)	37	41	49	70	39	43	48
Oct	(Apr 95)	40	44	46	68	42	46	45
Nov	(May 95)	41	45	46	69	42	46	45
Dec	(Jun 95)	38	45	45	72	38	46	44
1996 Jan	(Jul 95)	37	44	47	72	39	46	45
Feb	(Aug 95)	39	45	46	69	42	47	45
Mar	(Sep 95)	39	45	46	68	41	47	45
Apr	(Oct 95)	41	45	48	67	44	47	45
May	(Nov 95)	40	44	48	67	43	46	47
Jun	(Dec 95)	41	44	47	73	43	46	46
Jul	(Jan 96)	38	42	49	67	41	45	47
Aug	(Feb 96)	40	44	48	70	42	45	47
Sept	(Mar 96)	39	44	46	72	40	45	45
Oct	(Apr 96)	43	48	43	68	44	49	42
Nov	(May 96)	42	47	44	71	43	48	44
Dec	(Jun 96)	40	47	44	72	41	49	43
1997 Jan	(Jul 96)	43	49	42	71	45	51	41
Feb	(Aug 96)	45	51	40	71	47	53	38
Mar	(Sep 96)	44	50	41	70	46	52	40
Apr	**(Oct 96)**	**47**	**51**	**41**	**71**	**49**	**52**	**40**
Current and previous year to date								
May 95 to Apr 96	**(Nov 94 to Oct 95)**	**39**	**43**	**48**	**68**	**41**	**45**	**46**
May 96 to Apr 97	**(Nov 95 to Oct 96)**	**42**	**47**	**45**	**70**	**44**	**48**	**43**

* Leavers to December 1990 surveyed three months after leaving. Leavers from January 1991 surveyed six months after leaving.
# Training for Work (TfW) superseded Employment Training (ET) and Employment Action in April 1993.
  The figures in this table for leavers from April 1993 onwards include all those who joined Employment Action before 29 March 1993, and left after that date.
  This will have the effect of reducing the proportions going into a job or gaining qualifications for leavers from April 1993 onwards. Figures for 1990-1993 are for ET.
** In a positive outcome = in a job, full-time education or other government-supported training.
Those who responded positively to the question, 'When you left the Training Programme, had you completed the training that was agreed between you
  and the organiser of your training?' Note that many of those who did not complete their training nevertheless went into a job after leaving.

ENGLAND and WALES		All leavers Percentage of survey respondents who:			Completers Percentage of survey respondents who:		
Month of survey*	Month of leaving#	Tried for a qualification	Gained any full/part qualification	Gained any full qualification	Tried for a qualification	Gained any full/part qualification	Gained any full qualification
Jul 90 to Sep 91	(1990-91)	47	29	29	55	44	44
Oct 91 to Sep 92	(1991-92)	51	34	28	56	48	41
Oct 92 to Sep 93	(1992-93)	55	39	33	60	53	47
Oct 93 to Sep 94	(1993-94)	58	41	35	64	57	51
Oct 94 to Sep 95	(1994-95)	61	45	39	64	58	52
Oct 95 to Sep 96	(1995-96)	63	48	41	66	60	54
1994 Oct	(Apr 94)	56	41	35	60	54	48
Nov	(May 94)	57	41	34	60	54	48
Dec	(Jun 94)	62	47	39	67	60	53
1995 Jan	(Jul 94)	65	53	45	70	65	57
Feb	(Aug 94)	59	44	38	63	57	51
Mar	(Sep 94)	61	44	38	65	59	53
Apr	(Oct 94)	58	40	34	61	55	49
May	(Nov 94)	59	42	36	62	57	51
Jun	(Dec 94)	59	43	37	60	54	48
Jul	(Jan 95)	63	45	40	66	60	55
Aug	(Feb 95)	63	46	39	66	60	54
Sep	(Mar 95)	64	49	42	66	61	54
Oct	(Apr 95)	65	50	43	68	62	55
Nov	(May 95)	66	50	42	68	61	54
Dec	(Jun 95)	71	57	49	75	69	62
1996 Jan	(Jul 95)	67	53	46	71	65	59
Feb	(Aug 95)	64	48	42	67	60	54
Mar	(Sep 95)	66	50	44	71	64	58
Apr	(Oct 95)	60	43	38	64	56	51
May	(Nov 95)	56	40	34	58	52	46
Jun	(Dec 95)	59	44	39	61	55	49
Jul	(Jan 96)	62	44	38	66	59	53
Aug	(Feb 96)	59	43	38	63	55	50
Sep	(Mar 96)	59	45	39	62	56	50
Oct	(Apr 96)	59	43	37	61	54	49
Nov	(May 96)	59	44	40	61	54	
Dec	(Jun 96)	61	46	40	64	58	52
1997 Jan	(Jul 96)	61	45	39	64	57	51
Feb	(Aug 96)	58	43	38	60	54	49
Mar	(Sep 96)	59	44	38	62	55	50
Apr	**(Oct 96)**	**55**	**41**	**36**	**57**	**52**	**46**
Current and previous year to date							
May 95 to Apr 96	**(Nov 94 to Oct 95)**	**64**	**48**	**42**	**67**	**61**	**55**
May 96 to Apr 97	**(Nov 95 to Oct 96)**	**59**	**44**	**38**	**62**	**55**	**50**

* Leavers to December 1980 surveyed three months after leaving. Leavers from January 1991 surveyed six months after leaving.
# Training for Work (TfW) superseded Employment Training (ET) and Employment Action in April 1993.
  The figures in this table for leavers from April 1993 onwards include all those who joined Employment Action before 29 March 1993, and left after that date.
  This will have the effect of reducing the proportions going into a job or gaining qualifications for leavers from April 1993 onwards. Figures for 1990-1993 are for ET.

YT leavers gaining qualifications (smoothed); England and Wales

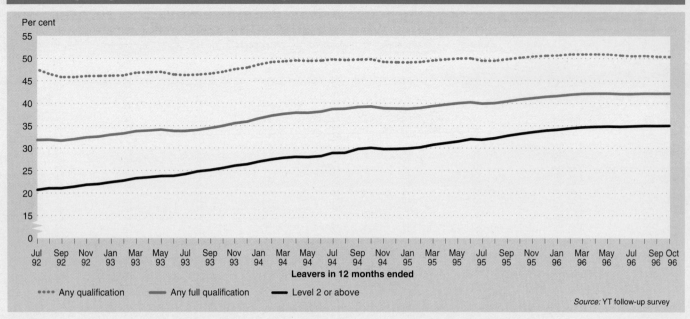

Per cent

Leavers in 12 months ended

•••• Any qualification —— Any full qualification —— Level 2 or above

Source: YT follow-up survey

Participation in youth programmes; England and Wales

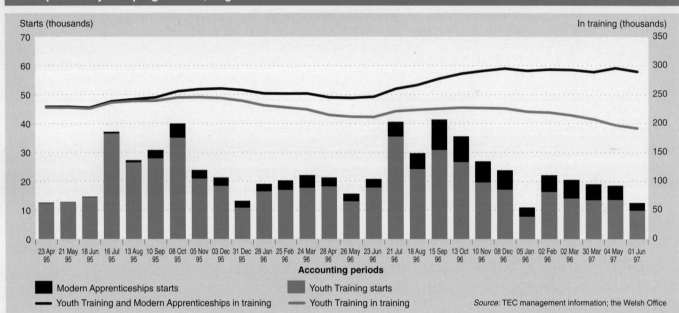

Starts (thousands)   In training (thousands)

Accounting periods

■ Modern Apprenticeships starts   ▨ Youth Training starts
—— Youth Training and Modern Apprenticeships in training   —— Youth Training in training

Source: TEC management information; the Welsh Office

Outcomes achieved by TFW leavers (smoothed); England and Wales

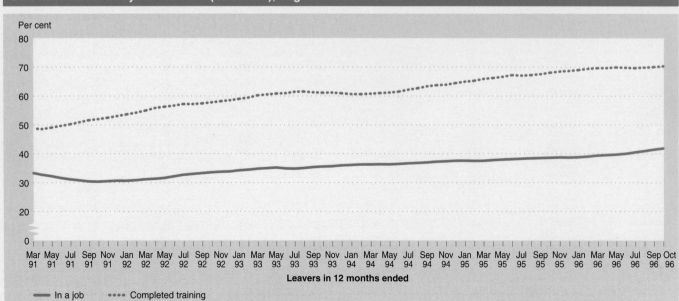

Per cent

Leavers in 12 months ended

—— In a job   •••• Completed training

Source: TFW follow-up survey

ENGLAND and WALES

Month of survey*	Month of leaving	All leavers Percentage of survey respondents who were:				Completers Percentage of those who completed who were:		
		In a job	In a positive outcome#	Unemployed	Completers**	In a job	In a positive outcome#	Unemployed
Jul 90 to Sep 91	(1990-91)	58	74	20	37	75	83	14
Oct 91 to Sep 92	(1991-92)	51	67	25	44	69	77	17
Oct 92 to Sep 93	(1992-93)	50	67	28	43	67	76	20
Oct 93 to Sep 94	(1993-94)	53	70	25	46	68	78	18
Oct 94 to Sep 95	(1994-95)	58	72	22	46	72	81	14
Oct 95 to Sep 96	(1995-96)	63	76	18	52	75	85	11
1994 Oct	(Apr 94)	54	67	27	35	67	75	20
Nov	(May 94)	53	66	28	37	66	74	21
Dec	(Jun 94)	63	74	21	59	73	81	14
1995 Jan	(Jul 94)	61	75	20	56	71	82	14
Feb	(Aug 94)	53	74	21	47	68	81	14
Mar	(Sep 94)	54	76	17	48	69	83	13
Apr	(Oct 94)	55	69	25	37	71	79	16
May	(Nov 94)	56	68	25	37	73	80	16
Jun	(Dec 94)	60	70	23	45	76	81	14
Jul	(Jan 95)	57	68	26	40	74	80	15
Aug	(Feb 95)	59	70	23	43	74	80	15
Sep	(Mar 95)	64	75	20	51	78	84	12
Oct	(Apr 95)	59	71	22	43	70	78	16
Nov	(May 95)	60	72	22	42	72	80	15
Dec	(Jun 95)	65	76	19	58	76	84	12
1996 Jan	(Jul 95)	61	76	18	55	72	84	12
Feb	(Aug 95)	57	76	17	50	70	85	10
Mar	(Sep 95)	57	79	15	53	70	85	10
Apr	(Oct 95)	63	75	19	46	80	86	9
May	(Nov 95)	64	75	19	48	78	85	10
Jun	(Dec 95)	68	77	16	57	79	85	10
Jul	(Jan 96)	64	75	20	49	78	85	11
Aug	(Feb 96)	67	76	18	54	79	85	11
Sep	(Mar 96)	68	79	15	56	79	86	9
Oct	(Apr 96)	65	77	16	49	77	85	10
Nov	(May 96)	65	77	17	48	77	85	11
Dec	(Jun 96)	68	80	15	60	79	87	9
1997 Jan	(Jul 96)	63	78	16	58	74	85	11
Feb	(Aug 96)	59	81	13	54	71	88	8
Mar	(Sep 96)	59	81	13	55	71	88	7
Apr	**(Oct 96)**	**64**	**77**	**17**	**49**	**77**	**86**	**9**
Current and previous year to date								
May 95 to Apr 96	**(Nov 94 to Oct 95)**	60	74	20	49	74	83	12
May 96 to Apr 97	**(Nov 95 to Oct 96)**	64	78	16	54	76	86	9

Note: From April 1995 the definition of YT leavers changed slightly - see *technical note* to Statistical Bulletin No. 4/97 for details.
* Leavers to September 1990 surveyed three months after leaving. Leavers in October and November 1990 surveyed in June 1991. Leavers from December 1990 surveyed six months after leaving.
\# In a positive outcome = in a job, full-time education or other government supported training.
** Those whose response to the question, 'Did you leave your last Training Programme before you were due to finish?' was 'No'.

ENGLAND and WALES

Month of survey*	Month of leaving YT	All Leavers Percentage of survey respondents who:				Completers Percentage of those who completed who:			
		Tried for a qualification	Gained any full/part qualification	Gained any full qualification	Gained any full qualification at Level 2 or above	Tried for a qualification	Gained any full/part qualification	Gained any full qualification	Gained any full qualification at Level 2 or above
Jul 90 to Sep 91	(1990-91)	54	49	39	..	70	70	62	..
Oct 91 to Sep 92	(1991-92)	58	49	34	20	73	71	57	37
Oct 92 to Sep 93	(1992-93)	62	47	34	23	76	70	57	42
Oct 93 to Sep 94	(1993-94)	64	49	38	28	76	71	61	47
Oct 94 to Sep 95	(1994-95)	65	50	39	31	76	71	63	52
Oct 95 to Sep 96	(1995-96)	66	51	42	35	74	70	63	53
1994 Oct	(Ap 94)	62	44	33	23	69	64	55	42
Nov	(May 94)	63	44	33	23	69	64	56	43
Dec	(Jun 94)	73	61	49	37	80	76	66	52
1995 Jan	(Jul 94)	72	59	48	38	82	78	68	55
Feb	(Aug 94)	66	52	42	33	79	76	67	55
Mar	(Sep 94)	64	49	40	32	77	74	65	54
Apr	(Oct 94)	60	40	31	24	72	66	58	48
May	(Nov 94)	59	38	30	23	70	65	58	48
Jun	(Dec 94)	62	46	36	28	70	65	57	47
Jul	(Jan 95)	61	43	33	26	71	66	59	49
Aug	(Feb 95)	62	46	37	30	72	69	63	53
Sep	(Mar 95)	66	53	43	35	72	69	62	52
Oct	(Apr 95)	65	48	39	30	73	68	63	52
Nov	(May 95)	65	49	39	30	73	68	61	51
Dec	(Jun 95)	71	59	49	41	78	74	66	56
1996 Jan	(Jul 95)	70	56	46	38	78	74	66	55
Feb	(Aug 95)	66	51	43	36	77	74	67	59
Mar	(Sep 95)	66	52	43	35	77	73	65	56
Apr	(Oct 95)	63	46	37	30	73	68	61	52
May	(Nov 95)	62	44	36	30	69	63	57	49
Jun	(Dec 95)	64	49	41	34	69	64	58	49
Jul	(Jan 96)	63	46	38	31	69	64	58	49
Aug	(Feb 96)	65	50	42	35	71	68	61	53
Sep	(Mar 96)	66	53	45	37	71	68	62	53
Oct	(Apr 96)	64	49	40	33	70	67	60	51
Nov	(May 96)	64	48	40	32	70	65	58	49
Dec	(Jun 96)	69	58	49	41	77	74	67	58
1997 Jan	(Jul 96)	67	55	47	39	76	73	67	57
Feb	(Aug 96)	66	52	43	37	76	72	65	56
Mar	(Sep 96)	65	50	42	35	75	71	64	55
Apr	**(Oct 96)**	**62**	**45**	**38**	**31**	**71**	**67**	**60**	**51**
Current and previous year to date									
May 95 to Apr 96	**(Nov 94 to Oct 95)**	65	50	41	33	75	71	63	54
May 96 to Apr 97	**(Nov 95 to Oct 96)**	65	50	42	35	73	69	62	53

Note: From April 1995 the definition of YT leavers changed, no longer counting those making planned transfers from one training provider to another as leavers. Many of these transferring trainees will not have gained a job or qualification or completed their training. Therefore the change in definition will increase slightly the proportions with jobs and qualification and completing their training. The way that data on qualifications gained are collected was changed from August 1991. The effect appears to have been to decrease the proportion recorded as gaining full qualifications, but to increase by a similar amount the proportion gaining part qualifications. Data for 1990-91 and 1991-92 leavers are not strictly comparable with those for later years.
* Leavers to September 1990 surveyed three months after leaving. Leavers in October and November 1990 surveyed in June 1991. Leavers from December 1990 surveyed six months after leaving.
.. Information on levels of qualifications is not available for 1990-91 leavers.

Placed into employment by jobcentre advisory service, 5 July 1997 - 8 August 1997 +

7,610

+ Not including placings through displayed vacancies.

DEFINITIONS

CLAIMANT UNEMPLOYED

The claimant count consists of all those people who are claiming unemployment-related benefits at Employment Service local offices and who have declared that they are unemployed, capable of, available for, and actively seeking work during the week in which their claim is made. All people claiming unemployment-related benefits are included in the claimant count. (Students claiming benefit during a vacation and who intend to return to full-time education are excluded.)

EARNINGS

Total gross remuneration which employees receive from their employers in the form of money. Income in kind and employers' contributions to National Insurance and pension funds are excluded.

ECONOMICALLY ACTIVE

In Tables 7.1, 7.2, 7.3, 7.5 and 7.6 (Labour Force Survey) people aged 16 and over who are in employment (as employees, self-employed, on government-supported employment and training programmes, or from 1992, as unpaid family workers) together with those who are ILO unemployed.

ECONOMICALLY INACTIVE

In Tables 7.1, 7.2, 7.3, 7.5 and 7.6 (Labour Force Survey) people aged 16 and over who are neither in employment nor ILO unemployed; this group includes people who are, for example, retired or looking after their home/family.

EMPLOYEES IN EMPLOYMENT

A count of civilian jobs of employees paid by employers who run a PAYE scheme. Participants in government employment and training schemes are included if they have a contract of employment. HM Forces, homeworkers and private domestic servants are excluded. As the estimates of employees in employment are derived from employers' reports of the number of people they employ, individuals holding two jobs with different employers will be counted twice.

FULL-TIME WORKERS

People normally working for more than 30 hours a week except where otherwise stated.

GENERAL INDEX OF RETAIL PRICES

The general index covers almost all goods and services purchased by most households, excluding only those for which the income of the household is in the top 4 per cent and those one and two-person pensioner households (covered by separate indices) who depend mainly on state benefits, i.e. more than three-quarters of their income is from state benefits.

H.M. FORCES

All UK service personnel of HM Regular Forces, wherever serving, including those on release leave.

I.L.O. UNEMPLOYED

In Tables 7.1, 7.2, 7.3, 7.5 and 7.6 (Labour Force Survey) people without a paid job in the reference week who were available to start work in the next fortnight and who either looked for work at some time in the last four weeks or were waiting to start a job already obtained.

LABOUR DISPUTES

Statistics of stoppages of work due to industrial disputes in the United Kingdom relate only to disputes connected with terms and conditions of employment. Stoppages involving fewer than ten workers or lasting less than one day are excluded except where the aggregate of working days lost exceeded 100. Workers involved and working days lost relate to persons both directly and indirectly involved (thrown out of work although not parties to the disputes) at the establishments where the disputes occurred. People laid off and working days lost elsewhere, owing for example to resulting shortages of supplies, are not included.

There are difficulties in ensuring complete recording of stoppages, in particular those near the margins of the definitions; for example, short disputes lasting only a day or so. Any under-recording would particularly bear on those industries most affected by such stoppages, and would affect the total number of stoppages much more than the number of working days lost.

MANUAL WORKERS (OPERATIVES)

Employees other than those in administrative, professional, technical and clerical occupations.

MANUFACTURING INDUSTRIES

SIC 1992 Section D.

NORMAL WEEKLY HOURS

The time which the employee is expected to work in a normal week, excluding all overtime and main meal breaks. This may be specified in national collective agreements and statutory wages orders for manual workers.

OVERTIME

Work outside normal hours for which a premium rate is paid.

The terms used in the tables are defined more fully in the periodic articles in **Labour Market Trends** *which relate to particular statistical series*

CONVENTIONS

The following standard symbols are used:

..	not available
–	nil or negligible (less than half the final digit shown)
P	provisional
—	break in series
R	revised
r	series revised from indicated entry onwards
nes	not elsewhere specified
SIC	UK Standard Industrial Classification
EC	European Community

Where figures have been rounded to the final digit, there may be an apparent slight discrepancy between the sum of the constituent items and the total as shown. Although figures may be given in unrounded form to facilitate the calculation of percentage changes, rates of change etc by users, this does not imply that the figures can be estimated to this degree of precision, and it must be recognised that they may be the subject of sampling and other errors.

PART-TIME WORKERS

People normally working for not more than 30 hours a week except where otherwise stated.

PRODUCTION INDUSTRIES

SIC 1992 Sections C-E.

SEASONALLY ADJUSTED

Adjusted for regular seasonal variations.

SELF-EMPLOYED PEOPLE

Those who in their main employment work on their own account, whether or not they have any employees. Second occupations classified as self-employed are not included.

SERVICE INDUSTRIES

SIC 1992 Sections G-Q.

SHORT-TIME WORKING

Arrangements made by an employer for working less than regular hours. Therefore time lost through sickness, holidays, absenteeism and the direct effects of industrial disputes is not counted as short-time.

STANDARD INDUSTRIAL CLASSIFICATION (SIC)

The classification system used to provide a consistent industrial breakdown for UK official statistics. It was revised in 1968, 1980 and 1992.

TAX AND PRICE INDEX

Measures the increase in gross taxable income needed to compensate taxpayers for any increase in retail prices, taking account of changes to direct taxes (including employees' National Insurance contributions). Annual and quarterly figures are averages of monthly indices.

TEMPORARILY STOPPED

People who at the date of the unemployment count are suspended by their employers on the understanding that they will shortly resume work and are claiming benefit. These people are not included in the unemployment figures.

VACANCY

A job opportunity notified by an employer to a Jobcentre or careers office (including 'self-employed' opportunities created by employers) which remained unfilled on the day of the count.

WEEKLY HOURS WORKED

Actual hours worked during the reference week and hours not worked but paid for under guarantee agreements.

WORKFORCE

Workforce in employment plus the claimant unemployed as defined above.

WORKFORCE IN EMPLOYMENT

Employees in employment, self-employed, HM Forces and participants on work-related government-supported training programmes.

WORK-RELATED GOVERNMENT-SUPPORTED TRAINING PROGRAMMES

Those participants on government programmes and schemes who in the course of their participation receive training in the context of a workplace but are not employees, self-employed or HM Forces.

	Frequency	Latest issue	Table number or page
SUMMARY TABLES			
Labour Force Survey: UK	M	Sep 97	0.1
Workforce: UK	M	Sep 97	0.2
Labour Force Survey: GB	M	Sep 97	0.3
Workforce: GB	M	Sep 97	0.4
BACKGROUND ECONOMIC INDICATORS	M	Sep 97	0.5
EMPLOYMENT AND WORKFORCE			
Workforce: UK and GB			
Quarterly series	M(Q)	Sep 97	1.1
Labour force estimates, projections		Feb 97	51
Employees in employment industry: GB			
All industries: by division, class or group	Q	Aug 97	1.4
: time series, by order group	M	Sep 97	1.2
Manufacturing: by division, class or group	M	Sep 97	1.3
Administrative, technical and clerical in manufacturing	D	Dec 94	1.10
Local authorities manpower	D	Jan 94	1.7
Employees in employment by region and sector	B(Q)	Aug 97	1.5
Census of Employment			
UK and regions by industry (Sept 1993)		Oct 95	369
GB and regions by industry (Sept 1993)		Oct 95	369
International comparisons	Q	Aug 97	1.9
Registered disabled in the public sector	A	Aug 96	325
Trade union membership	A	Jun 97	231
Tourism-related industries in Great Britain	Q	Aug 97	1.14
CLAIMANT UNEMPLOYMENT AND VACANCIES			
Claimant unemployment			
Summary: UK	M	Sep 97	2.1
: GB	M	Sep 97	2.2
Age and duration: UK	Q	Sep 97	2.5
Broad category: UK	M	Sep 97	2.1
Detailed category: GB	M	Sep 97	2.2
Region: summary	Q	Sep 97	2.6
Age: time series UK	Q	Sep 97	2.7
: estimated rates	Q	Sep 97	2.15
Duration: time series UK	Q	Sep 97	2.8
Region and area			
Time series summary: by region	M	Sep 97	2.3
: assisted areas, travel-to work areas	M	Sep 97	2.4
: counties, local areas	M	Sep 97	2.9
: parliamentary constituencies	M	Sep 97	2.10
Age and duration: summary	Q	Sep 97	2.6
Flows			
UK, time series	M	Sep 97	2.19
Age time series	M	Sep 97	2.20
Mean duration	Q	Jul 97	2.21
Claim history: number of previous claims	Q	Aug 97	2.22
Claim history: interval between claims	Q	Sep 97	2.23
By sought and usual occupation	M	Sep 97	2.24
Students: by region	D	Mar 93	2.13
Disabled jobseekers: GB	M	Sep 97	A.1
International comparisons	M	Sep 97	2.18
Ethnic origin	A	Jun 96	259
Temporarily stopped			
Latest figures: by UK region	D	Nov 93	2.14
Vacancies			
Unfilled, inflow, outflow and placings seasonally adjusted	M	Sep 97	3.1
Unfilled seasonally adjusted by region	M	Sep 97	3.2
Unfilled unadjusted by region	M	Sep 97	3.3
REDUNDANCIES			
In Great Britain	M	Sep 97	2.32
by region	M	Sep 97	2.33
by age	M	Sep 97	2.34
by industry	M	Sep 97	2.35
by occupation	M	Sep 97	2.36
EARNINGS AND HOURS			
Average earnings (index)			
Whole economy			
Main industrial sectors	M	Sep 97	5.1
Industries	M	Sep 97	5.3
Underlying trends	Q	Feb 96	75
Levels of earnings and hours for main industrial sectors and industries			
Manual employees	Q(A)	Aug 97	5.4
Non manual employees	Q(A)	Aug 97	5.5
All employees	Q(A)	Aug 97	5.6
Quarterly estimates of levels	Q	May 97	180
International comparisons (index)			
Manufacturing	M	Sep 97	5.9
Overtime and short-time: manufacturing			
Latest figures: industry	D	Dec 96	1.11
Regions: summary	D	Dec 96	1.13
Hours of work: manufacturing	D	Sep 95	1.12
OUTPUT PER HEAD			
Output per head: quarterly and annual indices	M(Q)	Sep 97	1.8
Wages and salaries per unit of output			
Manufacturing index, time series	M	Sep 97	5.8
Quarterly and annual indices	M	Sep 97	5.8
LABOUR COSTS			
Survey results 1992 Quadrennial		Sep 94	313
Annual update	A	Feb 96	5.7
RETAIL PRICES			
General index (RPI)			
Latest figures: detailed indices	M	Sep 97	6.2
: percentage changes	M	Sep 97	6.2
Recent movements and the index excluding seasonal foods	M	Sep 97	6.1
Main components: time series and weights	M	Sep 97	6.4
Changes on a year earlier: time series	M	Sep 97	6.5
Food prices	M	Sep 97	6.3
International comparisons	M	Sep 97	6.8
All items excluding housing costs	M	Sep 97	6.9
LABOUR FORCE SURVEY			
Economic activity: seasonally adjusted	M	Sep 97	7.1
Economic activity: not seasonally adjusted	M	Sep 97	7.2
Economic activity by age: not seasonally adjusted	M	Sep 97	7.3
Full-time and part-time workers	M	Sep 97	7.4
Alternative measures of unemployment (seasonally adjusted)	M	Sep 97	7.5
Alternative measures of unemployment (not seasonally adjusted)	M	Sep 97	7.6
Job-related training received by employees	M	Sep 97	7.7
Average actual weekly hours of work by industry sector	M	Sep 97	7.8
Additional Labour Force Survey tables	D	Dec 95	7.6-7.23
Labour market and educational status of young people	D	Mar 96	7.24
LABOUR DISPUTES: STOPPAGES OF WORK			
Summary: latest figures	M	Sep 97	4.1
: time series	M	Sep 97	4.2
Latest year and annual series	A	Jun 97	217
Industry			
Monthly: broad sector time series	M	Sep 97	4.1
Annual: detailed	A	Jun 97	217
: prominent stoppages	A	Jun 97	217
Main causes of stoppage			
Cumulative	M	Sep 97	4.1
Latest year for main industries	A	Jun 97	217
Size of stoppages	A	Jun 97	217
Days lost per 1,000 employees in recent years by industry	A	Jun 97	217
International comparisons	A	Apr 97	129
GOVERNMENT-SUPPORTED TRAINING			
Participants in the programmes	M	Sep 97	8.1
Number of starts on the programmes	M	Sep 97	8.2
Training for work: destination of leavers	M	Sep 97	8.3
Training for work: qualifications of leavers	M	Sep 97	8.4
Youth training: destination of leavers	M	Sep 97	8.5
Youth training: qualifications of leavers	M	Sep 97	8.6
Participants in the programmes	D	Jun 97	8.1
New starts on the programmes	D	Jun 97	8.2
Destinations and qualifications			
TFW/ET leavers	D	Jun 97	8.3
YT leavers	D	Jun 97	8.4
TFW/ET leavers completing agreed training	D	Jun 97	8.5
YT leavers completing agreed training	D	Jun 97	8.6
Characteristics of TFW/ET starts for England and Wales	D	Apr 97	8.7
Characteristics of young people leaving YT for England and Wales	D	Apr 97	8.8
Characteristics of young people starting Modern Apprenticeships for England and Wales	D	Apr 97	8.9
Destinations and qualifications of TFW/ET by their characteristics for England and Wales	D	Apr 97	8.10
Destinations and qualifications of YT leavers by their characteristics for England and Wales	D	Apr 97	8.11
DISABLED JOB SEEKERS			
Registrations and placements into employment	M	Sep 97	A.1
REGIONAL AID			
Selective Assistance by region	Q	Jul 97	A.2
Selective Assistance by region and company	Q	Jul 97	A.3
Development Grants by region	D	Aug 97	A.4
Development Grants by region and company	D	Aug 97	A.5

*Frequency of publication, frequency of compilation shown in brackets (if different).
A Annual. **S** Six monthly. **Q** Quarterly. **M** Monthly. **B** Bi-monthly. **D** Discontinued.

For the convenience of readers of *Labour Market Trends* who require additional statistical information or advice, a selection of enquiry telephone numbers is given below.

FOR STATISTICAL INFORMATION ON:

Earnings *(Tables 5.1- 5.9)*

Average Earnings Index (monthly)	**01928 792442**
Basic wage rates and hours for manual workers with a collective agreement	**01928 792442**
New Earnings Survey (annual): levels of earnings and hours worked for groups of workers (males and females, industries, occupations, part-time and full-time); distribution of earnings; composition of earnings; hours worked	**01928 792077/8**
Unit wage costs, productivity, international comparisons of earnings and labour costs	**01928 792442**

Employment *(Tables 1.1-1.5 and 1.9-1.13)*

Census of Employment	**01928 792690**
Employment and hours	**01928 792563**
Workforce in employment	**01928 792563**

Labour disputes *(Tables 4.1-4.2)*
	01928 792825

Labour Force Survey *(Tables 7.1-7.8)*
	0171 533 6176

Qualifications — **0114 259 3787**

Redundancy statistics *(Tables 2.32-2.36)*
	0171 533 6086

Retail Prices Index *(Tables 6.1-6.9)*
Ansafone service	**0171 533 5866**
Enquiries	**0171 533 5874**

Skill needs surveys and research into skill shortages — **0114 259 4308**

Small firms (DTI) — **0114 259 7538**

Trade unions	**0171 215 5999**

Training *(Tables 8.1-8.6)*

'Training for Work', 'Youth Training' and 'Modern Apprenticeships'	**0114 259 4027**
Workforce training	**0114 259 3489**

Travel-to-Work Areas (TTWAs), composition and review of	**0171 533 6113**
Unemployment *(Tables 2.1-2.24)* (claimant count)	**0171 533 6176**
Vacancies *(Tables 3.1-3.3)* notified to Jobcentres	**0171 533 6176**
Youth Cohort Study	**0114 259 4218**

(Note: The table numbers quoted relate to tables on the preceding pages)

FOR ADVICE ON:

Sources of labour market statistics — **0171 533 6107**

FOR ACCESS TO DETAILED INFORMATION, INCLUDING ON-LINE:

Nomis® (the Office for National Statistics' on-line labour market statistics database) — **0191 374 2468**

Quantime Ltd (on-line and other access of Labour Force Survey data) — **0171 625 7222**

Skills and Enterprise Network — **0114 259 4075**

STATFAX SERVICE FOR LABOUR MARKET STATISTICS

ONS STATFAX gives anyone with a fax machine instant access to the latest labour market statistics. The first two pages of the latest monthly LMS National Press Notice are available within moments of the official release time of 9.30am. The number to ring is **0336 416036**. Calls for the service are charged at 50p per minute. Contact ONS on 0171 533 6363 if you have any problems.